GLOBAL INDIGENOUS MEDIA

GLOBAL INDIGENOUS MEDIA

CULTURES, POETICS, AND POLITICS

EDITED BY PAMELA WILSON AND MICHELLE STEWART

DUKE UNIVERSITY PRESS · DURHAM AND LONDON · 2008

Frontis: Zorida shooting during First Women's
Video Workshop, Ejido Morelia, 1998. Courtesy
of Francisco Vázquez / Chiapas Media
Project / Promedios.

CONTENTS

Acknowledgements • vii

Introduction: Indigeneity and Indigenous Media on the Global Stage
Pamela Wilson and Michelle Stewart • 1

PART I: FROM POETICS TO POLITICS:
INDIGENOUS MEDIA AESTHETICS AND STYLE

1. Imperfect Media and the Poetics of Indigenous Video in Latin America
Juan Francisco Salazar and Amalia Córdova • 39

2. "Lest Others Speak for Us": The Neglected Roots and Uncertain
Future of Maori Cinema in New Zealand
Jennifer Gauthier • 58

3. *Cache*: Provisions and Productions in Contemporary Igloolik Video
Cache Collective • 74

4. Indigenous Animation: Educational Programming, Narrative
Interventions, and Children's Cultures
Joanna Hearne • 89

PART II: INDIGENOUS ACTIVISM, ADVOCACY,
AND EMPOWERMENT THROUGH MEDIA

5. Media as Our Mirror: Indigenous Media of Burma (Myanmar)
Lisa Brooten • 111

6. Transistor Resistors: Native Women's Radio in Canada and the Social
Organization of Political Space from Below
Kathleen Buddle • 128

7. Weaving a Communication Quilt in Colombia: Civil Conflict,
Indigenous Resistance, and Community Radio in Northern Cauca
Mario A. Murillo • 145

8. Outside the Indigenous Lens: Zapatistas and Autonomous Videomaking
Alexandra Halkin • 160

**PART III: CULTURAL IDENTITY, PRESERVATION,
AND COMMUNITY-BUILDING THROUGH MEDIA**

9. The Search for Well-Being: Placing Development with Indigenous
Identity
Laurel Smith • 183

10. "To Breathe Two Airs": Empowering Indigenous Sámi Media
Sari Pietikäinen • 197

11. Indigenous Media as an Important Resource for Russia's
Indigenous Peoples
Galina Diatchkova • 214

12. Indigenous Minority-Language Media: s4c, Cultural Identity, and
the Welsh-Language Televisual Community
Ruth McElroy • 232

**PART IV: NEW TECHNOLOGIES, TIMELESS KNOWLEDGES:
DIGITAL AND INTERACTIVE MEDIA**

13. Recollecting Indigenous Thinking in a CD-ROM
Priscila Faulhaber and Louis Forline • 253

14. Digital Tools and the Management of Australian Aboriginal
Desert Knowledge
Michael Christie • 270

15. Rethinking the Digital Age
Faye Ginsburg • 287

References • 307
About the Contributors • 335
Index • 341

ACKNOWLEDGMENTS

This collection took shape over a number of years and through the nurturing of many people. Thanks to the Internet, in early 1996 Michelle, then a graduate student at the University of Minnesota working on indigenous documentary film production in the United States and Canada, was excited to discover a graduate student at the University of Wisconsin who was completing a dissertation on a case study from the 1950s in which mainstream television journalism took a role in support of Native American rights.

After arranging to attend the "Console-ing Passions" conference in Madison so that they might meet, Michelle drove four hours in search of an interlocutor in a then much lonelier field. There we discovered that our interests truly intersected. However, as things go, we lost touch with each other for a number of years as we each began our teaching careers and our personal and professional lives moved us to different parts of the country.

In 2002 Pam attended the World Civil Society Forum and Indigenous Peoples Caucus in Geneva in conjunction with the UN Working Group on Indigenous Populations. There she met the Maori media producer and international law specialist Moana Sinclair, who at that time was heading an indigenous media initiative for the United Nations. Her new friendship with Moana inspired Pam to find a way to gather a group of indigenous media producers and scholars here at home.

During the process of organizing an indigenous media roundtable for the Society for Cinema and Media Studies (SCMS) conference in Minneapolis in 2003, Pam tracked down Michelle to ask her to participate. A new partnership was born at that conference, as was a wonderful intercultural dialogue between a handful of indigenous media producers and media studies scholars. Together we organized and chaired double workshops on global indigenous media at the 2004 SCMS meetings in Atlanta, as well as a series of indigenous screenings—and the conversations continued and spread.

We would especially like to thank those who participated in the discussions leading up to, during, and following these two conferences, since their participation convinced us that there was indeed a great interest in this topic in the interdisciplinary scholarly world as well as a need for collaborative and cross-cultural dialogue among indigenous media makers and especially between producers and scholars—a borderland not traversed nearly enough.

We owe an immeasurable debt of thanks to E. Ann Kaplan and Faye Ginsburg, two luminous scholars and amazingly strong women who have been beacons of light and support as we maneuvered through the academic and cultural systems. We are especially grateful for Ann's extraordinary support, during her term as president of the SCMS, to help us create a discursive space for this project. We would also like to give special thanks to Patty Zimmerman for her wise counsel and intellectual generosity to women in academia.

These exchanges of ideas among scholars and indigenous media producers—both at conferences and electronically—led to the current book project, and we owe great appreciation to Ken Wissoker of Duke University Press, who encouraged us from the very beginning and shepherded us through the publication process with his gentle wisdom.

In addition to those whose essays appear in this collection, our insights have been enriched by our interactions with Shirley Adamson, Donald Browne, Brenda Chambers, Kristin Dowell, Catherine Martin, Donald Morin, Clara NiiSka, Lorraine Norrgard, Lorna Roth, Anna Sherwood, Moana Sinclair, Beverly Singer, Mona Smith, Chris Spotted Eagle, Lisa Stefanoff, and Erica Wortham. We would like to thank a number of others for contributing to the ongoing dialogue that helped this book take shape, and for whose efforts and conversations the editors are genuinely grateful: Joline Blais, Malinda Maynor, Torry Mendoza, Andrew Jakubowicz, Houston Wood, Sigurjon (Ziggy) Hafsteinsson, A. Keala Kelly, Allen Meek, Judy Iseke-Barnes, Debbie Danard, Jim Fortier, and the readers for Duke University Press. Many thanks also to Amanda Cook Brown and Dave Boggess for their graphic skills and assistance.

Since our first meeting more than a decade ago, indigenous media studies have flourished considerably, and this book has meant for Michelle the chance to bring to fruition—in dialogue with Pam and the contributors to this collection—the global concerns that remained inchoate in her dissertation on sovereign visions in Native North American documentary. Michelle would like to thank those friends and faculty at the University of Minnesota who supported her early interest in indigenous media, particularly Mazhar al-Zo'by, Bruce Campbell, Laura Czarnecki, Andrew Kincaid, Richard Leppert, Ron Libertus, Peter McAuley, Steve Macek, John Mowitt, Paula Rabinowitz, Tom Roach, Dave Roediger, Adam Sitze, Chris Spotted Eagle, Elizabeth Walden, and the rest of her comrades in the Departments of Cultural Studies and Comparative Literature. Michelle would also like to thank her colleagues at SUNY, Purchase, for their practical advice, critical insights, and encouragement. She would like to express gratitude to Pam—for making everything seem possible, and above all for real collaboration, too rare in academia—and, finally, to Jason Harle—who reads everything with fresh eyes, for the thousandth time.

Pam would like to thank her mentors from throughout her academic career—notably Judith Shapiro, Dick Bauman, Beverly Stoeltje, Hap Kindem, Bobby Allen, and John Fiske—who nurtured and shaped her intellectual interests at that particular crossroads of cultural anthropology, communication, and media studies that locates indigenous media squarely in the scope of her passions. She thanks her friends and colleagues Greg Smith, Henry Jenkins, Aniko Bodroghkozy, Chad Dell, and Peg O'Connor for their ongoing support and encouragement of this project, and also those Reinhardt colleagues, Donald Gregory, Curt Lindquist, and Ken Wheeler, who were fellow participants in a Fulbright Hays Seminar on ethnic minority cultures in China in 2005, for their stimulating discussions and inspiration. Indispensable to her have been her two strongest pillars, Dave Boggess and Nolan Smith, for putting up with her intensive work and making sure that life kept going nonetheless. Pam dedicates this book to her parents, Linda and Bob Wilson, for their unflagging support. Finally this project would never have taken shape without Michelle, who has proven to Pam that collaborative projects are far more fulfilling than individual ones, especially if you find a kindred spirit with whom to craft a vision.

INDIGENEITY AND INDIGENOUS MEDIA

ON THE GLOBAL STAGE

Pamela Wilson and Michelle Stewart

In the dry, adobe-baking heat of a New Mexico summer, eighteen eager Native American writers, directors, and actors converged on the campus of the Institute of American Indian Arts (IAIA) in Santa Fe in 2004 to participate in what was promoted as a route to "Hollywood's fast track": the Summer Television and Film Workshop, a groundbreaking collaboration between the tribal arts college, ABC Television, and ABC's parent, the Walt Disney Company, to "raise the technical and creative skills of Native American filmmakers, screenwriters, producers, and actors, and to help them become more competitive in today's demanding marketplace." IAIA President Della Warrior proclaimed it an honor for Native American students to learn from "the decision makers who define excellence in the entertainment industry." Seven Workshop participants have subsequently received a yearlong apprenticeship with an ABC-Disney executive and full access to the corporation's extensive film production resources.[1]

The Sundance Film Festival has also provided major institutional support to Indigenous independent filmmaking by, according to Sundance promotions, "providing a world stage for their compelling and innovative stories" through the festival's Native American Initiative to "build connections between Native Cinema [and] the marketplace of independent film" as part of a "global filmmaking community." The 2006 Native Forum included panel discussions, such as "Native Cinema and the Marketplace" and "Investing in Indigenous Cinema," that emphasized the logistics of creating, funding, and marketing Native American and Indigenous films, while a grant from the Ford Foundation made possible a workshop for four Indigenous filmmakers to meet one-on-one with "established filmmaker and industry leaders . . . to strengthen the projects and help bring them to fruition." Sundance Festival Director Geoffrey Gilmore sees the project as "living proof of the dramatic evolution of indigenous filmmaking and filmmakers."[2]

Achieving this kind of "success" in the global media marketplace—with much emphasis in all public relations discourse on the terms *global* and *marketplace*—demonstrates the stakes of globalization for Indigenous cultural expression, both individual and collective. Young Indigenous media artists—considered "raw Native talent" by the Hollywood studios, according to the filmmaker and scholar Beverly Singer (personal communication, 2005)—navigate between their desires for major commercial industry support and their own artistic and cultural expression. At the same time, however, a good deal of Indigenous media is being produced for noncommercial purposes and beyond the reach of the mainstream media industries. Indeed, the major executives of the hegemonic media do not always define the terms of "excellence" for Indigenous media makers. Indigenous artists and activists are using new technologies to craft culturally distinct forms of communication and artistic production that speak to local aesthetics and local needs while anticipating larger audiences.

In recent years, Indigenous media—which we loosely define as forms of media expression conceptualized, produced, and / or created by Indigenous peoples across the globe—have emerged from geographically scattered, locally based production centers to become part of globally linked media networks with increased effectiveness and reach. Simultaneously, Indigenous media have begun to receive greater attention from scholars, critics, and global activists. These developments have called into question many previously held definitions and assumptions about Indigenous media and now call for a reexamination of how we think and talk about Indigenous media in an environment of globalization. Indigenous media now occupy a significant place not only in local cultures and communities but also in national and global media discourses, policies, industries, and funding structures. The need for a collection of essays representing a global, interdisciplinary perspective—as well as a mix of insights from both producers and scholars—has never been as urgent. This collection, by interdisciplinary scholars and media producers, both Indigenous and non-Indigenous, was born of a desire to address the changing environments in which Indigenous media are today being produced, shaped, and consumed.

Indigenous peoples have long had an ambivalent relationship with the mass media. Even though Indigenous groups and artists have produced their own expressive media for generations, the industrialized, mass-produced messages and images—and accompanying technologies—in most cases have represented the perspectives, values, and institutional structures of empire. "Mass media [have] long been a weapon of mass destruction for Native American people," explains the Pawnee / Yakama artist Bunky Echo-Hawk on his Web site. "[They were] used early on in American history to garner widespread public support for, and to justify the violent occupation of this land and policies encouraging the exter-mination of Native American people and culture. Currently, [they are] used to romanticize the culture, promote negative stereotypes, and main-tain the fallacy that Native Americans are a people of the past."[3] As Faye Ginsburg notes in her contribution to this book, Indigenous peoples have, until recently, been the object of other peoples' image-making practices in ways that have often been damaging to their lives.

Many studies exist of representations and stereotypes *of* Indigenous peoples by the dominant media;[4] this book's focus, however, is on the shift in the past few decades to the command of mass media technologies *by* Indigenous peoples as they have appropriated the technologies of the dominant society and transformed them to their own uses in order to meet their own cultural and political needs—what the visual anthropolo-gist Harald Prins (2004: 516) would call the Indigenization of visual media. A number of political, social, legal, and technological developments con-tributed to this shift. As we will discuss below, a burgeoning human rights discourse following World War II convinced many Indigenous activists of the need for a variety of forms of self-representation. In this context, the media became an important tool for bringing land claims and cultural histories to an international forum. Some Indigenous groups enlisted the aid of sympathetic anthropologists as both Indigenous peoples and an-thropology as a discipline began to question the ethnographer's role and responsibility in relation to Indigenous peoples. By the 1960s, civil rights movements in the United States and in Canada fueled significant calls for self-determination and a language of nationalism that insisted on the distinctness of Indigenous claims (beyond those of the demands for equal rights made by minority groups) (Fleras and Elliot 1992).

Concomitantly, the invention of a lightweight and portable film cam-era with synchronous sound took filmmaking into the street and the field. This gave rise both to the *cinéma vérité* movement (also known as direct or observational cinema; see Mamber 1976; O'Connell 1992; and Rouch and Feld 2003) and to a parallel ethnographic film movement among anthropologists (see Heider 1976; Loizos 1993; and MacDougall 1998). Some ethnographic filmmakers considered observational cinema to be the antidote to the crisis of representation: if the written monograph would inevitably betray the ethnocentric and subjective framework of the ethnographer, perhaps the camera could circumvent this bias. Thus, by setting up a camera and allowing the film to roll, some ethnographic filmmakers sought to document Indigenous cultural practices objectively. The excesses and absurdity of the worst of these practices led ethnographers and Indigenous groups to develop an ethos and practice of dialogic filmmaking and anthropological advocacy and convinced many of the necessity for self-representation (Weinberger 1994).[5] As Prins (2004: 518) explains of this turn that began in the 1970s, "In an intervention that paralleled the postcolonial move to 'write back' against colonial masters, Indian activists began to 'shoot back,' reversing the colonial gaze by constructing their own visual media, telling their stories on their own terms."

In Canada and Australia, the launching of satellites that stood to bring non-Indigenous media to the Arctic and the Outback for the first time spurred Indigenous groups to demand dedicated air time for the preservation and promotion of Indigenous languages and cultures (Michaels 1986; Roth and Ginsburg 2003). States made dispensations for "indigenous content" and, increasingly, national broadcasting offered grants and training to Indigenous producers. In this context, radio, television, and video all offered new means to connect communities and revitalize cultures.

In the 1970s and 1980s, a number of organizations, institutes, and foundations developed to provide support to this growing movement and to showcase Indigenous works in festivals and other venues.[6] Heralded by Paul Hocking's 1975 collection of seminal essays, the subfield of visual anthropology became an early academic locus for work on Indigenous media. Scholars in this interdisciplinary field began to address these new forms of cultural expression and turned their focus from ethnographic film produced by outsiders to the cultural politics of Indigenous media as produced by insiders—what Ginsburg calls the anthropology of media (see Michaels and Kelly 1984; Turner 1990; and Ginsburg 1991, 1994).[7] Scholars in other fields also began to give more attention to aspects of Indigenous media production such as community broadcasting and its cultural power and political efficacy. At the same time, the growth of community broadcasting organizations, government agencies, and scholarly journals reflected a broader interest in "community-based, citizen's and 'third sector' media and culture."[8] With this increased attention, the study of Indigenous media spread throughout the academy into many disciplines: from anthropology, communications, media studies, and cultural studies to such fields as literature, art, geography, linguistics, information technology, education, sociology, history, and political science.

Contemporary Indigenous media demonstrate the extent to which the hallmarks of an earlier regime of empire—colonization, forced assimilation, genocide, and diaspora—are being challenged and displaced by new constellations of global power. Indigenous media often directly address the politics of identity and representation by engaging and challenging the dominant political forms at both the national and international level. In this landscape, control of media representation and of cultural self-definition asserts and signifies cultural and political sovereignty itself. As such, Indigenous media are the first line of negotiation of sovereignty issues as well as a discursive locus for issues of control over land and territory, subjugation and dispossession under colonization, cultural distinctiveness and the question of ethnicity and minority status, questions of local and traditional knowledge, self-identification and recognition by others, and notions of Indigeneity and Indigenism themselves.

THE PROBLEM OF DEFINING INDIGENEITY
IN THE ERA OF GLOBALIZATION

In today's economic environment, marketing and selling "the Indigenous" through media, tourism, art, crafts, music, and the appropriation of traditional knowledges and Indigenous images has become a profitable enterprise that Indigenous peoples worldwide feel the need to monitor and protect. Indigenous styles and causes are now chic in the dominant cultures, especially in the West. This has led to new types of commercial market niches in the developed Western world for products marketed as Indigenous, ranging from import boutiques featuring tribal crafts (e.g., Ten Thousand Villages) to CDs of "world music" (e.g., those of Putumayo) and socially conscious charitable gift giving to "alleviate hunger and poverty" and promote "strong communities, sustainability, environmental protection, and peace" (e.g., Heifer International). As Nigel Parbury has noted, "The 'Indigenous Industry' is a global phenomenon that is worth billions and billions of dollars annually. In this context, it becomes an imperative to examine fundamental assumptions about what actually constitutes Indigeneity on the international stage, because that's where the major players . . . are conducting their business" (quoted in Onsman 2004: xv). Parbury's statement underscores the complexity and irony of the contemporary reality: not only are nation-states "putting up" with the presence of Indigenous peoples, but they may—under the auspices of "official" diversity—be competing not just for Indigenous land and resources, but also for the international "brand recognition" afforded by Indigenous cultural property. Thus, the question of Indigeneity as a distinct and significant category in today's global cultural politics is a complex one requiring careful analysis.

These considerations foreground the problem of defining Indigenous media—and Indigeneity itself—in this postmodern, globalized era, where the status of national identity and its relation to global institutions is itself being debated. When discussing Indigeneity, we encounter an intersection of many discursive paradigms in academia and also in cultural politics at all levels. In editing this collection, we have realized the lack of clarity that exists as to what does and does not constitute "Indigenous media," and this intellectual argument has shaped the collection itself. Should a collection on Indigenous media include articles on Welsh television? Or filmmakers of Indigenous ancestry who make Hollywood films? Or media that address Indigenous themes and issues but are produced by non-Indigenous artists? Is it important to distinguish Indigenous groups from other ethnic minorities in theorizing these issues? Indeed, is the question of Indigeneity a distinct and significant category in today's global cultural politics? Although we have come to understand that these questions do not have clear answers, we believe that an exploration of the paradigms that have defined the concept of Indigeneity will help frame the larger question of what constitutes "indigenous media." We and our contributors explore how these definitional questions bear on Indigenous activism and media activity on local, national, state, and global stages.

As we noted earlier, in the years following the Second World War, Indigenous groups began to lobby the newly formed United Nations and to form NGOs in order to advance land claims and secure sovereignty. The legal scholar S. James Anaya (2004) acknowledges that international law, once an instrument of colonialism, has continued to develop, "however grudgingly or imperfectly," to support the rights and demands of Indigenous peoples in their local and national struggles. He points out at least two distinct sets of Indigenous discourses in international law today: first, the rhetoric of international human rights principles and the subsequent rise of an international Indigenous rights movement in the late twentieth century, and, second, the political rhetoric of nation, focused on sovereignty issues of Indigenous nations in the context of the nation-states that now envelop and subordinate them.

The concept of the Fourth World (and, later, Fourth Cinema: see Jennifer Gauthier's essay in this collection) emerged in this context, both in response to the Third World liberation rhetoric of the 1970s and with a growing appeal (pursued by groups such as the American Indian Movement [AIM]'s International Indian Treaty Council and the World Council of Indigenous Peoples) to international political bodies as a way to stress prevailing rights to self-determination under treaty relations. In 1974 George Manuel and Michael Posluns were the first to use the term *Fourth World* in connection with Indigenous activism to indicate this growing international consciousness among "people who have special nontechnical, nonmodern exploitative relations to the lands which they still inhabit and who are disenfranchised by the nations within which they live" (Dyck 1985: 21). Today international Indigenous movements have widened their purview, emphasizing the realities of internal colonialism for Native peoples and strategizing cultural survival in the face of urbanization, relocation, and diaspora.

In late December 2006, for example, a number of news headlines from independent media sources announced the "First Encounter of the Zapatista Communities with the Peoples of the World." Held in Oventic, Mexico, this four-day series of workshops and intercultural sharing was facilitated by Zapatista Comandanta Sandra and Comandante Moisés, who hosted about two thousand participants from forty-four countries (see Encounter 2007). According to one report, the group was united by a desire to "construct a better world, where all worlds fit" and (quoting Comandante Moisés) "to get to know each other and share the experiences of how we are organizing and pushing forward the struggles of each group, each movement, each sector and each person" (Bellinghausen 2007).

This type of movement is at once both nationalist and antinationalist, in that it advocates for nationalism as well as a collaborative, collective global Indigenist appeal that takes the issues beyond those of the nation-state and earlier contexts of empire. It politically redefines the contours of Indigenous nationalism by fostering a coalition politics that is both local and international. Facilitated by globalization and the increasing transnational linkage of peoples, societies, economies, and governments worldwide, this international "pan-Indigenous" movement has brought together representatives of Indigenous nations and supportive NGOs (either particular to one Indigenous group, translocal, or transnational). At the same time, perhaps paradoxically, this type of international movement is also decidedly localist, respecting the autonomy and distinctiveness of disparate Indigenous groups.

International Indigenism—a term that, like *Indigeneity*, is used in various ways to fit diverse agendas—may at times appear to be strategically essentialist in its international appeals, identifying Indigenism as a philosophical and cultural attitude toward the world that is shared by all Indigenous peoples, a model for global conduct in its resistance to colonialism, imperialism, environmental destruction, and now, globalization. As Ravi de Costa (n.d.: para. 5) explains, "It is the fact that all Indigenous peoples can draw on their traditions as a mode of resistance that allows much broader identification to be made." In Ward Churchill's (1996: 512) formulation: "Indigenism offers . . . a vision of how things might be that is based on how things have been since time immemorial, and how things must be once again if the human species, and perhaps the planet itself, is to survive much longer. Predicated in a synthesis of the wisdom attained over thousands of years by Indigenous, land-based peoples around the globe—the Fourth World, or, as Winona LaDuke puts it, 'The Host World on which the first, second, and third worlds all sit at the present time'—Indigenism stands in diametrical opposition to the totality of what might be termed 'Eurocentric business as usual.' " In every regard, Churchill and others see Indigenous self-determination—sociopolitical, cultural, and economic autonomy (or sovereignty)—as the necessary response to the legacy of colonization and the only means to ensure the survival of Indigenous peoples.

Indigenous groups have become actively involved in the definition and assertion of the rights of Indigenous nations in international law. Many players are now addressing Indigenous issues on the world stage in transnational and international networks of advocacy and alliance: government agencies of the states in which Indigenous peoples are contained, as well as national, supranational, intergovernmental, and nongovernmental organizations (NGOs), foundations, and agencies. These groups are also in close dialogue with transnational corporations and funding agencies such as the World Bank and the International Monetary Fund, all of which have deep stakes in questions of the futures of Indigenous peoples, lands, and their resources—though not all have the same agenda.

Two of the major institutions in which the internationalization of Indigenous rights advocacy issues has taken place are the United Nations (primarily housed in the Commission on Human Rights and its various subcommissions until 2006) and the International Labour Organisation (ILO). As Anaya (2004: 7) explains, the principles on which this U.N.-based Indigenous rights movement has been based are distinct from the movements for national or tribal sovereignty:

> International law's embrace of human rights, however, engenders a discourse that is an alternative to the state-centered, historical sovereignty one, a discourse that has yielded results in the international system for Indigenous peoples. Indigenous peoples have seized on the institutional and normative regime of human rights that was brought in the fold of international law in the aftermath of World War II and the adoption of the United Nations charter. . . . Contemporary human rights discourse has the welfare of human beings as its subject and is concerned only secondarily, if at all, with the interests of sovereign entities.

Yet international Indigenism has pressured the United Nations to recognize collective group rights in addition to its normative focus on human rights. Ronald Niezen (2003: 4) uses the term *indigenism* to describe "the international movement that aspires to promote and protect the rights of the world's 'first peoples.'" As de Costa (n.d.: para. 2–3) explains,

> Embedded in this use of the term is the idea that local assertions of the cultural difference of Indigenous peoples, though frequently expressed in the language and symbolism of nations, only become fully visible through a global lens and can only be protected under a broadened understanding of universal principles of human rights. The strategy has been to bypass nation-states—who have rarely recognized Indigenous rights, sometimes even denying the existence of Indigenous peoples within their borders—and to present Indigenous concerns to higher political forums. Consequently the goals of this "indigenism" are largely institutional: the creation of formal measures of protection of Indigenous peoples' rights under international law.

In 1982, the United Nations established the Working Group on Indigenous Populations (WGIP) with the mandate to review developments regarding "the promotion and protection of the human rights and fundamental freedoms of indigenous people, giving special attention to the evolution of standards concerning the rights of indigenous people."[9] Six years later, the U.N. Economic and Social Council requested that the WGIP begin preparing a set of principles and preambles for a draft declaration of principles on the rights of Indigenous populations.[10] That document, the Draft Declaration on the Rights of Indigenous Peoples, was vigorously negotiated, and ratification began to seem elusive because of the vigorous objections of major settler states—in particular, the United States, Australia, and New Zealand—which stalled the finalization of this key instrument of international law setting forth covenants to protect the collective rights of Indigenous peoples.[11] In the meantime, some structural changes were under way. The United Nations in 2000 established the Permanent Forum on Indigenous Issues to serve as an advisory body to the council and to "(a) Provide expert advice and recommendations on indigenous issues . . . ; (b) Raise awareness and promote the integration and coordination of activities relating to indigenous issues within the United Nations system; and (c) Prepare and disseminate information on indigenous issues."[12]

In 2006, the United Nations disbanded the Commission for Human Rights and replaced it with the Human Rights Council. At its inaugural session in June of 2006, this new body approved the Declaration on the Rights of Indigenous Peoples and sent it to the General Assembly for ratification. After more than a year of frustration by Indigenous representatives during which time the vote was tabled and further delayed, the General Assembly of the United Nations finally ratified the Declaration on the Rights of Indigenous Peoples on September 13, 2007 by a vote of 143–4. The United States, Canada, Australia, and New Zealand voted against it, while eleven nations abstained. A news article quoted Victoria Tauli-Corpuz, the chairman of the U.N. Permanent Forum on Indigenous Issues, as saying that the declaration was "a major victory" for the United Nations in establishing international human rights standards since it "sets the minimum international standards for the protection and promotion of the rights of indigenous peoples. Therefore, existing and future laws, policies and programs of indigenous peoples will have to be redesigned and shaped to be consistent with this standard." However, Tauli-Corpuz emphasized that the most challenging issue would be to gain implementation by all countries, since the Declaration is not legally binding ("U.N. Adopts" 2007).[13]

The U.N. bodies also have served as important gatherings for historic intercultural dialogue among representatives of various Indigenous peoples to strategize about the future of Indigeneity in the face of globalization. In a 2004 report of a WGIP meeting, El Hadji Guissé asserted the need to defend the rights of Indigenous peoples, at both the local and national level, to their territories, resources, cultures, identities, traditional knowledge, and right to self-determination. Guissé (2004: 9) argued that Indigenous social, political, and economic systems, along with sustainable resource management practices, should be allowed to coexist alongside other systems rather than being forced to integrate into the global market economy. This included "recognition of prior rights of Indigenous peoples over lands and resources they have occupied and nurtured since time immemorial" (ibid.). Guissé's report noted that globalization "prioritize[s] profits over social concerns," increases disparities among and in nation-states, and has had long-lasting damaging impact on the environment.

Indeed, many Indigenous WGIP representatives spoke of "the negative effects of globalization on indigenous communities, particularly on their lands, cultures, identities and lives" (Guissé 2004: 3). They linked globalization with Indigenous poverty and expressed concern that globalization would lead to eventual assimilation into dominant societies, emphasizing the increasing political and economic exclusion of Indigenous peoples, along with the trend of younger Indigenous peoples migrating from rural to urban areas "as a force promoting assimilation that was generated by globalization" (ibid.). The representatives noted the severe and negative effects of transnational corporations on Indigenous peoples—especially extraction of natural resources and building of large hydroelectric dam projects on their lands. The WGIP discussed the role of the World Bank, the International Monetary Fund, and other financial institutions in facilitating access of transnational corporations and extractive industries to Indigenous peoples' territory, disregarding Indigenous rights. These actions have been coupled with a lack of respect for Indigenous traditional knowledge, environment, and human rights. WGIP participants called for the development and implementation of binding international standards for transnational corporate conduct, as well as strong rules acknowledging the specific needs of Indigenous groups in relation to looming international agreements regarding intellectual property.

At the same time, some WGIP representatives noted the more positive results of globalization, particularly improved communication and networking among Indigenous communities that "gave rise to a sense of belonging to a global society." They recognized, with some irony, that the mere existence of the Working Group contributed to this process, allowing Indigenous representatives to dialogue with each other and with governments and to develop an international perspective. In this sense, international Indigenism is another significant call for "globalization from below," or a globalization defined by the people affected, as opposed to a globalization determined by and serving corporate interests.

Still, the concept of "indigenous peoples" has largely been undefined in U.N. discourses, with significant disagreement over whether Indigeneity is necessarily place-based, to what degree Indigeneity ought to be tied to claims to primacy of mutual belonging in a relationship between a cultural group and a geographical territory, and to what degree claims of territorial (and cultural) autonomy define characteristics of Indigeneity. In the 1990s, the WGIP attempted to standardize terminology, requesting that the Greek legal scholar Erica-Irene A. Daes (1996: 4)[14] review prevailing definitions of Indigeneity[15] given that "the attendance at the Working Group of certain persons describing themselves as 'indigenous peoples' had been challenged by other indigenous peoples' representatives in the Working Group."[16] Daes, however, questioned the desirability of defining the concept, since "the concept of 'indigenous' is not capable of a precise, inclusive definition which can be applied in the same manner to all regions of the world" (5). Daes (1996: 12–13) noted that "'self-identification' as indigenous or tribal is usually regarded as a fundamental criterion for determining whether groups are indigenous or tribal, sometimes in combination with other variables" such as language or historical continuity in and ancient connection to a geographic location. In terms of individuals, the issue of subjective self-identification as Indigenous must also respect the community's right to define its own membership.

Most scholars agree that Indigeneity as we commonly conceptualize it is inescapably linked to either current regimes of colonialism or the legacy of empire. But which empires are considered to be those spawning Indigeneity and which are not? If we are consistent in our definition, then any cultural groups that meet the criteria for Indigenous peoples and that have been subject to empire might be eligible, no matter what period in history (or how far removed from the present time). In this case, many of the minority groups in China and groups in Europe such as the Welsh, Scots, and Basque would also be considered Indigenous as Donald

Browne (1996) sees them, or as Andrys Onsman (2004) considers the Frisians. However, for various reasons, the United Nations does not consider these groups among those it should shelter. Thus, even the self-identification of Indigeneity may be limited by the discourses, perceptions, and policies of the encompassing states and the refusal of certain states to accept the existence of any Indigenous peoples within them that use terms politically steeped in opposing ideologies.

For this reason, some Indigenous U.N. representatives from Asia have urged that a formal definition of Indigeneity is indeed necessary to prevent states from denying the existence of Indigenous peoples in their countries.[17] For example, the People's Republic of China, denying the history of Chinese colonialism—historically in the imperial eras and currently with internal colonialism of its geographic minority nationalities—conceptualizes Indigeneity as a phenomenon faced only by those carrying the legacy of European colonialist policies and claims that "there are neither indigenous people nor indigenous issues in China."[18] The Chinese argument is, in essence, a restatement of the "salt water thesis," which extended the right of self-determination *only* to former colonies.[19] Elaborating this argument, some delegations to the WGIP reasoned that "the concept of 'indigenous' is applicable only to situations in which the original inhabitants of the territory were subjugated and physically dispossessed by settlers *from overseas*, bearing alien cultures and values, and where these settlers, rather than the original inhabitants, have been the real beneficiaries of decolonization and independent statehood. These circumstances, the same delegations contend, have largely been restricted historically to the Americas and Oceania" (Daes 1996: 19). Daes argues that it is unfair to determine degrees of cultural difference solely based on whether "conquest, colonization, subjugation or discrimination [was] at the hands of persons from other regions of the world rather than [at the hands of] neighbours" (20). She points out that many African and Asian state governments conceptually critique the use of the term *indigenous* to distinguish between groups that have been neighbors for millennia (as in the case of China discussed above).[20] Instead, she advocates that "we think of 'indigenous' peoples as groups which are native to their own specific ancestral territories within the borders of the existing State, rather than persons that are native generally to the region in which the State is located" (20). Based on these discussions, the WGIP adopted a flexible approach to defining which groups are Indigenous (and therefore eligible to participate), relying on Indigenous organizations to draw attention to "any improper assertions of the right to participate as 'indigenous' peoples" (21).

In summary, the factors identified by the WGIP that modern international organizations and international legal experts consider relevant to understanding "indigenous"—but which do not and cannot constitute an inclusive or comprehensive definition, though they may provide some general guidelines—include: (a) priority in time with respect to occupying and using the resources of a particular territory; (b) the voluntary perpetuation of cultural distinctiveness (which may include language, social organization, religious and spiritual values, modes of production, laws, and institutions); (c) self-identification, as well as recognition by other groups or by state authorities as a distinct collectivity; and (d) an experience of subjugation, marginalization, dispossession, exclusion, or discrimination, whether or not these conditions persist (Daes 1996: 22).

THE RHETORIC OF NATION: INDIGENEITY AND/AS NATION

The policies of states or nation-states[21] regarding the management and administration of their internally colonized Indigenous peoples have shaped, and continue to shape, the daily lived experiences of the members of those Indigenous groups. Ideologies of assimilation and development often pervade academic as well as government projects and are frequently reflected in the creation and funding of outlets for mass media in a nation-state. Similarly, Indigenous media often must define themselves and their work against the idealized or stereotypical images that dominate the popular culture and discourses of mainstream societies. We often find such discourses situated in master narratives of evolution / progress in which Indigenous groups are seen as "simple," "primitive," or "backward." This condescending discourse justifies the "assistance" and intervention of the dominant state into, first, the management of the land and resources traditionally occupied and used by Indigenous peoples and, second, into Indigenous cultural practices and social / religious institutions.

Indigenous identities have, for several centuries, been predicated on relationships to the states in which they have been enveloped by colonization and under whose political control they have fallen. Duane Champagne (2005: 3), who identifies Indigenous peoples as "submerged nations," argues that "while native peoples have identities that predate the formation of nation-states, and many aspects of these pre-state identities continue to persist and make their weight felt in everyday life, native identity is largely defined in relation to colonizing cultures and state governments." In many cases, the nation-states have assigned, relocated, carved out, separated, labeled, defined, and imposed legal status on the identity of various Indigenous groups, with or without their input or consent, in order to establish official government recognition of and relations with these peoples, using domestic definitions of Indigeneity distinct to each nation-state. In states as wide-ranging as the United States and the People's Republic of China, for example, the decision of whether the government should officially recognize Indigenous groups (or minority nationalities, in the case of China) has been a controversial and ultimately flawed political process, with many cultural groups not receiving recognition while others have been lumped together arbitrarily or assigned labels reflecting dominant perception rather than local knowledge. Hundreds of Indigenous groups are still petitioning for official recognition by states around the world.

Interrogating how ethnic groups are constructed and maintained, as well as their processes and permutations, the social historian Paul Spickard (2005) underscores the fact that different ethnic markers have salience in different geographic contexts—to wit, in the United States, physical, "racial" markers that are "laid on the body" are the most powerful determinants of categories of difference, while elsewhere language, class, religion, and region may serve as important organizing principles, even for Indigenous groups. For example, Laurel Smith, in this collection, writes about Oaxaca, Mexico: "Often speakers of Indigenous languages identify themselves not as members of an ethnic group but as campesinos and / or as people from particular communities or regions. Ethnicity is difficult to isolate and identify in Oaxaca because it is not an essential category entered at birth but rather a constructed identity formulated in relations of power and difference." Spickard sees ethnicity as that "critical juncture between peoples when they come to see each other, and are seen by outsiders, as fundamentally, essentially, immutably different"; this inevitably results in attempts by one group to exert power over another or to highlight its own disempowerment. Discussing the common elements and models in colonial processes across the globe, Spickard notes the alternating attempts by nation-states to either (1) separate and restrict colonized groups (e.g., on reservations, often following the U.S.

Indian Affairs model), or (2) assimilate the colonized in an attempt to wipe out cultural difference and incorporate the colonized into the mainstream, dominant society of the colonizers (15).

States tend to deal with Indigeneity, minimally, at two levels: by officially recognizing and assigning political and legal status to particular cultural *groups or collectivities* (a political determination often couched in cultural and socioscientific terms); and by officially setting up criteria for *individuals* to determine who is Indigenous (either distinct from, or working in collaboration with, the internally determined criteria of the officially recognized groups). Although the politics of recognition and sovereignty has taken different paths in former English colonies (especially the United States, Canada, New Zealand, and Australia) as well as in Latin America and Asia, Augie Fleras and Jean Leonard Elliot (1992: 220–31) have noted the extent to which even the most seemingly progressive policies of liberal nation-states evince a double movement between the recognition of rights of self-government and policies that encourage forms of institutional assimilation. In Canada, such contradictions are visible in the distance between the establishment of Nunavut as sovereign territory (1999) and the completion of the Nisga'a Treaty (2000), on the one hand, and the persistence of land claims cases in British Columbia, on the other. For the Maori, the New Zealand government's decision to respect the Treaty of Waitangi (1840) and the subsequent establishment of a tribunal to determine Maori claims seemed like progress. Yet, as Fleras and Elliot argue, the record again has been mixed (190). Latin America has seen an increasing political participation by and influence of Indigenous people in recent years, including constitutional reform and / or the approval of ILO Convention number 169 in Colombia (see Mario Murillo's essay), Ecuador, Bolivia, Brazil, and other states; also, the elections of 2006 brought pro-Indigenous candidates into the presidencies of Bolivia, Ecuador, and Venezuela (the newly elected president of Bolivia, Evo Morales, is an Aymara Indian). However, as Gustavo González (2005) points out, these changes have "not yet led to a modification of their dire social and economic conditions or to a reduction in government resistance to addressing native peoples' demands for autonomy and respect for their cultures" (see also Kearns 2006).

In the United States, federal recognition is a formal political act that permanently establishes a government-to-government relationship between the United States and the recognized tribe as a "domestic dependent nation" and imposes on the government a legally defined relationship to the tribe and its members. Historically, tribes have been granted federal recognition through treaties, legislation, or administrative decisions.[22] However, in the United States, no single federal or tribal criterion establishes an individual person's identity as an "Indian." Each tribe has the authority and power to define its own eligibility criteria for membership. Concomitantly, there is also a federal definition of "Indian" for purposes of federal benefits. It typically requires membership in a federally recognized tribe or a particular blood quantum. Government agencies use differing criteria to determine who is eligible to participate in their "Indian" programs. Furthermore, the U.S. Census Bureau counts anyone an "American Indian or Alaska Native" who declares himself or herself to be so—yet many of these people who self-identify are not eligible for tribal membership or for federal benefits (see Stockes 2000). These examples illustrate the confusing, inconsistent, and often contradictory nature of the criteria used in the United States to determine who is an Indigenous person and which groups may be officially classified and "recognized" as Indigenous.

The People's Republic of China (a state that, as we have seen, officially denies the existence of "indigenous" peoples within its borders) does recognize minority nationality (*minzu*) status, indicating it on an individual's passports, identification cards, and all official documents. After the formation of the People's Republic in 1949, Mao's regime shaped and defined New China as a multiethnic, multinational state and undertook a project to officially classify the ethnic nations and peoples within it. Over four hundred groups applied for official recognition; in the end, the government's social scientists recognized fifty-six minzu, including the dominant Han, in an ethnic structure that has served as the framework for China's minority policies and governance for the past half century. Despite contention over the selection and naming of groups, according to anthropologists, most of the peoples have now accepted their state-assigned identities.[23] In time, over the course of several generations, these processes of internal colonialism often have an impact on the self-conceptualization of the people, whose identities are shaped by the colonizing labels and discourses. Today, states often adopt a discourse of official "diversity" that, paradoxically, in the name of the multiethnic state, forcibly contains and silences the claims for self-determination of disparate peoples that fall under the jurisdiction of official nationalism.[24]

Over the years, states have devised an array of strategies for managing the competing claims to sovereignty of Indigenous peoples. As a remedy, many Indigenous groups have adopted the mantle of "nation" as a direct appeal to international law meant to force settler states to acknowledge treaty relations entered into at the time of settlement. The last century has seen the rise of regional pan-Indigenous movements that have mobilized disparate organizations, networks, and sociocultural identities to challenge the state's power, to enforce treaty relations, and / or to support Indigenous groups recognized and unrecognized by the encompassing state.[25]

As Randel Hanson (2004) notes, the expansion of Indigenous sovereignty and discourses of self-determination in the era of globalization since World War II, especially in the decolonized settler states such as the United States, Canada, and Australia, has been intimately connected with globalization processes and related to the formation of a new global infrastructure in bodies such as the United Nations, in the pan-Indigenous movements, and in the rise of scores of NGOs and alliances for international activism. Hanson points out that the U.N. charter for the first time recognized that the concept of self-determination was a right not only of states but also of peoples, and that the implications of these new global developments widely challenged the colonial practices of the settler states and pressured them to begin to make structural changes in their domestic policies, marking a profound shift in the very notion of state sovereignty, since this was no longer seen as inviolable but was now being judged in terms of the legality and morality of its domestic practices (289–93). These developments afforded groups multiple venues for renegotiating their status in relation to encompassing states, but these opportunities were not without risks. Specifically, Hanson identifies the mixed blessing of development projects beholden to neoliberal agendas that might undermine Indigenous values while offering a measure of economic self-determination.

CENTRALITY OF MEDIA TO INDIGENOUS PEOPLES' MOVEMENTS

In the context of globalization and the rise of international Indigenism of the last two decades, the use and mobilization of media have become increasingly central at all levels of organization: local, national, and interior transnational. Media produced by and for Indigenous peoples, usually in their own languages and for internal consumption, under Indigenous control and funding, have come to exist alongside media produced in the media industries of the dominant society. In these cases, questions of ultimate control, funding, and editorial decision making are central. A third category of media often labeled "indigenous" (but which in many cases calls into question the definition of this term) is media produced in the mainstream, dominant industries that address Indigenous topics and issues or media that appropriate Indigenous knowledge and / or tell Indigenous stories, with or without the consent and involvement of those to whom that knowledge or those stories culturally, traditionally, or ethically belong. In recent debates in international law relating to Indigenous peoples, issues of appropriation and control of Indigenous knowledge and of cultural and intellectual property rights have become as important as questions of sovereignty over land and resources, "human rights and fundamental freedoms" protections, and cultural preservation.

Article 17 of the proposed U.N. Declaration on the Rights of Indigenous Peoples declared: "Indigenous peoples have the right to establish their own media in their own languages. They also have the right to equal access to all forms of non-indigenous media. States shall take effective measures to ensure that State-owned media duly reflect indigenous cultural diversity."[26] In January 1998 the Office of the U.N. High Commissioner for Human Rights, in cooperation with the government of Spain, organized a groundbreaking workshop for Indigenous journalists in Madrid.[27] A second U.N. workshop, "Promoting the Rights and Cultures of Indigenous Peoples through the Media," was held in New York in December 2000 (United Nations 2001). Participants included journalists, editors, filmmakers, photographers, academics, radio and television producers, communications consultants, public relations specialists, lawyers, students, and public information officers from the Americas, Europe, Russia, Australia, New Zealand, Africa, and Southeast Asia.

A major focus of both workshops was the role the United Nations might play in protecting the free flow of information—a fundamental condition for realizing and protecting human rights and international security—in an era of globalization, with an emphasis on the urgent responsibilities of both the mainstream and Indigenous media to cover Indigenous issues and voice the perspectives of Indigenous peoples. Participants emphasized the essential role of Internet-based media to create new information models through which Indigenous voices might be heard, viewing Indigenous media "as an indispensable tool to promote Indigenous identity, language, culture, self-representation and collective and human rights, and as a vehicle for communicating regional, national and international issues to Indigenous communities as well as conveying community concerns to a wider public." Workshop participants highlighted "the urgent need to strengthen Indigenous media," generally community-based rather than commercial, by building capacity, developing a sounder financial base, keeping up with technological developments, and building partnerships and networks (United Nations 2002).

Less than two years later, in July 2002, an Indigenous Media Dialogue was held in Durban, South Africa, during the World Conference against Racism, Discrimination, Xenophobia, and Related Intolerance. Focusing on strategies to strengthen Indigenous media and to improve coverage of Indigenous issues by mainstream media, participants called for the establishment of professional training and career pathways for Indigenous people working in the media industries, with a special emphasis on new media. Participants at this workshop also proposed the development of an international code of ethics for media personnel working with Indigenous peoples and issues. Further dialogue occurred when the United Nations and the International Telecommunication Union established the World Summit on the Information Society, with international meetings held in 2003 and 2005, and U.N. agencies helped organize the Global Forum of Indigenous Peoples and the Information Society in 2003.

The aim of all of these efforts has been to increase access by Indigenous peoples to new media technologies for production and distribution of their creative and political works, thereby raising the profile of Indigenous aesthetic perspectives and cultural / political issues both in the mainstream and in new venues for Indigenous media expression. The past decade has witnessed the establishment of a major presence for Indigenous visual media in a number of nations. In 1999, the Aboriginal Peoples Television Network (APTN) premiered as a cable network distributed across Canada, showcasing to a mainstream audience the artistic and cultural expressions of scores of tribal filmmakers and television producers. In 2004, after decades of negotiation and planning, Maori Television was launched in New Zealand. The following year saw the premiere of the first Indigenous television station in Asia, Taiwan's Indigenous Television Network, a mix of news and features originally funded by the Council for Indigenous Peoples and subsequently acquired by Taiwan's Public Television Service.[28] In Australia, the local Aboriginal television station Imparja began broadcasting in 1988 in central Australia as a project of a group of Aboriginal journalists, but the negotiations about developing a national Aboriginal television network have been clouded by complex politics.[29]

Recent international cinematic successes have propelled feature films by or involving Indigenous peoples, such as *Smoke Signals*, *Rabbit-Proof Fence*, and *Whale Rider*, into the mainstream limelight. Zacharias Kunuk's 2001 *Atanarjuat* (*The Fast Runner*) swept theatres and film festivals in North America and Europe, winning prizes at many international film festivals as well as six Genie awards in Canada. The favorable reception of these productions has helped bring the discussion of Indigenous cultures and Indigenous rights into the mainstream, while also helping to increase nation-state support for local Indigenous film industries. Local control over media has often fostered political and economic sovereignty, while also helping to forge international networks. Yet the crucial role of Indigenous media in communities around the globe tends to be obscured by the media exposure of the art-house successes. The complex dynamics of international Indigenous politics and Indigenous media have yet to receive sufficient and comprehensive attention.

The Internet and related technologies have been extremely important channels of media communication among Indigenous peoples politically, culturally, artistically, and commercially. As early as 1991, a listserv for international Indigenous issues, NATIVE-L, was launched by Gary S. Trujillo, inspired by discussions held at the "From Arctic to Amazonia" environmental conference of Native representatives from around the world in September 1989 at Smith College.[30] NATIVE-L spun into a number of different specialized listservs and also became the basis for NativeNet and later NativeWeb, Web portals on Indigenous issues that became central cyberspace gathering places and resource banks for Indigenous activists and scholars during the 1990s. Key members of these Native networks held the "Internet Native Peoples Conference" in 1994 in Berkeley, California. These virtual networks became the bases for global virtual communities whose participants shared common interests and goals, and in no small way this dialogue contributed to the international Indigenism movement we have discussed.

In 1994 the Oneida Nation was perhaps the first Indigenous nation to set up a tribal Web site, and many others soon followed. As Prins (2001: 520) points out, many are using the Internet to archive their written and visual records (see Woods 1996; Zimmerman, Zimmerman, and Bruguier 2000; d'Errico 2000; Prins 2001; Becker, Vivier, and d'Errico 2002; and *Cultural Survival Quarterly* 1998a). In 2001 Earthwatch Institute sponsored an online roundtable that questioned whether the dominance of English in Internet content promoted "the capitalist ideals and products of modern industrialized society." Key questions asked on the roundtable were: "Is the Internet just another example of Western domination that will speed cultural homogenization? Or can indigenous peoples and cultural minorities join the information revolution to ensure their cultural survival, thus protecting the world's precious cultural diversity?" (see Earthwatch Institute 2001).

In addition to these issues, Indigenous producers are concerned about funding, connectivity, and digital access—in short, the digital divide between those who are "connected" and those who are not (see Ginsburg's essay in this collection; and *Cultural Survival Quarterly* 2006). Kyra Landzelius (2006) offers the most recent research on Indigenous Internet use, providing a collection of ethnographic case studies of Indigenous and diasporic cyberactivism around the globe. Landzelius's collection details the ways cultural groups take up virtual media—both to enhance internal communication in their communities and to forge alliances across ethnic and tribal boundaries, including alliances between Native peoples and grassroots activists surrounding a common cause.

Given the resource-intensive nature of media production, Indigenous media producers often must negotiate the agendas and structures afforded by state institutions or granting agencies, whose interests do not necessarily harmonize perfectly with Indigenous goals and aspirations. As many of our contributors demonstrate (see, in particular, the essays by Murillo, Smith, and Halkin), negotiating does not inevitably entail "selling out" or assimilating. As Kathleen Buddle argues in her contribution to this collection, "Over the course of the colonial era, *engaging* rather than *resisting* larger-scale processes of change provided the means with which to reconfigure and productively expand on localized practices, thereby ensuring their relevance in the modern world."

GLOBAL INDIGENOUS MEDIA: A COLLECTION OF PERSPECTIVES

This collaborative anthology has grown out of a broader project to provide a cultural space for dialogue between Indigenous media producers, scholars, and activists who might otherwise not have the opportunity to come together and share their perspectives, visions, and works of art. As Ginsburg writes in her essay, "Increasingly, the circulation of these media globally—through conferences, festivals, coproductions, and the use of the Internet—has become an important basis for a nascent but growing transnational network of Indigenous media makers and activists. These activists are attempting to reverse processes through which aspects of their societies have been objectified, commodified, and appropriated; their media productions and writings are efforts to recover their histories, land rights, and knowledge bases as their own cultural property." This collection attends to the diversity of this expression by addressing as full a range of media production as possible: feature film, documentary, video art, multimedia works, television programs, radio broadcasts, Internet activism, and journalism. Clearly, growing international and national support has multiplied the distribution outlets for cultural expression, expanding the audience and strengthening global advocacy.

We have selected essays that not only speak to the particulars of their geographic and cultural contexts but also provide significant theoretical insights into the larger questions and processes of Indigeneity and media. We regret that limitations of space and access to the talents of a wider range of Indigenous producers do not allow us to be as comprehensive as we might wish and to cover every form of Indigenous media in every cultural corner of the globe, and we particularly lament the fact that we do not have case studies from India, Africa, or China. However, we hope that this work will inspire future collections that will continue to speak to the centrality of the media for Indigenous movements. This collection identifies the working goals of Indigenous artists and cultural activists in building community, in reenvisioning the political stakes of contemporary Indigenous aesthetics, in mobilizing movements for cultural survival and self-determination, in creating self-sustaining media institutions and places in government institutions, and in fashioning new technologies to articulate and negotiate the meaning of Indigeneity in the twenty-first century.

From Poetics to Politics: Indigenous Media Aesthetics and Style
The chapters in the first section focus on Indigenous media—particularly film, video, and animation—as artistic productions rooted in their culturally specific histories, offering distinct aesthetic and narrative perspectives while positioning themselves in dialogue with, and in contrast to, mainstream media forms and industrial products in both their modes of production and their stylistic elements. They frequently reflect culturally specific and localized Indigenous systems of knowledge and aesthetics adapted to the new technologies that media proffers. Exploring the work of individual artists and media collectives, these essays detail both the vibrancy of contemporary production and the way it opens up a dialogue

between generations and across communities: highlighting the emergence of new aesthetic strategies, the reworking of traditional forms, and the cultural politics of media making in larger regional, national, and global networks of funding and distribution.

Indigenous movements for self-determination require careful analysis of both the conditions of the Fourth World in general and the independent stakes of each group's struggle in particular. Juan Salazar and Amalia Córdova compare Indigenous media to the "imperfect cinema" described by the Cuban filmmaker and theorist Julio García Espinosa, emphasizing that the concept of a *poetics of media* may provide a way to identify the varied and complex Indigenous processes of making culture visible through media practice. Tracing several decades of the development of Indigenous video in Latin America, they provide a critical overview of the debates that have emerged in visual anthropology and Indigenous media activism. For Salazar and Córdova, the models of imperfect and Third Cinema may lead Indigenous filmmakers past the quest for the glossy production values of international art cinema and refocus the question of media in a movement for self-determination. As a movement dedicated to self-representation, "imperfect cinema" puts forth a powerful agenda for an anticolonial cinema. Salazar and Córdova provide a much needed history of how Indigenous media in Latin America have nurtured transnational Indigenous movements.

Jennifer Gauthier, a film scholar, focuses on the pioneering partnership of Barry Barclay with other Maori filmmakers to spark a rebirth of Maori cinema in New Zealand, coupled with increased state funding and creative support. Gauthier outlines Barclay's elaboration of Indigenous aesthetics in his definition of Fourth Cinema and his concept of "doing justice" by "tackling head-on questions of justice in land rights, civil rights, and cultural representation in the nation." Barclay works to produce a cinema that "does justice" to Maori on these terms: including as many Maori as possible on productions and transforming the style and aesthetics of filmmaking to respond to Maori economic, political, and cultural needs and values. As Gauthier explains, Maori cinema must navigate the particular institutions and models of identity and prestige in New Zealand. However, the successes of Maori cinema have opened it up to the dual pressures of commercialization and appropriation by the state.

Some Indigenous producers have responded to these pressures by turning inward and focusing on how media might first serve local needs.

The Cache Collective, a curatorial group of young scholars, examines how the Igloolik Isuma and Arnait Video collectives have adapted video technologies to invent hybrid temporal environments: the tapes store the past in the form of recorded memories while actors and videographers simultaneously use such archived "pasts" to discuss the present and to inform collective video practices. This chapter reveals the complexities of video production in Nunavut by exploring the social, political, and economic dynamics of contemporary Inuit artistic practices, arguing that the videos function as a new form of cultural memory. The collective's rich characterizations of Igloolik and Arnait production show how Indigenous media can reference mainstream genres and production techniques without surrendering to them, dynamically participating in the invention of Inuit tradition for present and future generations.

Examining issues of hybridity, representation, language, and pedagogy in her study of Indigenous-controlled animation production companies in the United States and Canada, Joanna Hearne, a film scholar, describes creative uses of animation to educate and entertain both Indigenous and mainstream audiences. Countering the legacies of intrusive pedagogies from the residential school systems, as well as mainstream media images of "vanishing natives," these short animated films reconstruct Indigenous cultural identities—and cultural futures—by redeploying both traditional oral narratives and Western image-making technologies. Hearne asserts that Indigenous animation intervenes in contested sites of education in several ways: by re-presenting pedagogical iconographies as scenes of storytelling rather than as classroom lessons and by presenting native-controlled images that counter stereotypical productions of "Indianness" in mainstream children's films. Bringing tales and characters of the oral tradition to life in contemporary settings, native animators assert the vitality of storytelling and dynamically preserve cultural continuity.

Indigenous Activism, Advocacy, and Empowerment through Media
The essays in the anthology's second section examine the role played by Indigenous media in cultural and political struggles such as combating discrimination, preserving Indigenous cultures and environments, and advocating for cultural rights—including the right to one's own language, the protection of Indigenous traditional knowledge, and the provision of sufficient resources to Indigenous peoples and their media, as well as mobilizing in advocacy for the ongoing movement for self-determination. These essays directly address the ways that Indigenous media serve local

struggles for recognition by nation-states. Moreover, these chapters emphasize the necessity for media self-representation in the international public sphere—representation that challenges mainstream and official state narratives, helps forge international solidarity movements, and often protects communities by bringing land claims and human rights issues to international attention.

Here, too, local movements strategically engage the state by mobilizing national and international resources and rhetoric whenever possible. As the media scholar Lisa Brooten's chapter on Indigenous media production in Burma suggests, Indigenous peoples must frequently bypass the nation-state in order to achieve international visibility and protection. Brooten examines the role of Indigenous media in a multiethnic opposition movement against the Burmese regime that is slowly changing not only the outside world's picture of Burma but also the self-image of many Indigenous groups. Brooten describes the work of two Indigenous video production groups, both tied to the work of NGOs protecting Indigenous communities and promoting human rights. This work entails great risk, but producers know that only the immediacy of the images and the stories of Burma's Indigenous peoples will bring international pressure to bear on the state.

Kathleen Buddle, in her anthropological study of the social construction of urban Aboriginal women's networks through radio programs in Ontario and Manitoba, provides case studies of the contemporary cultural and gender politics of local Indigenous media centers and projects, demonstrating how media projects themselves may become a focal point for community organization and detailing the complex negotiations between community media centers and state policies for minority cultural content. Buddle demonstrates how such resources can become crucial modes of sustenance and activism for disempowered sectors of Indigenous communities and can provide opportunities for political intervention. Buddle's work illuminates the ways urban radio and kinesthetic practices organize Native women's projects by resignifying the meanings of tradition, womanhood, home, and work, and by creating alternate sites for reception. Buddle examines the implications of Aboriginal women's radio interventions into political domains for the realigning of native nationalist structures of feeling. Thus, against both the mainstream and dominant Aboriginal media, women's community-access radio programs have helped Aboriginal women reimagine their social and political roles.

The contributions by Mario Murillo and Alexandra Halkin, focusing on Indigenous radio in Colombia and the media activism of the Zapatistas, respectively, demonstrate the critical function of the media in Indigenous resistance movements in Latin America, providing additional case studies to enrich and supplement the overview provided by Salazar and Córdova. Murillo's personal experience with Radio Payu'mat attests to radio's power to help sustain local organizing in northern Cauca, one of the most highly militarized and conflictive areas of the Colombian Andes. There, Indigenous communities use radio as a form of resistance to a Colombian national consciousness—a settler-state nationalism and mythology perpetuated by mainstream media and shaped by "materialism, militarism, and corruption." Existing within—or *engaging* (as Buddle would say)—a public sphere affected by both the state and commercial forces, Indigenous radio, Murillo argues, must be assessed in terms of how effectively it fosters not merely a space for Indigenous voices to be heard but also a space for genuine critique.

Halkin, a documentary filmmaker, offers a model of cooperative, transnational Indigenous media making through her experience as founder of the Chiapas Media Project / Promedios, a binational NGO providing video, computer equipment, and training to Indigenous Mexican (Zapatista) communities. Her story illuminates the complex interplay between Zapatista media production, state funding, and international support. The Chiapas communities have adapted video technology as an important tool for internal communication, cultural preservation, and human rights, a medium through which they communicate their own truths and realities to the outside world. A witness to some of the stunning international media interventions made by the Zapatistas in their struggle to promote the visibility of Indigenous people living in Mexico, Halkin illustrates some of the organizational intricacies and intercultural politics of establishing a sustainable local media training and production center.

Cultural Identity, Preservation, and Community Building through Media
The essays in the third section illustrate the critical role of Indigenous media in preserving and maintaining cultural identity and in building community, drawing attention to the interpersonal, local, and everyday aspects of media production and reception and to the connective links formed through such practice. Exploring a variety of community-based Indigenous media projects, these contributors provide a snapshot of the

vitality of Indigenous communities and their media. Given the reality of ongoing internal colonialism, Indigenous activists and filmmakers often operate in national or international institutions. Still, Indigenous media producers do not uncritically take up official categories of identity or the institutions and technologies that enable self-representation. These essays detail how Indigenous media operate in and against states around the world and articulate with different levels of nationalist discourse.

Laurel Smith interrogates the relationship between media, representation, and cultural identity in the Oaxacan pueblo of San Pedro Quiatoni. A cultural geographer, Smith investigates place-based identity by focusing on the production of a community-based video and the role of communications technologies in transnational networks of advocacy: a dialectic between local movements and global political rhetorics. Analyzing the politics of representation, Smith outlines how transnational relations and state institutions contribute to community development initiatives in rural Mexico. Deftly mapping the terrain of ethnopolitics, Smith demonstrates how Indigenous groups fashion politically savvy representations that engage larger translocal and transnational organizations by appropriating their terms for local ends.

The Finnish communication scholar Sari Pietikäinen examines the role of the Sámi-language media, serving a population spread across several nation-states in northern Scandinavia, in communal revitalization, considering such features as cultural renewal, language preservation, and transnationalism. Describing the range of Sámi media, Pietikäinen suggests that a population as "transnational, multilingual, pluricultural, and partly diasporic" as the Sámi require media that are able, as the Sámi say, "to breathe two airs." As such, Sámi media resonate locally *and* serve a specifically "pan-Sámi" function, nurturing broader, transnational needs throughout the diaspora.

Galina Diatchkova, a Chukchi cultural historian, asserts the increasingly vital role that Indigenous media have played in the growth of the Indigenous movement and the institutional and cultural politics in post-Soviet Russia. She chronicles the development of Indigenous broadcasting and journalism, particularly in Chukotka and Kamchatka, as well as the most recent mobilization of information technologies for cultural preservation and advocacy. Diatchkova delineates the political and financial challenges facing Indigenous media initiatives and the development of professional Indigenous media networks coupled with international networks of support. Diatchkova's personal experience with these movements provides valuable insights into how Indigenous groups have mobilized media over decades that witnessed tumultuous changes in state politics and policies. Against official policies of "integration" (assimilation), regional and federal paternalism, and economic crisis, indigenous-language newspapers, radio, television, and now the Internet have preserved language and rallied Indigenous groups.

The Welsh media scholar Ruth McElroy provides a case study challenging the received definition of Indigenous media in the shape of the Welsh-language channel, Sianel Pedwar Cymru (s4c), which began broadcasting in 1982 following an extensive political campaign conducted by both a political party and a social protest group. McElroy considers how discourses of Indigeneity in Wales operate politically in a predominantly white, nonsettler state, only relatively recently afforded a channel of its own and only just beginning to deal with its imperial past and established multiracial and multilingual communities. One of the earliest established European minority-language broadcasters, s4c offers a case study for the analysis of how changing media ecologies and cultural practices have been negotiated by broadcasters, audiences, and program makers alike. Rather than seeing cultural nationalism as necessarily fixing identity, McElroy problematizes the interlocking rhetorics of race, language, nation, and identity as they play out in Welsh-language media.

New Technologies, Timeless Knowledges: Digital and Interactive Media
The final section of the collection brings together exciting new work on the emergence of digital technologies and interactive media among Indigenous artists and in Indigenous communities. These chapters highlight the importance of new media to preserving and disseminating Indigenous knowledge. Demonstrating that new media function as more than mere storage devices for Aboriginal knowledge, these essays show the dynamic interplay between digital technologies and traditional forms of knowing and remembering. As in earlier chapters, these contributors address what Ginsburg (1991) has called the "Faustian contract" facing Indigenous media by demonstrating the vital ways Indigenous producers connect and reconfigure identity via digital technologies and new media, often in a tense partnership with government, academic, and / or commercial interests, yet still maintaining creative and editorial control to ensure representation of their culture. Such insights point again to the centrality of Indigenous poetics and aesthetics in organizing and expressing distinctive cultural ideals, logics, and knowledge. These

chapters also foreground the emerging role of Indigenous digital media in creating interconnected global networks as well as archiving and digitizing heritage and cultural knowledge, using new technologies for very local purposes. Rejecting both absolutist narratives of assimilation through technology and naive arguments about global villages, Indigenous media producers recognize both the pitfalls and promises of digital technology.

The scope of Indigenous media today vanquishes the old stereotype of the "vanishing native" standing passive in the face of the overwhelming forces of modernity. The anthropologists Priscila Faulhaber and Louis Forline detail the proactive self-positioning of the Ticuna Indians of Brazil in relationship to the global via the transposition of Ticuna Indigenous knowledge and rituals into a digitized form for the CD-ROM *Magüta Arü Inü: Recollecting Magüta Thinking*. For the Ticuna, magical thinking is associated with the possibility of reproduction of cultural information disseminated on a large scale. The Ticuna custodians who collaborated on the production of the CD-ROM consider the project an opportunity both to introduce Ticuna epistemology to the world and to be affected—on their own terms—by the world's reception of Ticuna magical thinking.

Michael Christie, a linguist writing about the databasing of Australian Aboriginal knowledge, tells the story of collaborations regarding the new Desert Knowledge Cooperative Research Centre in Alice Springs. Christie cautions that the institutional and technological parameters of "preservation" efforts can indeed affect traditional knowledge in ways not imagined or intended. Aboriginal ways of knowing and theories of knowledge are particularly compromised when information technologies are at work, bringing with them a bias toward Western assumptions about knowledge and its commodification and commercialization. Christie charts the complicated intersection of academic, commercial, state, and local goals, often encoded by the "scale" informing feasibility studies and public projects. For Christie, digital technology is more than a mere medium; it imports a host of assumptions about social relations and economies—about how communities relate to their own cultural production—that may not be compatible with Aboriginal forms of knowledge or Aboriginal desires. Thus he cautions that participants and researchers should ensure that initiatives emerge from local communities and that they begin with a critical analysis of scale.

In our closing chapter, Faye Ginsburg—the anthropologist widely regarded as one of the founding scholars of Indigenous media studies—draws together the themes laid out in this collection by providing some insights into the changing landscape of Indigenous media production in our twenty-first-century digital global village. In "Rethinking the Digital Age," Ginsburg examines how the concept of the digital age has taken on a sense of evolutionary inevitability, creating an increasing stratification and ethnocentrism in the distribution of certain kinds of media practices despite trends to de-Westernize media studies. Ginsburg notes that many Indigenous artists and activists not only dispute the logic of inevitability, but that, increasingly, Indigenous media makers are laying bare and rejecting the institutional and philosophical frameworks smuggled in with programs to bring Indigenous communities *into* the digital age. Indigenous media makers and activists recognize both risks and opportunities as they shout for audibility, desiring to be heard on their own terms, amid the triumphalist din of new media rhetoric. Critical of unadulterated techno-utopianism, Ginsburg argues that Indigenous groups must be the ones to determine their specific needs with regard to new media. Ginsburg seeks to reopen that space by discussing some of the work in new media being produced by Indigenous communities and to suggest how it might expand and complicate our ideas about the digital age in ways that take into account other points of view in the so-called global village. Ginsburg sees these efforts as ways "not only to sustain and build their communities but also to transform them through what one might call a 'strategic traditionalism.' "

Indeed, all of the contributions to this collection can be seen as strategically traditionalist in that they endeavor to protect the distinctive values of community traditions while simultaneously recognizing that culture itself is a living, dynamic organism. Indigenous media makers are producing such dynamic cultural and artistic works: works that question dominant worldviews while at the same time promoting a strategic, internationally conceived Indigenism. International Indigenism, as the contributors to this volume demonstrate, has forged a global support network for artists, activists, and communities. Using contemporary technologies as building blocks, producers dialectically engage Indigenous ways of knowing, being, and relating. In a world where perhaps no culture can hope to enjoy total isolation and autonomy, Indigenous media suggest a way to recognize and nurture local cultural distinctiveness while supplying resources for transnational affiliation.

NOTES

The authors wish to acknowledge those whose influences have led us from our previous research on the cultural politics of Native American representation in the mainstream news media (Wilson 1996, 1998 and 1999) and the rise of Native American filmmaking (Stewart 2001 and 2007) to embrace a global perspective and to see the connections between Indigenous issues and movements throughout the world. We have been especially inspired by Faye Ginsburg (1991, 1993, 1994, 1995, 1997, 1998, 1999, 2000, 2002, 2003, 2005a, b, and c), whose pioneering work has defined the field of indigenous media studies.

1. "ABC Television and the Walt Disney Studios Extend Partnership with the Institute of American Indian Arts to Offer Workshops for Talented Native American Students," ABC press release, June 6, 2005, www.thefutoncritic .com / cgi / pr.cgi?id=20050606abc01; "IAIA Forges Major Partnerships to Support 2005 Film and Television Workshop," IAIA press release, June 13, 2005, www.iaia.edu / apressrelease_63.php; see www.nativenetworks.si.edu / eng / purple / awards_honors.htm; "IAIA's Film and Television Workshop Places Four Students on Hollywood's Fast Track," IAIA press release, October 10, 2005, www.iaia.edu / cpressrelease_81.php.

2. "2006 Sundance Film Festival to Feature Native Forum Workshops along with 4 Native American and Indigenous Films," Sundance Institute press release, January 11, 2006; "2006 Sundance Film Festival Issues Call for Submissions from Native American and Indigenous Filmmakers," Sundance Institute press release, September 12, 2005, festival.sundance.org / 2006 / festival / press.aspx.

3. Profile of Bunky Echo-Hawk, retrieved November 2005 from www.thenaica .org / images / artists-in-residence / artists-in-residence_be.htm.

4. See, e.g., regarding the imaging of Native Americans by the dominant media: Bataille and Silet 1980; Churchill 1998; Deloria 1998; Kilpatrick 1999; and Rollins 2003.

5. Indigenous media activists have continued to work in partnership with nonindigenous specialists such as anthropologists and other community activists (see Alexandra Halkin's essay in this collection), and one training ground in the United States for aspiring Indigenous media makers was the Anthropology Film Center in Santa Fe, founded in 1965.

6. In 1972 a group of anthropologists founded the Society for the Anthropology of Visual Communication (SAVICOM), which became a section of the American Anthropological Association. In 1984 SAVICOM was replaced by the Society for Visual Anthropology (Prins 2002b: 304–5).

7. Another significant venue for advocacy reporting on Indigenous media issues around the world has been the work of Cultural Survival, an NGO founded by

the anthropologist David Maybury-Lewis in 1972 and dedicated to "promoting the rights, voices, and visions of indigenous peoples" (www.culturalsurvival.org). Beginning as early as 1983, this organization has focused a number of issues of its *Cultural Survival Quarterly* on issues related to media: "The Electronic Era" (1983); "Native American Journalism" (1994); "The Internet and Indigenous Groups" (1998a); "Aboriginal Media, Aboriginal Control" (1998b); and, most recently, "Indigenous Peoples Bridging the Digital Divide" (2006).

8. Quote is from the Web site of 3Cmedia, an annual scholarly electronic journal published by the Community Broadcasting Association of Australia; see www.cbonline.org.au / 3cmedia / . Although community broadcasting and Indigenous broadcasting share many of the same interests and issues, not all community broadcasting is Indigenous.

9. U.N. Document E-RES-1982-34. All documents from the U.N. Commission on Human Rights regarding Indigenous Peoples are available online in a database searchable by access number at ap.ohchr.org / documents / sdpage_ e.aspx?s=75. For sake of brevity, in subsequent listings only the specific information and access number will be provided rather than the search chain URL.

10. U.N. Document E-RES-1988-36.

11. United Nations Economic and Social Council 1994: 105–15. See also Daes 1993. For comments on recent sessions, see *Indian Country Today* 2005; Roy 2005; and c 2005.

12. U.N. Document E-RES-2000-22.

13. Macdonald 2006; Rizvi 2006.

14. For more on Daes's contribution to Indigenous rights work at the global level, see Alfredsson and Stavropoulou 2002.

15. Daes builds on two previous definitions of Indigeneity that laid the groundwork for the concept in international discourses. The first was in the International Labor Organization's (ILO) Convention no. 169 on Indigenous and Tribal Peoples, adopted in 1989 "to include the fundamental concept that the ways of life of Indigenous and tribal peoples should and will survive." Convention no. 169 set out a working definition of Indigenous peoples: "(a) Tribal peoples in independent countries whose social, cultural and economic conditions distinguish them from other sections of the national community, and whose status is regulated wholly or partially by their own customs or traditions or by special laws or regulations; (b) Peoples in independent countries who are regarded as indigenous on account of their descent from the populations which inhabited the country, or a geographical region to which the country belongs, at the time of conquest or colonisation or the establishment of present state boundaries and who, irrespective of their legal status, retain some or all of their own social, economic, cultural and political institutions, . . . self-identification as indigenous or tribal shall be regarded as a

fundamental criterion for determining the groups to which the provisions of this Convention apply" (www.ilo.org/public/english/indigenous). The second definition, formulated during this same period, appeared in José Martínez Cobo's five-volume U.N. *Study of the Problem of Discrimination against Indigenous Populations* (1986), which presented the first comprehensive definition of *indigenous* in a U.N. document: "Indigenous communities, peoples and nations are those which, having a historical continuity with preinvasion and precolonial societies that developed on their territories, consider themselves distinct from other sectors of the societies now prevailing in those territories, or parts of them. They form at present nondominant sectors of society and are determined to preserve, develop and transmit to future generations their ancestral territories, and their ethnic identity, as the basis of their continued existence as peoples, in accordance with their own cultural patterns, social institutions and legal systems" (Cobo 1986, quoted in Daes 1996: 9–10).

16. See Daes 1996 and an addendum to that Working Paper: "The Concept of 'Indigenous Peoples' (U.N. Document E/CN.4/Sub.2/AC.4/1996/2/Add.1).

17. As cited in Daes 1996: 13; see U.N. document E/CN.4, Sub. 2/1995/24, para. 41 for original.

18. David Goodman (2004) and others suggest a model of internal colonialism for the governing and development of many of China's ethnic minorities, even though Goodman surmises that such a concept does not sit well with the worldview of a communist regime. Quote is from Embassy of the Peoples' Republic of China in Switzerland 1997.

19. Although the U.N. Human Rights covenants are meant to support the right of self-determination to all peoples, the "blue water" or "salt water" thesis has been used by some nation-states to exclude peoples living under internal colonialism from the right to self-determination. Annette Jaimes (1992: 74) explained that the "Belgian Thesis" argued that "decolonization should extend to all colonized peoples, even if they are bound in enclaves entirely surrounded by colonizing states," such as those of Indigenous peoples: "Despite this attempt to extend decolonization to indigenous peoples, the 'salt water thesis' has predominated in international debate." The notion of the Fourth World was also meant to address the distinct conditions supporting the self-determination of Indigenous peoples often *against* postcolonial states.

20. Daes (1996: 23) hints that the inability of some governments to recognize the Indigeneity of groups within their states is not due to a lack of definition but rather to the "efforts of some Governments to limit its globality, and of other Governments to build a high conceptual wall between 'indigenous' and 'peoples' and/or 'Non-Self-Governing Territories.'"

21. In this book, we use the term *nation-state* (or *state*) to represent the sovereign political bodies, generally recognized by the international communities such

as the United Nations, within and across the boundaries of which Indigenous peoples and Indigenous nations have historically found themselves subsumed by conquest and empire. This does not negate the sense of nation, and sometimes (as in the case of many Native American tribal nations) the claims to sovereignty vis-à-vis their treaty status, that many Indigenous peoples embrace. It is a political designation that allows us to discuss the structures of power and governance in which Indigenous groups must negotiate their cultural and political status. As Gérard Chaliand (1989) notes, empires "gave way to states which sought to be nations," yet rarely has such a state been homogeneous and reflected a unified population. Rather, the irony of most modern nation-states is that they are primarily states exercising their power to attempt to either assimilate or manage the segments of their population who represent internal nationalities, or as Fleras and Elliot (1992) term them, "the nations within."

22. For a history of the evolving definition of aboriginality in Australia, see Gardiner-Garden 2000. For a history of these issues in Canada, see Asch 1997 and Hylton 1994.

23. For recent anthropological discussions of the classification of China's ethnic minorities, see Gladney 2003, 2004; Harrell 2001; and Schein 2000.

24. State-owned media in China promote such discourse in reports about the country's minority nationalities. For example, a 1999 article in the *People's Daily* anticipating the new *xibu da kaifa* (Great Western Development) program explained that such development would "help the people of various nationalities to speedily shake off poverty and become prosperous [and] will further the unity of the people of various nationalities and strengthening of national defense on the borderland in contribution to the building of a united stable motherland" (from *People's Daily* 1999).

25. In the United States, for example, the pan-Indian movement emerged in the early twentieth century with regional intertribal organizations leading to nationwide political advocacy groups by midcentury such as the Association on American Indian Affairs and the National Congress of American Indians.

26. United Nations, *Draft Declaration on the Rights of Indigenous Peoples* (1994).

27. For the report, see U.N. Document E / CN.4 / Sub.2 / Ac.4 / 1998 / 6.

28. Gluck 2005; Tsai 2007.

29. See Jakubowicz 2006; and the 2005 Indigenous Television Review Report from Australia's Department of Communications, Information Technology and the Arts ("Department of . . ." 2005).

30. This conference became the basis for an independent video, *Arctic to Amazonia* (1993), produced by Robbie Leppzer of Turning Tide Productions.

PART I

FROM POETICS TO POLITICS:

INDIGENOUS MEDIA AESTHETICS AND STYLE

IMPERFECT MEDIA AND THE POETICS OF INDIGENOUS VIDEO IN LATIN AMERICA

Juan Francisco Salazar and Amalia Córdova

In May 1998 the Eighth International Congress on Mental Health, Alcohol, and Drugs, held in Santiago, Chile, promoted its agenda with artwork featuring the image of a Mapuche woman superimposed on that of a brain. The woman's image had been grossly recontextualized, cut and pasted from a classic ethnographic photograph taken in the early 1920s. The Coordinadora Nacional Indianista de Chile (CONACIN, National Indigenous Corporation of Chile) delivered a strong public response to the organizers of the conference: "We were stripped out of our land. We were deprived of our gods and language. We were brought alcohol and venereal diseases. And after all the plunder, now they want to appropriate our images and treat us like drunks, criminals, and drug addicts. Our faces and ways of seeing have been taken away. Besides negating our images and usurping our archives of dreams, they have colonized our imagination through the mass media."[1]

While cases like this are commonplace in the region, the colonization of an Indigenous imaginary only recently became an issue of debate among scholars and media activists in Latin America. In fact, at a panel on Indigenous media at the Second International Film Festival of Morelia, Mexico (October 10, 2004), the Purehepecha director Dante Cerano distinguished Indigenous video or "Indigenous audiovisual artists" from the work of what he called "indigenist" Western documentary filmmakers. His comment sparked huge controversy among attending filmmakers who have been involved in collaborative projects for Indigenous communities in Mexico, yet it indicates the current push by many Indigenous filmmakers for independence and autonomy. Cerano was pointing specifically to the need to consider Indigenous media as an autonomous and independent field of media production distinct from non-Indigenous documentary or ethnographic film.

Over the past twenty-five years, Indigenous videomakers from Latin America have been "making culture visible" from their own perspective. In creating, imagining, and reinventing traditional social relationships through the moving image, Indigenous organizations are finding new forms of cultural resistance and revitalization. At the heart of this emerging Indigenous video movement in Latin America, we see a process grounded in local struggles for political self-determination, cultural and linguistic autonomy, and legal recognition, with potentially transnational and pan-American implications. This social embeddedness of textual practices—what Faye Ginsburg (1994) calls "embedded aesthetics"—is one of the critical aspects to consider when looking at the development of Indigenous video in Latin America.

We call these deep-rooted cultural aesthetics *the poetics of Indigenous media*. At the center of a poetics of Indigenous media, we locate socially embedded self-representation, or the active process of making culture visible. "Poetics" originates in the Greek notion of *poiesis,* meaning active making or the process of making. Our examination of media poetics draws from earlier conceptualizations of the notion as applied in film studies (Bordwell 1989; Ruiz 1995; Renov 1993) and expands it to encompass a notion of the poetics of Indigenous media that considers the social practices involved in making (Indigenous) culture visible through video media. The poiesis, or making, of media refers both to the processes and the products of representation, in what may be regarded as a particular cultural logic of Indigenous media—specifically, the way media practices become effective strategies for Indigenous peoples to shape counter-discourses and engender alternative public spheres.

Just as notions of Indigeneity and Aboriginality should be challenged in terms of how these categories are socially constructed, Latin American notions of Indigeniety should also be critically approached. In English, the terms *indigenist* and *indigeneity* do not convey the same degree of difference as is implied by the corresponding Spanish words. *Indigenismo* in Latin American history refers to a political and cultural movement that swept across most of Latin America during much of the twentieth century. Its origins may be traced back to the 1910s in the Mexican Revolution, when Latin American societies in ethnically diverse countries such as Mexico and Peru began to "look in the mirror" and construct themselves as mestizo societies. This non-Indigenous ideology crossed the fields of art, culture, literature, politics, and socioeconomics as an attempt to rescue the Indigenous subject from oblivion and oppression, acknowledge a rich and suppressed Indigenous heritage, assimilate Indigenous cultures as a key to social development, and ultimately reaffirm the complexities of Latin American modern identities. Across the continent, it influenced government policies that were applied to Indigenous peoples without consultation.[2] The fundamental criticism of the ideological construct of Indigenismo as it emerged in the 1970s was that it assumed a passive Indigenous subject that needed to be represented, rescued, and constructed from the enlightenment of Western values.

Latin American notions of *cine indigena* (Indigenous film), *video indigena* (Indigenous video), or *audiovisual indigena* (Indigenous media) also carry distinct social meanings. Much like the terms *native, indigenous*, and *aboriginal*, as Erica Wortham (2004: 366) asserts, "*Video indigena* has been appropriated and self-consciously resignified as a *postura* or political position vital to indigenous struggles for self-determination." Therefore, by tracing a genealogy of Indigenous video in Latin America, we endeavor to do more than map the origins of the Indigenous video movement per se; we also wish to attest to the "unveiling of the silencing, exclusion, and violence which are always, the genealogist contends, the condition of possibility of the origin, the origin of the origin, so to speak" (Avelar n.d.).

Based on our involvement with different organizations, festivals, and media makers in the past few years, we believe that Indigenous video in Latin America can be characterized as *imperfect* media that respond in a constructive way to calls for unthinking the Eurocentric foundations implicit in many of the Latin American cultural and creative industries (see Shohat and Stam 1994). In the larger picture, Indigenous video calls for the decolonization of media practice from the dominant industry's film and videomaking conventions to the sometimes overshadowing involvement of non-Indigenous producers, funding agencies, and nongovernmental organizations (NGOs). While contemporary mainstream Latin American cinema has moved away from many of the ideologies of the Latin America Cinema movement of the 1960s and 1970s (i.e., Third Cinema, imperfect cinema, cinema of underdevelopment, revolutionary cinema, aesthetics of hunger, etc.), Indigenous media embody and enact a much more radical and sustainable model of such community-based media. This movement challenges not only the dominant politicolegal structures of the Latin American states but also their cultural foundations. Indigenous organizations and individuals in Latin America are creating distinctive media projects, structures, and networks that demonstrate how effective and coordinated local mobilization and transnational networking might allow indigenous peoples to challenge the "indigenist" rhetoric of development, modernization, and citizenship perpetuated by laws, treaties, and constitutions across all Latin American nation-states. What we see happening today across the region is not only the emergence of new Indigenous videomakers but the formation and shaping of a whole new wave of communicators who are taking the question of media democracy to the next level.

TOWARD AN *IMPERFECT* VIDEO

By updating and recontextualizing Julio García Espinosa's notion of *imperfect cinema,* we hope to illuminate contemporary Indigenous media practice in Latin America and its arrested development through the past twenty years. García Espinosa's manifesto "For an Imperfect Cinema" (1983 [1970]), along with Glauber Rocha's "An Aesthetics of Hunger" (1965) and Fernando Solanas's and Octavio Getino's "Towards a Third Cinema" (1966), laid out the polemical goals of the New Latin American Cinema. This loose movement of (mainly male) filmmakers established the political and aesthetics foundations of "Third Cinema," emphasizing an ideal of social change beginning with the subversion and overthrow of the hegemonic structures of film production, distribution, and consumption dictated by the Hollywood system. These strategies reimagined what a national cinema might be—envisioning a national-popular cinema. To a much lesser extent, this position or *postura* also explored alternative forms of storytelling. Imperfect cinema, for example, warned against the illusion of technical perfection fostered by hegemonic cinema. For García Espinosa, any attempt to match the perfection of commercial films contradicted the implicit objective of a revolutionary cinema—that is, the call for an active and participatory audience. García Espinosa was interested in a new poetics of cinema and a different mode of film practice based on a consciously and resolutely "committed" cinema.

By no means should we assume that Indigenous filmmakers cannot pursue more creative aesthetics or industrial modes of production, or that political documentaries are the only route ahead. As Antoni Castells i Talens (2003) suggests, mixed modes of production might work on several levels. Political denunciation videos play a key role in Indigenous mobilization, he reaffirms, "yet a culture that only represents itself as activist cannot achieve normalization." This realization is perhaps the greatest strength of a new wave of Aboriginal and Indigenous filmmakers coming out of Australia and Aotearoa / New Zealand.

Indigenous media have forced the discussion of political production to move beyond the well-worn poles of the debate: mass cinema versus auteur cinema, or a cinema of naive liberation versus one that destroys tradition. In fact, these polarities continue to obscure the complexities of community media production (Rodríguez 2001: 6). On a similar note, discussing Indigenous media in Australia and the South Pacific, Helen Molnar and Michael Meadows (2001: xi) have demonstrated that Indigenous people throughout the world "do not necessarily see themselves as imprisoned by the dominant culture of the mass media and, in fact, find their own 'spaces' in which to produce alternative viewpoints and cultures."

Indigenous video production in Latin America, in other words, is positioning itself as a distinct field of cultural production—as a signifying practice separate from national cinemas, popular and community video, and tactical media practices. It inhabits its own representational space and is starting to create parallel circuits of production, dissemination, and reception of cultural materials, which for some indicates the end of the hegemony of the literate and the beginning of a decolonization of the intellect (Ticona and Sanjinés 2004).

We must note, however, that many obstacles remain. Indigenous producers work in a landscape that differs considerably from other forms of audiovisual production. They often work collectively, without training, infrastructure, or equipment. What training is available must be compressed into short workshops, and the dearth of funding opportunities usually means that there are long gaps between productions. Finally, unlike commercial media, Indigenous production stresses the producers' ties and accountability to communities.

In the following pages, we describe some of these projects and cases in more detail and offer a genealogy of Indigenous video in Latin America. Based on our participation in the process during the last few years, we map the contemporary Indigenous media landscape in the region by tracing the development of the Consejo Latinoamericano de Cine y Comunicación de los Pueblos Indígenas (CLACPI, Latin American Council of Indigenous Film and Communication).[3]

However paradoxical as it may seem, the force of the New Latin American Cinema started to wane quite rapidly sometime in the mid-1980s, coinciding with the rise of grassroots and independent video collectives in many Latin American countries (see, e.g., Festa and Santoro 1991; Aufderheide 1995; and Roncagliolo 1991). Perhaps not coincidentally, the formal beginnings of Indigenous video production in Latin America may be traced back to the booklet *Toward an Indigenous Video,* first published in Mexico in 1983 by the government's Instituto Nacional Indigenista (INI, National Indigenous Institute) (INI 1990). In a sense, this rather official launch of Indigenous video in Mexico also came to redefine the use of *video popular* in the political and cultural agenda of several video collectives of the time. The context in which Indigenous video in Latin America surfaces is not just intimately tied to exemplary cases of participatory media beginning with the indirect legacy of "Third Cinema" in the 1960s and 1970s, but it is also linked to more direct experiences of *video popular* and radical community video in the 1980s (Thede and Ambrosi 1991) and video collectives organized in the 1990s. We think the surge of Indigenous video in Latin America in the last twenty years is not confined either to the sympathetic legacy of participatory methods in ethnographic film or to the interests of ethnographic filmmakers in the Indigenous struggle for cultural survival. This first impulse stemmed from the concern of applied anthropologists working in the early 1980s in NGOs—and not just from ethnographic filmmakers working at the community level—who perceived the particular interests and demands of Indigenous activists turning to radio and video as instruments of political action.

The beginnings of the 1980s were marked by severe economic crises sweeping a region already affected by political nationalism, right-wing military dictatorships, social inequality, and cultural paternalism (i.e., misleading policies) toward Indigenous populations. Until the early 1990s, Indigenous peoples were not constitutionally recognized in any Latin American country, and it has only been in the last decade or so that some countries, such as Colombia, Mexico, and Peru, have reformed their national constitutions to include their respective Native peoples. Other countries have legally recognized the existence of ethnic minorities but not of Indigenous nations, and, until recently, the legacies of *indigenismo* have still been felt strongly across a wide range of fields.

Responding to generations of invading ethnographic, documentary, and commercial film crews, Indigenous communities began to take up the means of audiovisual production and to generate their own narratives and images of themselves. Against this backdrop CLACPI was created in 1985 by a group of committed media makers, anthropologists, and Indigenous activists in Mexico, launching a festival to strengthen the training, development, production, and exposure of Indigenous film and video by, about, and for Indigenous peoples. CLACPI surfaced to gather the scattered but emerging audiovisual efforts (mainly film and video) in Latin America, with the aim of channeling the growing demands for more valid, vetted means of communication among and emanating from, by, and for Indigenous communities.

The first CLACPI festival was swiftly organized in 1985 in Mexico City, primarily around a showcase of mostly non-Indigenous 16-millimeter films shot in the late 1970s and early 1980s by documentary and ethnographic filmmakers interested in Indigenous politics. In this first festival, awards for excellence in cinematographic production went to such films as *Nuestra voz de tierra, memoria y futuro* (*Our Voice of Earth, Memory, and Future*) (Jorge Silva and Marta Rodríguez, Colombia, 1973), *Los hieleros del Chimborazo* (*The Icemen of Mount Chimborazo*) (Gustavo Guayasamín, Ecuador, 1980), and *Mara'acame, cantador y curandero* (*Mara'acame, Singer and Healer*) (Juan Francisco Urrusti, Mexico, 1982).

Despite the good intentions, Indigenous organizations and media makers were still outsiders in the process of appropriating moving images, with their own voices and point of view. This tendency continued well into the mid-1990s, with CLACPI festivals held in Brazil (1987), Venezuela (1990), and Peru (1992) following the inaugural format established in Mexico.[4] The second festival, held in Rio de Janeiro in 1987, coincided with the public presentation of two groundbreaking processes of Indigenous video production founded some years earlier. One was a project with Kayapó people in the Brazilian Amazon, Mekaron Opoi D'joi (He Who Creates Images),[5] originated by Brazilian photographer / filmmaker Mônica Frota with the assistance and vast documentation of the U.S. anthropologist Terence Turner. The other is the ongoing project Vídeo nas Aldeias (VNA, Video in the Villages), headed by photographer Vincent Carelli and originating at the Centro de Trabalho Indigenista (CTI, Indigenous Work Center), a Sao Paulo–based, non-Indigenous NGO that Carelli had helped to create after he had left the state-affiliated Indian office, Fundação Nacional do Indio (FUNAI, National Indian Foundation).[6] As Carelli (2004) recently has recalled, "It was not going to be the state that would change the situation of Indians, but they themselves who must take their destiny in their own hands. . . . We took part in the general movement of Brazilian civil society in search of alternatives." Although VNA began at the CTI, it is now an independent media center where Indigenous organizations have today a more prominent involvement, though still under Carelli's charge.

In 1989 another exemplary event took place when Mexico's INI implemented a historic Native media training program called the Transferencia de Medios Audiovisuales a Organizaciones y Comunidades Indígenas (Transfer of Audiovisual Media to Indigenous Communities and Organizations). As part of this project, state-sponsored video centers called *centros de video indígena* (CVIS) were established in four Mexican states. These video centers coordinate much of the Indigenous video production in Mexico today, but their influence and omnipresence has decreased in recent years, giving way to Indigenous-owned or -coordinated video centers like Ojo de Agua Comunicación (Eye of Water Communications) in Oaxaca. The CVIS provide a good example of the complex entanglement of Indigenous video and national politics across the region. Erica Wortham (2004: 363–64), for example, has demonstrated that this project originated "at the height of official pluralism in Mexico" after 1987, whereby a "government video program created in a transitional institutional setting colludes with the indigenous autonomy movement— through the work and visions of individual video makers and cultural activists—to produce a social form and process that has gained international recognition while confronting particular challenges in indigenous communities." By 1992 several Indigenous videomakers in Mexico were forming the independently run Organización Mexicana de Videastas Indígenas (OMVIAC, Mexican Organization of Indigenous Videomakers) in an effort to create a national organization of Indigenous communicators. It eventually dispersed, leaving videomakers to work with independent Indigenous media production centers or with the CVIS channeled through the Mexican state.

In June of the same year, during the fourth CLACPI festival held in Cuzco and Lima, the organization was restructured to encompass the demands of Indigenous producers for better access to audiovisual tech-

CLACPI festival poster, 1996. COURTESY OF CAROLINA SANJINÉS / CLACPI.

nology and for a voice in the processes of decision making, coordination, and programming. These changes would crystallize in two different ways. First, Indigenous communities in Ecuador took a different route from CLACPI, founding the Abya Yala Network and organizing the Indigenous Abya Yala video festivals. The Confederación de Nacionalidades Indígenas del Ecuador (CONAIE, Confederation of Indigenous Nationalities of Ecuador) played a fundamental role in this process, organizing four Abya Yala video festivals and issuing the Quito Declaration of 1994, a foundational document which asserted the right of Indigenous peoples to the creation and recreation of their own image.[7]

Second, between CLACPI's 1992 festival and the following festival held in Santa Cruz, Bolivia, in 1996 (see figure), Indigenous groups forged a national strategy for the production of Indigenous video. The festival in Bolivia was launched along with a consultative, long-term strategy of building a national plan for Indigenous media training and production, including international and regional workshops. This model marked the beginnings of what we consider to be the paradigmatic experience: the Plan Nacional Indígena de Comunicación Audiovisual (PNICA, National Indigenous Audiovisual Communication Plan) in Bolivia and the formation of the Coordinadora Audiovisual Indígena-Originaria de Bolivia (CAIB, Bolivian Indigenous-Aboriginal Audiovisual Council). The PNICA was implemented following a nationwide consultation, becoming an extensive nationwide media training and production initiative to support Indigenous self-representation, and training Indigenous people from different nations and communities in video production. The PNICA is jointly coordinated by the media training center Centro de Formación y Realización Cinematográfica (CEFREC, Center for Cinematographic Training and Production) and CAIB, which includes three of Bolivia's primary Indigenous organizations. Productions address community needs and seek to counteract the effects of mass media on the communities. Themes range from journalistic reportage to traditional stories, told through short fictions, documentaries, news programs for television, music videos, and video letters. The resulting work—though widely acknowledged and circulated at Indigenous film and video festivals in Bolivia and throughout Latin America—is not in distribution. Paradoxically, in La Paz, CEFREC houses the most extensive Indigenous video archive in Latin America, making it CLACPI's main centralized media collection site.

By the seventh CLACPI festival, held in Chile in 2004 (see fig. 1.2), festival coordinators had consolidated a different approach to recognizing the contribution of works screened at these festivals. This new form of appraisal, which had been in development since the 1992 festival in Peru and had been influenced by the Abya Yala festival's award system, finally acknowledged the notion of imperfect video and the distinct cultural poetics of Indigenous media practice. Looking at the awards for best films granted at CLACPI festivals from 1996 onward, we see a significant shift away from rewarding impeccable technical *products* toward praising *processes*. Festival organizers chose to prioritize and acknowledge agents of social change and cultural transformation affecting Indigenous peoples across the region. This shift is exemplified by the categories for awards in place after 1996: the preservation of cultural identity; the defense of Indigenous peoples' rights; the social organization of indigenous com-

CLACPI festival poster, 2004. COURTESY OF GUIDO GUTIÉRREZ / CLACPI.

munities; artistic creation; best fiction with Indigenous participation; testimonial and documentary value; trajectory in Indigenous communications; and best *mise en scène*. No other film or video festival in the world places as much emphasis on the creation process.

So when we attempt to "unpack *video indígena*" in Latin America (Wortham 2004), the notion of imperfect video reminds us that there is no such thing as an absolute or perfect televisual language. Imperfect media is about the constant search for new languages, languages unconcerned with technical perfection or conventional rules and modes of representation and narrativization. It reflects and is grounded in the needs of its users in a communal setting, but with an eye turned toward intercommunal and transnational contexts. The Cochabamba Declaration[8] of the 1996 festival in Bolivia summarized these ideals, which have become the point of reference for Indigenous media practice in Latin America, grounded in the specific cultural logic of Indigenous videomaking processes.

CLACPI's festivals have not only consolidated CLACPI as a pan-Indigenous organization, they also have strengthened the social spaces of Indigenous media production and the position of Indigenous media makers in the management of their organizations. Like the Bolivian experience, past festivals in Guatemala (1999) and Chile (2004) have ended with important political declarations demanding attention to Indigenous peoples in social processes, such as in Colombia and Guatemala's peace processes and the situation of Mapuche political prisoners in Chile. In addition, these festivals saw the emergence of a new group of *auteur* videomakers, such as Marcelina Cárdenas (Quechua), Dante Cerano (Purhepecha), Mariano Estrada (Tzeltzal),[9] Juan José García (Zapotec and CLACPI president until 2006), Alberto Muenala (Quichua), and Jeannette Paillán (Mapuche), among many others. The festival in Chile in 2004 brought together a large group of Indigenous videomakers and audiences to public screenings, including a program devoted to CEFREC-CAIB productions and several videos from Indigenous Zapatista communities in Chiapas.

Digital video technology has greatly contributed to this surge of production. More affordable than film, digital technology has enabled communities with limited resources to produce high-quality video. All of the award winners of the 2004 CLACPI festival were shot on digital formats. As more and more videos are shot in Mini DV and DVcam / DVCPro, the irritating notion of "broadcast quality" has once more revealed its ideological origins. Still, the jury's special mentions awarded to works dealing with the struggle of women and of urban gay and lesbian Indigenous people; the acknowledgement of emergent themes such as genetic engineering, environmental disasters, and their impact on Indigenous communities; and the recovery of traditional music all indicate attention to process (mobilization) rather than product.

During the 2004 festival in Santiago, mornings were devoted to the first symposia on new technologies, audiovisual industries, technological convergence, and community media, as well as to panels on local projects, marking the potential of Indigenous video in the years to come. These panels gave an overview of the Indigenous communication processes in progress across the region and delineated sustainable and enduring models of media production. Two main issues concerning product and process were identified: (1) in terms of product, the problem of the distribution of videos, and (2) in terms of process, the question of autonomy.

AUTONOMOUS PRODUCTION: THE FUTURE COORDINATES
OF INDIGENOUS VIDEO IN LATIN AMERICA

Addressing the future of Indigenous video practice in Latin America will require attention to problems of funding dependency and of the technological sustainability of projects. Most projects depend heavily on either state or international cooperation funding, or rely completely on the committed work of certain nongovernment organizations and the leaders of the few media centers devoted to Indigenous-produced video, such as those already mentioned.

The Indigenous video landscape in Latin America can be roughly sorted into three tentative groupings: (1) a group of projects that have achieved continuity in time and space, producing and circulating works steadily; (2) organizations or projects that have a more sporadic flow of production and circulation but remain in existence; and (3) those areas where production is scarce or very discontinuous.

The first group includes the cvi (Indigenous video centers), now run by the Mexican government's Indigenous commission, the Comisión Nacional para el Desarrollo de los Pueblos Indígenas (cdi, National Commission for the Development of Indigenous Peoples); the training and production initiative Promedios de Comunicación Comunitaria / Chiapas Media Project (cmp) in southern Mexico; vna in Brazil; and the pnica of Bolivia. These four cases offer different models, but each is far from an industrial or commercial mode of production. What they have in common is that they all offer a representational space from which to debate and present an alternative modernity for Indigenous peoples. All of them open new windows of opportunity for generating an audiovisual and oral collective process for reflection and community mobilization.

Production in Mexico is relatively prolific; Indigenous Mexican work circulates more widely than any other Latin American Indigenous productions through regional Latin American, "Latino," and international Indigenous documentary and ethnographic film festivals, and increasingly through informal binational (U.S.-Mexico) migrant circuits. Documentary is by far the strongest genre, with few but quite innovative Indigenous-produced fictions.[10] Indigenous directors from Mexico have traveled to other Latin American countries to receive training and also to teach at Indigenous video workshops coordinated by CLACPI or regional media organizations.

While the National Plan (PNICA) in Bolivia has nationwide aspirations but remains completely independent of the government, the Mexican experience has had strong state involvement. As Wortham (2004) acknowledges, "*Video indígena* was given *carácter nacional* (national character) by INI" through the founding in the mid-1990s of the CVIs, giving rise to the question of Indigenous autonomy and communication independence. State control over the CVIs has decreased in the past years due to financial constraints, political disputes, and mismanagement. Simultaneously, nonprofit Indigenous media organizations have emerged, such as Ojo de Agua Comunicación, with Zapotec founding member Juan José García as its recent president. Initiated by Indigenous videomakers and their non-Native collaborators, Ojo de Agua Comunicación provides many Indigenous media makers with alternative social spaces from which to work and communicate.

Promedios de Comunicacion Comunitaria / Chiapas Media Project (see Alexandra Halkin's essay in this collection) has achieved a successful partnership with autonomous Indigenous Zapatista communities since 1998. Based in Mexico and in the United States, the organization subtitles the productions in English, enabling the work to screen at festivals, conferences, and tours, and is the only Latin American project that self-distributes its work internationally. Promedios considers autonomous community video production to be the foundation for the communication of an Indigenous perspective at every level. The project is autonomous from any government involvement, though it does rely on foreign cooperation.

The PNICA in Bolivia, VNA in Brazil, and to a lesser extent, Promedios in Chiapas, rely fundamentally on international cooperation funding (Norwegian, Dutch, Spanish, Swedish, Canadian, and U.S.) and international agencies such as UNESCO as well as, in recent years, the World Association for Christian Communication (WACC). They are coordinated by a core group of selfless local organizers, including Ivan Sanjinés, director of CEFREC in La Paz, and Vincent Carelli of VNA in Olinda.

VNA remains an independent and ongoing training, production, and circulation initiative that works with community-based Indigenous video producers in Brazil. Works are screened regularly in indigenous villages and communities as part of the training programs. Over the past decade, VNA has produced some of the most widely circulating Indigenous videos, which have won major awards at international Indigenous film festivals.

The National Plan in Bolivia is a partnership between the grassroots Indigenous organizations in Bolivia that form CAIB and the independent media center CEFREC. Since its launch in 1996, the National Plan has relied on nongovernmental funding generated from grassroots Indigenous organizations (such as CAIB) and international funds raised through CEFREC. The CEFREC-CAIB partnership also sustains CLACPI's Indigenous media archive, publishing a catalogue of works every few years.

In general, the four projects mentioned above engage in national and regional workshops, in both rural and urban contexts, producing programs that range from feature-length documentaries to community television programs, video letters, short fictions, and special series portraying important conflicts taking place in their territories. Some of the resulting works are safeguarded in video libraries around the world. Many have been subtitled into several languages and are screened at international festivals, yet only a few titles have had international distribution. If Indigenous videos are to circulate to wider audiences, communities, and audiovisual markets, the lack of existing distributors dedicated to Indigenous productions will have to be addressed urgently. This issue was strongly raised at one of several roundtables during the CLACPI festival in Chile in 2004.

A second tier of media organizations includes those that generate works somewhat sporadically. The Communications Department of the national Indigenous organization of Colombia, the Organización Nacional Indígena de Colombia (ONIC, National Indigenous Organization of Columbia), and the state-supported Indigenous Communication Office of CONAIE in Ecuador have been instrumental in the development of programs and festivals at both a local and international level. Both organizations house important yet precarious media archives. Unfortunately, both rely heavily on the fluctuating politics of the government administration currently in power and on the delicate balance between local Indigenous organizations.

On a third level, small independent Indigenous and non-Indigenous production companies—dispersed throughout Argentina, Chile, Guatemala, Peru, and Venezuela—support or produce Indigenous media production more irregularly. There are no nationwide media centers to coordinate the efforts of Indigenous media makers in these areas. Supported by CLACPI, a network is in progress in the Southern Cone to bring together Indigenous producers from Argentina, Bolivia, Chile, Paraguay, and Perú.[11] Despite having fragile structures of production and different forms of organization and representation, Indigenous video is also being produced even in less documented areas such as Paraguay, Nicaragua, and Panama.

With the limitations and conditions mentioned above, to a Western eye, the independent production route might appear to be a more viable way of acquiring audiovisual training and funding for media production, but few countries have an independent film community that is responsive to the community concerns articulated by Indigenous videomakers. Few Indigenous videomakers are trained at film schools, and they rarely participate in large-scale productions or in their national film festivals. Productions often result from training workshops or are created and developed collectively, sometimes under pressing political and economic circumstances or for organizational and advocacy purposes. Many videos from more remote communities stem from human rights awareness projects and serve a specific purpose, targeting a specific, usually foreign audience. These audiovisual experiences sometimes constitute the way an Indigenous videomaker first interacts with audiovisual media making. In other cases, video workshop participants have had radio experience at a community level. Workshop participants are often chosen for their leadership skills and experience and are expected to maintain a connection to their community.

Generally speaking, most producers still expect some form of state intervention. Many communities prefer to sidestep any state involvement in the development of their media; videomakers will use the state media center's equipment at off hours, or only seek technical advice. State-run facilities tend to produce more celebratory works that focus on cultural preservation and tend to avoid more politically oriented work. An autonomous approach to production rests on the organized deployment of community resources, spaces, and engagement. Thus, we identify as *autonomous collaborative production* what the film industry might term *independent production*.

CONCLUSIONS

Indigenous media in Latin America do not follow conventional production processes. They inhabit a wide range of platforms, including film festivals, international meetings on Indigenous rights, academic conferences, and local community meetings. They use various production methods, styles, and formats. Lack of funding, the collective nature of production, and a lack of project continuity have limited the kind and number of films produced. A general lack of infrastructure and equipment, limited training (usually compressed into short workshops), and the community obligations of Indigenous producers generally distinguish Indigenous media production from commercial production. We must bear in mind that Indigenous media constitute a system of social relations and networking aimed at reaffirming communal social solidarities, where local conjunctures are increasingly strengthened and linked through transnational strategies and cross-cultural collaborations across national borders.

We think of Indigenous film and video in particular as "imperfect media" whose locally based "embedded aesthetics" and concern for making political and cultural interventions may contribute to the theorization of a politically emancipatory form of citizens' media. The notion of a poetics of media identifies the varied and complex Indigenous processes of *making* cultural objects (videos) and forging cultural processes through media practice. Based on our engagement with the Latin American Indigenous video movement over many years, we argue that Indigenous peoples take up audiovisual technologies of information and communication according to their own cultural logics. Thus, the *structuration* of Indigenous media as discursive practices must be contextualized in these broader and complex processes of cultural activism, including the new processes of ethnic resurgence sweeping the region. This discursive and signifying practice of "making videos" is often an active communal process for making culture visible for strategic political purposes.

The future of Indigenous video in Latin America will be marked by the need to empower communities, organizations, and individual videomakers to manage and determine self-consciously where the road ahead lies. There needs to be a system in place that will permit less reliance on external funding and distribution, as both can compromise the autonomy and independence of Indigenous productions. As Indigenous video becomes an independent field of cultural production by and for Indigenous peoples, the complexity and fluidity of their experiences will offer new guideposts for all media producers working outside a hegemonic order of mass, corporate media.

NOTES

1. The full quote and the image are both available online as part of Alvarado's exhibition "Fotografía mapuche: Construcción y montaje de un imaginario," at www.puc.cl/proyectos/mapuches/html/imagi1b.html. See Alvarado, Mege, and Baez 2001. Translation by the authors.

2. Indigenismo as a movement was most prominent in Mexico and Peru. However, the uneven influence of indigenismo across Latin America should be noted: political and cultural elites in other countries, such as Costa Rica, Uruguay, and Argentina (for instance), refrained from constructing their nationalist ideologies as those of mestizo societies.

3. After the eighth CLACPI festival, held in Oaxaca in June 2006, the organization renamed itself as the Coordinadora instead of the Consejo.

4. The films receiving awards in the festival held in Brazil in 1987 were also primarily by non-Indigenous Latin American filmmakers such as Gustavo Guayasamin or the Argentinean Raul Tosso; Tosso's classic epic *Gerónima* (1986) received an award and also had its theatrical release. During this festival, a special mention was awarded to the Ecuadorian film made by Camilo Luzuriaga in 1983, *Así pensamos* (*That's How We Think*), produced in cooperation with the Unión de Organizaciones Campesinas del Azuay (UNASAY, Union of Campesino Organizations of Azuay) and funded by Swiss Aid. At the Venezuelan meeting of 1990, an Indigenous feature-length drama shot in Ecuador in 1989, *Sahuari* (coproduced communally by the Balda-Lupaxi), was one of the first Indigenous films to receive an award and the first award for a film shot on video (U-Matic). The festival in Venezuela was also the first to showcase and award mentions to animated cartoons and clay animation: e.g.,

El mito de Peribo (1988), based on Yanomami mythology and produced by a university student, Félix Nakamura.

5. For a description of Frota's film, see Communication Initiative 2002. See also Frota n.d.

6. See the Centro de Trabalho Indigenista Web site at www.trabalhoindige nista.org.br and the Video in the Villages site at www.videonasaldeias.org .br/home_ingles.htm.

7. We thank the director Alberto Muenala for his insight into the process in Ecuador. For more information on the Abya Yala festival, also known as the Festival de la Serpiente, see CNC n.d.; CONAIE n.d.; and Llacta n.d.

8. For the text of the declaration, see European Commission 1996.

9. We must note Mariano's rejection of the term *independent videomaker*: "In reality I am not an independent videomaker—while the technical questions of videomaking are resolved alone, the feeling and content of my videos belong to the people" (quoted in Córdova and Zamorano 2003).

10. See the videography of Dante Cerano of Exe Video at www.moreliafilm fest.com or at www.nativenetworks.si.edu.

11. The network has been named Red Regional de Comunicación Indígena Kuj-kuj Zugun, as stated in the declaration of the regional coordination meeting: "Unidos por una comunicación propia: Memoria del taller de identificación y coordinación regional en communicación y desarrollo," held in Iquique, Chile, and published in La Paz, Bolivia, in 2002 (see "Declaración de Iquique de los Pueblos Originarios" 2002).

CHAPTER 2

"LEST OTHERS SPEAK FOR US": THE
NEGLECTED ROOTS AND UNCERTAIN FUTURE
OF MAORI CINEMA IN NEW ZEALAND

Jennifer Gauthier

The Indigenous peoples of New Zealand, the Maori, became the subject of global fascination recently with the success of *Whale Rider*, a 2003 film directed by the Pakeha New Zealand filmmaker Niki Caro.[1] *Whale Rider* is based on *The Whale Rider*, a novel by acclaimed Maori writer Witi Ihimaera. The film tells the story of Pai, a Maori girl who struggles to come to terms with her culture and identity in contemporary New Zealand. Caro's film garnered attention and awards all over the world, including an Academy Award nomination for actress Keisha Castle-Hughes.[2] At the time of its release, members of the press, the New Zealand government, and Caro herself viewed *Whale Rider* as a symbol of the rebirth of Maori filmmaking. A July 2003 article in the *Guardian* reported that although Maori filmmaking had been "in hibernation," Caro hoped that this would change with the release of *Whale Rider* (Fickling 2003: 1). The reviewer compared Caro's film with such landmark New Zealand features as *The Piano* (Jane Campion, 1993), *Utu* (Geoff Murphy, 1983), and Barry Barclay's films *Ngati* (1987) and *Te Rua* (1991).

While celebration was the prevailing mood in many New Zealand film circles, in other, specifically Maori, ones the mood was abiding sadness. *Whale Rider* was made by neither a Maori director nor a Maori producer. It does not feature a Maori crew, and moreover, it does not embrace a Maori aesthetic. Caro's film made visible, to all who cared to notice, the glaring omission of Maori filmmakers from the history of New Zealand national cinema. While Maori filmmakers have had mixed reactions to the global success of *Whale Rider*, the film's media hype ultimately opened up a space for public discourse and activism.

New Zealand and the rest of the world have largely ignored Maori cinema, with the exception of Lee Tamahori's *Once Were Warriors* (1994), based on a novel by Maori writer Alan Duff.[3] Recently, the inclusion of films by Barry Barclay and Merata Mita in the First Nations / First Features exhibition at the Museum of Modern Art in New York (May 2005) introduced Maori filmmaking to a U.S. audience, but its history is still buried.[4] This essay seeks to unearth the neglected roots of Maori film-making in New Zealand and to place Maori cinema in the context of the development of New Zealand national cinema. The main goal of this project is to examine the work of Barclay, a Maori filmmaker, writer, and activist, whose contribution to Indigenous cinema has received scant attention from film historians and scholars. In partnership with other Maori filmmakers, Barclay is at the forefront of efforts to spark a rebirth of Maori cinema.

A SHORT HISTORY OF NEW ZEALAND NATIONAL CINEMA

In terms of cinema, New Zealand is perhaps best known as the training ground for Peter Jackson and as the home of Middle Earth.[5] In fact, a recent sales brochure put out by the New Zealand Film Commission featured a fantasy-inspired drawing with the text, "New Zealand: Home of Middle-Earth" inscribed on a stylized manuscript page. When the New Zealand Film Commission (NZFC) was founded in 1978, no thought was given to the multicultural nature of the country or to the role of Maori in the new national cinema. The government entrusted the NZFC with the following functions: "To encourage and also to participate and assist in the making, promotion and distribution and exhibition of films; to promote cohesion in the NZ film industry; to promote the proper mainte-nance of films in archives; to promote the study and appreciation of films and filmmaking; to gather and publish information related to the mak-ing, promotion, distribution and exhibition of films" (Government of New Zealand 1995: 9). The government would make funding available only to films that had significant New Zealand content as judged accord-ing to their subject, their shooting locations, the nationalities and places of residence of the main crew and cast, the sources of funding, and the ownership of the facilities and equipment. Coproductions would also be eligible for support (ibid.). In creating the NZFC, the government intended to stabilize the haphazard state of production financing that had existed in the 1960s and 1970s with the work of the National Film Unit (part of the Tourist and Publicity Bureau) and independent producers like Rudall Hayward and John O'Shea (see Waller 1996).

Until the *Lord of the Rings* trilogy, the hallmarks of New Zealand national cinema were little-known films by the male Pakeha filmmakers Roger Donaldson (*Sleeping Dogs*, 1977; *Smash Palace*, 1981), Geoff Murphy (*Goodbye Pork Pie*, 1980; *Utu*, 1983), Ian Mune (*Came a Hot Friday*, 1984; *The End of the Golden Weather*, 1991; and *What Becomes of the Broken-Hearted*, 1999—the follow-up to Lee Tamahori's *Once Were Warriors*), and Vincent Ward (*Vigil*, 1984; *The Navigator: A Medieval Odyssey*, 1988).[6] Many of these films share a distinctly masculine ethos, projecting a New Zealand national identity founded on physical power, fear of the "Other" (women), and a cultivated distrust of authority figures. They are also largely Pakeha in their content and ideology, with the exception of Murphy's *Utu*, which chronicles the clash of white settlers and Maori in 1870.[7]

The NZFC caters mostly to first-time filmmakers whose budgets are small; the commission caps its investment in a single film at $1.8 million and has been able to support on average four films per year because their budgets are often less then $1 million (Government of New Zealand 2000). To encourage feature film production, in 1999 the government established the Film Fund, a separate initiative of $22 million to fund feature film projects, run by an independent charitable trust. In April 2005, the NZFC took over the management of the Film Fund, which had originally been developed to support the production of larger-scale projects than those funded by the NZFC. The Film Fund today allows for support of experienced filmmakers who want to make "more complex and textured films which speak with a New Zealand voice" (ibid.: 3). Its initial goal was to support ten feature films in eight years. To date, five feature films made with money from the Film Fund have been completed: *Whale Rider, Perfect Strangers* (Gaylene Preston, 2003), *River Queen* (Vincent Ward, 2005), *The World's Fastest Indian* (Roger Donaldson, 2005), and *Perfect Creature* (Glenn Standring, 2005).

The founding documents of the NZFC and the Film Fund make no mention of the diversity of New Zealand's culture or society. Although New Zealand is a country of many cultures, "as the *tângata whenua*, the indigenous population, Mâori people occupy a unique place in New Zealand society" (Statistics New Zealand 2005). According to the 2001 census, the Maori numbered 526,281 out of a total population of 3,737,277, or one out of every seven people (Statistics New Zealand 2002).[8] Maori was declared an official language of New Zealand in 1987, yet the funding structure of the government film agency does not reflect this diversity. Nor are its two founding cultures equally represented on screen; in its first nine years, the film commission invested in thirty feature films, yet not one of these was made by a Maori.

EARLY MAORI CINEMA

Historical accounts of Maori cinema often begin with Barclay's work. But in a talk that he gave at the National Endowment for the Humanities Summer Institute in Hawaii in July 2003, Barclay pointed out that Ramai Hayward, the Maori wife of Pakeha filmmaker Rudall Hayward, who codirected and coproduced films with her husband in the 1970s, may actually have been the first Maori filmmaker. While scholars tend to minimize Ramai Hayward's contribution to her husband's work, Barclay notes that she took on a more active role in filmmaking as her husband aged. *To Love a Maori*, made in 1972, concerns two young Maori men who leave their village for the city and must fight to resist the temptations of a life of crime. One of the young men falls in love with a white girl and must face the prejudice of her parents. Eventually, when her parents die in a car crash, the girl goes to live with her boyfriend's Maori family, where she learns the benefits of Maori community and culture.

According to Barclay, the educational value of this dramatic feature film is the result of Ramai Hayward's Maori influence. He has suggested that fundamental to Maori filmmaking, and perhaps to Indigenous film-making in general, is a lesson or purpose. As he describes it, "There is a social point to a Maori tale; a spiritual point, for through our stories, we locate ourselves, we link ourselves with the past, to the present and to the future. Maori rarely toss off stories for the hell of it, just to tell a great yarn" (Barclay 2003). *To Love a Maori* was, in fact, based on actual case histories of Maori and Pakeha youth, so it makes sense that it would reflect the Maori's struggles to balance their cultural heritage with mod-ern urban culture. As a lesson about the importance of cultural identity, the story has real value for both Maori and Pakeha viewers.

More officially, we might point to Barclay's *Tangata Whenua* as a point of origin for Maori cinema. *Tangata Whenua* was a series of documen-taries made for television in 1974 about Maori life and culture. Produced by John O'Shea and Pacific Films, the series was the first to present aspects of the Maori world on television. It was based on a text by the Pakeha writer and historian Michael King, who brought a specific ethos to the project. In a recent interview, Barclay described the show's focus on Maori voices and images: "The old ladies would be allowed to speak for themselves, in their own language if they preferred. He [King] would be a listener and mostly off screen. Commentary would be at a bare minimum. This was revolutionary in its day. To some extent, it still is. Each time I have been interviewed for New Zealand television in recent years, I have been looking at know-it-all interviewers with clipboards" (personal communication, September 2005). While some critics might argue that this approach replicates a voyeuristic colonial gaze, it is important to note that in the New Zealand context, Maori had never been able to speak for themselves in the Maori language on screen. The absence of a Pakeha commentator in this documentary series allowed the Maori a measure of control over their own representation. It is this sense of self-determination and control that Barclay sought to augment in his feature films.

NGATI

After his work on *Tangata Whenua*, Barclay (1992: 124) directed what he refers to as "Pakeha documentaries" and then lived outside of New Zealand for several years. When he returned in 1983, he recalls being "shocked to see how little progress had been made in Maori filmmaking" (ibid.). In 1987, Barclay directed the first dramatic feature film by a Maori filmmaker, and, according to some sources, the first feature film anywhere in the world made by a member of an Indigenous culture living in a majority white culture (see Cairns and Martin 1994; and Martin and Edwards 1997). Based on a semiautobiographical screenplay by Tama Poata, and produced by John O'Shea, *Ngati* utilized a crew of young Maori who were part of a training collective, Te Awa Marama, and a cast of mostly nonactors. The film was well received both critically and by audiences around the world—it screened during the Critics Week at Cannes and won the grand prize at the 1987 Taormina Festival in Italy. In its home country, *Ngati* sparked a national debate about the role of Maori films in New Zealand national cinema.

The film is set in 1948 and tells the story of a young Australian doctor, Greg Shaw, who returns to the small (fictional) New Zealand town of Kapua, on the East Coast of the North Island, where his father had worked as an attending physician. The residents of Kapua are dealing with the possible closing of a local freezing plant that provides work, as well as with the impending death of one of the village children, Ropata. The film's story is a meandering tale centered on the community and its natural surroundings. Barclay's cinematic style allows for the slow unfolding of the characters' lives and their relationships to one another, during which time Greg is ultimately forced to confront his mixed heritage. He learns during his stay that his father was married to a Maori woman, so his ties to the community are stronger than he had imagined. With *Ngati*, Barclay highlights the connections between the past, present, and future, and he pays homage to the dignity of the Maori people and their culture. In using the cinema for these ends, Barclay was a pioneer.

First and foremost, Barclay works with a unique filmmaking style rooted in the Maori emphasis on community. The narrative focuses on a group of people living together, sharing space, and drawing strength from each other and from their participation in the community. While the young doctor is the primary focus, he is not the traditional "star" of the film. As the actor Wi Kuka Kaa, who plays Iwi in the film, has remarked, "The 'white hero' part of the story is differently told in *Ngati*. The guy is not the hero of the film like the [Kevin] Costner character is in *Dances with Wolves*. He's one part of the wider story. The Pakeha is swept along by events like all the other characters; he merges rather than standing out. That's what happens when you get a Maori, like Tama, who knows his own history. You get a very different story" (quoted in Cairns and Martin 1994: 128). Moreover, the film focuses on community values rather than individual success. Barclay documents the Maori respect for elders, the sacred quality of knowledge passed on from generation to generation, and the practice of communal decision making and shared power. The male protagonist's "hero" role in the film is problematized. He is not the all-knowing or powerful man; instead, he is on a journey of discovery and knows very little, as the women of the community remind him.

Although *Ngati* is a fictional film, not a documentary, its narrative unfolds slowly and deliberately and not according to some Hollywood conception of the five-act story. It is not a linear progression; the goal is not to get from here to there or to create a chain of cause and effect. Instead, Barclay's storytelling style encourages us to settle into a community and watch what unfolds, even if nothing (in terms of traditional narrative action) does. The structure of the narrative is much like the circularity in conversations that Barclay (1988: 8) identifies as a Maori characteristic. The anthropologist Dorothy Lee (1960: 137) has noted that "each culture has phrased [its] reality differently," and the structure of cinema is bound to reflect these differences. As Barclay (1988: 11) describes, "The Pakeha linear style is reflected in much Pakeha filmmaking where the argument is thrust forward with punch and assertiveness." *Ngati* challenges this aesthetic by refusing to privilege the linear development of a single storyline. Greg's journey to self-knowledge does not take center stage, nor does it progress in a straightforward manner. The film focuses equally on Ropata's condition and his friend Tione's attempt to come to terms with it, as well as on the economic situation of the village. Another recurring thread throughout the film is the clash between Ropata's father, Iwi, and his sister Sally, whose urban-inflected ideas contrast with Iwi's staunch adherence to Maori traditions.

Ngati weaves these stories and characters together into a kind of "visual tapestry," a strategy that Barclay (1988: 14) uses to reflect the physical details of the Maori community. For *Ngati*, Barclay wanted to borrow aspects from documentary, to catch the community members as they lived their daily lives:

> Day and night there are always people about. In the middle of an important conversation an aunty might come in carrying a toddler that needs to be put to bed. Somebody in the background might be wiping off the kitchen table, preparing for a couple of young men who have just returned from gathering seafood. A young girl might have dropped by to raid her friend's collection of T-shirts before taking off for a game of netball. The normal tapestry of life, but how to capture it on the screen? (ibid.)

Alternating between scenes depicting Greg as he gets to know the villagers and shots of the villagers rallying around Ropata, the film creates a balanced narrative. Moreover, the focus on Maori activities such as making horseshoes, catching urchin, sheep shearing, playing cards, and preparing the *hangi* complement the scenes of conversation that communicate the story. These actions are filmed lovingly with attention to detail, and they help to fill out the picture of Kapua.

The inclusion of rich documentary detail in Barclay's drama might help to explain the film's success. However, this hybrid quality may also make it difficult for some viewers to enjoy the film, as it focuses more on minutiae than on action. As Bill Nichols (1994: xiii) has observed, "The categories and boundaries surrounding documentary and reality, fact and fiction, defy hard and fast definition." In many ways, *Ngati* borrows elements of ethnographic film; more specifically, it is akin to autoethnography, as Barclay and the film's writer, Tama Poata, set out to capture and tell the story of their own people, or *iwi*. Barclay's work is rooted in John Grierson's original notion of *documentary*, a term that Grierson coined in his review of Robert Flaherty's *Moana* (1926). History tells us that Grierson later defined *documentary* as "the creative treatment of actuality." *Ngati* is a fictional story that is embedded in an actual location, with fictional characters who enact actual Maori cultural traditions. The film embodies the hybridity that many visual anthropologists and film scholars identify as an emerging trend in ethnographic film.

Barclay's documentary aesthetic relies on production practices rooted in Maori culture. "To be any sort of a Maori," he has observed, "you have to be a listener. You do not interrupt a person who is talking, no matter how humble that person may be" (Barclay 1988: 11). In order to be better listeners, Barclay and his crew perfected a system that allowed them to be invisible. He utilized zoom lenses and sound rigs, including a slanting microphone that enabled the director and crew to shoot at a distance from the subjects. This distinctive approach to cinema draws on the traditions of the *marae*—the gathering place in front of the Maori meeting house. As Barclay (1992: 11) describes it, "On a *marae*, there is opportunity for all to speak." Barclay chose to use a long lens to film *Ngati*, rather than a dolly, which is more intrusive and can hinder the action. Rather than replicating a (neo)colonial gaze, this strategy ultimately gives power to the characters and their environment; the cast members are left to talk among themselves as they might normally (Barclay 1988: 11–12). For Barclay, the camera should be both a listener and a patient observer, waiting for the right material to emerge. Conversations form the bulk of the film's action; some people are filmed from a distance, others from in the midst of the discussion.

In scenes set in cramped rooms like Ropata's bedroom and various kitchens, the sense of closeness created by the camera's proximity underscores the tight bonds between the community members. To capture larger group gatherings, the camera is generally stationary and positioned off to the side. Occasionally, Barclay positions the camera slightly above the action, as if to let us get a good sense of the whole and to underscore the communal nature of the village. Moreover, Barclay is fond of using the long take, a choice that helps to establish the slow pace and meditative quality of the film. As David MacDougall (1992–93: 42) has noted, the long take serves several important purposes in documentary filmmaking: it helps to reveal the relationships between the background and the foreground, it reemphasizes the "objective presence of disparate physical objects in the shot," and it "provides a 'stage' for the enactment of human behavior which reveals individual identity." A crucial feature of *Ngati* is its portrayal of the Maori and their specific material conditions; the long take allows for the anonymous actor to become human (43). This particular cinematographic choice has not historically been the sole province of documentary film; as MacDougall notes, some of its most proficient practitioners have been directors like Jean-Luc Godard, Michelangelo Antonioni, Alain Resnais, and Roberto Rossellini (44).

With all of Barclay's cinematic work, and with *Ngati* in particular, the film's formal elements and production style go hand in hand. The spirit of cooperation and shared responsibility that is depicted on screen—the principle of *tatau tatau*, meaning "all together"—guides the filmmaking process as well. He uses as many Maori crew members as possible and does not stride onto the set as the all-powerful director but works in close communion with his actors and technicians. Barclay suggests that the individual artist is not what filmmaking is about, as he compares the role of the film to that of the carvings on the Maori meetinghouse—the images are for the people, for the community (personal communication, June 2003). He infuses the filmmaking process with Maori values and traditions; although the crew on *Ngati* was mixed, all crew members gathered each morning for a prayer. "Each day the cast and crew assembled in the open for ten minutes *karakia* (prayer) before the camera was set up and shooting commenced. The *karakia* was conducted, not by an elder we had brought along, but by a religious man of that area. To this day there is a strong sense among those people that *Ngati* belongs to them and that makes me very proud" (personal communication, October 2005). The film grew out of a sense of community and shared history that united the Maori and Pakeha participants.

MAORI CINEMA AND THE STATE

After Barclay's *Ngati* came three other Maori feature films: *Mauri* (Merata Mita, 1988), *Te Rua* (Barclay, 1991), and *Once Were Warriors* (Tamahori, 1994). These are the only Maori films that have been made with the support of the NZFC in its twenty-five-year history. *The Maori Merchant of Venice*, directed by Shakespearean Maori actor Don Selwyn and released in 2002, was financed by the Maori TV fund with the NZFC providing only marketing assistance. The film is based on an adaptation of the Shakespeare play translated into the Maori language by the Maori scholar Pei te Hurinui Jones in 1945. Despite winning awards in both New Zealand and at the Hawaii International Film Festival, the film has had problems gaining wide release, most likely because of its use of traditional language.

The neglect of Maori cinema by the state is undoubtedly linked to economic goals and the power of the expectations that Hollywood has created in the minds of cinemagoers. As one New Zealand writer has observed, "In an industry which recognizes and endorses a Eurocentric world view, it has been almost impossible to form films' crews with both the necessary technical skills and a meaningful range of cultural perceptions unconditioned by dominant Pakeha ideology" (Parekowhai 1987–88: 75). Although *Ngati* was a critical success, it took another five years for Barclay to find the support to make another feature film. This experience suggests, as Parekowhai has noted, that "few individuals with the power to invest in the New Zealand film industry will put money into productions that derive from a noncommercial cultural perspective outside mainstream Pakeha assumptions" (75). When making money is a primary goal, national cinemas are often forced to compromise their aesthetic and cultural goals. As Stephen Crofts (1993: 56) remarks, some of these nations try to "second-guess the desires of the U.S. market" and end up making poor imitations of Hollywood films. In this situation, "a fantasy of a foreign market can, then, exercise inordinate influence over 'national' product" (ibid.).

Maori cinema flies in the face of mainstream expectations, as *Ngati's* editor Dell King has noted:

> What I like about Maori filmmaking is that in contrast to Pakeha filmmaking, generally speaking there is space for resonance. In the Maori vision of the way the universe works, the interaction of all things, and the fact that people are pushed by forces which are emotionally powerful but not necessarily logical, means that you use that, and give the audience a chance to respond. You actually take them into something, and when they've just got there it's like a note that hangs and hangs and then you nudge them on. In New Zealand Pakeha filmmaking, there's a tendency not to wait for the resonances, always to be driven by some quite narrow idea of what's going on. (quoted in Cairns and Martin 1994: 131)

Maori filmmaking does not rush the audience; its pacing is slow compared to the mass-produced films that glut the global market. Barclay does not pander to the audience with Americanized versions of Indigenous stories but creates his own unique aesthetic that is true to his roots.

FOURTH CINEMA

In addition to his work as a filmmaker, Barclay has lectured and written about the concept of Fourth Cinema. Barclay's (2003) framework is based on the following definitions: First Cinema is American (or Hollywood) cinema, Second Cinema is art house cinema, and Third Cinema is the cinema of the Third World. Third Cinema is often more specifically associated with Latin American filmmakers of the 1960s, especially Glauber Rocha, Fernando Solanas, and Octavio Getino. Their Marxist-inflected work was explicitly "democratic, national and popular," according to Paul Willemen (1994: 182), who has addressed at some length the issue of how First, Second, and Third Cinemas are defined by scholars.

Fourth Cinema is cinema made by First Nations peoples, according to Barclay (personal communication, October 2005). Fourth Cinema films have a kind of Indigenous essence to them.[9] This essence, Barclay (2002) suggests, may only be understood by Indigenous people, but like all cinema, Fourth Cinema works on many different levels. Also important to Barclay's concept of Fourth Cinema is the idea that filmmakers can use the medium as a popular court of appeal; they can infuse their work with larger political goals. This act is what he calls "doing justice," referring not only to getting the depiction of a people right—to do justice to their image on screen—but also to tackling head-on questions of justice in land rights, civil rights, and cultural representation in the dominant society.

The conditions of production in Fourth Cinema are different from those of First, Second, and Third Cinemas. According to Barclay, the conditions of exhibition might be different as well. When he talks about Indigenous cinema, he often discusses his vision of the Fourth Cinema film event—a communal gathering where people watch the film, eat a meal together, and generally share each other's company. He even suggests that filmmakers might pay people to come to the film, arrange transportation for them on a bus, prepare the meal for them, and make the occasion into a kind of *hui* (gathering). This idea, he says, fits into the Maori tradition of hospitality and gift giving; rather than asking the audience to go to the film, you bring the film to them (personal communication, June 2003).

In every way, the notion of Fourth Cinema turns First Cinema on its head. Barclay has used a scene from *The Mutiny on the Bounty* (Lewis Milestone, 1962) to illustrate his ideas. In this scene, Captain Bligh (Trevor Howard) orders Fletcher Christian (Marlon Brando) to go ashore and have sex with a Native woman. Breaking down the scene, Barclay (2002: 14) notes, "Within the context of First Cinema, this is a very rich scene— imperial power, white male hunk, the navy uniform, and sex in the tropics. . . . The Bounty scene is from the camera of the ship's deck. The camera is owned and controlled by the people who own the ship. It takes pictures of those who sail the ship. What happens when the camera is shifted from the deck onto the shore?" He goes on to suggest that

> the Bounty mythology only works if the Indigenous world is kept ashore and the camera does most of its work on the deck, where white imperial men scheme their schemes. The camera, cut loose from First Cinema constraints and in the hands of the natives, does not work anything like as well away from the ship's deck (as the ship men see it), because allowing the camera to operate ashore under God knows whose direction would defeat the purposes of those in control of the First Cinema, whose more or less exclusive intention has been, over one hundred years of cinema, to show actions and relationships within Western societies and Western ideological landscapes. Furthermore, the First Cinema enterprise is likely to be greatly deflated if there is a camera ashore, a camera outside First Cinema, a camera with a life of its own, watching—if it can be bothered to watch—who comes ashore. . . . The First Cinema Camera sits firmly on the deck of the ship. It sits there by definition. The Camera Ashore, the Fourth Cinema Camera, is the one held by the people for whom "ashore" is their ancestral home. "Ashore" for Indigenous people is not usually an island. Not literally. Rather, it is an island within a modern nation state. (ibid.: 14–15)

For Barclay, filmmaking is a political act, one that empowers Indigenous peoples and cultures. In his Fourth Cinema aesthetic, the act of taking back the camera is likened to an act of revolution. Maori cinema rewrites not only New Zealand history but the history of the cinema. Regarding *Ngati*, he has remarked:

It's about being Maori—and that is political. It's a determined attempt to say what it's like being Maori. . . . It is politically deliberate—political in the way it was made, a serious attempt to have Maori attitudes control the film. Political in having as many Maoris as possible on it or being trained on it. Political in physically distributing the film or speaking about it and showing it in our own way. Political in going in the face of a long tradition in the film industry here and abroad saying these simple things, without car chases or without a rape scene, actually have appeal, maybe it won't work. . . . I think a lot of the political struggle is to get through to Pakehas and Pakeha institutions that this is the way we think, therefore change your manners. This is the Maori world, take it or leave it. (Lomas 1987: 5)

With its political undertones and effort to speak back to Pakeha representations of the Maori, Barclay's work exemplifies Faye Ginsburg's (1998: 190) arguments about the connection between Indigenous media and "broader social and political movements for cultural autonomy and self-determination."

Because Barclay is documenting the lives and culture of his own people, his camera work encourages viewers to identify with the Maori characters. We see their daily lives as well as their rituals, their public and their private moments. *Ngati* rarely uses point of view shots, perhaps in an effort to situate the viewers as members of the community rather than as the main characters. We are alternately watching the Maori and identifying with them, depending on the camera's placement. This strategy helps to highlight the fact that for non-Maori viewers, although the film can help us to understand their lives and draw us into the activities of the community, we can never be Maori.

Barclay's Fourth Cinema calls attention to the conflicted nature of New Zealand's postcolonial identity. It strives to tackle the issue of identity as it is linked to the community, and in this way it challenges the hallmarks of national cinema that came before it. As Merata Mita (1992: 47) notes, the common themes of early New Zealand films, the white man or woman at odds with nature, country, or self, have become "deeply etched into the national psyche," but these films also "fail to analyse and articulate the colonial syndrome of dislocation" that they voice. She goes on to suggest that characters in Pakeha films "never question their survival on a political level, only a personal one" (48).

In contrast, Barclay's films demonstrate the powerful link between the personal and the political, the experience of Maori living today in a postcolonial, yet still colonized, society. The issues of identity at stake in *Ngati* resonate beyond the individual, beyond the personal; they suggest the ongoing struggle of Maori to nurture and preserve their culture in a modern, increasingly urbanized New Zealand. It is unclear whether or not Maori will have the opportunity to portray this struggle cinematically in the years to come.

THE FUTURE OF MAORI FILMMAKING

Does Maori filmmaking have a future? What is being done today to support the efforts of Maori filmmakers? Te Manu Aute was founded in 1986 as an advocacy and support organization for Maori professionals in the film and television industries. Today that organization is called Nga Aho Whakaari (or Maori in Film and TV Inc.). Nga Aho Whakaari has approximately one hundred members and is growing steadily. The organization, along with Te Mangai Paho (the Maori Broadcasting Funding Agency), was involved in the review by the New Zealand Ministry of Culture and Heritage of government screen funding in 2004, calling for greater recognition of Maori peoples and principles in film and television funding policies.[10]

In 2003, Barry Barclay, along with Merata Mita and Tainui Stephens (a radio, television, and film producer and NZFC board member), submitted a proposal to the NZFC for funding specifically for Maori film projects. The proposal, Mana Maori Paepae (MMP), draws on Maori culture and language to communicate its message; *mana* in Maori means spiritual power or authority, while *paepae* refers to the threshold of the meeting-house where a ceremonial welcome takes place. The document refers to the MMP as "an idea: a response to our need and duty to grow a unique Maori cinema voice" (Barclay, Mita, and Stephens 2003: 1). It acknowledges the powerful and important role of cinema, likening it to a *hui* in a theater; both are experiences of storytelling. In this act of storytelling, the proposal strongly argues that Maori must speak for themselves, "lest others speak for us" (3). The document defines a Maori film as one that is made by Maori and reflects the Maori spirit and culture; it also stresses the roles of the writer and director in communicating in a Maori voice (ibid.).

The proposal lays out a process for the support of Maori filmmaking, establishing a committee, or *paepae*, that will accept feature film proposals from the Maori creative community and recommend them to the NZFC for funding. This plan calls for an annual fund of $3 million for the production of at least one Maori film. The money will come from the Film Fund and the NZFC. The document stresses issues of guardianship and support, making clear the writers' belief that Maori are the best judges of proposals for Maori films. The main goal of the proposed system is to "make more and better Maori feature films" (Barclay, Mita, and Stephens 2003: 4). Projects must have a Maori writer and director attached, and the MMP will help secure a Maori producer if needed. The MMP will also act as an advocate for the filmmakers, securing relevant property rights, permissions, and recognition of Maori cultural standards. Just as Maori cinema foregrounds the connections between the past and the present, the MMP also highlights this important aspect of Maori culture: "Our movement into the future remains enabled by our knowledge of the past" (2).

The MMP initiative can only succeed if there is a critical mass of well-trained Maori professionals working in New Zealand in all aspects of the film industry. In New Zealand, the Film Commission has given financial support to the Maori in Film and TV group and has sponsored various workshops for writers and directors, both Maori and Pakeha. The outcome of the review of government screen funding has not been made public, but the NZFC was given a $10 million boost to its budget in 2004. It is not yet clear whether some of this money will be set aside for Maori projects, but Maori filmmakers like Barry Barclay are hopeful that it will be.

NOTES

1. The term *Pakeha* refers to the descendants of the European settlers of New Zealand. *Maori* refers to the *tangata whenua* or Indigenous people—in other words, Indigenous Polynesian inhabitants and their descendants. See Ausubel 1960; King 1985; and Statistics New Zealand 2005 for additional information about these terms.
2. Awards include the British Academy of Film and Television Arts (BAFTA) Children's Award for Best Feature Film, the Independent Spirit Award for Best Foreign Film, Audience Awards at the Rotterdam and San Francisco International Film Festivals, the Audience Award in World Cinema at Sundance, and the People's Choice Award at the Toronto International Film Festival.

3. Until the release of *Whale Rider*, *Once Were Warriors* held the distinction of being the most successful New Zealand film in its home market. This honor now belongs to *The Lord of the Rings* films.

4. "First Nations / First Features: A Showcase of World Indigenous Film and Media" was an exhibition at the Museum of Modern Art in New York, May 12–23, 2005. See www.moma.org / exhibitions / film_media / 2005 / first _nations.html.

5. Peter Jackson chose to film *The Lord of the Rings* trilogy (*The Lord of the Rings: The Fellowship of the Ring*, 2001; *The Lord of the Rings: The Two Towers*, 2003; *The Lord of the Rings: The Return of the King*, 2003) in his native New Zealand. Middle Earth is the setting for several of J. R. R. Tolkien's novels, the source material for Jackson's films.

6. Ward and Donaldson migrated to Hollywood but recently returned to New Zealand to work on *The Fastest Indian in the World* and *River Queen*, respectively. Tamahori has worked in the United States since 1996, directing several action features and an episode of *The Sopranos*.

7. Merata Mita acted as a consultant for the film, in addition to her work as casting director and playing the part of Matu.

8. According to Statistics New Zealand, "a Maori is a person who identifies with or feels they belong to the Maori ethnic group." See Statistics New Zealand 2005.

9. Barclay distinguishes between "Indigenous cinema," or films made by First Peoples, and "indigenous cinema," a term that he observes is used by the New Zealand Film Commission to describe any film made in New Zealand, set in New Zealand, and produced and written by a New Zealander. As he rightly notes, these "indigenous" New Zealand films are most often made "by the Invader" (personal communication, October 2005). His notion of Fourth Cinema may also be drawn from the tendency to refer to Indigenous peoples globally as the Fourth World. See Prins 1977.

10. For more information on Nga Aho Wakaari, visit www.ngaahowhakaari .co.nz / ; for Te Mangai Paho, visit www.tmp.govt.nz / .

CHAPTER 3

CACHE: PROVISIONS AND PRODUCTIONS IN
CONTEMPORARY IGLOOLIK VIDEO

Cache Collective

Should I catch game that I cannot take with me all at once, I should cache it for future use. Should the camp come into a situation where food must be found, this cache will come in handy, as it will be only a matter of returning for food, for you will not be required to hunt it. These are the things I used to be told about.

—George Agiaq Kappianaq, elder, Amitturmiut (cited in Bennett and Rowley 2004: 246)

When reflecting on his goals and process of production, video artist Zacharias Kunuk (n.d.) asks, "Can Inuit bring storytelling into the new millennium? Can we listen to our elders before they all pass away? Can producing community TV in Igloolik make our community, region and country stronger? Is there room in Canadian filmmaking for our way of seeing ourselves?" As a founding member of Igloolik Isuma Productions and cocreator of the Cannes smash *Atanarjuat* (*The Fast Runner*), Kunuk's story is probably as well known as he is. Kunuk was born in 1957 and lived off the land in what is now northern Nunavut until 1965, when the Canadian government sent him, along with many other Inuit children, to boarding school in Igloolik. There, for the first time, Kunuk viewed "southern" cinema and, in 1981, bought a video camera with the profits from selling his own carvings. Isuma (which means "to think") was incorporated in 1990 by cofounders Zacharias Kunuk, Paul Apak Angilirq, Pauloosie Qulitalik, and Norman Cohn in an effort to broadcast northern video production to an Inuit audience.

The historic and political circumstances surrounding Isuma's foundation should not go unremarked, as they point to the need to maintain video production made for and by Inuit. The legislation creating the territory of Nunavut in 1999, although intended to provide Inuit with control over the economic, political, and social situation of their own communities, remains fraught with unfulfilled promises. The Canadian federal government continues to maintain jurisdiction over the territory while curtailing Inuit access to the funding and administrative resources necessary to sustain cultural production, a restrictive process that affected Isuma from its beginnings. Indeed, while the creation of Nunavut promised Inuit more direct control of their own communities, fruitless negotiations with federal representatives and an often untenable bureaucratic and administrative system prove that Inuit leaders must still push for social and creative rights.

Since the late 1970s, members of the community of Igloolik have initiated a series of reforms, including important provisions for video- and filmmaking. A prolific video practice in Igloolik has not emerged in isolation but has instead been consistent with cultural developments in communications technology in the north. Unique in Nunavut for refusing television broadcasting until 1983 on linguistic and cultural grounds, the community of Igloolik only agreed to broadcast television under the stipulation that it incorporate the Inuktitut language and address issues relevant to people living in Nunavut.

This agreement led Inuit film- and videomakers to take cultural production into their own hands and resulted in the creation of Isuma and a second Igloolik-based video collective, Arnait Video Productions. When it was incorporated in 1990, Isuma created a nonprofit video equipment facility called Tariagsuk, which sponsored a women's video workshop in 1991 that eventually led to the creation of Arnait. The women who first participated in videomaking in Igloolik include Susan Avingaq, Marie-Hélène Cousineau, Matilda Haniliaq, Julie Ivalu, Madeline Ivalu, Mary Kunuk, Martha Maktar, and Celina Uttuigak, though individual involvement in Arnait varies according to the women's activities outside the collective (Fleming 1996). Arnait approaches videomaking as a medium to integrate Inuit women's voices into debates of interest to all Canadians. The artists of this collective ask: "How does one experience the dawning of the third millennium in a small Inuit community which is in the midst of political and social change?" (Arnait n.d.). Susan Avingaq describes Arnait as a "women's video workshop [that] can help people communicate with each other. That can be useful. It can make them understand. A long time ago, just with words and language, people believed stories and legends, they saw pictures in their imagination. Our stories are useful and unforgettable" (ibid.). By creating videos that express the benefits of community and of the creation of working relationships among people, Arnait produces work that generates great interest from outside Igloolik.[1]

This chapter develops in the sphere of external interest in videos produced by both Isuma and Arnait. Its content draws from a curated program titled "*cache*: three contemporary videos from Igloolik" that was held at the Agnes Etherington Art Centre in Kingston, Ontario, on March 20, 2005. The *cache* program, composed of three artists' tapes, presented the video practices of two Igloolik-based collectives as ongoing, never completed storage projects. Like the caches in which Inuit hunters stored food and supplies when they were plentiful, the selected works from this program act as caches for shared memories, knowledge of skills, oral storytelling, and traditional values. These works also store abstract concepts for future generations to draw on: among them ideals, values, the cultural importance attached to traditional skills, concepts embodied in recounted stories, and historical reenactments. Stuart Hall (2001: 89) describes such archival projects as "not an inert museum of dead works, but a 'living archive,' whose construction must be seen as an on-going, never-completed project."[2]

This chapter considers the three videos presented in *cache* and reads these tapes as an archive of activities, stories, and approaches to artistic production built through collective video practices in Igloolik. This reading is informed by Hall's concept of the living archive; it also adapts existing scholarship on Third Cinema and diasporic production to meet the needs of a minority group; it considers the videoscape as an environment of memory that challenges temporal and spatial categories; it addresses the influence of northern spatial orientation, as described by Edmund Carpenter, on video structures; and it presents oral tradition as something that memory producers value as a negotiated recollection, over, for example, an indexical image of the past. Like a computer's fast-access memory, these caches continually build up and are constantly reaccessed as artists and community members collectively construct, produce, and share these videos.

Today, both Isuma and Arnait develop video projects primarily for an Inuit audience. As Marie-Hélène Cousineau, former coordinator of Arnait, explains, "It was just a matter of showing [work] to the community, the people in town. When Susan [Avingaq] makes a video about caribou clothing, she's not thinking that someone in Montreal will be interested in it, or someone in New York will enjoy it. She's making it for people in town to learn how to do caribou-skin clothing" (quoted in Fleming 1996: n.p.). Although members of Isuma and Arnait see their main goal as producing for Inuit audiences, it is, paradoxically, precisely this local address that they feel makes their work suitable for travel. After completing a video workshop for Aboriginal women in Montreal, the participants screened their work, and members of Arnait also took advantage of opportunities to show elsewhere (Fleming 1996). Isuma, as a professional production house, produces standard-length features for television channels available in the south as well as for the Inuit Broadcasting Corporation (IBC). The tapes from both collectives are available for consultation or purchase from Isuma and Arnait's archives or from a video distribution facility in Toronto called Vtape. The tapes have been sought out by southern curators and screened in galleries and festivals in Canada and the United States, as well as abroad. As these tapes travel, they educate and engage audiences in Inuit histories and "preserve and enhance Inuit culture and language" (Kunuk n.d.).

As an audiovisual vehicle for storage in Igloolik, video serves as a storage method that allows aesthetic, artistic, and interpretative practices to be reaccessed as mnemonic records of place deeply rooted in community.[3] In doing so, these works resist categorization; they share characteristics of, but never fully fit in, genres of contemporary video practices: in particular, experimental video, conventional television, ethnographic documentary, and dramatic narrative. Some videos coming out of Arnait and Isuma record oral histories in the form of interviews with elders, while others do so by reconstructing Inuit life in 1940s Igloolik. Artists from Isuma and Arnait loosely consider these two major tendencies as categories or genres that fulfill a common motivation to engage a primarily Inuit audience with local histories. To slot these tapes in any Western genre would be to position them as dependent on contemporary Western video practices. Examined in this light, these productions never will meet the criteria defining any of these categories (Banning 1991).

In this way, Isuma and Arnait create local categories of video production that draw on many different genres and that function for a specific purpose in Igloolik. By drawing on oral traditions that historically store Inuit knowledge, Igloolik video artists create pieces that expand conventional ways of transferring ideas and stories through interviews with elders, storytelling, and historical recreations. In considering this approach, Kass Banning (1991: 28) observes, "Initially, it is difficult to detect anything uniquely non-western about the use of the video medium," as the medium is exploited for its conventional, time-based, and hence dramatic narrative potential; however, other devices resist a southern economy. Western audiences may consider pacing in the videos slow and, although the tapes are organized around a dramatic scenario, they seldom display the conflict-resolution patterns familiar in Western plots. However, Banning notes that these "stylistic choices are precisely qualities by which the Inuit judge these media to be positioned successfully within their own discourse" (ibid.).

For instance, members of Isuma construct stories that remain open and fluid, with storylines that are subject to inevitable changes in weather conditions. In a proposal to Telefilm Canada, the members of Isuma explain why they do not write final scripts: "Our NUNAVUT programs have a different narrative structure. . . . The changing rhythms of weather, wind, snow, light and animals so determine how people behave that this natural rhythm may in fact be the central story line of every program; and that 'action' is actually more about doing and making things to stay alive, than arguing about them. Cooperation is the story, rather than conflict" (Igloolik Isuma International 1996: 70–71).[4] These distinctive features—slower pace and lack of conflict in an otherwise conventional narrative structure—resist cinematic categorization; seen on their own terms, these tapes positively embody, if not invent, "a mixed economy" (Banning 1991: 28). Film and video theorist Laura Marks (2000) calls this kind of work—production consisting of mixed genres and styles—*hybrid cinema*. For Marks, this cinematic hybridity emerges in intercultural contexts and produces reflection on "the encounter between different cultural organizations of knowledge" (1). While Marks focuses mostly on diasporic artists, Inuit artists experience modes of diaspora and exile given the realities of life in the north. In Zacharias Kunuk's words, "Today we are living two lives—one in Inuktitut, the Inuit way, and one in the white culture" (Kunuk 1992: 14). In our analysis, we foreground the mixed cultural experience reflected in Isuma and Arnait videos rather than positioning the dominant culture as the invisible norm against which neocolonial societies judge cultural minorities (Marks 2000: 8).[5]

The *cache* tapes also challenge temporal and spatial categories as they represent lived experience in the past and present. Each video performs an archival act by recording and storing memories, texts, and objects, whether such processes are carried out by actors or narrated by Igloolik elders.[6] For example, Arnait's 1993 Qulliq (Oil Lamp) uses a historical reenactment to record the lighting of a seal-oil "lamp and stove of the old days, the only source of light and warmth" (Igloolik Isuma Productions n.d.). The lighting of the qulliq was an important activity practiced by Inuit women and is here cached because it is deemed to have value as a memory aid. The video's opening sequence shows Susan Avingaq outside in the snow pulverizing seal blubber in a soapstone container until it becomes a sticky gelatinous substance (fig. 3.1). The camera follows her as she moves inside the igluvigaq and zooms in on her hands as she places Arctic cotton, a shrubby plant found wild in Nunavut, around the rim of the container to act as a wick.[7] The camera moves across the surface of objects and provides an intimate sense of touch. These close-ups are juxtaposed with medium shots and distant views of igluvigaq on the horizon, creating an uneasy push and pull in the visual field, simultaneously enticing viewers while distancing them from the image (Marks 2000: 132–33, 162–63).

Likewise, in Qulliq, the camera moves to a close-up shot and then back to frame an image of Susan Avingaq and Madeline Ivalu as they light the oil lamp and build a support structure for the container (fig. 3.2). Meanwhile, the voices of the two women, singing, provide a soundtrack to the action. The subtitles to the song indicate that the women are telling a story about hunting for caribou on the Arctic tundra and seeing the light of the oil lamp from far away. The song renders the visual image more complex by marking a trajectory from the outside to the inside; it juxtaposes the interior domestic scene against the harsh winter climate. At the same time, the song also underscores the importance of the oil lamp, which serves as a source of heat and light during the months of subzero darkness. The video's final sequence shows a panoramic view of fields of ice with the horizon line melting into the sky. The video presents the practice of preparing the oil lamp in a series of intersecting spaces that traverse the artificial division of the interior and exterior, the close up and far away, and the intimate and distant.

To create temporally composite environments, the three videos in cache record reenactments and stories about the past and simultaneously use such "pasts" to discuss contemporary society. In the words of Victor Masayesva (2001: 232), "The wick saturated in fat is a sophisticated

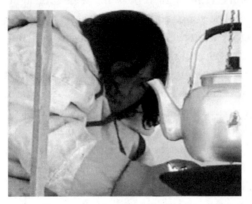

(*top*) Susan Avingaq lighting an oil lamp.

(*middle*) Susan Avingaq and Madeline Ivalu building a support structure for an oil lamp container.

(*bottom*) Susan Avingaq boiling a kettle of water over an oil lamp.

Arnait Ikkagurtigitt Collective, *Qulliq*, 1993. STILLS COURTESY OF V TAPE.

metaphor of television technology used to illuminate a Native value, that of patient observation." The use of video technology to store a traditional practice while representing a transtemporal *value* denotes contemporary presence as well as a record of the past; *Qulliq* positions Inuit culture as "struggling between two ways" by alluding to Inuit values that sometimes conflict with Western sensibilities (Zacharius Kunuk, quoted in Hendrick and Fleming 1991: 26). *Qulliq* simultaneously houses the past and the present as we hear the voices of Susan Avingaq and Madeline Ivalu recounting such traditional practices as lighting the seal oil lamp, building igloos, and hunting caribou. The actors, while discussing the position of the qulliq, wear costumes designed from the dress of "the old days" as well as contemporary jewelry (fig. 3.3). Here, past and present are not separated but exist in the same hybrid temporal environment staged in the video (Igloolik Isuma Productions n.d.).

Qulliq, in this sense, is an environment of memory.[8] While *Qulliq* is certainly constituted through acts of remembering, it is not a nostalgic representation of a lost past. It is not marked with regret for an old way of life; instead, it portrays the lighting of an oil lamp unceremoniously, interwoven with contemporary song and original script. Memory, here, is not attached to any specific site—no museum exists to house recreations of qulliq lighting; no monument commemorates such an activity. Videos such as *Qulliq* are meant for storage but not through a connection to specific sites, unlike museums that exist as fixed sites with collections that are transposed and changed. Whereas, in the words of Stuart Hall (2001: 89), museums act as *sites* for the storage of "dead works," the videos produced by Arnait and Isuma re-create *environments* of the past in and around Igloolik—whether this is achieved through a fictional re-creation or by evocative storytelling. *Qulliq* is a real environment of memory, where memory acts as ongoing phenomena, occurring simultaneously with contemporary events as actors, scriptwriters, and videographers gather to reenact the lighting of the oil lamp and then preserve it through video technology.

At both Arnait and Isuma, artists remain unsure of the accuracy of such reconstructions; they have been built after careful consultation with Inuit elders who recall and share their personal experiences. The video itself does not represent memory. Instead, it stores a memory environment, acted out at a particular time, when particular information was known about qulliq-lighting from a particular source. The actors question themselves in their actions—"Where would qulliq be? . . . This, what is it for? Maybe like this. . . . This should be here."—as they position a pole on which the lamp will hang. Through negotiation with sometimes competing recollections, a consensual archive is built from the accumulated knowledge in the present. The process itself acts as a mnemonic device; it is a cache-storage of that day's memory environment.

Such memory environments are undoubtedly temporal. Video technologies have stamps of time, and screens might even be marked with the date of a tape's production. However, *Qulliq*'s hybrid temporal structure does not situate this work in the past; its cache is not one of "tradition." Indeed, such temporal categories as tradition and past place anything classified in their realm in such cultural constructions; a "tradition" can only exist because it is dependent and contingent on its binary opposite: an antitradition or a modern experience that denotes something "of the past." Of course, certain ideas of qulliq-lighting are of the past, in that this activity is no longer practiced for the same reasons it once was. Most Igloolik women no longer light seal-oil lamps in igloos to warm their homes or to cook their food. Rather than light the seal oil for warmth, as in *Qulliq*, they now do so for purposes of cultural survival and continuity, in order to demonstrate how it was done. Thus, the video *Qulliq* is not strictly of the past, nor is it a memory of the past; rather, it is a work of living memory, a textual record produced in a memory environment by actors and writers in the present.

A memory environment is simultaneously temporal and spatial. Since "environment" connotes images of "place," it is necessary to consider the ways in which "place" acts on remembrance in the constitution of a memory environment. Isuma's 1995 *Qarmaq* (*Stone House*) recreates a historical scenario set in the year 1945. *Qarmaq* is part of the video series *Nunavut* (*Our Land*), which provides historical recreations of the past focusing on the traditional ways of Inuit people living on the land in the 1940s and 1950s, before the period of government resettlement. From 1950 to 1970, the Inuit were removed from the land and transferred to permanent settlements. Meanwhile, their children were sent to residential schools with lessons conducted in English, based on a southern Canadian school curriculum (Wachowich 2004).

At the beginning of *Qarmaq*, a female elder scans the land looking for the right spot to build a house to serve as shelter for the coming winter. According to Edmund Carpenter (2004: 152), who writes about the Aivilikmiut living in the eastern Arctic, Inuit knowledge of topography and sense of spatial orientation depend on keen observation skills to identify reference points in the land that mark out relationships "between contour, type of snow, wind, salt air, ice crack."[9] Similarly, in the video *Qarmaq*, the female elder observes the geological layout of the hilly shores before she eventually chooses a flattened area of terrain and tells the men where to place the rocks that will mark the entrance and outer circumference of the walls. The men then begin to collect large boulders, carefully selecting them according to shape, size, texture, and flatness to ensure that they are suitable supports that fit together properly. Meanwhile, the women go out into the hills to gather moss that serves as insulation and to prepare sealskins to form a roof covering for the house. Isuma's video archive caches a sensuous geography formed by a working process based on experiential knowledge. In her analysis of video production in Igloolik, Marks (2000: 217) suggests that the works provide insight into systems of understanding: "Awareness of the temperature and dryness of the air, for example; a keen sense of the distance vision and hearing necessary for hunting on vast treeless areas; the pleasure and warmth of food. The screen of vast landscape and quiet real-time activity may look sparse to outsiders, but is full of implicit presence."

In *Qarmaq*, the men and women construct a shelter that takes shape bit by bit as people gather the necessary building materials. The structure is transformed as the men place the rocks side by side to create the walls and floor. The women fill the cracks between the rocks with moss and help put the large canvas of sealskin over the rafters, securing it along the sidewalls. The activity of building this enclosure exemplifies an experience of space that is dynamic and processual, one shaped by a series of shifting relationships between players negotiating roles in their relationships to one another and to their environment (Carpenter 2004: 155). The actors in this video perform an interconnecting series of tasks, as the house-building process is facilitated by people who group and regroup at various points and locations along the shore, by the campground, and in the fields as they do their work. In this way, narratives of place are rooted in multisensory experiences of the body moving through space (Malpas 1999). *Qarmaq* is a cached memory environment negotiated by this dynamic interchange, through the positioning and repositioning of community members across different spatial locations.[10]

Qarmaq's memory environment is fused with oral traditions that expose systems of knowledge and shared learning among the family and its wider community. To this end, the videos produced by Isuma and Arnait serve as educational tools to inform people about Inuit social and cultural practices. They are representative of wider political reform in Nunavut that has seen the establishment of broadcasting companies devoted to maintaining Inuit language and culture. Isuma and Arnait's production can be distinguished from that of such organizations as the Canadian Broadcasting Corporation (CBC)'s northern services (established in 1958) and the IBC (established in 1981), both of which focus on issues relating to southern Canada and the United States, with only a small percentage of airtime devoted to Inuit content (Alia 1999). When Igloolik accepted broadcasting in 1983, there were a number of organizations in Nunavut with goals to produce videos and films by and for Inuit people. Among these has been Project Inukshuk (established in 1978), which aims to establish Inuit production centers in the north to serve as training sites for Inuit video and filmmakers (ibid.). Following the initiatives of these companies, Arnait and Isuma include predominantly Inuit members who control the decision-making process for production and distribution.

Both companies work in consultation with elders who recollect personal experiences that provide evidence of familial and community relations. This partnership between memory environments and intergenerational crossover is also seen in Arnait's 2001 *Anaana* (*Mother*). It focuses on Vivi Kunuk, who recounts her relationship with her father, her mother, her husband, and her in-laws (fig. 3.4). *Anaana* presents the sensibilities of the younger generation by exploring the lives of Kunuk's nieces, nephews, and grandchildren. In one scene, Kunuk's granddaughter recounts growing up with her cousins, aunts, and uncles on the land, hunting for caribou. She compares this to her experiences of living in Igloolik and then moving to southern Canada to be with her mother, where she felt isolated and alone. Her voice-over recollections play against video images of the granddaughter and her cousins swimming in the water and running across the grass on the Ivalu campgrounds. Set in contrast to this scene of youths at play is the story of a father's death as told by one of the granddaughter's cousins. Throughout this moving account, close-up shots of the cousin's face alternate with panoramic views of the water glistening in the sunlight and a field of Arctic cotton moving in the breeze. In *Anaana*, families and friends experience life and death on the Arctic tundra and tell the complex stories of mothers, daughters, fathers, sons, aunts, and uncles.

Narratives of place are played against each other in *Anaana* through the diverse perspectives of the younger and older generations of women. Memories are revealed as much by what is seen as by what is not seen, presented through the layering of spoken word, poetry, and song. This type of intersection between the visual and the oral conveys the disjunctive nature of conflicting knowledge systems, such as those offered by official histories and private memories, by positioning the various orders of image and sound against one another in ways that do not necessarily correspond (Marks 2000: 31). By avoiding direct polemics, the videos produced by Arnait and Isuma present new histories as they come into being through the combination of images and sounds. This leaves the audience to look for what is left missing or unexposed in the story itself, hence the significance of unfinished translations, soundtracks that are mismatched with their corresponding images, or distracting activity in the background.

Employing an experimental strategy that leaves the audience looking for what is unexposed, *Anaana* is grounded in visual, poetic, and oral imagery. The artists use such images to transfer intergenerational memories from elder to community, thus refusing a chronological storyline based on conventional written histories. According to Carpenter (1973: 26), again writing of the Aivilikmiut, time is understood to be dynamic rather than measured in static units, and is inexorably linked to place.[11] In this way, place expressly informs memory. Vivi Kunuk recounts childhood memories of hunting on the land with her father, who treated her like a boy until she reached marrying age. Her husband, Enuki Kunuk, describes their married life together when they lived in a tent and survived on bare essentials until eventually they built a sod house on the land where his family had lived for generations (fig. 3.5). As he recalls the stories, Enuki Kunuk walks around the hilly terrain, pointing out areas in the grass, rock, and soil that show remnants of their home. The land holds memories of former times, providing evidence of personal and familial relations that expose the past and the present, some lost and others ongoing in the lives of children and grandchildren.

Anaana's reminiscences about particular events allow past experiences to be revived when, for example, Enuki Kunuk picks up a runner from a toy sled that was left in the area his family once inhabited. This connection to objects and to place becomes a virtual image that stands in for actual events that remain preserved in Kunuk's mind.[12] In this case, the past is preserved when embodied in Enuki Kunuk's childhood stories of his experience on the land and in his family's temporary dwellings. While the actual experience as remembered by Kunuk is absent from the video screen, it is not completely lost to the viewer, since it is

(*top*) Vivi Kunuk recounting memories from her childhood.

(*bottom*) View of Etuki Kunuk.

Mary Kunuk, *Anaana*, 2001.
STILLS COURTESY OF V TAPE.

still partially accessed through the split in time presented by *Anaana*. Past (Enuki Kunuk's memory) and present (his experience of walking through the land where he once lived) are split into two parts, yet both are partially visible through the visual rendering of *Anaana*. There is no doubt that discrepancies exist between the actual event as experienced in Kunuk's past and its resurrection through storytelling, but this is not up for debate in *Anaana*. The tape focuses on Kunuk's past and his understanding of his own surroundings, and the way this knowledge fluctuates and changes as it is transferred to those around him.

At both Arnait and Isuma, the artists will never be sure of the accuracy of reconstructions based on knowledge summoned from a past experience that is itself indeterminate. The videomaking process is the result of teamwork, as cast and crew debate a scene and recollect oral tradition. In *Anaana*, for instance, Vivi Kunuk tells the story about falling off a dog sled as a child and, once she finishes her story, says, "I don't know if my version is correct but I remember it that way." In this case, Kunuk's family and friends value this story neither for its correctness or accuracy nor as an inventory, annal, or register of the past. Like the videos in *cache*, the story is stored for future access, as a living archive that is always in the process of being constituted, formed, and contested in the ever changing present, just as culture is always in the process of production.

NOTES

In keeping with the ideals of communal production and authorship put forth by both of the video collectives we examine here, the cache curatorial initiative has produced all aspects of this chapter collectively. This essay was collectively re-searched and written by Lindsay Leitch, Erin Morton, Emily Rothwell, Taryn Sirove, Andrea Terry, and Michelle Veitch. We would like to thank Lynda Jessup and Marie-Hélène Cousineau for their inspiration and support.

1. For more on Arnait's history and development outside the community of Igloolik, see Cache Collective 2005.
2. Hall's (2001: 89) notion of "living" archive "is strongly counterposed to the common meaning accorded to 'tradition,' which is seen to function like a prison-house of the past." According to Hall's strategy, to posit Igloolik video practices as reenacting "tradition" would be to deny the "modern" function of these tapes, thereby occluding their experimental status. In this essay, we seek to disrupt such classifications to show the difficulties in assigning a category to these videos. See Fleming 1996.
3. See Himani Bannerji's (1999) discussion of the legal, administrative, and gov-ernment institutions that essentialize and establish communities as homoge-neous groups linked to primitive traditions.
4. Rather than composing completed scripts for their video productions, the members of Isuma write a general story outline and then improvise the lines and the details of the action. See Igloolik Isuma International 1996: 69–71.
5. As Marks (2000: 8) notes, foregrounding a mixed cultural experience calls into question "the norms and knowledges of any culture presented as discrete, whole, and separate." In other words, these videos make explicit the impos-sibility of an untouched and so-called authentic culture devoid of outside influences or of the potential to exist in a contemporaneous context. To this end, the videos produced by Kunuk contrast sharply with films produced by North American settlers, such as Robert Flaherty's 1922 *Nanook of the North*. Although Flaherty worked with Inuit filmmakers and actors, he assumed control over production and misrepresented traditional customs by establish-ing the Inuit as an "untouched" or isolated culture. See Alia 1999: 15–20; and Howell 2002. Even Asen Balikci's 1967 Netsilik Eskimo film series, which was filmed in cooperation with Inuit participants, focuses on historical ways of life

from the perspective of an ethnographer whose imperative was to prepare for the disappearance of these practices by making a record for posterity. See Margaret Mead's foreword to Balikci 1970.

6. These practices of archiving memories are common to the body of Isuma and Arnait video work, not just the three videos in *cache*. For example, Arnait's 1992 *Attagutaaluk* (*Starvation*) is a documentation of an interview with Rose Ukkumaluk, an Iglaolik elder who recounts a story of a woman who survived starvation. And Isuma's 1989 *Qaggiq* (*Gathering Place*) is a reconstruction of several families building a communal dwelling for a celebration.

7. In the video, the women explain that, in former times, a snowhouse that was in use was referred to as an *igloo*, while a snowhouse that was empty and discarded was referred to as an *igluvigaq*. Today, however, they use the term *igluvigaq* to refer to both a snowhouse in use and an empty snowhouse.

8. The wording for "environment of memory" comes from the historian Pierre Nora's (1989: 7) *milieux de mémoire*, which is dependent on his concept *lieux de mémoire* (sites of memory) as places "where memory crystallizes and secretes itself." Nora's sites of memory are connected to specific "sites," such as monuments or museums, that exist "because there are no longer *milieux de mémoire*, environments of memory" (7). Thus, the Igloolik video collectives do not create memory sites but rather memory environments.

9. *Aivilikmiut* refers to Inuit living in the eastern Arctic. The Inuit from Igloolik, on the other hand, live in the central Arctic and are referred to as either *Amitturmiut* (meaning people from the Igloolik / Hall Beach region) or *Iglulingmiut* (meaning people living in and around Igloolik). We examine the crossover between Avilikmiut and Amitturmiut experiences of place, while recognizing that these experiences are individual and specific to different Inuit groups. See Robinson 2004: 8, 225.

10. Notions of memory and their connection to narrative structures have been examined by Jeff Malpas (1999).

11. For more on Carpenter's analysis of Aivilikmiut conceptions of time and place, see Carpenter 1955, 1956, and 1973.

12. This perspective is informed by the work of Gilles Deleuze (1989), who describes "recollection-images" as those which cannot be captured on camera and that are based entirely on acts of remembrance.

CHAPTER 4

INDIGENOUS ANIMATION: EDUCATIONAL
PROGRAMMING, NARRATIVE INTERVENTIONS,
AND CHILDREN'S CULTURES

Joanna Hearne

> *I wonder what Disney's going to think?*
> —*Norval Morriseau*

Recent Native-produced animated films recover and claim cultural continuity in the intersections of education and entertainment. Films about Indigenous peoples by outsiders—including Hollywood Westerns, documentaries, and children's programming—have tended to function both pedagogically and ideologically. They have educated (and miseducated) generations of young viewers about the nature of cultural difference and the histories of settler nations such as the United States and Canada. This chapter explores developments in Indigenous animation in the context of historical attempts to assimilate Native children through residential boarding school policies and mainstream educational and dramatic films. The "vanishing Indian" tropes that have structured both mainstream visual representations and government policies have aggressively denied what Eric Michaels (1994) has called a "cultural future" for Indigenous communities by refusing to imagine Indigenous children as contemporary receivers and producers of knowledge and identities. New Indigenous animation productions intervene in the contested sites of media and education in several ways: (1) the films re-present pedagogical iconographies as scenes of storytelling rather than scenes of classroom education, (2) they draw on and redirect the conventions of animated media, including opening and closing credits and images, voice acting, and trickster and storytelling characters, in ways that assert Native control over visual and aural representations, (3) they acknowledge children—especially Indigenous children—as producers and receivers of knowledge embedded in narratives and languages from culturally specific tribal traditions, and (4) they offer alternatives to English-language, acculturating, mass media cartoons by presenting Native-controlled images that counter productions of stereotypically noble or villainous Indianness in Disney and other animated films.[1]

Native American and First Nations production companies such as Blackgum Mountain Productions in the United States and Raven Tales Productions in Canada address Indigenous concerns about social accountability both in the languages and cultural values that children learn from visual and narrative content as well as in production issues of direction and casting. Crucially, many new animation films are primarily in Indigenous languages. They redeploy both traditional Indigenous oral narratives and Western image-making technologies not as separate or oppositional binaries but rather as coterminous, mutually embedded, politicized modes of address.

Indigenous animations are produced and received in a complex and diverse field of media spaces. Although some productions, funded by educational grants, are developed specifically as instructional materials for use in schools, many are intended for television broadcast in the United States, Canada, and internationally, on networks such as the Public Broadcasting System (PBS) and Canadian Broadcasting Corporation (CBC). Grants and other funding from private foundations as well as from government-funded media organizations such as the Aboriginal Peoples Television Network (APTN) and the National Film Board (NFB) in Canada and PBS and the Native American Broadcasting Corporation (NABC) in the United States have resulted in a range of new training, production, financing, exhibition, and distribution opportunities.

What issues of hybridity, representation, language, and pedagogy come into play when tribal oral narratives become the basis for animated films for children, and when local ethics and aesthetics determine production practices? Episodes of *Stories from the Seventh Fire* (in Cree and English) visualize and foreground the scene of storytelling itself as a basis for educational and familial relations, and the new, independently produced series *Raven Tales,* by the Kwakwaka'wakw director Simon James, imagines a Haida story of the creation time through computer animation. The Cherokee artist Joseph Erb, working with the American Indian Resource Center in Tahlequah, Oklahoma, has developed educational programming for K–12 public schools that combines Indigenous language preservation with media literacy skills; films authored by youth are then integrated into the curriculum of language-immersion classes for preschool and kindergarten classes.[2]

These Cree, Kwakwaka'wakw, and Cherokee films all adopt cross-culturally popular forms—such as hip hop culture, 3-D computer-generated imagery (CGI) used for computer gaming, and references to mainstream animation—while restoring the cultural education embedded in creation stories about trickster figures. This story genre fully exploits the stylistic possibilities of clay, cell, and computer animation that lend themselves to the morphing, humorous exaggeration, and emphasis on innovation, physical creation, and cultural survival that have always characterized trickster stories. Indeed, the broader history of animated cartoons has involved precisely the "style of character-driven, anarchic comedy" embodied in Native trickster stories (Wells 2002: 2). At the level of production, the films have cast actors who are bilingual in English and Cree, Cherokee, or Muscogee Creek, and visual designs have been tied to specific tribal artistic patterns, such as the painting of the Anishinaabe artist Norval Morriseau (innovator of the "woodlands" school of painting) and the carvings of the Kwakwaka'wakw artist Simon James.

These productions are made for children by industry professionals or by youth for themselves and for younger children. Often produced through educational arts and language immersion programs, as well as independently for television, these media forms intervene in the "children's cultures" of mainstream media with alternative Indigenous modernities for youth. The stories make both linguistic and cultural resources available to children and youth as part of their creative repertoire as they navigate life in and beyond educational institutions. The work of Indigenous animated children's programming is not only to record traditional stories using new technology, as was the goal of many kinds of recordings made under the auspices of salvage anthropology. Here the notion of "tradition" as material that could be stored in transcribed texts and ethnographic films has been supplanted by tradition-as-action, a set of living and dynamic cultural practices. Works of Indigenous animation support the view that Indigenous media should be seen not just as content but rather as a process of "mediation"—an act of exchange between speaker and audience (Ginsburg 1991, 2002). The Laguna Pueblo actor and director Larry Littlebird, who in the 1970s collaborated with the Blackfeet filmmaker George Burdeau to produce and direct the first all-Native-produced television series (*The Real People* series, broadcast by KSPS-TV in Spokane, Washington), asserts: "I believe that the oral tradition—the spoken word—is alive, and that it frees you to action. It's not like you have all these stories, and so they're in your memory. No, the words free you to be reminded of all the stories that you have as a resource, from which you can make choices that give you action toward freedom" (personal communication, September 25, 2003). Littlebird's characterization of his own storytelling is in keeping with theories that underscore the practical work of speech as "artisan communication" from tellers who, as Walter Benjamin (1968: 86) described them, have a form of "counsel" for listeners that resembles a present-day "proposal concerning the continuation of a story which is just unfolding."

The film theorist Ella Shohat (1991: 109) addresses this issue of tradition and the past as part of her broader intervention in postcolonial theory and strategic identity politics. She writes, "For communities which have undergone brutal ruptures, . . . the retrieval and reinscription of a fragmented past becomes a crucial contemporary site for forging a resistant collective identity. A notion of the past might thus be negotiated . . . as fragmented sets of narrated memories and experiences on the basis of which to mobilize contemporary communities." In circling back to creation stories, Native filmmakers neither reify essentialist cultural identities nor elaborately "invent" traditions and communities; instead, they kindle and transmit stories as resources. Both Littlebird's description of Keresan oral narratives and Shohat's reassessment of the place of tradition in postcolonial theory suggest a politicized, active relation of the past to the present (see also Dirlik 2000: 222–23).

The *Oxford English Dictionary* defines the verb *to animate* as both to give life through action and to simulate action, to "breathe life into, quicken, vivify, enliven . . . give (a film, cartoon figure, etc.) the appearance of showing movement, by using a quick succession of gradually varying images [; or to] fill with boldness, courage, or spirit; excite (a person) to action; inspire, actuate . . . put in motion" (Simpson and Weiner 1989). Animation as a concept and a visual technique has the capacity to "actuate" stories from and about the past, providing individuals and communities with the means for "mobilization" and "action toward freedom." In each of these formulations, the traditional, as it defines a relationship with the past, is not invented in the present so much as it is *animated* or activated as an imaginative framework for current and future cultural survival.

CINEMATIC CONTEXTS

Indigenous producers and directors situate animation in the context of a range of other strategies used to confront media and pedagogical environments perceived as hostile to Indigenous families and children's cultures. This new wave of animation parallels the emergence of nonanimated dramatic and documentary films that explore the destructive community, familial, and emotional repercussions of residential-school education and foster-care systems that were designed to de-Indigenize Native children. These films are part of a prominent thread in Indigenous studies engaged in the necessary work of confronting and exposing the cultural and interpersonal ruptures wrought by these harsh policies. One of the most powerful recurring images in recent feature films that revisit Indigenous boarding-school experiences (in the United States, Canada, and Australia) is the scene of removal. Two films by non-Native filmmakers, *Map of the Human Heart* (Vincent Ward, 1996) and *Rabbit-Proof Fence* (Phillip Noyce, 2002), dramatize forced removal, each film depicting the children looking back through a car's rear window as they are taken away from relatives and other loved ones. These scenes of family breakup and the institutionalization of Native children also resonate with larger issues of tribal removal and relocation, while dramatizing the domestic consequences of assimilationist policies. Documentaries by Native filmmakers often include evocative reenactments, as do Alanis Obomsawin's short film *Richard Cardinal: Cry from a Diary of a Métis Child* (1986), Loretta Todd's *The Learning Path* (1991), and Pamela Matthews's *Only the Devil Speaks Cree* (2004). Some of these films also include scenes of foster homes and residential-school education, with military-style drills, rows of beds in the dormitories, and graphic portrayals of punishment in the classroom for speaking Native languages or speaking English incorrectly.

A second, quite separate, trend is the competing tradition of animated and live-action representations of Indigenous peoples by cultural outsiders. These programs have presented images of Native people to generations of white and Native children, from mid-twentieth-century Disney films such as *Peter Pan* (Clyde Geronimi et al., 1953) and television Westerns, to the more recent Disney products *The Indian in the Cupboard*

(Frank Oz, 1995) and *Pocahontas* (Mike Gabriel and Eric Goldberg, 1995).[3] Those media, especially in children's cartoons, often omit images of Indians altogether, or represent them as either threatening aggressors or passive, wise sages. Even in shows with no Indian characters, cartoon villains often speak an accented English, potentially producing negative associations with Indigenous and / or foreign languages and accents (Geiogamah and Pavel 1993; Dobrow and Gidney 1998). Scholars have intervened in this field of mainstream children's programs by advocating for a "critical pedagogy" (the application of cultural studies theory in education) that teaches students to become active and critical readers of the media that saturate their worlds (Grande 2004; Giroux 1998).

Indigenous animation represents an interruption of mainstream political and representational address to children that is different from either the work of filmmakers reflecting on institutional interference in Native families through boarding schools or the recent emphasis on critical readings of mainstream animations and film stereotypes. Instead, recent Indigenous programming has involved the creation of alternative representations for children—a strategic intercession in prior and ongoing educational paradigms that is constituted in the act of filmmaking itself— and this dynamic has emerged from its own historical context. Efforts to provide positive alternatives to mainstream animated representations of Native peoples began in Canada and the United States in the 1970s, primarily in the arena of fine arts rather than children's media. Among early high-quality animations of traditional stories are those by the non-Native artists Faith Hubley (*Starlore*, 1983) and Barbara Wilk (*Emergence*, 1981, and *Letter from an Apache*, 1982). In the late 1960s and early 1970s, Canada's NFB expanded its sponsorship of experimental animation to include individual First Nations artists such as Duke Redbird (*Charley Squash Goes to Town*, 1969) and Alanis Obomsawin (*Christmas at Moose Factory*, 1971) as well as community media training venues such as the Sikusilarmiut studio workshops for Inuit youth that resulted in *Animation from Cape Dorset* (1973), a series of films initially intended for television broadcast (Roth 2005). In the United States, some independent filmmakers began to incorporate animation into their films, as Victor Masayesva did for his experimental film *Ritual Clowns* (1988) and Patricia Albin for her film *Popol Vuh* (1989). J. Leonard Concha's short film for children, *Coyote Goes Underground* (1989), features the Taos Pueblo elder Pete Concha telling a Coyote story in the Tiwa language to four children. The film alternates between this scene of the storytelling and clay-animated sequences that depict the events of the story. These innovative efforts prefigure later, more systematic, productions by companies controlled by Native artists who make films targeted for Native youth as well as for broader national and international audiences.

THE SCENE OF THE STORY

Indigenous-controlled children's productions consistently reimagine the figure of the storyteller and the act of storytelling, or what I call the "scene of the story," as a symbolic iconography of the site of education that intervenes in the historically assimilationist educational models of institutional schooling systems. Yet the image of an Indian elder telling stories to children around a campfire has become a cultural cliché in part through the appropriation and commodification of this image by non-Native filmmakers and advertisers. Hollywood Westerns such as *Hondo* (John Farrow, 1953) and many others, as well as mainstream children's productions, often present Indian knowledge as available to young white male characters, and to the spectators themselves, through the act of viewing and listening. Sympathetic, "pro-Indian" Hollywood films are full of wise Indian characters who are forever imparting New Age wisdom to white protagonists. Given the dislike for romantic stereotypes in Native discourses, the efforts of Native animators to remember and reclaim the figure of the storyteller attests to the importance of the scene of storytelling for contemporary Native cultural identities.[4] This dynamic visual reframing in Native media is analogous to what Chadwick Allen (2002: 161, 132) describes as the "scene of indigenous instruction" in post-WWII Native American and Maori activist and literary texts, moments characterized by an "idealized grandparent-grandchild relationship" and characters who engage in "rebuilding the ancestor." The way many animated films reimagine storytellers—including an outdoor setting and campfire—represents an effort to take back the means of cultural production and the ownership of tribal knowledge.

In each of the examples that I discuss in the profiles that follow, the storyteller introduces the story with information that signals the specific linguistic, cultural, or geographic origins of the story, as when the storyteller in Joseph Erb's *Messenger* (2004) explains the different Cherokee words for "owl." In the digitally animated *Raven Tales*, producer / director Simon James used his experience as a mask carver to indicate the Haida and Kwakwaka'wakw origins of story through the visual style of the animated figures. In addition, he replicated the textures of traditional materials by scanning and digitizing 150-year-old woven hats and clothing from the collections in the Museum of Anthropology at the University of British Columbia (personal communication, March 3, 2006). This investment in the authority and particularity of the cultural past, then, takes place in the politicized context of the media present, with its concomitant technologies of reproduction that raise issues, inherent in broadcast dissemination, of both cultural property and cultural sharing.

While outsiders imagine Indian sages as dispensers of knowledge, mainstream children's literature, video, and animated films have frequently appropriated "traditional" and/or "anonymous" tribal narratives without citation of print sources or individual storytellers (Hearne 1993; Reese 1998; Keeshig-Tobias 1997). Revisiting these issues of intellectual property rights, cultural protocols, and royalties, Native producers of animated films are especially concerned with locating the origins of stories in individual performances, in families, in clans and communities, and in specific geographic areas. Film credits, claiming various forms of authorship and ownership, as well as attributing the performances to named actors, appear at the beginning and endings of films and take on special significance for Native production, especially in light of a cinematic history in which Native actors have often remained unnamed on credits lists.[5]

In their efforts to reclaim Indigenous education and the image of storytelling, contemporary Native filmmakers have constructed embedded, metacommunicative frames—such as production footage, carefully constructed animated "outtakes," and other opening and closing narratives, imagery, and credits—that interpret the story for the viewer. Barbara Babcock (1977: 71) was one of the first to call attention to metanarration and interpretative frames in oral literatures, suggesting that "'beginnings' and 'endings' are of crucial importance in the formulation of systems of culture." Frame narratives and their interrelationships with embedded narratives are forms of self-designation and self-commentary; they mark narrative points at which issues of identity, identification, and self-representation are particularly freighted and visible.

Embedded in the story as a character, the storyteller alludes both to the animator/director, visualizing the story, and to oral storytelling as an interpersonal mode of transmission. Animation as a form highlights this relationship between the storyteller and the story, making manifest the film's mode of production. Paul Wells (2002: 11) suggests that authorship is crucial in animation because through reflexive discourse "within and about the very language of animation, animated films recover the idea that such discourses must be created, and beg the question 'who by?' "

One of the most prominent threads of criticism in animation studies weaves through this issue of self-reflexivity (Lindvall and Melton 1997; Wells 2002; Polan 1985). Brechtian direct address is commonplace in the medium, as are "double-coding, intertextuality and carnival comedy," along with techniques of "pastiche and parody, of extended quotation and of multiple perspectives" (Linvall and Melton 1997: 212–17). Although all animated films have these capacities for self-conscious reflection on issues of authorship and discourse, Native American and First Nations animations harness these aesthetic qualities for the politicized work of cultural survival, foregrounding issues of authenticity, copyright, language, and cultural memory that are particular to Native communities. This claim to ownership of Native cultural production insists on recognition in a political sense, relating visual storytelling to other kinds of narrative claiming, such as testimony, and to the process of "passionate research" that is important to the historicizing work of projects such as reclaiming rights to land and sovereignty (L. T. Smith 1999: 143–44; Hall 2000: 705).

A particularly powerful example of experimentation with diverse animation techniques to engage these issues of cultural claiming through storytelling comes from *Two Winters: Tales from above the Earth* (2004), written and directed by the veteran documentary filmmaker Carol Geddes (Tlingit and Tutchone). The frame story is set in the winter of 1816, when the volcanic eruption of Mount Tambora in Indonesia sent clouds over northern Canada that extended the winter weather and caused widespread hunger and hardship for the southern Tutchone people. Geddes evokes the intricately related story worlds of Tutchone history by combining 3-D rotoscope animation for the frame narrative, live actors working in a bluescreen studio, original watercolor paintings of the Yukon landscape, and 2-D flash animation to convey dreams, visions, and creation stories.[6] The realistic figure movement and beautifully rendered settings of the rotoscoped sequences contrast very compellingly in visual style with the stories the characters tell about the origin of animals and seasons. Drawn from stories told by Yukon elders, these embedded narratives (along with dreams about hunting and the coming of the Europeans) help to sustain the characters' relationships with one another and with their environment. The film can be played in English or Tutchone, thus encouraging both language rejuvenation and accessibility to outsiders. The complex arrangement of animated narratives relates Tutchone history to multiple time frames (creation time as well as pre- and post-contact histories) while locating the tribe's homeland in the context of global events.

Creation stories, in particular, articulate Indigenous primacy on tribal homelands and in relation to specific ecologies. The continuation of these stories can contribute to legal claims based on cultural continuity over time. Animation provides unique opportunities to subvert and re-invent visual codes and vocabularies, which is why it is a valuable form for work in minority Indigenous languages. Animation also disrupts lin-ear time, because, unlike photography, it has no anterior referent, giving it an especially flexible relationship to issues of historicity and tradition. Thus, Native animators' return to the "scene of the story" raises issues and questions about the way knowledge is made and shared, and about the origins and endurance of Indigenous epistemologies.

CHEROKEE AND MUSCOGEE CREEK CLAY ANIMATION

Media literacy school programs for Native youth have resulted in produc-tions such as *The Trickster* (2003), a clay animation film made by Cherokee students through the American Indian Resource Center in Tahlequah, Oklahoma. In working with clay as a storytelling medium, these young filmmakers engage in a material form that turns away from realism. In fact, nothing highlights the constructed nature of visual storytelling more than clay animation, which involves the painstaking work of creating and manipulating physical models that often carry the actual fingerprints of their makers, foregrounding the physical traces of their artistic cre-ation. Although Joseph Erb's first film, *The Beginning They Told* (2000; see fig. 4.1), is computer-animated, his work in the schools has been in clay animation, in part because of the medium's modest space and budget requirements.

The Cherokee and Creek students in Erb's clay animation classes also provide the voices for the films, bringing together film production, film text, and language preservation. Over the past few years, Erb and his students have produced over eighteen clay-animated shorts, and Erb has completed a twenty-six-minute film called *Messenger.* "I had never really thought of animation before college," he says, "but some of the ideas that I had and some of the stories I knew were better implemented in anima-tion. If you watch animation from different cultures it manifests itself

From *The Beginning They Told*. IMAGE COURTESY OF JOSEPH ERB.

differently, even though it's the same medium. I think we're at the beginning of something exciting because Native culture will re-define animation for itself" (quoted in Murg 2004).

In one short animation by Muscogee Creek students at Morris High School, *Day and Night* (2005), nocturnal and diurnal animals must come to a compromise about the duration of night and day. When voting does not work (since there are equal numbers of day and night animals), they find a model for dividing day and night equally based on the even numbers of light and dark rings on Raccoon's tail. The film closes with the animals happily playing ball during their designated times. Following "The End" is a "bridge frame": Mouse reappears with a radio and begins to break dance, joined by day animals Turtle and Chipmunk, who tackle the night animals and exit the stage. The same electronic music of the break dancing routine lends continuity to the credits and production scenes, which were shot in black and white digital video. After a shot of the "Morris High School" sign outside the school building, the scene switches to a school hallway. A young man leads the audience through a door to a small supply room, where, in cramped quarters, students practice their Creek dialogue, work on computers, and manipulate clay models. The double self-inscription of the credits and production footage—a technique used in *Atanarjuat / The Fast Runner* (2001) to assert the modernity of that film's Inuit filmmakers and cast—brings together the scenes of storytelling and education, reclaiming school grounds as a space for the intergenerational relations of storytelling rather than the site of familial rift.

As Mouse, Turtle, and Chipmunk switch from speaking Creek to the kinetic language of break dancing that emerged from urban African American communities, they model the way their Muscogee teen animators are seeking to master multiple communicative conventions, moving between cross-cultural and tribally specific forms of address. The "bridge frame" is an extended instance of code-switching, in which the Muscogee animals' break dance represents an alternative, artistically specific deployment of tribal and performative languages. It is impossible to parse the blurred boundaries between "tradition" and "modernity," and in fact such efforts seem irrelevant to the story's meaning. Instead, the animators are interested in drawing other kinds of boundaries, employing their powers of cultural hybridity in the work of shoring up their Muscogee identities.

In other films, such as *Cufe Totkv Svtetv / The Rabbit Gets Fire*, the closing production shots of the student animators, which accompany the credits, include their perspectives on the film project, its meaning, and why it is valuable. The film tells the story of Rabbit traveling to France to steal fire from Creek-speaking Parisians, bringing back fire and a celebratory dance to the Creek people. For the Ryal School students, both insider and outsider audiences are important. One student notes, "It's fun showing it to most of my friends and family, 'cause they're like, the same—they have the same Creek culture as mine and they understand it—the Creek words—real well, and they liked it." Another student values the ability of the films to travel: "Because I've never been out of state, and it's pretty cool that something I made is going out of state." The students also identified with Rabbit, who proves he can do something that people did not think he could do. The ability of Rabbit—and the film—to travel "out of state" is crucial to the way the films establish an adaptable, contemporary Indigeneity using "old" stories. Although many of the films tell creation stories, they are always imagined in the context of recent history, signified by contact with Europe, grocery stores, pickup trucks, Euro-American style houses and furniture, and radios and break dancing. The work of the students as creators of their worlds is represented as current as well as historically and politically situated; one Bell Elementary student says, at the end of *Trickster:* "Indian power!"

Erb's own film, *Messenger*, tells the story of a Cherokee family visited by a *skilly*—an owl that is a messenger of death and sickness. The father dies after the owl visits the family, but the owl, seeing the grieving daughter, falls in love with her and courts her in human form. This visit, too, ends in tragedy as he accidentally shoots her while hunting on the eve of their marriage. In the opening frame narrative, a Cherokee narrator (sitting by a computer-animated campfire), describes the different Cherokee words for owls—the *skilly* or screech owl (the "messenger" of the story), and the *ugukuhi* and *wahu*. The opening credits dedicate the film to the memory of Billy "Snow" Fields, who voiced the Storyteller in the film, thus remembering and simultaneously modernizing him as part of the production team for the claymation film.[7]

As the film begins, before the narrator begins to speak, we hear an owl calling, and as he begins the story about a Cherokee family long ago, we see a cabin reflected in his eye. The audience actually enters the world of the story at the beginning through the eye of the storyteller, and as the story ends, the teller undergoes a metamorphosis and becomes the skilly—feathers grow out from his sleeve to cover his hands, and his hair becomes streaked with white, a physical characteristic of the skilly in human shape. He flies away, and in the closing credits, footage from the production again emphasizes the contemporary work of the Native animators. Thus the teller literally embodies the shape-shifting skilly, marking the creative and potentially destructive power of storytelling as a relationship between tellers and listeners—in this case a visual as well as aural relationship. The final frame of the credits is a quotation from Chad Smith, principal chief of the Cherokee Nation, emphasizing in life-and-death terms the importance of language preservation: "If we lose our language, we will have no culture and people will say—there once was a great and powerful Cherokee Nation, but it is no more."

Opening and closing credits play a special authenticating role in Native animation films. While Rabbit and other animals seem to make light of this moment and pay homage to mainstream popular culture in their on-screen shenanigans, the transition from constructed "outtakes" to live-action black-and-white footage does a different sort of work than the "outtakes" from such Pixar / Disney films as *A Bug's Life* (1998) and *Monsters Inc.* (2001), which introduced and perfected the technique for mass audiences. The serious work of attribution and identification in the listed credits and the playful acknowledgment of the performative qualities of identity in the "outtakes" unite to situate Indigenous cultural identity in the realm of both genealogy and staging, bringing these vexed and contested models of ethnic affiliation together to activate and visualize Native futures.

RAVEN TALES

Raven Tales Productions represents a middle ground between the government-funded, community-based Creek and Cherokee films by Joseph Erb (and his students) and the more industry-based production of

Stories from the Seventh Fire. The twenty-two-minute pilot episode of *Raven Tales*, "How Raven Stole the Sun," was partly funded in 2004 by a $10,000 completion grant from the All Roads Film Project, a program through National Geographic developed to foster Indigenous filmmaking globally. The pilot has already appeared on Access TV in Canada and on Maori TV in New Zealand, and the success of the pilot show has led to a license for potential television broadcast as a series in Norway, Japan, France, Germany, and the United Kingdom (*Animated News* 2004a; Miller 2005).[8] The series was picked up for broadcast on APTN in October 2006, with plans to broadcast twenty-six episodes over the next three years.

Raven Tales' producer, Simon Daniel James (Winadzi)[9], comes from a family of political leaders, performers, and artists of the Kwakwaka'wakw tribe in the Pacific Northwest. An artist and mask carver (the Raven Tales animations are based on his carvings), James for many years earned his living as a salmon fisherman before the decline of the salmon population in the Northwest drove him to change careers and to attend the Vancouver Film School. He and the codirector, Chris Kientz (Cherokee), have worked with the Charles River Media group to develop a book project documenting the production for a general audience (*Animated News* 2004b). James's and Kientz's production work represents an Indigenous influence in mainstream computer animation, including military CGI industries, gaming, and university-based creative media programs, while at the same time locating the authority, control, and intellectual ownership of the stories with tribes in two ways. First, the production reflects long-standing intertribal exchange in the Pacific Northwest—for example, the Haida story of "How Raven Stole the Sun" includes influences from Salish and Kwakwaka'wakw cultures. Second, the story and production acknowledge internal tribal systems of intellectual and artistic property rights. In addition to textual sources such as Bill Reid's and Robert Bringhurst's *The Raven Steals the Light* (1984), James works with elders from tribal nations to obtain permission to animate their stories, and stresses his own cultural training by his grandfather James Aul Sewid, a chief of the Kwakiutl Reserve at Alert Bay, British Columbia: "My grandfather taught me everything, and I tried to learn every story from him while he was living" (quoted in Miller 2005).

The pilot episode of *Raven Tales*, "How Raven Stole the Sun," takes place in the "creation time" when most of the world was still unformed (see figs. 4.2 and 4.3). The landscape of rain, volcanic rock, and unformed animal shadows is presided over by the elders Frog (Carmen Moore), Raven / Tlesla (Evan Adams), and Eagle / Nusi (Ian Reid)—viewers see footage of Evans and Moore voicing their characters in the sound studio in the film's closing credits. Frog, the storyteller, is both a character and the narrator, voiced in different styles by Moore. The opening credits appear with stylized portraits of the characters on painted banners, images that serve as a transition to the opening sequence, when they become part of the storyteller's cloak.[10] Viewers see Frog from above, her face hidden by her traditional woven reed hat as she sits in front of a fire; the stick she throws in the fire sends up a spiritual shape of a raven, the logo for the series. This "scene of the story" frames and introduces the action that follows with Frog's description of creation: "It was a dark time . . . the rain never stopped. All things were bound then by their shadow forms—whale and seal, bear and beaver—waiting, awake but unable to move, aware but unable to act." As the screen goes dark, the film begins again with the antics of Raven, introduced by the storyteller's voiceover: "The Raven, who of course existed at this time, because he had always existed and always will, was somewhat less than happy with this dark and wet state of affairs." The Frog reappears in the narrative as well and is addressed as "Storyteller" by Raven, who is always surprised by her appearance. Although Raven's acts of disruption release the light of the sun and moon so that animals and plants can live, it is Frog's story that gives Raven the initial idea. "No story is ever just a story," she says. "Some are true, and some are inspiration, and . . . this one is both." When Raven, having taken the form of a human child, lets the light out of its box, he inadvertently animates the world, giving "the lumps"—the shadow forms of the animals—the power of movement.

In the context of the filmmakers' claim to have made the "first all–Native American computer animated short film," the characters Raven and Frog, animators of life on Earth in the story, double as embedded commentaries on the film's production as an intervention in an emerging digital imaginary dominated by computer games and the massive budgets and commodity tie-ins of Disney-Pixar feature films (*Animated News* 2004a). James's and Kientz's film, with its hermeneutic performances, "resignifies" the traditional in the media landscape while insisting on the authority of contemporary Indigenous interpretations of the past (see Ginsburg 2002). Unlike the transcriptions and translations by Franz Boas and other anthropologists, whose important efforts to record Kwakw*aka*'wakw

(*top*) Raven and Eagle, from *Raven Tales*.

(*bottom*) Raven and Eagle look into a shell, from *Raven Tales*.

myths in the Pacific Northwest nevertheless resulted in texts removed from historical and contextual interpretive framing, James's and Kientz's animation inscribes modern claims to self-representation and visual discourse.

STORIES FROM THE SEVENTH FIRE

The series *Stories from the Seventh Fire*, produced as family television programming for general broadcast, combines several animation styles with wildlife footage. The series is a creation of Storytellers Productions —a collaboration between the Métis Cree director Gregory Coyes, Ava Karvonen, and Gerri Cook—and includes animation based on fifteen paintings by the Anishinaabe artist Norval Morriseau to tell Cree stories about the trickster Wesakechak, live-action wildlife footage by the cinematographer Albert Karvonen to depict legends from the West Coast, and a 3-D computer-animated Wolf Mother as a storyteller. This complex array of styles, reflecting the collaboration of several producers and a multilingual, multigenerational cast, translates into a feeling of poly-vocality and shared perspectives at the level of the film text, which also brings together Anishinaabe and Cree cultural references. Each half-hour episode, including one Wesakechak tale and one Wolf tale, cost approximately $400,000, with 2-D animation by Bardel in Vancouver, and 3-D CGI by Bioware in Edmonton (a computer games company; see Decker 1999; Dinoff 2000). The DVD version of the series can be played in English or in Cree and comes with extensive teachers' guides that include background information, suggested activities in different class subjects, and a bibliography of print and Web resources.

Bilingual performers—Tantoo Cardinal, Gordon Tootoosis, and Johnny Waniandy, as well as a group of Cree youth—created the voices in each language. Cardinal stressed the importance of the production for the children who played the wolf cubs, the listening audience for Cardinal's Wolf Mother storyteller:

> Cree, in this society, normally is something that you have to hide. You put it away some place, you know, you stick it in a box in the closet because you're not going to have a chance to use it, you don't even find anybody that you can talk Cree *with*. And here, they were using their Cree in a studio. It was being recorded, being put to stories, you know, the traditional stories, and it's very exciting, very empowering for them. (Coyes 2003)

The nested frames that introduce and conclude the animated and live-action legends begin in outer space, moving toward Earth as the narrator (Tootoosis) describes the Anishinaabe seven fires prophecies that foretold the coming of the Europeans and the loss and recovery of Anishinaabe traditions. As the stars or "fires" become a constellation on the planet Earth, a wolf howls as a meteor shoots past, and through trees viewers see a storyteller, a campfire, and the shadowy figures of listeners; by the end these listeners are revealed to be people and animals sitting together. The storyteller introduces the story as Cree, and when the story is over, he asks, "So, what have we learned from this story?"—reinforcing the storytelling as education. The parallel storyteller from the animal world, a 3-D computer-animated Wolf Mother (Cardinal), promises her cubs that stories will entertain and scare them, help them become better hunters, and teach them about the big world outside the den. The director, Gregory Coyes, notes in an interview,

I was looking at [*Stories from the Seventh Fire*] as an alternative to what else was on the menu for kids as far as animation goes. . . . What I wanted was to create something that my kids would enjoy that was good for them. And I don't mean 'okay swallow this. You won't like the taste but it's good for you.' I mean media that nurtures them. . . . that nurtures an audience and doesn't rob an audience. . . . It informs you, it makes you laugh, it feeds your spirit and it does all the things that good stories do. (personal communication, March 6, 2006)

Finally, the Wesakechak stories themselves are metamyths that reflect on how language and storytelling originated. "How Wesakechak Got His Name" describes how the "trickster-teacher" figure Wesakechak, unhappy with his name and unable to change it to something more noble-sounding, ends up becoming the teacher of the first people, someone who wields language for the sake of others (personal communication, March 6, 2006).[11]

In the Wolf Tales segments of the *Stories from the Seventh Fire* series, Cree youth literally voice the characters being narrated by an elder storyteller; in Coyes's words, the visual and other elements followed "from the energy and spirit and performances [of] this process of recording these voices." In this way, the filmmakers and vocal performers present alternative teaching and learning models to the institutional interventions in Indigenous families carried out by residential schools and other educational systems, and call into question a series of assimilationist assumptions—including blood quantum identity politics and the erosion of Indigenous land bases and treaty rights—based in the ideology of the "vanishing Indian." Their productions honor children as bearers of Indigenous cultural, political, and linguistic futures by strategically reimagining youth as both film authors and as listening audiences. Controlled by Indigenous directors and producers in collaboration with outsiders, these films intervene in an otherwise often homogeneous field of mainstream animated and live-action children's programs. Through metanarrative framing devices, film credits, and other references to the communicative, culture-bearing, and pedagogical work of visual storytelling, these media makers alert us to attend to conditions of production, performative artistry, and tribal copyright, as well as to intergenerational relations, both imagined and ongoing, between tellers and listeners at the scene of the story.

I would like to thank the editors as well as the filmmakers Greg Coyes, Joseph Erb, Simon James, and Larry Littlebird for their insights and suggestions. Millie Seubert and Chris Turner of the National Museum of the American Indian (NMAI) helped to arrange screenings from the NMAI collection, and support for research and travel came from the University of Missouri-Columbia's Arts and Science Alumni Organization and Center for Arts and Humanities.

1. I use the terms *Native American* and *First Nations* to refer to Indigenous peoples in the United States and Canada, respectively, while I use *Indigenous* and *Native* to refer more generally to Indigenous peoples across tribal and national boundaries. Although *Indian* is still widely used in Native communities, here I use the term to refer to mainstream visual images of Native people.

2. For DVD sales and other information about Cherokee and Creek clay animated films by Joseph Erb and his students, see the Web site for Blackgum Mountain Productions, www.blackgummountain.com. Episodes of *Raven Tales* and *Stories from the Seventh Fire* are available on DVD and VHS from Film West Associates, www.filmwest.com. *Stories from the Seventh Fire* is also available from Green Planet Films at www.greenplanetfilms.org, and *Raven Tales* is also available from www.raventales.ca / .

3. Among the many excellent scholarly analyses of the animated *Pocahontas*, as well as *The Indian in the Cupboard*, are articles by Strong (1998) and Kapur (2005).

4. Chadwick Allen's term *"re-recognition,"* describing native literary and activist efforts to remind U.S. and other governments of historical treaty obligations, or "treaty discourse" (2002; 19), is also useful in this context; Native mediamakers politically "rerecognize" the figure of the storyteller in their productions.

5. *Nanook of the North* (Flaherty 1922) is one example. The actor Allakarialak, who played Nanook, and the other Inuit actors never appeared in the credits, while non-Native music composers were credited. For further discussion of crediting Indigenous actors, see Hearne 2005 and Hearne 2006.

6. *Two Winters: Tales from above the Earth* is available on DVD from FilmWest, www.filmwest.ca. Produced in association with APTN, the film has won eleven awards (including top honors for experimental animation and sound at the Nextfest Digital Motion Picture Festival). Rotoscoping is a technique that involves drawing or tracing over live-action film movement, frame by frame, either by hand or using computer programs.

7. The scriptwriter for the film is Bob Hicks, the Muskogee Creek director of the film *Return of the Country* (1984).

8. The filmmakers, after winning the Best Native Film award at the 2004 Santa Fe Film Festival, donated $10,000 to the Media Rights Foundation in Albuquerque to create the New Mexico Film Production Grant.

9. "Winadzi" is James's tribal name, and he discusses the meaning and importance of this name: "My name is 'Winadzi,' which means The Raider, a name given to me by my Grandfather, Chief James Aul Sewid, of the Kwicksuteniuk / Mamalelakala clan of the Kwakw*aka'*wakw people. My nickname, however, is 'Simon Daniel James,' given to me by my mother, Mabel Sewid and my father, Tahnis, Simon Dick." (James, n.d.).

10. The description of "How Raven Stole the Sun" in this chapter is based on the pilot version screened at film festivals. The version of this episode broadcast on APTN and currently available on DVD features a slightly different opening credit sequence, one that omits the figure of the Frog Storyteller at her campfire (although Frog remains a central character in the narrative).

11. Greg Coyes notes that he did not hear the Wesakechak stories himself as a child but rather came to the stories as an appreciative parent who recognized them as "very effective, entertaining, fun teaching tools." He adapted the stories from versions translated by the Métis writer and elder Maria Campbell and the Cree elder Stan Cuthand, both from Northern Saskatchewan (personal communication, March 6, 2006). Other Cree / English language productions include the stop motion animation film *Christmas at Wapos Bay* (2002), by the Cree director Dennis Jackson, which was funded in part by the NFB of Canada. A complete season of the Wapos Bay series was produced for broadcast on APTN in 2006 and 2007. The Wapos Bay Series Kit is available on DVD from www.nfb.ca. *Christmas at Wapos Bay* is available from www.filmwest.ca.

PART II

INDIGENOUS ACTIVISM, ADVOCACY, AND
EMPOWERMENT THROUGH MEDIA

MEDIA AS OUR MIRROR:

INDIGENOUS MEDIA OF BURMA (MYANMAR)

Lisa Brooten

Maybe we can solve problems in this way, to show, like a mirror. . . .
We hope that when they watch this movie, this documentary, they will
understand more about themselves . . . to find the real solution, in this
mirror.

—*"Saw Eh Th'Blay," Karen filmmaker, Kawlah Films*

The Indigenous media of Burma, also known as Myanmar, reflect both
the country's diversity and the needs of its Indigenous groups to protect
themselves against the assimilationist policies of a brutal military regime.[1] They are also part of a multiethnic opposition movement against
the Burmese regime, and in this context, the Indigenous media help
protect the dignity of Indigenous peoples against being overlooked by
their partners in this opposition movement, the ethnic majority Burman
dissidents. These media complicate notions of "Indigenous media" by
drawing information from a variety of non-Indigenous sources, by targeting multiple audiences, and by involving and / or working with nongovernmental organizations (NGOs) and outsiders.

Burma's Indigenous media aim to hold a mirror up not only to their
own communities but also to the larger Burmese opposition movement,
to the Burmese regime, and to the international community. In doing so,
they also walk a fine line between representing Indigenous peoples as
victims in order to evoke sympathy among outsiders and victimizing
themselves rhetorically out of agency to the extent that their Indigenous
readers become despondent and lose motivation for action. Part of their
job, then, is to identify the patterns of resistance and survival that begin

to alter stereotypes of Indigenous people as helpless, hopeless victims. But they are also beginning to challenge outsiders to think beyond charity and to embrace solidarity and political action.

These media have developed a great deal since my own introduction to Burma in 1989, when I began teaching English in a school, run by Karen refugees from Burma, that was housed in a refugee camp in western Thailand. Here I learned about the situation in Burma, the plight of the country's Indigenous minorities, and their alliances with other Indigenous groups and with Burman dissidents, many of whom I have met as my involvement with Burma has continued in the intervening years.[2] Indigenous media have grown right along with the opposition or independent media of Burmese-in-exile: promoting, reinforcing, and reflecting the growing influence of Indigenous peoples in Burma's political development. This chapter provides an overview of Burmese Indigenous media and the functions they perform for their communities and for the Burmese opposition movement as a whole. It also profiles two Indigenous video production groups that have emerged recently to provide perspectives of rural Indigenous peoples, who are not generally the focus of videos about Burma. The desire of these groups to be heard is long unfulfilled in the history of Burma and its opposition movement.

BURMA/MYANMAR AND THE BURMESE OPPOSITION

Burma is a country of great ethnic diversity in which over one hundred different languages and dialects have been identified (Smith 1999) despite the fact that population statistics in Burma are generally unavailable (and are contentious when they exist). The 1974 constitution identifies seven ethnic states—Chin, Kachin, Karen, Kayah (Karenni), Mon, Rakhine (Arakan), and Shan. There are several other large minority groups in the country as well, such as the Lahu, the Naga, the Pa-O, and the Wa, and there are many Chinese, Tamils, Bengalis, and others of Indian origin living in the country. The most recent figures available, from 1983, list the majority Burmans as comprising 69 percent of the population (Steinberg 2001).

In the early nineteenth century, the British colonized Burma as a province of India, dividing its administration into Ministerial Burma (in the central part of the country) and the Frontier Areas, in which the Indigenous peoples remained semiautonomous. The British exacerbated existing tensions between the groups, using Indigenous minority soldiers to police the Burmans agitating for independence in central Burma. During World War II, the Burmans fought with the Japanese while the Indigenous hill peoples such as the Karen and Kachin sided with the British, a situation that affected ethnic relations long after Burma's independence in 1948. Burma experienced only a few years of civilian rule before a coup brought the military to power in 1962 under the leadership of General Ne Win, who led the country to languish in isolation. In 1987, Burma was accorded Least Developed Country (LDC) status by the United Nations, which recognized it as one of the world's ten poorest nations.

Massive protests broke out in 1988. Initially led by students, these demonstrations eventually brought hundreds of thousands of civilians to the streets to protest conditions in their country. The Burmese military reacted with violence, gunning down thousands of people during protests that, with few exceptions, were nonviolent.[3] Many of the students who led the protests fled to the border areas, where they met Indigenous peoples who had long been struggling against the regime. One student activist, Mi Sue Pwint, admitted that even though she had grown up in the Karenni state, she worried about meeting the insurgent groups at the border. "We saw from the picture books and the movies about the rebels, so we worried about meeting them. We thought they were always ready to kill people," she told me, laughing (personal communication, July 3, 2000). She told me that her fears were small compared to those of students from the urban areas. And even though he is Karen himself, the young farmer (later turned filmmaker) Eh Th'Blay[4] was also afraid of the Karen "insurgents," given the portrayal of them in the Burmese media as "wild people . . . not normal people, with long hair and dirty, dirty teeth . . . Their shirts were also not very good and they spoke with rude words" (personal communication, July 30, 2005).

Yet once the students reached the border and began meeting Indigenous people, their views changed. As student activist Win Min put it, "They weren't fighting to break up the country, but because they were really suffering. What they were saying was that if [they] don't get equality, [then they] will break up the country. We could now see that their position was a fair one . . . and that we can solve the country's problems" (personal communication, March 6, 2000).

Since 1988 the Burmese students and the leaders of the country's largest opposition party, the National League for Democracy (NLD), have effectively used the global discourses of democracy and human rights to express the Burmese people's plight and to gain support for their struggle.

This discourse has fit very well with the foreign policy concerns of the United States and its allies, and the Burmese democracy movement has attracted U.S. and world media attention. This is in stark contrast to the U.S. media's comparative inattention to the Indigenous groups' calls for self-determination in the decades since Burma's civil war began in 1948.

In 1990, elections were held in which the NLD won in a landslide that included substantial support from the Indigenous groups. It soon became clear, however, that the military regime had no intention of handing over power. It has retained power since, despite a spirited Burma activist campaign that has increased pressure on the Burmese regime to improve the human rights situation both in Burma's cities and rural areas.

VIOLENCE AND INDIGENOUS PEOPLES

Human rights groups have dedicated volumes to documenting abuses by the various incarnations of the Burmese regime, including the current State Peace and Development Council (SPDC). According to Human Rights Watch (2005),

> The SPDC restricts the basic rights and freedoms of all Burmese. . . . [and] continues to commit systematic, widespread, and well-documented abuses in ongoing conflicts with ethnic minority rebel groups, including extrajudicial executions, rape, torture, forced relocation of entire villages, and forced labor. As of late 2004, an estimated 650,000 people were internally displaced in eastern Burma alone, and at least 240 villages have been destroyed, relocated or abandoned since 2002. Some 2 million Burmese have moved to Thailand, including 145,000 refugees living in camps.[5]

In addition to the struggle for their survival, Burma's Indigenous groups are concerned about preserving their cultures, especially since many are convinced the military regime is conducting a campaign to "Burmanize" the country.

The SPDC refers to the Indigenous peoples of Burma as "national races" (Kampe 1997) and promotes (apolitical) cultural diversity by celebrating public Indigenous cultural performances while committing abuses against these peoples in the rural areas. While many of the Indigenous groups prefer to be known as "ethnic nationalities" of Burma, others recognize the term *Indigenous* as spelled out in the Indigenous Peoples Forum of August 1988 and the Conference on Indigenous Peoples of

October 1995, both held in Chiang Mai, Thailand (Asian Indigenous Peoples Pact 1988; Kampe 1997). In this definition, *Indigenous peoples* are defined as cultural groups that have "a common heritage, language, and culture, are generally indigenous to the land (but not necessarily), or at least inhabit and identify with some territory, are only partly integrated into the dominant nation-state, are usually discriminated against or put at a distinct disadvantage with respect to the national majority population, and share a common desire to affirm their identity and self-determination" (Kampe 1997: 4).

Worldwide, Indigenous media have been important vehicles for the expression of identity and self-determination, yet scholars and activists have raised questions about their authenticity, especially those in which Indigenous peoples collaborate with "whites" (Ginsburg 1997; Michaels 1994; Pack 2000). Such a pursuit all too easily leads to an essentialism that ignores the hybrid cultural formations inevitable in a globally interconnected world, and is itself ethnocentric, as Sam Pack (2000: 274) points out, demanding an authenticity of Indigenous media as "cultural artifacts" that is not demanded of other media. Another argument, that Indigenous media should target only Indigenous communities (Michaels 1994), fails to consider the political nature of these media, despite their focus on the "cultural." Faye Ginsburg (1997) reminds us to ask questions about the actual authorship of media productions, but it is also clear that many outsiders working with Indigenous producers are careful to emphasize reciprocity so that they speak "with" rather than "for" the people with whom they work (Lansing 1989). Many of these outsiders have become long-term residents of the communities in which they work (see, e.g., Ginsburg 1997). Other scholars argue that authenticity is found only in hybrid media forms themselves (Jhala 1998). Media representations, like ethnographic representations, are subjective, based on a producer's reading of a situation from a particular location in levels of power relations (Narayan 1993). In my view, Indigenous media are "authentic" to the extent that they provide a forum for perspectives of Indigenous peoples rather than of society's dominant group(s).

INDIGENOUS MEDIA OF BURMA

The Thai-Burma borderland has for decades provided Burmese activists with the freedom to develop and distribute alternatives to the highly censored media in Burma. Numerous clandestine radio stations have operated from these border areas, the earliest of which was the Karen-controlled Radio Kawthoolei, which began broadcasting in 1949 and continued intermittently during the 1970s and 1980s (M. Smith 1999). Both armed and nonviolent resistance groups inside Burma have used wireless transmitters for local radio communications, and several reporters and stringers for international broadcasting networks are based along the border.

Journals and information sheets in a range of languages have long been published on the border and can now be broadly divided into two categories. One category consists of a few well-funded, widely read, and increasingly professional opposition media that are "unmarked" in terms of ethnic identification. These media's writers, like those of the *samizdat* media of the former Soviet bloc, are primarily urban-based intelligentsia with connections to Western journalists (Downing 2001: 358). *The Irrawaddy* magazine, based in Chiang Mai, Thailand, is a good example of such media.

The second category of print media, which has grown since the mid-1990s, includes those media identified with Indigenous nationality groups. These publications perform the type of *cultural activism* described by Ginsburg (1997: 123), self-consciously using hybrid cultural forms as a means of social action that is highly political, while not always recognized as such. These Indigenous media demonstrate how, especially in repressive regimes, "informal cultural spaces may become politicized particularly through the effective use of small media" (Sreberny-Mohammadi and Mohammadi 1994: xxi). Several of these media have become significant voices for the Indigenous nationalities, putting them "on the map" both for outsiders and for other groups in the opposition.[6]

Burma's Indigenous media target both their own group and outsiders and perform several functions. According to their staff members, these include the promotion of Indigenous self-determination, cultural preservation, education, action, participatory communication, and the use of human rights discourse to educate Indigenous peoples, majority Burmans, and outsiders about what is happening in the rural areas of Burma, and to advocate for change.

Self-Determination
Burma's Indigenous media respond to the need that non-Burmans feel to protect their identity against the regime's assimilationist policies and their dignity against feeling overlooked by the Burman opposition groups, who

they argue are not especially concerned with Indigenous peoples' rights to self-determination. Some Burmans perceive this desire for autonomy as a threat to the strength of the opposition, a distraction from the most pressing issues of political change. The non-Burman students involved in the 1988 protests often felt their loyalties divided once they reached the border areas, when they had to decide whether to affiliate primarily with the struggle for democracy or with their Indigenous group's struggle for self-determination. Nai Kasauh Mon, for example, was a student in Rangoon in 1988 when he became involved in the demonstrations. When he returned home afterward, his Mon family and friends challenged his loyalty to his people. "Many people asked me, 'You are for democracy, so you don't work for the Mon people? Are you sure [this is good] for the Mon people?' " (personal communication, July 22, 2000).

Nai Kasauh Mon decided to work with the statewide Mon organization created a few weeks after the demonstrations, the Mon National Democratic Front (MNDF). But the Burman students criticized the formation of the MNDF. "They said, 'You are Mon, you should join our democracy movement, you should not create your own separate group," Nai Kasauh Mon told me. "They said, 'Democracy must come first, and then we can talk about self-determination later.' . . . So that's why many ethnic people were confused. 'Should we participate in this struggle or not?' " (ibid.). While there is increasing cooperation between Burman and Indigenous political groups, it is not surprising that a motivating factor in the development of Indigenous media in the last decade has been the desire to maintain Indigenous cultural identities and the demand for self-determination.

Cultural Survival

These media clearly perform a "cultural transmission" function of ethnic media (Viswanath and Arora 2000), reviving or reinforcing ethnic identity and passing it along to the next generation (Aufderheide 1995; Prins 1989). The Karen journal, *Kway K'Lu*, for example, is primarily committed to informing Karen people of the situation of other Karen. The journal is named after the *kway*, a horn made from the tusk of a wild animal such as a boar. Varying sounds to represent different meanings, the player of the kway would inform the Karen in neighboring villages about community projects or celebrations. As *Kway K'Lu*'s editor, Saw Thaw Thi, explained, "We want to let the people know each other by reading this newspaper. . . . People in Papun can know what happened to the Karen people in the southern part, like this, Mergui-Tavoy. And people here can know what happened to the Karen in Chiang Mai or Chiang Rai, and what the Karen people in America or Australia are doing. So this is something like the *kway*, or Karen horn" (personal communication, July 24, 2000).

But a culture under threat must be protected before it can be transmitted to a younger generation, and thus a concern for literacy and the preservation of their languages motivates many of the groups publishing Indigenous media. The Human Rights Foundation of Monland (HURFOM) publishes some of the few regular Mon-language publications, as well as reports on the suppression by the Burmese military government of Mon-language training. In the October 30, 2000, edition of *The Mon Forum*, for example, HURFOM reported on the SPDC's attempts to close down the Mon National schools in Kawkareik Township, Karen State. The report pointed out that although the Burmese regime agreed in its 1995 ceasefire with the Mon to allow the teaching of the Mon language in both government and private schools, in reality the military rulers "never kept their promise for the promotion of Mon literature" in the Mon community and "still operate their assimilation policy" (*Mon Forum* 2000).

Saw Thaw Thi told me that his objective in publishing *Kway K'Lu* was to "raise the level of Karen literature and culture in the Karen society" (personal communication, July 24, 2000). He said that long ago, Karen literature used to be taught in Karen schools through high school, but that nowadays the Karen cannot teach their language in the schools in Burma except for some Christian groups who teach Karen in Sunday school. Many older Karen believe that the standards of Karen literature have been declining and are alarmed that many Karen young people "do not know exactly that we have a good culture" (Saw Thaw Thi, personal communication, July 24, 2000). These examples of Indigenous media alert us to the fact that in a militarized setting where one's group is under attack, this function of cultural transmission becomes more clearly a matter of cultural survival, closely linked with the need to maintain Indigenous languages and to educate Indigenous peoples on issues that affect them.

Education

Many Indigenous media work to educate their people about the relevance of international politics to the Burmese situation. To this end, in 1999 HURFOM began publishing a Mon-language independent newspaper, *The Guiding Star*, the first of its kind for the Mon people. This newspaper, like others, often includes information on the Burmese political situation translated into Mon from other news sources such as the online BurmaNet News, the Mon listserv, *The Irrawaddy*, the two Thai English-language dailies (the *Bangkok Post* and *The Nation*), and other sources, further complicating questions of the "authenticity" of Indigenous media. Yet the use of information from outside sources is placed in a local context in this and other Indigenous media, since it is often rewritten for the specific audience or with background information added so that readers can see their own situation in a larger context.

Indigenous media also provide information about how readers' own actions can have an impact on the situation in Burma. One campaign that has gathered momentum over the past few years educates and organizes villagers in response to the proposed dam on the Salween River, which flows through Burma and forms a portion of the border between Burma and Thailand. The Karen journal *Thulei Kawwei*, produced by the Karen Environmental and Social Action Network (KESAN), an Indigenous NGO, has informed Karen villagers about the proposed dam and its potential impact on the environment and on villagers' lives. A key goal of *Thulei Kawwei*, according to KESAN founding member Paul Sein Twa, is to highlight Indigenous knowledge regarding the environment and sustainable forestry and agriculture, a valuable resource that KESAN believes is underutilized by both the Karen villagers and policymakers (personal communication, July 26, 2005). This emphasis on the value of Indigenous knowledge is part of a larger goal of these media to motivate Indigenous peoples to see themselves as having a role to play in the movement for change in Burma.

Call to Action
Many of these media work to maintain their readers' motivation to struggle on behalf of their people in whatever ways they can while resisting a dependence on outside forces. This could be termed a "call to action" function of Indigenous media, which combines the functions described by K. Viswanath and Pamela Arora (2000) as "boosterism" and mobilization. These media help their readers feel good about themselves and motivate them to support initiatives to improve the *group* situation. The cartoon in figure 5.1 is an example from *Kway K'Lu*, produced primarily for Karen inside Burma and along the border in refugee camps.

Saw Thaw Thi explained that Karen people living in their own villages bury their dead in cemeteries, but that at the refugee camps they must

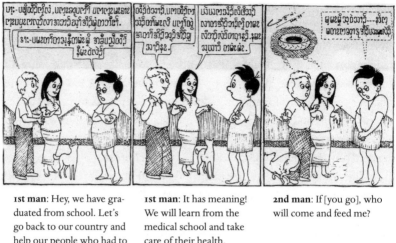

1st man: Hey, we have graduated from school. Let's go back to our country and help our people who had to run away [to the jungle].
2nd man: Oh, I can't do anything, so it would have no meaning.

1st man: It has meaning! We will learn from the medical school and take care of their health.
Woman: Oh, I'm going to teach the young people who have no chance to go to school. You can do something!

2nd man: If [you go], who will come and feed me?

Cartoon from *Kway K'Lu*, May 10, 1999.

burn the corpses using old tires. "So [the cartoon] means, 'Oh, you are fit for this tire, you are not fit for the country,'" he told me, laughing amiably (personal communication, July 24, 2000). *Kway K'Lu* readers are encouraged to get involved in efforts to improve their situation, although Saw Thaw Thi insisted that the magazine does not tell them specifically what to do. "We just encourage them, we don't show the way, because some will want to fight by means of arms, some will want to fight by means of politics, like that. Let it be, whatever they want to do" (personal communication, July 24, 2000). What is clear is the expectation that they will work in some way for the Karen *as a group*.

Participatory Communication
These Indigenous media involve their communities in the production process to varying degrees. The staff of HURFOM, like that of *Kway K'Lu*, aims its Mon-language publication at the grassroots and tries to get content and ideas directly from its Mon readers by providing space in its publications for villagers to express their views. They encourage readers to write in, and they receive between fifteen to twenty letters a week,

many delivered by hand from inside Burma. Saw Thaw Thi emphasizes the readers' role in the production of *Kway K'Lu*. "They also can respond to each other by sending their articles or their news to this newspaper, and we include them" (personal communication, July 24, 2000). *Thulei Kawwei* relies on contributions from its audience of rural Karen, who provide the bulk of the published information that does not come from other media sources.

These media have employed various strategies to reach out to larger audiences, such as printing their magazines in several languages and adjusting their physical shape for easier distribution inside Burma. The Shan newsletter, *Independence*, for example, is printed monthly in three sections, using the Shan, Burmese, and English languages in a single issue. And HURFOM is now printing four pages of Burmese-language information in *The Guiding Star*. Because *The Guiding Star* is dangerous to carry inside Burma, the staff has changed its design several times to make the newspaper easier to fold and conceal. In different ways, Indigenous media are encouraging the development of a more participatory communication environment that includes their readers inside Burma as much as possible under the circumstances.

Human Rights

These Indigenous media have made clear the value of human rights abuse documentation as a basis for advocacy campaigns targeting the international community. For example, Nai Kasauh Mon's decision in 1988 to work for Indigenous self-determination led him to work with several NGOs and human rights organizations, which in turn led him to document the human rights abuses against the Mon and to disseminate this information to the outside world. He helped to found HURFOM in 1995 for these purposes, and the group began publishing its information in both Mon and in English in *The Mon Forum*, which provides monthly coverage of human rights abuses in Mon areas and describes conflicts between Mon people and the SPDC. HURFOM also maintains *The Mon Forum* Web site, which provides online access to back issues of HURFOM's publications, information on the Mon people and Mon history, and photographs of victims of human rights violations.

Many of the new Indigenous media aim to educate the Burmese peoples about their rights under international law. *Kway K'Lu*, for example, discusses the rights of women, children, and Indigenous peoples, along with issues such as genocide, ethnic cleansing, and democracy. As

Nai Kasauh Mon told me, "We try to show our people what are the international principles for human rights protection." For example, he said, "The ILO has decided that Burma still has not stopped using forced labor . . . so we translate it and inform our people about how the international community is trying to protect [their] rights" (personal communication, July 22, 2000). These media at times provide information used as evidence, for example, by the U.N. special rapporteur for Burma, various government bodies, politicians, and international organizations including the International Labour Organization.

I have written elsewhere about the danger of an overemphasis on individual civil and political rights, characteristic of coverage by Western, and in particular U.S. media, and the resulting marginalization of minority groups' social, economic, and cultural rights (Brooten 2004). Unacknowledged correlations between various types of human rights abuses and different groups of victims tend to make the abuse of Indigenous people's individual civil and political rights invisible, emphasizing instead violence targeted at the group of which they are members. Their individual agency is in this way obscured, and this is perhaps why those portrayed as victims are generally the first to critique their portrayal as helpless or hopeless. At the forefront of those critiques are recent video projects aimed at challenging the stereotypes of Indigenous peoples as backward, simple, hapless victims.

THE EMERGENCE OF INDIGENOUS VIDEO

Thanks to the surge in Indigenous video over the past several years, depictions of the situation in Burma are no longer the province of outsiders, or of the majority Burmans, but also of Indigenous peoples, who can now influence their own representations in the media. In addition, these videos are challenging the idea of a monolithic "Karen" identity, not least by differentiating the perspectives of villagers from (and often challenging) those of the leadership of the Karen National Union (KNU). I will profile two of the most prominent groups that have recently emerged: Kawlah Films and Burma Issues. While both work primarily with the Karen, Burma Issues works with Karenni and Shan peoples as well.

Kawlah Films
Kawlah Films grew out of a video documentation project for a Thailand-based Karen NGO.[7] This organization had initiated a video documentation

project in 2003 to assess the work of their mobile teacher-training units operating inside the Karen areas along Burma's border with Thailand. The NGO invited Saw Eh Th'Blay, a young Karen refugee who had had some training in photography, to come and join them as the camera operator. Eh Th'Blay accompanied one of the mobile teacher-training units during its summer vacation teacher training inside Burma. Using a small Sony handycam with twelve hours of battery and four hours of film, Eh Th'Blay taped footage of the group's long days of trekking through the jungle, the dangers they faced, the training itself, and interviews with trainees about the situation for the schools in their area, their reasons for attending the training, and their hopes for the future.

When he returned from this trip, Eh Th'Blay watched the film he had collected with John, a Canadian colleague who had by that time been living in Thailand for nearly eight years, volunteering with the NGO they both worked for.[8] As John remembers, "We looked at what he had. It was fantastic, and that's when we decided to make a movie" (personal communication, July 24, 2005). Eh Th'Blay had never used a computer, and while John was comfortable with a computer, he had never edited video. But with a donated computer, a copy of digital editing software, some training from local NGOs, and a visit from a friend with a bit of editing experience, they muddled through until, after a few months of hard work, they had a film they liked.

Because the organization is a Thailand-based NGO staffed by refugees and is therefore vulnerable to the actions of the Thai government, Eh Th'Blay and John had to keep a low profile. The Thai government is especially keen to remain on friendly terms with its neighbor to the west and is therefore sensitive to any indication that it is helping the dissident Burmese on Thai soil. Because their film was in many ways overtly political, John and Eh Th'Blay decided they needed to split from the NGO officially and form their own organization. Late one night, when it came time to add the title to their first finished film, Kawlah Films was born.

That first film, *Karen Education Surviving*, was released to some acclaim. It has been shown at film festivals in Scotland, Greece, and Canada, as well as at the World Social Forum in Mumbai, India, in 2004 and Porto Alegre, Brazil, in 2005. Kawlah Films' second effort, *Ceasefire*, documents the situation in an area ostensibly free from fighting under a ceasefire agreement between the KNU and the SPDC. This film calls into question the value and legitimacy of the ceasefire and can be seen as critical of both the KNU and the SPDC. *Ceasefire* has been screened at the Indigenous People's Forum in Chiang Mai, Thailand, at the Wild Spaces Forum in Australia, and at a film festival in Bangkok focusing on issues of war and peace. Kawlah Films has recently been commissioned by the United Nations High Commission for Refugees (UNHCR) to produce a film in cooperation with the Karen Women's Organization (KWO) that will focus on sex- and gender-based violence in the Karen areas.

Despite attention from international audiences, Saw Eh Th'Blay sees Kawlah Films as producing for a few different audiences: "For the Karen audience, we hope that when they watch this movie, this documentary, maybe they will understand more about themselves, right? To find the solution, to find the real solution through this mirror. . . . We also focus on the military. Even when they did wrong, but they said they didn't do anything, so this one is like, 'See what you are doing?' [It's] like a mirror for the SPDC" (personal communication, July 30 2005). Eh Th'Blay also explained that for audiences internationally, Kawlah Films is less like a mirror and more a means for people to learn about Burma's Indigenous peoples. These goals—both internal analysis in the group and external advocacy work—are shared by the NGO Burma Issues.

Burma Issues
Burma Issues is "devoted to a peaceful resolution to Burma's struggles for human rights and democratic rule" and focuses on the most marginalized of Burmese peoples, primarily the country's internally displaced persons (IDPs) (Burma Issues 1994a). The group was founded in 1990 and later became a project of the Peaceway Foundation, formed to give Burma Issues legal status as an NGO in Thailand. Burma Issues' philosophy is that marginalized people can and should be "major actors in bringing about much needed political, economic and social change in the country" (ibid.). The organization focuses on long-term change through community-building efforts in which the process of speaking critically and working together to create change in a community is as important as the actual results, if not more so. As a founding member of Burma Issues explains, for example, about a project to develop gardening techniques to improve food, "The goal is not to improve food but to get people together talking, strategizing as they do that. They get confidence as they do [this], they recognize their own skills . . . that they are already doing these things. They're not just passive victims, they're active" (Max Ediger,

personal communication, July 14, 2000). While founded with significant help from outsiders, Burma Issues is now run by people from the various Indigenous minority groups of Burma (mostly Karen, Karenni, and Shan), with occasional help from foreign volunteers.

Because of Burma Issues' commitment to nonviolent change through its work with people at the grassroots level, Saw Kweh Say joined the organization over ten years ago, not long after he graduated from high school in a refugee camp in western Thailand. He is now the Burma Issues video project coordinator, overseeing the production of videos intended to be "a voice for the people's movement in Burma to the international community" (Burma Issues 2004b). He has also worked as a member of Burma Issues' adult literacy unit, and as a community organizer, spending from several months to over a year in each village in order to get to know the villagers, understand their situation, contribute to the village school, and gain their trust. Kweh Say says that this work requires that Burma Issues staff act primarily as listeners, and that neither they nor their films conceptualize the villagers as victims. "For the media work," he explains, "we also want to encourage the awareness of the audience that if you look at them as victims, you will feel sorry and you will only want to support them with relief" (personal communication, July 13, 2005).

Kweh Say and others at Burma Issues are urging people to look to their own involvement in Burma's situation in a gesture of solidarity rather than just donating money as a gesture of charity. For example, people could volunteer to work with Burmese or they could examine the relationship between their governments or corporations and the SPDC. They could then apply pressure through lobbying, consumer boycotts, or however is most relevant to help those who are suffering. As Kweh Say argues, "If you understand that [the IDPs] survive, they are there, and they are still living there, and they are still struggling for their life, for their freedom, then maybe you [will] have another idea to support them, to participate in their struggle. . . . [You will think] 'If it's true that they are still alive and they are struggling, then I want to be a part of them for their struggle'" (personal communication, July 13, 2005). Burma Issues' films are intended for international advocacy but are also meant to challenge audiences in more comfortable circumstances to reflect on the ways we are implicated in the suffering of the Burmese peoples, however indirectly, through the products we buy or the policies of our governments.

Burmese Indigenous media function as a mirror in multiple ways, reflecting for the SPDC a significant challenge to official accounts of the situation in the country's rural areas, and reflecting for the international community the impact of its policy decisions on the ground. Perhaps most important, they reflect for Indigenous peoples the patterns of oppression that lock local communities into narrow understandings of their plight as a result of failure on their part; they show Indigenous peoples how their situation is the result of political and structural forces beyond their immediate control. But they also reflect Indigenous peoples' strength and perseverance and reframe Indigenous knowledge from its marginalization as "backward" to its acceptance as valuable and necessary to the struggle for Indigenous survival. In the end, any sustainable change in Burma will come about not through top-down policies implemented by authorities or outsiders but by the slow alteration of the patterns of submission and resistance by people in their daily lives, accompanied by acceptance that it will be a long process continually promoted, reinforced, and reflected by the Indigenous media of Burma.

NOTES

To the peoples of Burma (Myanmar), whose struggles continue.

1. The country's name has taken on especially political connotations since 1989, when the military government changed it to the Union of Myanmar. While the government claimed the new name is ethnically neutral and would provide a greater sense of national unity, the opposition movement opposed the name change, since it was made without consulting the people through a referendum. While the United Nations has accepted the name change, the U.S. government has not, and the terms have become an indicator of one's political position in the struggle for control over the country. Since this chapter focuses on the work of Indigenous groups in opposition to the country's military regime, *Burma* will be used here. The term *Burman* is used to refer to the ethnic majority of the country, while *Burmese* is used as an adjective to refer to the language and Burma's indigenous peoples.

2. As a graduate student, I was active in the Free Burma Coalition, an umbrella organization of groups dedicated to political change in Burma, and I deepened my understanding of the situation through doctoral research on Burma's opposition movement and its media and technology use. My study of the

country and my commitment to political, social, and economic change there continue.

3. The number of people killed in 1988 is unknown, but according to reports published in the London *Times* and the *Guardian*, between two thousand and three thousand people were killed by riot police between August 8 and 13, 1988 (cited in Kraeger 1991: 332). Estimates of the total killed during three months of unrest range as high as ten thousand people, including thousands of monks (M. Smith 1999).

4. "Eh Th'Blay" is a pseudonym, used by request given the precarious security situation in Thailand in which these activists find themselves. The dissident and Indigenous Burmese remain officially stateless in Thailand, although their activities are often tolerated as long as they remain low profile.

5. For extensive documentation of human rights abuses in Burma, see the annual country reports on human rights from the U.S. State Department (available at www.state.gov / g / drl / hr / c1470.htm), and reports on Burma from Amnesty International (available at web.amnesty.org / library / eng-mmr / index), Human Rights Watch (available at hrw.org / doc?t=asia&c=burma), and the Online Burma Library (available at www.burmalibrary.org / index.php).

6. Burmese Indigenous media also include websites and information posted regularly to the Burma-related listserves, where the number of postings by Indigenous media organizations has increased significantly in the past ten years.

7. For security purposes, the organization will remain unnamed.

8. Like "Eh Th'Blay," "John" is a pseudonym, used by request for security reasons.

CHAPTER 6

TRANSISTOR RESISTORS:

NATIVE WOMEN'S RADIO IN CANADA

AND THE SOCIAL ORGANIZATION OF

POLITICAL SPACE FROM BELOW

Kathleen Buddle

Women's life stories in urban Indian Country are rife with "route" meta-phors. Contemporary urban Aboriginal[1] identities appear to be inti-mately tied up with and evaluated in terms of where one has been, where one is headed, and how one organizes these elements into narratives. Broadcasting from London, Ontario, Mary Lou Smoke tells her radio audience that from the Anishinabe reserve of her youth, she moved to and through the neighborhoods of Toronto, eventually distinguishing her "path" in pursing the "Red Road" or "Indian Way." Her tales of traversing the bar circuit with her guitar, dancing the powwow trail, or marching with fellow members of the Canadian Indian Movement and touring with the "White Roots of Peace" Iroquoian traveling school provide fodder for the weeks to come. Smoke has assumed multiple positions at every point along this "journey." Through her words and actions, she has now amassed sufficient cultural capital to conduct herself in the capacity of elder, and she is widely recognized for her radio activism.

A number of her talents would come into play as Smoke visited Six Nations, the home reserve of her husband Dan Smoke, to conduct a Feast for the Dead ceremony and to cover a story for the Smokes' weekly Native community radio program. Amnesty International and the Native Women's Association of Canada sponsored this 2004 event as part of the Stolen Sisters campaign to open discursive space concerning the epidemic of violence against Aboriginal women and the problem of "missing" Aboriginal women in Canada.[2] Mourners flocked from across Canada to offer final farewells to women relatives who ostensibly had vanished, leaving traces that civic authorities could not, or perhaps would not, decipher. Mary Lou Smoke, still recovering from the recent discovery of her own sister's remains in a Toronto back alley, talked about the ways that popular constructions of Native women structure their capacities for sociability at work, on the street, and at home. The participants discussed the ongoing contests between Aboriginal nations and the Canadian state as well as the complex array of actors and interests that contend for authority in Aboriginal community settings. Six Nations, home of the Iroquois Confederacy in Canada, provided an appropriate setting for the gathering, since women have traditionally held, and continue to wield, considerable local authority in their roles as clan mothers, faith keepers, ceremonial leaders, and, more recently, as band councilors and band chiefs.

The attendees resolved to find ways to "turn up the volume" on Native women's voices. They vowed to intervene to ameliorate Native women's issues of disengagement as well as to problematize the ways that bureaucratic regimes of power effectively discipline women's movement and activities and regulate their civic participation. They sought ways to identify and to *valorize* the unique ways that Native women are weaving links between themselves and others and between the different arenas in which they make their lives. Mary Lou Smoke highlighted radio's potential to exert an important diacritical force in women's self-making projects.

Through their radio program, *Smoke Signals*, Mary Lou, who is Anishinabe (or Ojibwe), and Dan Smoke, who is Seneca—Haudenosaunee (or Iroquois)—expose Canadians to Native renditions of reality and to promote symbolic "healing" in, and social justice for, Aboriginal peoples at large. Over the years, a number of women listeners have approached Mary Lou at powwows and other community events to meet with someone, they often say, that they feel they already know. Rendering her both accessible and familiar, *Smoke Signals* may help break down barriers to sociability, including shyness, though still respecting local cultural protocols that call for reticence in early social encounters between strangers (Buddle 2005). In fact, the emerging friendships that resulted from meeting her listeners led Mary Lou to form a women's network.

Much like women's affiliations, Native radio represents a protean contact zone where new politics and forms of collective expression are constantly generated. With little gap between the makers and consumers,

Native radio merges the fields of production and reception, providing an important context for the construction and reconstruction of cultural agency. Native women's radio activity is both active and social. What distinguishes this communicative activism is the way that the women's ideas of interactiveness are articulated with a more general theory of social agency and power (cf. Ang 1991). The communicative "habitus" emerging from women's radio practices intersects with local histories and issues to inform *gendered* differences in Aboriginal media practice and decision making.

DISTANT AND DEAUTHORIZED SITES

Aboriginal media organs, and the political organizations out of which they emerged, have historically performed in an adaptive fashion. Advancing new informational flows, they have achieved community recognition because they have selectively incorporated certain culturally transformative practices in social projects that appear on the surface to be predominantly conservative (Buddle 2004). Over the course of the colonial era, *engaging* rather than *resisting* large-scale processes of change provided the means with which to reconfigure and productively expand on localized practices, thereby ensuring their relevance in the modern world.

Operating below the threshold of visibility, Native women's ways of affiliating contrast markedly with the styles of affiliation that characterize modern Native political and media organizations. Tacitly illegible and therefore not subject to the juridical controls of more solemnized movements, Native women's organizations have been able to establish new corridors for communication and novel means for determining the direction and the value of information carried along their currents while eluding certain disciplining influences.

Here, I am directly concerned with two sets of intertwined communicative contexts. Both represent arenas wherein Aboriginal women are reclassifying and attaching new definitions to women's roles in civic processes. The first concerns those practices involved in the publicizing of the Aboriginal domestic realm, as women take worldly "political" work, normally considered a male preoccupation, into their homes. The second concerns the feminization of public political space, as Native women weave unique forms of, and frames for, social networks while traversing the field of Aboriginal media production. One of the outcomes of the interpenetration of these apparently disparate nodes is discernable in the capacity that Aboriginal women's media proffer for "refunctioning" Aboriginal women's roles, for creating new possibilities, images, subjectivities, and cultural practices, and for facilitating greater mobility across these performative spaces and relational terrains.

This investigation of boundary-marking practices is embedded in the literature on media, gender, and cultural production (Imam 1991; Mankekar 1999; Rofel 1994; Sreberny 2001; Yang 1999). In drawing attention to the encoding of radio practices and products by Native women media activists, the research identifies and begins to account for an emergent Aboriginal professional subculture while amplifying suppressed and subordinate discourses and elucidating local and wider approaches to gendered politics and social transformation.

Communications media provide new arenas in which cultural practices and culturalist discourses can be elaborated (see Ginsburg, Abu-Lughod, and Larkin 2002; and Askew and Wilk 2002). I look to some of the idiosyncratic ways that an emerging class of urban Aboriginal women is valorizing new forms of cultural production through a variety of spatial practices (cf. de Certeau 1984)—embodied acts that etch in lived space much as the speech act marks a performative moment of language. Additionally, I trace women's transgressive travel between regions that were delimited through colonial processes as well as movement between different domains of knowledge: the official and the embodied, the propositional and the practical, the mapped and the storied. My intention is to show that Native women's discursive and gestural mediations are reconfiguring the ways that members of the urban Aboriginal population stratify access to symbolic resources.

OFFICIATING SPACES

Several province-based Aboriginal women's coalitions in Canada have identified an implicit ideological link between women's uneasy political integration into urban Aboriginal institutions and their failure to access—or, rather, to adjust their dispositions to—the "consecrated" forms of "paleo-traditional" cultural capital that the dominant Aboriginal political organizations, and many other formally recognized or institutionalized Aboriginal action groups, seem to inherit.[3] These very social premiums are championed in the mainstream of Aboriginal political and communications organizations. Native politics and media are predominantly male-dominated fields in Canada—contexts that have been shaped through particular local and historical responses to domination and that have come to valorize certain resolutely *adaptive* dispositions toward knowing and acting. One demonstrates competency in these fields largely by performing a masterful blending of "the traditional" with "the modern." In some instances, however, attempts to co-opt the power of dominant groups have resulted in the re-production of practices subtly complicit with paternalistic politico-management practices or modernization schemes. These are instances of discursive formations taking shape as the discourses combine, cut through, and consume each other.

Pan-Aboriginal nationalist discourse frequently places the symbolic construct of "the Native woman" into productive relation with a host of "natural" metaphors to redeem the connection with the traditional. The attribution of feminine kin terms to the land, as in "Mother Earth," is a clear example. Accordingly, Aboriginal women are availed of subject positions or symbolic participation in public political space solely by harnessing their productive energy toward reproducing *tradition*. In addition to their "traditional" contributions, however, Aboriginal women today are becoming more forceful and visible public actors, entering national political space through media work. This is producing mixed or even contradictory results, sometimes altering the structure of gender relations in which they live, sometimes reinforcing the very inequities that true self-determination would require they stamp out.

The stories that follow speak to the creation of new fields of action for Aboriginal women and to the new and distinctive symbolic modes of affiliation and belonging governing their social formation. Organizing their "connecting" projects in articulation with, or, rather, as traversed by, a variety of discursive practices while holding their own ground, the emerging women's coalitions seem to be striving to shift First Nations' gender debates from consecrated space and time into new dimensions.

HEARTH SPACE FOR *SMOKE SIGNALS*

By engaging in certain activities and not others, Aboriginal women collectively reconfigure the symbolic repertoires through which Aboriginality and womanhood can be thought and formulated—shaped by discourses on duty, family, and tradition. Far from abstract ideologies, these connote powerful discursive practices with actual material consequences in the lives of Aboriginal women. Therefore, when Aboriginal women act outside of the spheres in which they have been positioned historically—when, for example, they speak out about their experiences of "tradition" as oppressive or of traditionally valued women's work as nongratifying, when they challenge the grounds on which their authority is disqualified in policy-making locations—they broaden the scope of possible roles for Aboriginal women. When social actors recognize and authorize new behaviors as acceptable, they authorize and recognize their selves and each other (cf. Butler 1999).

These actions make statements about their actors, to be sure, but they also act as a call to arms, hailing other girls and women into action to take on roles as the bearers and educators of future generations, as modern subjects who act as the defenders and progenitors of emerging customs or neotraditions, as political interveners, or as champions of nonofficial orders of knowledge. As Judith Butler (1999: 122–23) contends, however, it is not simply enough for these realities to be performed or pronounced into being, for they do not become fully realized, they do not succeed, they do not work, unless women can compel the collective recognition of this performativity. When considering what Aboriginal women's agency might connote, it is therefore useful to think about the ways that Aboriginal women create the authoritative in social contexts. In other words, what does it take to animate that social magic that compels collective recognition in Aboriginal social circles? What constitutes this power, knowledge, or adeptness? In brief, how do Aboriginal women create relatively discrete gendered social environments and authoritatively confer values in them?

Smoke Signals is a low-cost community access radio program that Mary Lou and Dan Smoke produce and fund mainly for the urban Aboriginal population of London, Ontario, the surrounding reserve area, and the fifty or so international audience members who listen via the Internet each week. The Smokes introduced the program shortly after the Oka Crisis—an armed confrontation between the Mohawk peoples of Kahnesatake near Montreal and the Sûreté du Québec and Canadian Army in 1990 that mobilized Aboriginal groups across Canada in defense of their rights. Aboriginal media continue to play a prominent role in the Aboriginal Rights movement. The Smokes use their home to coordinate their production activities.

Mary Lou Smoke's subsequent resolve to form a women's Drum grew out of the emerging friendships with her listeners. The decision to employ individual hand drums following northern customs did not directly contradict men's practice in southern Canada, where, on the powwow circuit, for example, all male drummers beat one drum—and women form a surrounding wing singing harmony. A Drum ensemble, called into being by a radio announcement, began to meet weekly at Smoke's house. The gathering provided a space in which only the drummers determined the requirements for participation and membership. The group, Smoke tells, gathered individuals who, in addition to a shared interest in drumming and singing, felt "hailed" to the task of formulating ideas for improving urban Aboriginal community life. This was, minimally, the formal theme delimiting membership. Over the course of the meetings, many would concede that avoiding household duties provided an important motivating factor for joining the cohort. Smoke took on the initial leadership role, teaching the women how to make hand drums and to sing the songs that had been passed down to her. The group, which included her husband Dan, collectively negotiated matters such as determining the events at which to drum, the outfits to wear, and the order of songs. Drummers took on driving, hosting, and drum-keeping roles on a rotating basis. Often, the Drum would perform at events that the Smokes aimed to cover journalistically for their radio program—in which case, fellow drummers would volunteer as coproducers of radio segments.

The participants acquired new skill sets—from computer know-how to public speaking prowess—in addition to the social capital they amassed through singing. One unintended consequence was the reconfiguring of a somewhat rigidly structured set of kin relations; this reconfiguration rather successfully enabled the selective exclusion of nonrelations and nonresidents from community planning projects. By gathering a group of women and selectively incorporating men around interest-driven initiatives—singing, drumming, and the radio program—this more malleable configuration of affiliations opened corridors for communication and possibilities for identification between individuals who otherwise likely would not have interacted. The ensemble gradually created a number of institutions and practices that manifested their membership, from training programs for teens to organizing an annual "gathering of good minds" festival. The group also now works closely with the Native Women's Association of Canada and Amnesty International on the "Stolen Sisters" campaign.

The capacity to meet and exchange information with distant others may generate levels of consciousness beyond one's immediate circumstances, thereby increasing choice and empowerment. This, in turn, may translate into the improvement of democratic potential and into capacity

development. When women gather to deliberate over community matters and share their strategies and solutions with other women's collectivities across cultural boundaries, the networks established become not
merely a means of exchanging ideas but themselves the *ends* of social
action. The provisional engagements Aboriginal women activists make
in those organizational activities, which require highly developed embodied competencies, are themselves critically important forms of cultural
production.[4]

Radio facilitates this process of community formation by making it
possible to carry out public life in more than one place at one time. This
is critical, given the physical mobility of the urban Aboriginal population,
but also given that "being women" is not the only framework in which
Aboriginal women make their lives. Their identities as women are always
defined in relation to their other identities as well as to their simultaneous
memberships in and movement through multiple local, cultural, and
national communities.

Few Native women I know would self-identify as "feminists," yet
many speak of their activities as "women's work." What empowers their
collective movement to embrace new forms of labor is the drive to create
new authorial dispositions for Aboriginal women. What the processes of
embodied nondiscursive action point to, then, is that women's refusal to
limit themselves by, or to subject themselves exclusively to, the subject
positions to which they would be relegated by others does something in
the world. It calls into being new forms of subjectivity and action, and
with them come new collective senses of belonging.[5]

MOBILITY AND THE SEARCH FOR PLACES OF RECOGNITION

Michel de Certeau's (1984) concept of "pedestrian speech acts" helps us
approach Aboriginal urban migration in communicative terms, elucidating the idea that human movements through time have an "enunciative"
function. Despite the historically heavy traffic of goods, ideas, and people through them, reserves in the popular imagination are bastions of
Aboriginal tradition. However, we might profitably understand reserve
communities as interlocuting senders and receivers. Moreover, because
urban migrants are not simply unbounded social actors but remain connected to "home" communities through a variety of local social moor-
ings, we might approach the new forms of "Indianicity" they enact in
urban areas as local processes of making meaning and discipline.

Some Aboriginal women experience urbanization as disconnecting them from their cultural traditions; circular migration to recharge their symbolic resources is commonplace. However, 1996 Canada Census figures reveal that women predominate in reserve out-migration and are the group most likely to move in and between cities. They are also the group least likely to move back to reserves. The data indicate that movement away is sometimes voluntary but often economically propelled and possibly politically coerced.

What are women communicating through such "kinesthetic acts"? Some tell me they leave their reserve to explore cities, to take advantage of services not offered in rural locations, or to cope with the realities of raising young children on their own. Others intimate that they leave to find jobs, further their education, or improve their children's options. Some frame their moving from the reserve as an opting out of oppressive kinship politics that exclude some Aboriginal nuclear families from certain local and regional circuits, invalidating both the kin-based information corridors and the messages carried along them (Albers and Medicine 1983; K. Anderson 2001; Maracle 2003; Weaver 1993). Many concede that, failing to find a voice "at home," they have physically absented themselves to express their dissent. When they leave, Native women often sacrifice—because of prevailing Indian Act policies—their homes, financial security, and the rights they may have enjoyed on the reserve while in family homes or in marriages.

Increasingly, many of the younger women frame their departures from the reserve as a necessary rite of passage, as a quest that must be accomplished to attain what is necessary to do battle in contemporary domains of cultural politics. Their movement likely signifies a new structural feature of society, therefore, rather than simply ongoing "resistance." Cities may well afford Aboriginal women with opportunities to gain what Saskia Sassen (1998) refers to as "greater sense of presence" or a greater capacity to emerge as subjects. Migration to cities may therefore mark a strategy allowing Native women to become direct actors in the arena of politics the city represents. Cities also afford Native women with greater opportunities to take on roles on an international stage—relocating the nexus of Native politics from band councils and regional governments to the digital and electronic spaces that increasingly orient activity in Aboriginal domestic spaces.

Creating institutions in cities is one way that Aboriginal women seek to reconfigure authoritative spaces. The emergence of Aboriginal women's radio programs clearly evinces this tendency. It is both historically and politically significant that Aboriginal women, who are structurally more susceptible to alienation from national Aboriginal political participation, have recently begun to experiment *collectively* with radio to ameliorate communicative ruptures.

IMMATERIAL INDUSTRY

In 2000, the Winnipeg-based program *Not Vanishing* was the first Native women's call-in radio show to take to the air in Canada. A group of first-generation reserve migrants to the city of Winnipeg created it to accommodate the growing city population and to incorporate the women's participation in the most remote parts of the province—many of which had no telephone access. Native Communications Inc. (NCI) broadcast the program for three years (the management officially terminated the program in 2003).[6]

In the late 1990s, the Native Media Network (NMN) had been producing a one-hour Cree-language radio program that did not involve women. A group of concerned Native women, after many meetings at Ivy Chaske's house, approached the organization, offering to help the men meet their mandate to cover women's issues. The NMN board refused and suggested that the women create their own show. The group of volunteers sought their own training and funding and shamed the NMN into sharing their studio space. Each trainee was expected to learn all of the technical aspects of radio production in order to find for herself an activity well-suited to her particular disposition. Many of the women simultaneously served on the board of the Original Women's Network (OWN)—a nonprofit charitable resource center for Aboriginal women. Collectively, these women would contribute to the development of a variety of community organizations, including Payuk, an intertribal housing complex for women, the Neechi Food Co-op, the Aboriginal Centre, the Ma Mawi Wi Chi Itata Centre, the Native Women's Transition Centre, and a Native women's shelter. The credibility of the program was closely linked with the sorts of activities in which its producers engaged in Winnipeg's broader Native community.

The hosts derived the name *Not Vanishing* from a poem penned by Chrystos as a rejoinder to Edward S. Curtis's *The Vanishing People*. The women sought to assert their capacity for meaningful agency not merely in the face of colonizing forces that would sooner have them fade into oblivion, but in response to injurious inside pressures—namely, the exclusionary practices of mostly male-led local Aboriginal organizations. *Not Vanishing* took shape as a means of amplifying the concerns of a particular subculture of Native women activists who were determined to defy those who would deny women access to social and political parity in the Aboriginal community. Middle-aged, working-class, single mothers comprised the activist cohort. And, because mentoring figured so prominently in their productive processes, a second wing of support later established itself among a younger cohort of women. This addition would eventually form a controversial all-women's Drum.

In contrast to other areas, such as southern Ontario, where gender relations in the civic sphere are considerably more harmonious, Native women's forays into media production in Winnipeg mark a direct contest to carefully guarded male authority. Ideally, so the plan went, interventions would redirect male-centered social agendas that often seemed to take shape in the form of economic development projects by shifting the focus toward projects with greater human capacity-building potential. In voicing their dissent, however, the women placed the Aboriginal solidarity movement itself at risk, since it draws its power from the presumed unified nature of Aboriginal people's collective movement to oppose oppression by outsiders. Pointing out problems internal to the movement threatened to weaken the overall force of its ideally consensus-driven efforts to assert Aboriginal distinctiveness from the Canadian masses. Although the women's coterie was a tremendously diverse group whose members ranged from fervent civil rights activists to assimilationists, achieving consensus was seldom an issue. The women applied their knowledge of the political process and played to the moderates, using individual women's gifts tactically in each situation toward the collective benefit of the whole.

A notable feature of local Aboriginal gender politics in the Winnipeg area is the women's appropriation of "men's skills" by attaining mechanical proficiency in media technologies and men's drumming style. Achieving technological mastery appears to provide a credential of competence, allowing women to demonstrate their own embodied capabilities while accessing traditionally "male" opportunities. The activists frame their involvement in media work in terms of a deliberate attempt to create an autonomous feminized Aboriginal public sphere—a place for women at the table. The strategies the Native women's group employs are cautious and subtle and geared toward effecting change over the long term, owing to the realities of ongoing repression by some male leaders and given the impossibility of easily eliminating the lingering residue of colonial projects that sought to reproduce Euro-Canadian gender relations in Native contexts. The production practices associated with *Not Vanishing*, as much as the actual program itself, were designed to attain strategic goals.

Native women's industry in the Winnipeg collective prefigured a global civil society with lines of solidarity that cut across national boundaries. The hosts of *Not Vanishing*, for example, frequently played segments of programs by its sister station in Ecuador,[7] seeking to build networks of solidarity around events and issues. In Winnipeg, to protest the oppression they were experiencing in national Native political space and to form both support and action groups, Native women from both urban centers and reserves across the province listened to and telephoned the show, emphasizing its direct communicative function. *Not Vanishing* hosts used airtime to discuss their circumstances anonymously, to listen to solutions, and to organize clandestine meetings at centrally located grocery stores and coffee shops during a time when Native women's assemblies were actively discouraged. Women called in anonymously to tell their stories and to comment on the predicaments of other women. Many claimed that the opportunity to have their issues heard and their choices validated by the hosts and other listeners helped them find the resolve to act—to leave abusive situations, seek medical advice, or take a job-skill training course, all acts of embodied agency.

The hosts regularly promoted services specifically aimed at Native women, including healthy-baby, job-skill, and other education programs, as well as information about safe houses, transportation options, and other means of improving the mobility and sociability of Native women, who often find the symbolic and material constraints of the "domestic" realm—a site socially engineered through a variety of colonial projects— entirely too constraining. Representing a call for reform, the grievances aired over the program caused unease in traditional gender circles. The women therefore assessed the value and function of publicizing their predicaments over the radio according to a pragmatic rationality.

With *Not Vanishing*, women deployed communications technologies to overcome the impasse between state efforts to create modern citizens and societal pressures to uphold "traditions." While modern subjects certainly enjoyed the benefits of pursuing individual career advantage and prestige, they sacrificed communal capital. As such, the hosts opened themselves to charges of diminishing Aboriginal difference. Native women's networks, nonetheless, sought to maintain a space for the reconstitution of symbolic repertoires with which an urban Aboriginal community could think and formulate a unified image of its difference from the non-Native public.

In bringing to light the systemic nature of the women's erstwhile "individual" predicaments, *Not Vanishing* helped to place urban Aboriginal women at the center of policy discussions, giving the category a statistical force that political leaders could no longer ignore. Using radio to channel social change, Aboriginal producers pushed the parameters of the medium, "refunctioning the apparatus of cultural production" (cf. Benjamin 1999 [1934]). Bending it to local bidding, these cultural agents deployed radio to chart internal and terrestrial journeys, to cultivate and to validate undervalued registers of knowledge and nonofficial dispositional locations so as to recover their "selves." Exposing audiences to a wider range of ways of being Aboriginal, and of being women—to a grander repertoire of possible identifications and possible futures—*Not Vanishing* enhanced the capacities of its producers and its listeners, extending to them the tools with which to metaphorically redesign their interiors. The project also linked local women with centers of decision making, facilitating ordinary Native women's participation in national and global issues and in transnational social movements.

At the level of program content or text, *Not Vanishing* presented complexities that some would rather have glossed over, primarily in its refusal to present Aboriginality as a unitary essence and as a necessarily consensual construct. Instead, the program's cultural producers rabble-roused, presenting "tradition" as a site of conflicting discourses and competing voices by situating "the cultural" as a domain of contest and by deploying community radio as a forum for its debate.

What would justify the erasure of *Not Vanishing*, however, was the more deeply sedimented set of presumptions governing a particular economy of practice. On the air, the women had managed to create a social field and to confer values in and socially profit from it. Yet on the ground, the program's worth would be evaluated according to divergent sets of convictions and multiple "laws of recognition" (cf. Povinelli 2002). *Not Vanishing* did not meet the station's criterion for marketability, the broadcast community's standards for professionalism, or the business community's qualifications for profitability. Instead, the women worked in an alternative economy of practice characterized by the very forms of every-day agency that would constitute Aboriginal "feminism" as a power.

Both *Not Vanishing* and *Smoke Signals* demonstrate that Native wom-en's everyday engagements with media are socioculturally embedded and are conceived in specific locales. In pursuing pan-Aboriginal themes, *Smoke Signals*, for example, receives its share of criticism from those who would preserve the inviolability of discrete cultural traditions and prac-tices. In terms of gender issues, however, it has met with considerably less controversy. This is partly attributable to the regional culture in which it is set, with a vastly different history of gender politics than that of *Not Vanishing*. It is circulated, moreover, at times and along routes etched in the air by a noncommercial university radio station. As the only Aborigi-nal program in the area, it could not focus on women's issues exclusively. The large non-Native audience also proves the program's success both in restoring corridors of communication between Aboriginal polities that were disrupted by colonial projects and in creating new connections with communities of shared experience or sentiment.

Operating from deauthorized sites on the social map, both radio proj-ects denote significant efforts to secure social recognition by individuals who are at risk of being disenfranchised from political in-groups. These are instances whereby Native women and their aides de camp engage in important cultural work, acting concertedly to travel beyond roles pre-scribed for them and create new authoritative spaces from which to speak and act. The social movement to secure social justice for Aboriginal peoples is predicated on proving Aboriginal unity. Yet, the radio practices described above destabilize this notion of an undisputed traditional soli-darity. This radio activity illuminates the ever complex nature of symbols and their discursive conduits, which must be negotiated by situated social agents in urban Indian Country. Finally, the practices highlight the uneasy tension that exists between the tropes of tradition at regional and na-tional levels.

CONCLUSION

I have sought to contextualize here the ideological projects of actively interpreting social actors (cf. Bourdieu 1977; and Thomas 1994) who are enmeshed in dense social ties and intense exchanges and whose activities constitute complex structures of meanings. Theorizing the notion of "flexible alliance" (cf. Ong 1999) requires elucidating some of the connections between the local and wider constraints on Aboriginal social justice projects. It requires holding the analytic concept of the "imaginary" in productive tension with concrete material forces. I am centrally concerned with the particular forms of communicative activism and boundary-crossing activities that Aboriginal women enlist: collectively, to encode forms of Aboriginal women's agency with value and, individually, to make sense of the particular circumstances in which they find themselves. I have considered some of the implications of changing forms of cultural communication and of shifting boundaries around gendered workplaces for the formation of new sorts of group affiliation, specifically as they relate to urban Aboriginal women's action networks.

Unique power structures and social dynamics pervade Native women's radio production spaces. Forging new fields and locations as "transistor resistors," Native women are calling into being new subjectivities— tactically invisible, yet audible and mobile public selves. Native women's radio practice locates and organizes particular evaluative processes. This arena of practice provides the ground on which an accounting can occur for the ways ideas are produced and expressed about subculturally relevant demarcations of "alterity."

While Aboriginal women endure an additional order of subjugation *as* women, Native peoples on the whole in Canada continue to wrestle with multiple forms of oppression. By incorporating radio into their customary practices, Indigenous social actors avail themselves of opportunities to circulate their preferred readings of treaty texts more widely, to press for the recognition both of Aboriginal rights and of a wider repertoire of ways of being Aboriginal in a modern world. Programs such as *Not Vanishing* and *Smoke Signals* and Native communications societies such as NCI each ultimately aspire to advance the cause of social justice for Aboriginal peoples in registers of Aboriginal choosing.

Still, women's unique paths into Aboriginal radio speak to the need for a more nuanced understanding of the nature of the linkages between cultural expression, gender issues, and political practice in urban Aboriginal contexts. *Smoke Signals* and *Not Vanishing* provide important clues as to the ways that gendered connectivity is imagined and performed in the context of two First Nations locations. The contexts of their production show how Native women are customizing Aboriginal political processes and spaces and alternatively encoding cultural capital and labor.

Across Canada, radio continues to serve as the most ubiquitous and accessible medium of telecommunication between cities and reserves in First Nations contexts. For the moment, Aboriginal women's talk radio remains poised at the threshold of "exilic" space and the axis of decision-making power. Drawing power from this interstitial positioning, rather than simply surrendering to marginality, Native women communicators perform their invisibility as a tactical overture, removing themselves from unjustly authorized fields of view and taking up positions in "no man's land." Programming radio and the nation from their kitchens, Aboriginal women are intervening in politicized contact zones, seeking to elude the disciplining power of "tradition" while operating in the domains in which it is exercised.

NOTES

I am deeply grateful to Bea Medicine (1923–2005), Mary Lou Smoke, Ivy Chaske, Sandi Funk, and Nahanni Fontaine for their support of and contributions to this research. The Social Sciences and Research Council of Canada generously provided the funding.

1. The fact that there is no consensus regarding appropriate terminology for the Indigenous population in Canada speaks to the complexities that inhere in all endeavors to represent the many polities comprising it. *Indigenous* and *Aboriginal* are the sole terms in use covering Status and non-Status Indians, Métis, *and* Inuit peoples. *First Nations* (a term recently coined by the former Assembly of First Nations head, Ovide Mercredi), *Indian*, and *Native* are used tactically in various regions by different groups to represent Status and non-Status Indians. Finding the aforementioned objectionable, many prefer local or linguistic identifiers. My usage of terms thus shifts as a concession both to the contested nature of ongoing debates in Indian Country and in resistance to the generalizing of nongeneralizable experiences that the use of one term encourages.

2. According to a public brief by the Stolen Sisters, young Indigenous women are five times more likely than other women to die violent deaths. See the official report at www.amnesty.ca / campaigns / sisters_overview.php.

3. Pierre Bourdieu (1993: 40–45) uses the terms *consecrated* and *paleo-* to discuss the values and authority upheld by the old guard in a given field. These tend to be directly contested by the "heretical," devalued, or not-yet-valued expectations and unrecognized knowledge bases of the newly arriving cultural producers.

4. I build here on the argument of Terence Turner (2002: 77) that the term *media* ought to refer to the social processes of mediation that occur through Indige-

nous video production rather than to the technologies of representations or to the representations themselves.

5. Strategies to bring Aboriginal women into focus have situational relevance; at times, this is a discourse that defines its difference in opposition to white feminism, maleness, age, cultural, and class distinctions, partly defining itself through what it is not.

6. NCI is a network that maintains 57 FM transmitters and reaches listeners in 70 Native communities in Manitoba.

7. In 1991 Kathy Mallett and Sandi Funk of OWN received a grant to travel to Ecuador to provide media skills training to Indigenous women there. The trainees recorded women's stories in their communities and sent interpreted versions to be aired on *Not Vanishing*.

CHAPTER 7

WEAVING A COMMUNICATION QUILT
IN COLOMBIA: CIVIL CONFLICT,
INDIGENOUS RESISTANCE, AND COMMUNITY
RADIO IN NORTHERN CAUCA

Mario A. Murillo

It was a typically hot day in the southwestern Colombian department of
Cauca, home to one of the largest populations of Indigenous peoples in
the country. On September 15, 2004, about seventy thousand Indigenous,
peasant, and Afro-Colombian protesters were marching north on the Pan
American Highway toward Cali, Colombia's third largest city, to protest
the government's bilateral negotiations with the United States over a
regional free trade accord, among other issues.

The marchers had left a few days earlier from the town of Santander de
Quilichao, despite the government's attempt to prevent them from carrying out the weeklong protest. Members of the Guardia Indigena, or
Indigenous Guard, wooden staffs in hand, walked in a long file, maintaining a watchful eye on would-be outside troublemakers along the march;
young men and women enthusiastically waved the red and green flag of
the Indigenous movement, while mothers carried their infant children
on their backs. Colorful buses—known locally as *chivas*—trekked slowly
alongside the main line of protesters, as weary passengers on board
sprayed their friends marching on the street with cold water they squeezed
out of small plastic bags.

It was the latest in a long history of what Indigenous leaders call their
"mobile congresses": massive, high profile marches and gatherings that
bring together Indigenous and peasant communities from throughout
the region to address grievances about economic development, militarism in their territories, and disrespect for their collective rights. In the

past, similar gatherings—referred to as *mingas* by the Nasa people—were organized to plan community development projects and to denounce violence carried out against Indigenous peoples by government, guerrilla, and paramilitary forces.

What made this mobilization different from dozens of similar protests in previous years was how it utilized radio in covering the march. An Indigenous reporter riding up and down alongside the march on a *radiocicleta*—a tandem bicycle with a loudspeaker and a small transmitter—sent reports back to a student-run radio station at a university in Cali, which in turn redirected the signal via telephone to Radio Payu'mat, the local station in Santander de Quilichao, licensed to the Asociación de Cabildos Indígenas del Norte del Cauca (ACIN, Association of Indigenous Councils of Northern Cauca). The station broadcast the reports live over its two-thousand-watt transmitter and eventually streamed much of the coverage on its Web site. As a result, a much larger audience suddenly had access to an event that in the past was traditionally reported only marginally by Colombia's commercial mass media.

Radio Payu'mat is part of the ACIN's comprehensive communication project, which encompasses an Internet "telecenter," video production, printing, and publishing, and two other smaller radio stations. They call it their *tejido de comunicación* (communication quilt). It is integrally linked to the ACIN's broader strategy for improving the lives of the Nasa people, applying traditional cultural practices and organizational structures with modern technologies.

Today, the tejido represents a major component of the community's *plan de vida* (life plan): a comprehensive community development program that hatched from the Indigenous movement's initial attempts at mobilizing over land, cultural, and civil rights in the early 1970s. It is designed to strengthen the level of organization of the Indigenous communities of northern Cauca while simultaneously resisting the unilateral imposition of external development projects from the state and other entities in Indigenous territories. Among the objectives of the "life plan" is to democratize community life, allow the communities to take control of their territories and the natural resources in them, awaken the critical conscience of the community, make Indigenous culture visible, and export the Nasa model to other regions of the country (Dorado 2004, written in conjunction with the Radio Payu'mat Staff).

Radio has become a principal component of the movement's strategy to communicate its message to Nasa audiences and to other local communities in northern Cauca, including peasant and Afro-Colombian people. Radio Payu'mat and two other smaller community radio stations operating in the mountainous region have become central spaces where the community gathers in a virtual *minga* to discuss and listen to issues affecting them directly.

Just as radio was used by governments in the past to create a sense of Colombian national culture and identity in a country traditionally divided by regions, the Indigenous communities of Cauca—like many Indigenous groups in other parts of the country—are using radio as a form of resistance to that same national consciousness, which they see as being shaped by materialism, militarism, and corruption.

WHY FOCUS ON THE NORTHERN CAUCA REGION?

The Nasa—erroneously referred to as Páez by the Spanish colonizers and today by a large sector of the non-Indigenous population—are among the largest of Colombia's eighty-four Indigenous nationalities, with a presence on a vast swath of national territory encompassing several departments (provinces), including Cauca, Tolima, Valle del Cauca, Nariño, and Putumayo. For decades, the Nasa have been at the forefront of Colombia's contemporary Indigenous movement. To understand the function of the ACIN's communication quilt, then, one must place it in the context of the larger experience of Colombia's diverse Indigenous communities and their long struggle for land and civil rights, political autonomy, and cultural affirmation.

The specific focus of this chapter is Indigenous radio, and in particular the case of Radio Payu'mat and its two sibling stations, Radio Nasa and Voces de Nuestra Tierra, in northern Cauca, located in the Andean region of southwestern Colombia. There are many other rich experiences of Indigenous radio throughout Colombia. Even in the department of Cauca itself, a diverse cross section of community and public interest radio stations serve distinct constituencies confronting a wide range of social conditions. Each one can serve as a viable case study to understand the evolution of Indigenous radio, its local impact, and prospects for the future. Though most of these community media experiences came about as a result of specific national political developments that converged in the early 1990s, each one has a distinct function in its respective communities and reflects the incredible cultural diversity of Colombia's Indigenous population (Unidad de Radio del Ministerio de Cultura 2000).

The origins, mission, and organizational structure of the ACIN's radio project provide a measure of its qualities as a public sphere for the communities it represents. Radio Payu'mat and the other elements of the ACIN's tejido are both a viable public sphere to discuss issues that affect people in their territory and a space that serves as a true alternative medium countering conceptions of nationhood, development, and security embraced by the mass commercial media and, in turn, the broader population.

Despite comprising a small percentage of the country's population, Colombia's Indigenous people have been relatively successful at influencing public opinion. The Indigenous movement has inserted itself into the national Colombian dialogue through its broad-based political organizing, high-profile mobilizations, and dynamic, charismatic leadership (Rappaport 2005; Murillo 2004). The movement emerged in Cauca in the early 1970s, with various Indigenous ethnicities—such as the Kokonuco and Guambiano people, along with the Nasa, the largest of Cauca's Indigenous nations—taking the lead. The ACIN's tejido, therefore, is a solid example of the larger movement of Indigenous community media in Colombia, especially since it is a component of the "life plan" that the Nasa feel could serve as a model for the entire country.

THE INDIGENOUS MOVEMENT IN COLOMBIA

Colombia's eighty-four different Indigenous groups are organized in a complex system of traditional communal councils, or *cabildos*, populating every department. Sixty-five have maintained their native non-European language. Although a vast majority of Colombians have some degree of Indigenous blood, most of them are considered *mestizo*, or mixed race, including large numbers of peasants who are not members of officially recognized traditional communities tied to specific territories. Numbering about one million out of a total Colombian population of over 44 million, Colombia's Indigenous people continue to be threatened almost daily by the violence of the decades-long internal conflict (Murillo 2004; Villa and Houghton 2005). On a local, regional, and national level, Colombia's original inhabitants have struggled against the state for years over land rights, autonomous governance in their territories, defense of their cultural and religious traditions, and recognition of Indigenous education and health practices.

The contemporary Indigenous movement in Colombia dates back

to the late 1960s and early 1970s. The first efforts began in northern Cauca, when the young, activist Indigenous leadership launched a series of land occupations in areas controlled by cattle ranchers, the church, and other wealthy landowners. The dramatic nature of the land recuperation process galvanized Indigenous communities in Cauca and throughout Colombia. It led to widespread government repression against the Indigenous leadership, including assassinations, mass arrests, and physical displacement (Villa and Houghton 2005).

In February 1971, in the town of Toribio, the Consejo Regional Indígena del Cauca (CRIC, Regional Indigenous Council of Cauca) was formed. It was the first major organization in the country to mobilize Indigenous communities on a massive scale and is today one of the most important Indigenous organizations in Latin America. CRIC's organizing platform included seven key points relating to the rights of Indigenous people: (1) recovery of Indigenous land / territory; (2) demarcation of Indigenous reserves; (3) fortification of Indigenous councils, or cabildos; (4) resistance to land-lease payments to landowners; (5) promotion and defense of Indigenous laws; (6) defense of the history, language, and customs of Indigenous people; and (7) the training of Indigenous professors to educate the community, through their native language, about the situation they face (Controversia 1978).

Over the years there have been many other formations and groupings using a diverse array of strategies to confront state policies toward Indigenous people. In the late 1970s in Cauca, another group made up primarily of Guambiano leaders formed the Autoridades Indígenas de Colombia (AICO, Indigenous Authorities of Colombia); they continue to wield influence in the department and on a national level. Another important group was an armed militia that emerged in the mid-to-late 1970s, also in Cauca and the neighboring department of Tolima, that served as a self-defense force for the communities involved in the land recovery campaigns. The Movimiento Armado Quintín Lame (MAQL, Quintín Lame Armed Movement) was named after the Nasa leader who resisted European encroachment on Nasa territory in the early part of the twentieth century. The MAQL eventually signed a peace agreement with the government in 1990, demobilized as a fighting force, and was instrumental in getting Indigenous representation in the Constituent Assembly of 1991.

Indigenous political groups later launched candidates for public office at nearly every level of elected government. Other organizations started development projects in Indigenous communities based on principles of environmental sustainability, equitable distribution of resources, self-sufficiency, and community participation.

All of these efforts culminated in the 1991 Constituent Assembly, where Indigenous leaders directly participated in the rewriting of the antiquated Constitution of 1886. For the first time in Colombia's history, Indigenous communities became equal partners in the makeup of the nation. The 1991 constitution finally recognized the territorial, cultural, and religious rights of Indigenous peoples as inalienable and proclaimed the country a multicultural and pluriethnic republic. Suddenly, Indigenous representatives were being elected to the national legislature in both the Senate and the Chamber of Representatives in seats specifically allotted to the Indigenous population.

As part of these political advances, the 1991 constitution officially recognized Indigenous territories as autonomous zones where Indigenous laws, customs, and languages (in cases where the native tongue still predominated) would supersede national norms. The government could now only exploit the natural resources in Indigenous territories, including oil and natural gas, after direct consultation with the Indigenous leadership.

However, as is the case with many of Colombia's laws, most relating to Indian rights have not been fully implemented, and in many respects, conditions have worsened for Indigenous communities over the last fifteen years. The internal armed conflict, pitting left-wing guerrilla organizations against government security forces and right-wing paramilitary groups tied to the drug trade and the Colombian Army, has escalated in some regions, directly affecting Indigenous communities (Caldón 2005). The government of President Alvaro Uribe, reelected to an unprecedented second term in May 2006, launched legislative efforts to roll back many of the gains made by Indigenous people in the 1991 constitution. These measures sought to limit the autonomy of Indigenous territories in order to create favorable conditions for the passage and implementation of bilateral and regional free trade agreements (Mondragón 2005). As the U.S.-Colombia Free Trade Agreement was being hammered out in the summer of 2006, the government perceived the Indigenous community as an obstacle to the agreement's approval. Mobilizations of the kind I described at the beginning of this chapter continue to demand the implementation of rights spelled out in the constitution and of laws resulting from those rights. National, regional, and local assemblies are held regularly to plan strategies of action. And now, as is the case with

Radio Payu'mat and the ACIN's tejido, radio has become an essential tool to further this agenda, both internally—in the community, as an organizing tool and a space for deliberation and discussion—and externally, to the public at large, as a vehicle for denunciation and resistance.

COLOMBIAN MEDIA: FOR ELITES ONLY?

Behind this backdrop we find the Colombian mass communication system. Colombia's media institutions have been described as an "imperfect duopoly" where two major groups control the majority of the information industries (Waisbord 2002). Although not officially tied to the state, the intermingling of both state and powerful private interests with the people who control the major media makes any attempt at differentiation almost meaningless.

The commercial mass information and cultural industries continue to perpetuate myths about Colombian democracy and society both by embracing the institutional definitions used by the establishment to describe the fringes of society and by limiting the spaces whereby these voices may be heard (López de La Roche 2001; Convenio Unión Europea 2004). When it comes to coverage and representation of Indigenous communities, the tendency of the mass communication system has been consistent: it either ignores the communities by making them invisible, lumps them all together, homogenizing them and negating their diversity and complexity, or presents them as nothing more than passive actors, the victims of an unjust system. When the communities take matters into their own hands, the dominant media usually represent these situations as acts of criminality, emphasizing the tendency to break the law— block highways, occupy territory "illegally," etc.—as a way to express grievances. The Colombian mass media rarely represent the complex organizational structures of Indigenous communities, characterized by consensus-building, grassroots participation, and leadership accountability (Convenio Unión Europea 2004).

Radio traditionally has served as the echo chamber of both television and the press, reaching many more people in the countryside because of the accessibility of the technology. Much as in the United States, daily national radio talk shows regularly take the lead from the mass "elite" media, providing important spaces for the government, the business class, and the traditional political parties to set their respective agendas, while marginalizing (if not altogether ignoring) truly oppositional perspectives.

This should come as no surprise if one considers the ownership of the press, radio, and television in Colombia, a list that reads like a who's who of the dominant families in politics and business, including a number of former presidents. The highly concentrated ownership of Colombia's mass media system is a significant mechanism used by the political and economic elite to maintain its grip on power.

In Colombia, alternative media models did emerge to challenge this hegemony. Independent presses were started over the years, clearly partisan in their oppositional approach, functioning as a "political and literary public sphere" for the Left. But as Silvio Waisbord (2001: 29) points out, these presses did not "match Habermasian standards of bracketing political interests or advancing the force of the best argument," because their primary goal was to "express the voices excluded from a public sphere that, under authoritarian regimes, could only live in alternative and underground spaces." Too often, the leaders of these presses have been physically silenced through assassination, forced disappearance, or exile. This occurred in the print media as well as in the earlier experiments with community radio.

RADIO PAYU'MAT AND THE ACIN'S "COMMUNICATION QUILT"

Radio Payu'mat came about as a result of the Programa Comunidad (Community Program) launched by the Ministry of Communications and the Ministry of Culture in 2000. Prior to this, there were other low-power stations operating in different regions, including Radio Nasa (an unlicensed, community station broadcasting in the town of Toribio since 1995) and Voces de Nuestra Tierra (a licensed community station in the town of Jambaló that first went on the air in 1997), both of which were established by the cabildos of these two towns.

In order to strengthen the communication program that was started with these low-power community stations, the cabildo of Jambaló established the "School of Communication" in 1999, a three-year plan to train and expand the capacity of the members of the community charged with working in communication. The school eventually trained seventy-five people in radio, video, and print media, as well as in the Nasa communication philosophy and the current political situation facing the country and the communities.

While the communication school was in its early stages, word arrived about the Programa Comunidad for Indigenous areas, launched by the ministries of communication and culture. The general objective of the program was to facilitate internal communication for the Indigenous communities in their specific territories and in neighboring regions and to support their "life plans." The ultimate goal was to support the communities' communication strategies, provide the basic infrastructure for radio transmissions, and initiate training programs spearheaded and directed by the Indigenous communities themselves according to their cultural traditions and their community needs. The legitimacy of the program would be guaranteed through direct participation of the Indigenous organizations and traditional authorities (Unidad de Radio del Ministerio de Cultura 2000).

The effort stemmed from two important constitutional breakthroughs, recognizing (1) the collective rights of Indigenous communities and (2) the right to create and receive information/communication. In essence, this was a governmental response to years of activism by both the Indigenous movement around cultural and civil rights, and the media reform movement about opening up democratic communication spaces for marginalized communities. The "public interest" designation for these Indigenous radio stations was granted based on the status of Indigenous territories as public administrative structures that, like municipalities and provinces (departments), represented legal state entities, however autonomous they may have been from the central government. Public interest stations outside of the Programa Comunidad include the National Police and Armed Forces radio stations, operating throughout the country but ostensibly with different missions. Programa Comunidad facilitated the establishment of twenty-four public interest stations that catered specifically to a cross-section of the Indigenous population in various parts of the country. The consultation process was intense and deliberative, with the Ministry of Communication working directly with the Indigenous authorities to see what kind of radio, if any, each wanted to establish for its respective community. Some communities rejected the idea of starting a radio station out of hand as counter to traditional practices and beliefs (Unidad de Radio del Ministerio de Cultura 2000).

Regardless of the relatively open consultation carried out by the government institutions behind Programa Comunidad, some observers saw the program as an example of the government's political opportunism. This was particularly true in northern Cauca. Radio Payu'mat was established during the administration of President Andrés Pastrana in 2000. At the time, Pastrana was conducting a controversial peace dialogue with left-wing rebels of the Fuerzas Armadas Revolucionarias de Colombia (FARC, Revolutionary Armed Forces of Colombia). Some Indigenous activists perceived the radio project as a way for the government to curry favor with popular movements in the countryside, especially those not so comfortable with the direction of the peace talks and with the exclusion of civil society from the negotiating table. From the very beginning, the Indigenous community in northern Cauca was divided as to whether to accept the offer from the Ministry of Communications, precisely because of concern that accepting the license would be perceived as being co-opted by the government (Dorado 2004). In short, there was an immediate concern that as autonomous entities, the Indigenous communities could not afford to accept any program coming from the state, especially in a place where the organization was so strong and independent, as was the case in northern Cauca. Eventually, after intense consultation with the community, the ACIN decided to accept the license and committed itself to starting up the radio station.

In 2002, the Nasa "life plan" (community development program) was awarded the UNESCO Peace Prize, recognizing it as one of the most significant community development programs in the world. The initial funding for equipment and basic infrastructure had come from the Colombian government, but the prize brought the Nasa Project an instant influx of cash: $25 million Colombian pesos (over US$10,000), more than half of which was directed to the station. Whereas initially the cabildos were reluctant to budget their money to fund the radio station, this money was immediately redirected to get the project up and running.

An interesting part of the early history of the station was the difficulty in setting up the transmitter. On three occasions between 2002 and 2003, lightning strikes destroyed the transmitter. The Nasa spiritual leaders accused the station management of not consulting with them about the suitability of setting up the antenna where they had initially placed it. After recognizing that everybody had been mistaken about the proper location for the transmitter, the The Walas (spiritual leaders) conducted a traditional Nasa cleansing ritual to synchronize the transmitter with the land and the sky, thereby protecting it from future lighting strikes or other natural calamities. The station finally went on the air in 2002. The Walas continue to conduct regular cleansing rituals of the transmitter, the studios, and the entire staff of programmers and producers.

Today, Radio Payu'mat transmits news, interviews, music, and community announcements from 7:00 a.m. to 8:00 p.m. from their studios in Santander de Quilichao, the principal city of northern Cauca. Programs are recorded on a minidisc or CD and broadcast on the other stations run by the ACIN, an informal network that duplicates the message from the regional station to the local ones. Broadcasting at two thousand watts, Payu'mat's signal reaches the many small towns that pepper the region's mountainous terrain, and on some days it reaches as far north as Cali. The station regularly schedules live broadcasts of special events in the community. In August 2005, for example, the ACIN, the CRIC, and other local groups held a mass protest to denounce controversial statements made by a local army commander, who linked the Indigenous leadership with the FARC guerrillas. The Indigenous leadership denounced the charges as highly irresponsible, given the history of the violent backlash directed at alleged guerrilla "collaborators." The all-day rally held in Santander's town square was broadcast live, with a long list of speakers who had strong words of criticism for the army commander as well as for the government of President Uribe. Some staff members later expressed concern to me that the government would pressure them because of the harsh tone of the rally and broadcast.

When the Indigenous communities held a public, nonbinding referendum about the U.S.-Colombia free trade agreement in March 2005, government officials debated the ACIN leadership on the air about the merits and drawbacks of free trade and its potential impact on the countryside. The referendum results later showed that 95 percent of the Indigenous population opposed the free trade accords, leading one government official to insinuate that "dark forces" (i.e., guerrillas) were manipulating Indigenous voters. The ACIN denounced the accusations on the air. These and other instances over the first three years of operation demonstrate clearly that, notwithstanding the government's role in providing the community with a radio station, Radio Payu'mat acted independently and broadcast first and foremost with the ACIN's activist mission in mind.

Radio Payu'mat's programming and administrative staff is small, with only eight people working there at any one time. One of the major challenges they face is getting more people involved from the many small towns that the station serves. The long travel distances, the difficult security situation in the area, and the poverty of the potential volunteers make it very difficult to get more people involved with the station, whether as production staff, news reporters, or technical or administrative support. The problem of staffing has also affected the two smaller stations, Radio Nasa and Voces de Nuestra Tierra, despite efforts to increase the training program coordinated by non-Indigenous advisors to the ACIN.

To measure the actual impact of these three stations on the community would involve a much more thorough analysis of the listening audience. During several visits to the area and in conversations with many people in the communities served by the stations, I observed that people are tuning in and that they perceive the stations as true alternatives to the large commercial stations in the area. I would frequently hear people express strong feelings that the stations "belong to them," or that "those kids are good" (referring to the mostly young staff of each station). Indeed, there is a tremendous sense of ownership of the stations. They have become their communities' public spaces, where community members can announce public events, celebrate birthdays, or alert people about the death of an elder. Little children regularly come into the studios of all three stations to send greetings out to their families and friends. And the cabildos of the ACIN recognize, after more than three years of operation and a good degree of initial skepticism, that there is no better way to get the word out about a mobilization than on the airwaves of the three stations.

MEDIA MARKETS, INDIGENOUS RADIO, AND THE PUBLIC SPHERE

Numerous scholars have rigorously criticized Jürgen Habermas's bourgeois public sphere model. Although Habermas's analysis is directed at Western-style democracies like those of the United States and Europe, his model of the public sphere may be applied in the context of Colombia's mass communication system and its broader political framework (Murillo 2003). Nicholas Garnham (1992) highlights three virtues in Habermas's approach to the mass media that make it particularly applicable to a case like Colombia. First, Habermas's model focuses on "the indissoluble link between the institutions and practices of mass public communication and the institutions and practices of democratic politics" (361). This has been one of the fundamental operating principles of the global movement for democratic communication over the past several decades. Second, Habermas forces us to focus on the material resources needed for any public sphere to be effective, on how those resources are made available, and to whom. And finally, Habermas escapes "from the simple dichotomy of free market versus state control that dominates so much thinking about media policy," showing us how both market forces and state bureaucratic control of media can result in profound threats to democratic discourse (360–61).

Garnham's analysis is applicable to the emergence of Indigenous radio in Colombia, its function as an expression of democratic discourse, its capacity to operate independently in a very difficult economic and political environment, and its role as an alternative to the broader commercial media. As I described above, Indigenous radio resulted in part from a societal acceptance of the "indissoluble link" between media institutions and political institutions. That is, in order to expand democracy, one needed to increase access to media forms free from direct political influences by traditional sources of power. Indigenous radio clearly serves that function, providing diverse communities with a media voice not tied to the major political parties or economic interests. This coincided with a number of political changes in the constitutional order that led to the recognition of both Indigenous people's rights and rights regarding access to and control of mass communication systems.

In the late 1980s and early 1990s, it became apparent to many, with considerable reluctance on the part of the commercial media system in Colombia, that resources and spaces needed to be made available to traditionally excluded sectors of the public. That the commercial media system for the most part was free from direct government intervention and control did not mean that a democratic communication system existed, since these media outlets were deliberately exclusive in nature. In the wake of the Constituent Assembly of 1990–91, a consensus emerged that the state had the responsibility to help jumpstart other outlets by allocating resources and technical training, with the understanding that these new media institutions would remain autonomous from state interference in programming decisions, management, and direction. Community radio and the Indigenous radio stations that fall under the regulatory rubric of "public interest" radio were the gradual result of this realization.

Nevertheless, because Indigenous and community radio would not escape the pressures of both state and market influences, Habermas's observations about this existing dichotomy allow us to critique objectively Indigenous radio's capacity to create, on the one hand, a truly open space for the community to deliberate issues affecting the public good and, on the other, a radical alternative public sphere challenging the status quo, regardless of their primary sources of funding. As numerous scholars have written, both state-controlled and corporate-controlled media have the potential to restrict or enhance free speech, notwithstanding the general tendency to embrace one over the other as providing the ideal model.

The market versus state dichotomy manifests itself in some fundamental characteristics of Indigenous radio in Colombia. For one, the public interest stations first established in the late 1990s as part of the licensing process received development assistance from state institutions to get off the ground and to pay for production and transmission equipment, as well as for very rudimentary training. This might discount their claims of independence from the state. But as I have sought to demonstrate, Radio Payu'mat has repeatedly shown an unabashed independence from the state and has not hesitated to critique, on many levels, government policy vis-à-vis Indigenous communities and the nation as a whole. True, this cannot be said about all twenty-four of the public interest stations that emerged under the Programa Comunidad. And given the very volatile nature of Colombia's conflict, there are no guarantees that the ACIN can continue to sustain this level of critique without suffering regulatory or violent retaliation. But in the end, the level of independence will always correspond to the strength of the organization controlling the stations.

On the other end of the state-corporate seesaw is the deliberate acceptance by some Colombian community radio practitioners of commercial radio principles in order to maintain independence from the state. Community radio stations are forced into a never ending struggle between their desire to produce relevant public affairs and cultural programming and the need to maintain a listening audience sufficiently large for them to compete with commercial broadcasters whose signals reach the farthest corners of Colombia (Murillo 2003). In many cases, the commercial format has won that struggle. For Radio Payu'mat, the dilemma is in a sense resolved for them in the regulation itself. It is illegal under the public interest licensing structure to sell commercial advertising space. These stations are only allowed to sell underwriting credits or sponsorships, much like the public radio system in the United States. The issue of commercialism becomes more relevant for the ACIN's community stations such as Voces de Nuestra Tierra, where the rules are different and on-air commercial space may be sold. In the ACIN's communication mission, commercialism has been explicitly rejected, as the association sees itself as providing an alternative in every sense of the word.

However, it would be shortsighted to think that the pressures do not exist, given the prevalence of commercial popular culture even in very traditional Indigenous communities. It is a struggle that Mauricio Dorado (2004: 14) recognizes as one of the fundamental challenges of the entire Indigenous movement in Colombia as it navigates between cultural tradition and political autonomy, on the one hand, and the influences of "Western modernity" and all its representative by-products, on the other. The question of commercialism inevitably returns us to what Garnham (1994: 359–60) describes as Habermas's failure to accept "playful aspects of communicative action" as a possible link to citizen participation. The Indigenous stations in northern Cauca balance this by avoiding popular, commercial music on their play lists, such as salsa or merengue hits, filling the airwaves instead with songs by local artists who play mostly Andean folk music, very often with protest themes—music that is very popular among the many communities they serve. So they deliberately target audiences with their own popular music, bringing in listeners through music that by its nature incorporates citizen participation. As one Nasa programmer told me, "We have to give the people what they like, otherwise they won't listen."

The point is that Indigenous radio is clearly a response to demands from a community seeking its own space in a media environment seen to be undemocratic. That it was established with the support from various sources including the state does not necessarily make it dependent on the state. It also maintains an alternative mission to the commercial marketplace. That it is still influenced by the market in some ways is more a reflection of the much larger and more complex negotiation that goes on constantly in the Indigenous community as it struggles to maintain its traditions against the backdrop of a highly mediated popular mass culture. None of these traits diminish its role in the community as a type of public sphere and as a tool for broader resistance.

CHAPTER 8

OUTSIDE THE INDIGENOUS LENS:

ZAPATISTAS AND AUTONOMOUS VIDEOMAKING

Alexandra Halkin

We are Indigenous people of different languages and cultures, descen-
dents of the ancient Mayan people. The Indigenous people of Chiapas
and all the Indigenous peoples of Mexico have been suffering great
injustices—plundering, humiliation, discrimination, and marginalization—for several centuries; many other peoples around the world also
live in the same situation, in the Americas and beyond. This is a consequence of the violent Spanish conquest and, after that, the North American invasions. This left us living in complete misery and on the way to
being exterminated. These are the reasons that forced us to rise up in
arms on January 1, 1994, and say, "Enough!"
—Comandante David, Oventic, Chiapas, 2003, from the CMP/Promedios
video of the announcement of the formation of the Caracoles and Good
Government Assemblies

On January 1, 1994, the Ejército Zapatista de Liberación Nacional (EZLN,
Zapatista National Liberation Army),[1] a Mayan Indigenous organization
based in Chiapas, Mexico, declared war on the Mexican government in an
armed uprising that took over six towns in Chiapas. The international
press blasted news of the uprising over broadcast media and the Internet,
and for weeks analyses of the underlying causes of the Zapatista revolution jumped off the pages of the international press: the Mexican Constitution had failed to recognize Indigenous peoples, their rights, and their

cultures. The Mexican government therefore was treating Mexico's Indigenous peoples as second-class citizens, socially and through legal fiat, effectively denying Indigenous peoples the rights guaranteed to all Mexicans under the Mexican Constitution. With a strong sense of the importance of media events, the Zapatistas chose January 1, 1994—the date that the North American Free Trade Agreement (NAFTA) went into effect—for the uprising.[2] Since the Zapatistas are primarily an agricultural people, they argued that NAFTA would have a significant impact on Indigenous peoples throughout Mexico. Yet the Zapatista concerns were never heard, let alone solicited, by either the Mexican or U.S. negotiating teams.[3]

In addition to guns, the media were always an important part of the Zapatista "arsenal"; in fact, in the days immediately following the uprising, the Zapatistas (via sympathetic supporters) used the Internet to broadcast their cause to the world. They employed as their spokesperson a charismatic mestizo,[4] Subcommander Marcos. Through his savvy use of the Spanish language, Marcos was able to capture the attention of the international news media, which then declared Marcos to be the "leader" of the Zapatistas when in fact they had no leader per se.[5] This strategic appropriation of the mainstream news media and the Internet allowed the Zapatistas to call to international civil society to join them in "building a new world." With appeals made via the Internet, they focused international attention on the uprising and, in so doing, used the resulting international pressure to force the Mexican government into negotiations, and a subsequent truce, by January 12, 1994. It is, then, by their own design that the Zapatistas have become something of a "spectacle," spawning everything from PhD dissertations to conferences to rock music.[6]

This chapter focuses on both the product and process of Indigenous media and offers a "best practice" model of cooperative, transnational, Indigenous media making, based on my personal experience with the Chiapas Media Project (CMP) / Promedios, a binational nongovernmental organization (NGO) that provides video and computer equipment and training to Indigenous communities in the states of Chiapas and Guerrero. From my perspective as the founder, former director, and now international coordinator of the Chiapas Media Project / Promedios, it is clear that the CMP / Promedios model is not the only means of facilitating and promoting Indigenous media; rather, my hope is that our story, including our mistakes, over the past ten years, might encourage others to join in this struggle. Here I emphasize the local, domestic, and global contexts in which media operate as agents of social change.

The difference between the videos the communities produce about themselves and what "outsiders" produce about them is notable. There has been a tendency for "outsiders" to focus on the militarization and violence in Chiapas, while the communities portray themselves as survivors involved in the next level of the struggle and resistance to neocolonialism / globalization. In the category of self-produced videos, there is also a notable distinction between the Zapatistas' videos produced to tell the world about their issues and those produced for internal community use and local circulation. CMP / Promedios productions— documentaries focusing on collective projects such as coffee, textiles, education, and organic agriculture—circulate internationally chiefly via universities and film festivals. In contrast, the vast majority of videos produced for internal consumption focus on meetings, celebrations, and religious and cultural gatherings. These internal videos are almost exclusively in the Tzeltal, Tzotzil, and Tojolabal Mayan languages, addressing an audience assumed to be Mayan. Thus, while the Zapatistas strategically use the media for international recognition, videos produced for local circulation demonstrate the integration of media into the Zapatista-Mayan cultural fabric.

The Zapatista-produced videos have a powerful effect on outside viewers. Audiences in the "developed world" are seeing ordinary Indigenous people (with no stereotypical ski masks or guns, as they are seen in the outsider-produced images), organized collectively to work in their organic municipal garden and talking about how they want to be self-sufficient and neither use chemical fertilizer nor take government handouts—something that contradicts the image, produced by corporate media, of the Zapatistas as armed guerrillas only interested in state power. For other Indigenous communities in Mexico and beyond, the videos offer an example of successful Indigenous resistance to globalization and present a sustainable agricultural model for collective survival. This paradigm shift benefits CMP / Promedios in many ways: by increasing video sales, providing word-of-mouth promotion for future presentations, recruiting student interns, and creating sensitivity to Indigenous struggle and self-representation. As I will demonstrate, there are ways that "outsiders" can help to facilitate the process of Indigenous media production and distribution that not only document and educate but that will also help to integrate new media into other forms of cultural production.

> What we ask from those who are not Zapatistas, who do not agree with us or do not understand the just cause of our struggle, is that you respect our organization, that you respect our communities and Autonomous Municipalities and their authorities. And respect the Good Government Assemblies in all the regions, which have been formally constituted today, witnessed by many thousands of indigenous and nonindigenous brothers and sisters from our country Mexico and from many countries around the world.
>
> —Comandante David, Oventic, Chiapas, 2003, from CMP / Promedios video

Not every Indigenous community in Chiapas is Zapatista. The communities with which CMP / Promedios works are communities that clearly identify themselves as Zapatista, also known as "Zapatista civilian communities," thereby distinguishing them from the armed wing of the Zapatistas, the EZLN. These communities organize themselves via local, regional, and municipal authorities, elected through community consensus. They also have a rotating governance board, the Good Government Assembly (*Junta de Buen Gobierno*), which deals with all matters of decision making for their given autonomous municipality. The members of the Good Government Assemblies rotate out every fifteen days and are members of the communities that are part of each particular autonomous municipality. In some regions, the Good Government Assemblies have been so successful at mediating local conflicts (cattle theft, land disputes, etc.) that local Mexican government judiciary now refers to them to mediate between Zapatista and non-Zapatista individuals.

Other communities support the Zapatista cause but do not identify themselves as Zapatista. And there are non-Zapatista communities, ranging from ones that self-identify with political parties (especially the Partido de Acción Nacional [PAN], Partido de la Revolución Democrática [PRD], or Partido Revolucionario Institucional [PRI]) to communities that support paramilitaries. Many of these paramilitary organizations receive support from local ranchers and, in many cases, state and federal governments.

This larger sociopolitical context is key to understanding the environment in which the CMP / Promedios operates. In December 1997, a month before the first CMP / Promedios workshops were to take place, government-trained paramilitary forces killed forty-five Indigenous people, mostly women and children, in what is now referred to as the "Acteal Massacre." This bloody event received much international mass media attention that mostly reiterated the Mexican government's version of the story: that the massacre was a result of long-standing intercommunity conflict—not government-sponsored violence against Zapatista supporters. The story and perspective of the communities were not present in the coverage. Concurrent with this, the Mexican government began to expel foreigners, including human rights workers, from Chiapas under the pretext that they were violating the constitution by involving themselves in internal politics. Against this backdrop, CMP / Promedios made its first, formal, binational media exchange.[7]

PERSONAL INVOLVEMENT

> With the purpose of creating an intercultural dialogue from the community level up to the national level, that may allow a new and positive relationship between the various indigenous groups and between these groups and the rest of society, it is essential to endow these communities with their own means of communication, which are also key mechanisms for the development of their cultures. Therefore, it will be proposed to the respective national authorities, to elaborate a new communications law that may allow the indigenous towns to acquire, operate, and administrate their own means of communication.
> —From Article 3 of the San Andrés Accords, 1996

It was in this environment and under an apparently impenetrable cloak of censorship that the Zapatistas recognized the power of the media.[8] In the spring of 1995, I made my first trip to Chiapas while producing a documentary for a U.S.-based NGO taking a humanitarian aid caravan to a Zapatista region. During the production, our caravan arrived in a community that was swarming with press (both national and international): photographers and TV news cameras all "capturing the story" of the Zapatista representatives and community members who were present. It is important to note that this media presence was not a by-product of the Zapatista struggle; rather, the Zapatistas themselves had initiated and directed this international media presence, recognizing their dependence on outside (both mass and independent) media for visibility, for a degree of protection, and for leverage. The Zapatistas understood the power of their story; what was lacking was the means of transmitting that story themselves.

While the "external" journalists were "getting their story," several people in the community came up to me to ask about my Hi8 camera (where I bought it, how much it cost, etc.), clearly demonstrating an interest in and awareness of this technology and an obvious desire to communicate their message to the outside world. It was clear that the Zapatistas would benefit from access to video technology. Before leaving Chiapas, I began a discussion with Zapatista authorities, who expressed a strong interest in bringing video technology to their communities, and with representatives of local NGOs who had a working relationship with the Zapatista communities; their preexisting relationships with the Zapatista communities helped facilitate our communication and gave us credibility in the communities.[9] I returned to the United States with the kernel of an idea for a project and with the Zapatistas' encouragement to move ahead. In this stage of the project, I really only envisioned a workshop or a series of workshops in one region—I never imagined what the project would become.

GETTING ORGANIZED

> I have always wanted to provide the people in the Zapatista region with video equipment so that they can communicate, with sounds and pictures recorded by them, what is happening and what is NOT happening in their communities. I am immensely pleased to know that it's finally going to happen.
> —Guillermo Monteforte (personal communication, October 1997)

In the fall of 1995, I returned to Mexico and began meeting people who would be crucial to the success of the project. Through a series of transnational connections, I met Guillermo Monteforte, a Canadian Italian videomaker and trainer who turned out to be indispensable. Monteforte was involved with a government-funded initiative administered by the Instituto Nacional Indigenista (INI, National Indigenous Institute), a government institution that provided training and video technology to Indigenous communities throughout Mexico in the late 1980s and early 1990s.[10] He was also the founding director of Oaxaca's Centro de Video Indígena (CVI, Indigenous Video Center), created as part of the INI program. Not only did Monteforte have experience working in Indigenous communities in Mexico, but he was also a skilled video professional with sensitivity in teaching these skills. Based on his many years of working successfully with Indigenous videomakers and their communities, Monteforte was able to provide contacts for potential video instructors. At the time, we were still thinking that this would only be a two-week workshop. Since he was the expert, I deferred to Monteforte to organize the training program, while I focused on logistics and financing the donated equipment as requested by the communities.

After some extensive conversations with Monteforte, we decided that we needed to present a formal proposal of a media training strategy to the Zapatistas. Several people had suggested that we go and speak with David, a Zapatista authority who lived in Oventic (in the Highlands region). David was extremely supportive of our proposal for the workshop and offered to facilitate the negotiating process with various Zapatista communities.

KEY ACTORS

> It is deeply encouraging to see young people come together to build bridges of friendship, cooperation and communication. I applaud your vision and I hope this project will inspire future cross-cultural exchanges with youth groups around the world.
> —Carol Moseley-Braun, former U.S. Senator (personal communication, January 7, 1998)

This project could not have "gotten off the ground" without the support of many activists, NGOs, and media makers in the United States and Mexico. As in any process of social change, it is the individual, the community, and the vision that create the ability for sustainability. We welcomed the opportunity to work within already-existing connections while keeping our vision of media activism. Besides Guillermo Monteforte, other people were essential to getting CMP / Promedios off the ground. Tom Hansen (currently national coordinator for the Mexico Solidarity Network) was at that time the director of Pastors for Peace, a U.S.-based NGO that had been working in Chiapas since the uprising. Hansen helped me make initial contacts with Chiapas NGOs and shared his contact list to raise funds for the first equipment. This primary list of individuals was the initial direct mail list that provided significant support early on and that we still use to this day. Via one of Hansen's contacts in Mexico City, I met Jose Manuel Pintado, an independent video producer based in Mexico City, who had earlier introduced me to Monteforte and to Fabio Meltis, an Indigenous youth organizer in Mexico City, who encouraged many Indigenous young people to participate in the first workshop.

Another key actor in the formation of the CMP / Promedios was Francisco (Paco) Vázquez, a Nahua youth from near Mexico City, who participated in the first workshop. Vázquez had been involved in his community's collective projects and had a built-in sensitivity about dealing with the communities in Chiapas. Without Vázquez, the project would never have advanced beyond the first workshop. When I met him, he was a self-taught, fluent English speaker, and he became my default translator/partner, since I could barely speak Spanish during the first one and a half years of the project. Vázquez helped me navigate the Indigenous cultures, understand Mexican bureaucracy, and in many ways served as my protector the numerous times the Mexican military and immigration authorities stopped me at roadblocks and checkpoints.

FIRST WORKSHOP

For me it is an awakening, because before we've never even seen this kind of equipment that is now in our hands. But now we see we can do this work.
—Emilio, Zapatista participant in the first workshop in Ejido Morelia (personal communication, February 1998)

The first workshop was held in February of 1998 in the town of Ejido Morelia. Through our existing network of contacts, we met Miguel, a Zapatista authority who served as our link to the local and regional authorities and who was key in planning the project. Through Miguel we began to understand the governing structure of the Zapatista civilian authorities. We found that communication and logistics were much smoother when one person per community served as a "key person."

From the beginning, we realized that we had to work in the given organizational structure of the Zapatistas.[11] There is no cookie-cutter "Zapatista structure"; each community and each region differ, and it is crucial to understand the dynamics on a local level. By respecting how each individual community works, we were able to work with them. This was only possible by asking and listening to the experts who were living in that community.[12]

Due to the larger political and military actions undertaken throughout Chiapas by the Mexican government, it took two years to fund and organize the first workshops. Street Level Youth Media was a Chicago-based youth organization that I contacted to participate in the first workshop. It was made up of inner-city, mostly Chicano, youth. Street Level provided me with a 501(c)(3) tax-exempt status in the United States that was helpful in soliciting funds. However, the Acteal Massacre in 1997 created panic in the Street Level Youth Media group, and we had to reorganize some of our initial plans.[13] In February 1998, we held the first binational workshops as part of a youth intercultural exchange project under the name Chiapas Youth Media Project; the participants were Street Level Youth Media from Chicago, Meltis's group of Indigenous youth from Mexico City, and Monteforte's group of Indigenous video-makers from Oaxaca. A grant from the U.S.-Mexico Fund for Culture, based in Mexico City, funded these first workshops.

During our time in Ejido Morelia, there was a lot of tension due to non-Zapatista illegal logging in the community. This situation resulted in a rock-throwing incident in which a Zapatista member of the community was hit in the head. Miguel and other local authorities asked us to assist them in documenting the injury and, if necessary, to help transport the person to a hospital in a nearby town. The staff of Street Level, the Chicago group, fearful of the violence, did not want any of their youth involved and forced them to stay behind, locked up for safety. The staff of Street Level wanted constant assurances that "nothing would happen," and even very minor incidents added tension to an already tense situation. The entire situation illustrated the difficulty of organizing cultural exchanges in a highly conflicted area.

WHAT CAN WE PLUG IN AND WHERE?

> [We are giving a hand to the compañeros here in Chiapas who are interested in receiving this video workshop]. . . . We lost the lights and we had to use the electrical generator from the clinic, then we got started. And the dogs ate our food last night and we had to return [to San Cristóbal] to get more food. These are the different problems that we've had in doing these workshops.
> —Sergio Julián, Oaxacan Indigenous video instructor during first workshop in Oventic (personal communication, February 1998)

During the first meetings with the Zapatista authorities David and Miguel, we asked many questions about infrastructural issues such as electricity, (relatively) weatherproof buildings, security for the equipment, and so on. In both Oventic and Ejido Morelia, only ungrounded electricity was available—lines pulled from the government electricity grid in the area. Community leaders explained that there was no guarantee of consistent electricity or voltage. We understood this to mean that there would be inevitable interruptions of the workshops.

The first equipment we purchased consisted of s-vhs and vhs camcorders and s-vhs editing systems. Early on, we accepted used equipment from sympathetic U.S. supporters, but we quickly realized that these donations had a very short life span and were too hodge-podge. We recognized that people were attempting to be altruistic by sending us their used equipment, but we quickly learned to say, "If you won't use it, we don't need it!" The Zapatistas needed good equipment and training, not the castoffs from technology-saturated American consumers.

HOW DO WE ORGANIZE?

> We decided that the television was saying pure lies about what happens in our Chiapas. Or they add or take out words but never say the truth. We also thought that it would be good to have a camera because there are so many soldiers on our lands, at any moment something could happen. This means that when the soldiers are beating us you can enter with the camera and shoot it, record testimony—denounce it.
>
> —Moisés, Zapatista videomaker interviewed in *La jornada* (personal communication, October 2000)

After the success of the first video workshops in Ejido Morelia and Oventic, the Zapatista communities indicated their interest in continuing with the video training. In March of 1998, we decided to formalize the project as the Chiapas Media Project (CMP), a nonprofit organization based in the United States. Early on in the project, it became clear to me that there were certain aspects of my cultural conditioning (white, middle-class, college-educated North American female) that were causing conflicts in the project. My own cultural style of decision making—and my frustration at the long meetings with local Zapatista authorities and the slowness of decision making in the communities—created friction in our organization. Realizing that my strengths could be better utilized elsewhere, I removed myself from the day-to-day decision making in Mexico and focused on international distribution and promotion.

In 2001, the organization incorporated in Mexico as Promedios de Comunicación Comunitaria and became CMP/Promedios. CMP/Promedios is organized as a collective with no director or hierarchical structure but with three full-time staff members in Chiapas and one full-time and one part-time staff member in the United States. This organizational structure attempts to reflect that of the Zapatista communities with which CMP / Promedios works. Currently, CMP / Promedios is assisting the communities in Chiapas to build and equip four regional media centers. We see ourselves as working for the communities, taking their lead and working with them to create an autonomous media network that reflects their needs.

HOW DO WE TEACH?

> It isn't easy to translate Indigenous Spanish into English. There is a complex, sometimes unclear mixture of expressions and sentence structures that on the surface shows inability of precise expression in a language that is not their own, and one that fills them with a complex of being dominated by mestizos who scorn them for not speaking it "properly."
> —Guillermo Monteforte (personal communication, April 1998)

I came into this project with very little knowledge of Indigenous media or its processes. My primary vision of the CMP / Promedios came from my background as a documentary videomaker / artist with my interest and curiosity focused on discovering what kinds of videos the Zapatistas would produce once they had the equipment and training. In my mind, I was facilitating the education of videomakers by transmitting technical skills to my peers. In the summer of 1998 we held our first video production workshop in the village of La Realidad. I was sitting next to Manuel, a local Zapatista authority who had a camera in his hands, when he turned to me and asked, "Don't we need special government permission to use this equipment?" I was surprised at the question and asked him why he was asking. He replied, "Because all of the people who come here always have *credenciales* hanging around their necks, given to them by the government." He was referring to the press and, after further discussion, I realized that Manuel thought ownership of video equipment had to be authorized by the government. After this, we made sure during the workshops to reiterate that the equipment belonged to the communities, that no government permission was needed, and that the training we were providing was professional and no different from what the people with the credenciales had received. Put simply: the villagers had just as much right as the people with the credenciales to tell their story and distribute it as they saw fit.

In the beginning of the video training process, we were all aware of the pitfalls of bringing in temporary "outsiders" to do the training, particularly as "instructors." Bringing in people from outside of Mexico would not work from either a sociopolitical or economic standpoint—we did not want to replicate the colonial model. With very rare exceptions, all of the introductory video and computer workshops the first two years were taught by either Indigenous videomakers from Oaxaca or by Mexican CMP / Promedios staff.

CMP / Promedios staff felt that it was extremely important for the instructors to be Mexican—preferably Indigenous Mexican—in order to provide a continuity of process and to connect Zapatista videomakers to the broader network of Indigenous videomakers in Mexico and Latin America. The development of a network of media centers is a long-term commitment that can only succeed if it is self-sustaining. In this respect, CMP / Promedios relies on good relations with Indigenous videomakers in Oaxaca and elsewhere who strengthen and broaden CMP / Promedios as a link in the larger network of Indigenous media organizations.

In the first workshops, the students were primarily local authorities, put there to check us out and make sure we "weren't up to no good." We found this out later after working in the communities for a while, when we noticed that certain people were dropping out of the courses whom we would later encounter in leadership positions. Another dynamic operating was the presence of so many "outsiders." Many people of goodwill came (and continue to come) from around the world to Chiapas with the intention of assisting the communities. Yet many broken promises have left locals wary of first-time visitors. We knew from the beginning that we could not make any promises we could not fulfill and that the most important thing was continuity—to maintain a presence (see figs 8.1–8.5).

THE HYDRA OF FUNDING

> The Funds Executive Committee has agreed on a grant of $21,400 for the development of the above mentioned project (Chiapas Youth Media Project). The award of the funding assigned to the granted projects is established through an agreement signed by the Fund and the person appointed as project manager, who will be responsible for signing the agreement, receiving the checks and keeping the Fund informed on the development of the project as well as the application of the funds granted.
> —Marcela S. Madariaga, program coordinator, U.S.-Mexico Fund for Culture, notification letter of first grant to CMP / Promedios, August 1997

(*this page and opposite*) Zapatista Women, First Women's Video Workshop, Ejido Morelia, 1998. COURTESY OF FRANCISCO VÁZQUEZ / CHIAPAS MEDIA PROJECT / PROMEDIOS.

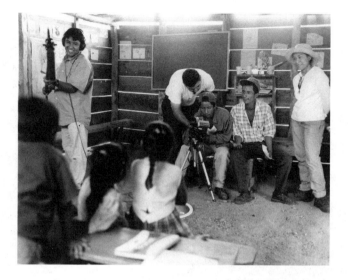

(*top*) Zapatista and non-Zapatista video makers during the production of the video, *Education in Resistance*, 2000.

(*above*) Zapatista video makers editing, 1998.

(*left*) Zorida shooting during First Women's Video Workshop, Ejido Morelia, 1998.

COURTESY OF FRANCISCO VÁZQUEZ / CHIAPAS MEDIA PROJECT / PROMEDIOS.

We entered the project knowing that neither goodwill nor passion would buy us a video camera or a Final Cut Pro editing system. Self-sustainability also requires a media product that can be shown, distributed, and sold. Unfortunately, selling Indigenous-made videos does not often generate enough revenue to support the project on its own. Working in a political movement that offers a potent critique of international capitalism means that organizers and participants are suspicious of both government support and corporate interests. We needed to respect this political framework, balancing it with the need for consistent funding. Therefore, for the first five years, the U.S. side of the project took full responsibility for securing funding.

The costs involved in equipment maintenance alone necessitated some creative strategies for self-generating funds. In addition to foundation / corporate funding and personal altruism, we also created a system of self-generating income: video sales and university presentations. It is in this element of structural financial solvency—a sustainable infrastructure — where outsiders can provide the clearest support. But it is also one of the most complicated aspects of Indigenous media making.

When we first began discussions with the communities about the project, we explained that the equipment was theirs to do whatever they wanted with, but that if they decided not to produce videos for outside consumption (a product to *sell* to the outside world), it would be hard to maintain financing. In the spring of 1998, in Ejido Morelia, workshop participants made the first video produced by the communities, *La familia indígena* (*The Indigenous Family*). It was a very simple, straightforward video about the differing roles / jobs of men and women in the community. People on the tape spoke Spanish rather than a Mayan language; this was a long time before they began recording in their own language for international distribution.[14] The tape was well received, and we sold at least 150 copies in the first six months. CMP / Promedios used this tape as our first promotional video. We organized our first U.S. tour with this video and developed a viable model for doing presentations that generated income and raised the visibility of the project.

CMP / Promedios is currently distributing more than two dozen videos internationally produced in Chiapas and Guerrero, with most distribution done via our Chicago office. Video sales in 2005 exceeded seventeen thousand dollars, with university sales making up the majority of the income. The presence of CMP / Promedios at large academic conferences like the American Anthropological Association (AAA) and the Latin

American Studies Association (LASA) has been instrumental in raising our visibility in the academy, greatly increasing our video sales, and adding names to our direct mail list. One of our other main sources of self-generated funding is honoraria from university presentations. Currently, video sales cover the monthly satellite Internet connection fees in all four of the regional media centers.[15]

CMP / Promedios also seeks funding via philanthropic resources. At the beginning of the project, we decided that we would apply for grants only when no strings were attached and only when the foundation had no political agenda that conflicted with our agenda or the community's. We have found that we are indeed able to secure funds that will allow us to maintain our artistic and political freedom. It took us a while to identify which foundations had funding priorities that matched our work and were willing to take a risk on a project such as ours. Support from private foundations has made it possible for us to grow as an organization, although, at times, it has also proved a source of tension. These problems were often premised on a foundation's desire for us to recreate its preconceived cultural context, one that was often totally unrelated to the cultural context in which we are operating. A good illustration of this is that many foundations want a certain level of gender equality in the composition of workshops. In the early days of the CMP / Promedios project, we spent a lot of time talking with local Zapatista authorities about the need for women's participation. We would then see women participating in the introductory workshops but not returning to subsequent workshops. We soon understood that our input really made no difference and that women's participation was the decision of the communities, not that of outsiders, however well meaning. We realize that foundation support will not last forever, and we are hoping that we will be able to maintain our funding relationships long enough to finish the infrastructure needed to make all of the regional media centers completely operational and self-sufficient.

CONCLUSION

We set up the projector and a white sheet over the wall of one of the classrooms. It was getting dark and people started to come out and sit on the grass. . . . Out came the first image: color bars. I heard "oohs and ahhs" . . . but what was even more impressive than the response to the color bars was to see

these people moved by a video produced in their own language by their own people: men, women, and children [showing] a sense of pride as well as excitement to be able to see themselves speak about their work, their organization and their struggle.
—Cruz Angeles, filmmaker and CMP / Promedios intern (personal communication, 2000)

Over the past ten years, CMP / Promedios has trained more than two hundred Indigenous men and women in basic video production; built and equipped four regional media centers in Zapatista territory with digital video production, postproduction, audio, and satellite Internet access; enabled the production of twenty-four videos for international distribution; and provided the means to make hundreds of videos utilized internally by the Indigenous communities in Chiapas.[16] Over the years, there has been a significant improvement in the quality of production in the videos. All productions (those intended for both external and internal use) go through some type of community consensus about topics and content.[17]

As I have noted, CMP / Promedios is not the only model for supporting Indigenous media initiatives; the possibilities are myriad. In Latin America, there are a number of important and successful Indigenous media projects (see Salazar's and Córdova's essay in this collection). In addition to the better-known organizations, such as the Coordinadora Audiovisual Indígena Originaria de Bolivia (CAIB, Indigenous Audiovisual Coordinator of Bolivia), Brazil's Vídeo nas Aldeias (VNA, Video in the Villages), and the Confederación de Nacionalidades Indígenas del Ecuador (CONAIE, Confederation of the Indigenous Nations of Ecuador), there are a number of smaller initiatives whose work does not receive wide recognition or distribution. Video production and dissemination in the communities has become a regular feature of Indigenous life.

There is an important role for "outsiders" to play as collaborators with Indigenous communities / organizations in fostering media initiatives—namely, in the initial transfer of media technology and the creation of infrastructure and sustainability. My own most important contribution has been my ability to raise the initial funding that supported the creation of a permanent infrastructure and my current role in getting the videos distributed to the widest audience possible.

The communities in Chiapas have adapted video technology as an important tool for internal communication, cultural preservation, and defense of their human rights. They also have used it as a vehicle for communicating their own truths, stories, and realities to the outside world. The ability of Indigenous communities and other marginalized groups to record, edit, and distribute their own story is vital to a functioning society. Indigenous-controlled video has the power to make connections in communities and to extend communication / information internationally to non-Indigenous people. All of us have a role to play in supporting these important processes.

> The work of video has really moved us; it has a great importance in helping us to construct our indigenous history. We can see that we will be able to do many things for our well-being and the future of our children.
> —Estella, Zapatista videomaker, April 2003, letter written to CMP / Promedios

> With this group of young people or not so young people, it's my intention to insist that they learn more, that they prepare more, in order to be able to make a testimony or tell a story, all of this is recorded so that the town can see that the work is moving ahead.
> —Miguel, local Zapatista authority, Ejido Morelia (personal communication, February 1998)

NOTES

I would like to thank Shayna Plaut, Guillermo Monteforte, and Luisa Ortiz Pérez for their generosity and help in writing this chapter.

In this essay, I use only first names to refer to Zapatista persons. All of the Zapatista authorities and many of the Zapatista videomakers only use a first name, a *nombre de guerra*, which usually has no relation to their actual name.

1. The origin of the Zapatista name is worth mentioning. From 1910 until his assassination by the Mexican military in 1919, a charismatic farmer, Emiliano Zapata, took up the revolutionary struggle for agrarian reform during the Mexican Revolution. Zapata's Ejército Libertador del Sur (Liberation Army of the South) claimed that "land belonged to those who worked for it"—quite a revolutionary statement coming from those who worked the land and endured the hardships of exploitation by the *hacendados* (landowners). Since that time, Zapata's legacy has inspired many of the campesino grassroots movements and provided the name for the EZLN, which publicly appeared in Chiapas during the presidency of (and in response to the policies of) Carlos Salinas de Gortari in 1994, calling for the agrarian struggle and political

respect for Indigenous peoples. This rebel movement not only took Zapata's name for its struggle but also embraced the task of guarding and preserving the Zapatista spirit, a task the Zapatistas have honored to the present day.

2. The Zapatistas had been organizing secretly for many years before their public appearance on January 1, 1994.

3. The EZLN said that NAFTA was not going to benefit Mexico's Indigenous peoples in particular or its poor people in general—unfortunately, this unheeded warning has proven accurate.

4. This term refers to those of mixed European and Indigenous ancestry.

5. The Zapatista communities make decisions through consensus, and local leadership is rotated on a monthly / yearly basis.

6. Our office has been inundated with requests for interviews, office visits, and access to the communities.

7. Tom Hansen, instrumental in helping start CMP / Promedios, was kidnapped and expelled by Mexican immigration authorities during a delegation bringing video equipment to Ejido Morelia in February 1998.

8. The San Andrés Accords were an agreement signed between the Zapatistas and the Mexican government in 1996. Even though the accords were never formalized into the Mexican Constitution, the Zapatista communities used them as a framework for actions / work they have assumed since 1996. Video is one example of these actions.

9. The project would not have been possible without developing relationships with NGOs in the area, and we work hard to maintain those relationships.

10. The National Indigenous Institute is now known as the Comisión Nacional para el Desarrollo de los Pueblos Indígenas (CDI, National Commission for the Development of Indigenous Peoples).

11. Although the Zapatistas' first language is Mayan, in order to facilitate communication with us, they decided to hold their meetings in Spanish, the default lingua franca.

12. Our contacts initially were with local authorities and now are via regional media coordinators and the Good Government Assemblies.

13. In reaction to the increasingly volatile internal Mexican political environment, we decided to insure the safety of the youth delegation by asking PRD deputies to escort our group through immigration checkpoints to Ejido Morelia.

14. In the first video productions, Spanish was used, because the videos were seen as productions for all of the Zapatista autonomous municipalities, where Spanish is the common language. As the project became more integrated on a local and regional level, local languages began to be used.

15. The regional media centers are equipped with satellite Internet access. This involves a computer that controls the positioning and programming of the satellite dish. The communities use the Internet for e-mail correspondence

with fair-trade projects that distribute their products, for news gathering, and for communicating with the other regional media centers.

16. In 2000, we began work in Guerrero with the Campesino Environmentalists of the Sierra de Petatlán.

17. The Zapatista videomakers produce videos in collaboration with their community, region, and / or municipality.

PART III

CULTURAL IDENTITY, PRESERVATION, AND
COMMUNITY-BUILDING THROUGH MEDIA

CHAPTER 9

THE SEARCH FOR WELL-BEING: PLACING

DEVELOPMENT WITH INDIGENOUS IDENTITY

Laurel Smith

In 1997, members of Grupo Solidario de Quiatoni, an Indigenous community-based organization in the southern Mexican state of Oaxaca, produced the video *Buscando bienestar (Searching for Well-Being)*.[1] Early in this video, group member Pedro Santiago explains: "The little we plant here isn't enough to live on—that's why people go elsewhere to earn a living. But some of us think that there are ways to work together: to live better, to find well-being for our community." Later, when the group's founding leader, Eucario Angeles Martínez, speaks to the camera, he says that the Grupo Solidario thought outside-orchestrated development projects would "put an end to the crisis, scarcity, to the sadness and poverty that our fellow community members suffer." However, he notes, things did not work out as anticipated, and he explains how, after collective reflection, the group turned their attention to studying "the signs, the stories, the ways of the past, the knowledge of how to live." Angeles Martínez tells viewers why group members have chosen this pathway to community well-being:

> We think that this is how we must work in order to get ahead. We shouldn't bring things from outside, but take advantage of what is ours. We should revive and use the customs of the past. It would be good if the only things brought from the outside were things we cannot make here. . . . we want to depend less on outsiders. We also need to know who we are today in order to study our own knowledge and wisdom. This is how we want to progress.[2]

Delimited through these evocations of "elsewhere," an "outside," and "outsiders," is a place called Quiatoni. San Pedro Quiatoni is the name of a *municipio* (a geopolitical unit) in the mountains of southeastern Oaxaca, as well as the name of the pueblo serving as its administrative seat. According to the 2000 Census, almost all (98.9%) of the 9,570 inhabitants of this municipio speak an Indigenous language, a distinctive form of Zapoteco. Local authorities are elected by *usos y costumbres*, a catch-all legal term referring to open elections in which community assemblies select representatives. Oaxaca de Juárez, the state capital, is six hours away from the pueblo of San Pedro Quiatoni; it takes three hours of traveling up and down dirt roads to reach the highway. The members of thirty-four families from settlements sprinkled throughout the municipio of San Pedro Quiatoni came together to establish Grupo Solidario de Quiatoni in 1984. Like them, I use *Quiatoni* to refer to a place that is spread unevenly, a place that embodies the sense of community summoned forth by the above quotes. Despite the cartographic distance and cultural differences that mark Quiatoni, these quotes (and their translations) indicate how ideas, images, practices, commodities, technology, and people travel from, into, and out of this place. They also suggest how some residents represent and grapple with the uneven processes of globalization currently changing the place in which they live.

NETWORKING INDIGENOUS IDENTITY

Latin American social movements presently use *indígena* as a category that connects ethnic groups to territorial claims, cultural heritage, and socioeconomic location. These ethnopolitics locate Indigenous identity in an ongoing struggle to maintain place-based values, practices, and knowledge while grappling with the violent change wrought by centuries of genocide, economic exploitation, and forced acculturation intensified by the processes of globalization (Kearney and Varese 1995; Varese 1996). Such politics of representation establish a position for challenging state policies on a historical and moral basis and, at the same time, for asserting citizenship rights with demands for greater inclusion in the formulation of state programs, particularly those relating to development. With the strategies of ethnopolitics, Indigenous movements refashion development practices, restructure state institutions, expand the spaces of democratic participation, and reimagine national identities (Yashar 1999; Radcliffe 1999). Place-based Indigenous identity in Latin America should not, however, be essentialized as inherently inclusive or isolated from other political currents (Calderón, Piscitelli, and Reyna

1992). The global politics of local identity rely on shared images of custom, community, and ethnicity, and though these may be marshaled in defense of cultural resources, they may also be reactionary and deeply gendered, classed, and racialized (Paulson and Calla 2000). Furthermore, Latin American ethnopolitics intersect (sometimes successfully, at other times uneasily or not at all) with national-popular political initiatives such as labor and peasant movements (Hale 1994).

Increasingly, Indigenous activists and organizations link place-based collective action to projects undertaken by state agencies and national, supranational, intergovernmental, and nongovernmental organizations (NGOs), foundations, and agencies with specific interests such as the environment, agriculture, women, education, and religion. Their work taps into transnational networks of advocacy (Keck and Sikkink 1999) that stretch their sociospatial relations and amplify the impact of ethnopolitics (Brysk 2000). Daniel Mato (1997: 184) notes how making such transnational connections requires "negotiations, social and institutional learning, and transformations of all the actors' self-representations and agendas." Mato's research on Latin American Indigenous organizations and their more globalized allies reveals similarities between sociopolitical agendas and the language used to express them and underscores how Indigenous leaders critically appropriate ways of speaking and bargaining in order to understand and address threats to territorial and cultural autonomy (Mato 2000a). Mato (2000b) also points out that differentiated access to technology and uneven levels of knowledge about network mechanisms and modes of operation characterize activist-advocate relations.[3]

If and when groups gain access to them, communication technologies (hereafter comtechs) can enhance dialogue and the exchange of information among grassroots organizations, international NGOs, and other sources of support that comprise transnational networks of advocacy. They have, for example, played an important role in protecting and empowering the grassroots Zapatista movement (Froehling 1997; see also Alexandra Halkin's essay in this book). Comtechs channeled through advocacy organizations also provide the means to market the crafts and commodities of marginalized communities far beyond their site of production. Additionally, with comtechs, data based on local knowledge may be authoritatively rendered and then mobilized in the interest of those who, until recently, have not had a voice in planning development projects. In short, comtechs can relocate the politics of representation at a variety of scales: community, regional, national, and global. Video technology operates in this fashion when it aids Indigenous communities fighting to assert local autonomy and territorial integrity. Indigenous cultural activists use the social relations of media to negotiate alternative images designed to rework power relations from their own perspective (Ginsburg 1997). Video self-representations thus displace the authority of social scientists to represent people and processes (Turner 1990; Ruby 1992). Due to its high cost, the use of video technologies is an inherently collective process, and rare is the individual or organization that can rally these resources alone. Research on Indigenous video illustrates how the governing bodies that are largely responsible for the marginalized social location from which these cultural interventions are produced are often also responsible for the access to comtechs by Indigenous communities (Ginsburg 1993; Langton 1993; Michaels 1984). Furthermore, the prominent role played by advocates working to make video technology and skills available to cultural activists complicates matters of authorship (Ginsburg 1997: 127).

THE CULTURAL POLITICS OF INDIGENOUS IDENTITY IN OAXACA

After the Mexican Revolution in the first decades of the twentieth century, Indigenous identity demarcated an anthropologically defined category of difference that functioned as a key component in the scripting of both state and popular Mexican nationalisms (Hernández Díaz 1993). Based on evolutionary assumptions about an inevitable pathway to assimilation, the state policy of *indigenismo* was designed to acculturate Indigenous peoples into the dominant mestizo national "imagined community" (B. Anderson 1983; Parra Mora 1993) through education and development (Favre 1999). Development programs formally recognized Indigenous peoples as campesinos: a production-based identity that emphasized their role in feeding the industrializing cities, seen as the engines of national progress. The imposition of a nationalist peasant identity denigrated Indigenous cultural practices and values and helped solidify the social location of Indigenous peoples at the bottom of Mexico's politico-economic hierarchy (Kearney 1996).

Some Mexican intellectuals and academics evoked idealized images of "the Indian" as models for revolutionary politics or modern citizenship, but these constructions also identified Indigenous peoples that failed to fit the models as backward, irrational, and in need of paternalist uplift

(Maldonado 2000; Dawson 1998). Hegemonic representations disseminated by the cultural industries, such as radio and television, have valorized, exoticized, or ridiculed Indigenous identity as national patrimony (Pérez Montfort 1994). For example, Néstor García Canclini (1995) argues that the National Museum of Anthropology in Mexico City exhibits Indigenous identity as a pacified and "pure" heritage that is frozen in time. Such representations erase historical and contemporary conditions of cultural violence, deny the cultural hybridity and socioeconomic diversity arising from the process of translating tradition through modernity, and thus silence contemporary Indigenous peoples. It is exactly these politics of representation that Indigenous cultural activists in Mexico seek to rewrite with the strategies of ethnopolitics (e.g., Garduño Cervantes 1985).

Because its large continuous Indigenous population negated evolutionary narratives of nationhood, the southern state of Oaxaca has historically been represented as the opposite of modernization, an obstacle to progress and a site devoid of agency (Chassen-López 2001). Recent census data indicates that 7 percent of the Mexican population over the age of five speaks an Indigenous language; Oaxaca is home to half of Mexico's speakers of an Indigenous language, and they comprise 37 percent of the state's population over the age of five. Although most researchers classify these peoples into sixteen different ethnolinguistic groups, there has been extensive debate over how the character trait of speaking an Indigenous language structures ethnic and peasant identity in Oaxaca (e.g., Campbell 1996). Often speakers of Indigenous languages identify themselves not as members of an ethnic group but as campesinos or as people from particular communities or regions. Ethnicity is difficult to isolate and identify in Oaxaca because it is not an essential category entered at birth but rather a constructed identity formulated in relations of power and difference (Stephen 1996). In Oaxaca, grave socioeconomic inequalities and ongoing racist denigration of Indigenous cultural practices have shaped the growing influence of ethnopolitics (Hernández Díaz 1992).

In the late 1980s the Mexican state began to modify its policy of repressing nonstate-sponsored social movements; and Indigenous organizations were able to extend their regional and local linkages (Sarmiento Silva 2001). The expansion of Indigenous collective action at the national level contributed to the modification of the Mexican constitution, which on the five-hundred-year anniversary of the arrival of Europeans recognized the nation's multicultural composition. In 1994, the Zapatista uprising in

Chiapas garnered wide popular support and resulted in the signing of the San Andrés Accords.[4] The state of Oaxaca has been the most responsive to the Indigenous movement's demands for self-determination and autonomy. Its constitution was reformed in 1995 with an article acknowledging the state's extensive cultural diversity. Later that same year, community elections based on usos y costumbres were legalized. Furthermore, the growing transnationalism of Indigenous migrants from Oaxaca has contributed to "the appearance of ethnicity as a self-conscious sense of peoplehood" (Kearney 2000: 177). Dismal working conditions and racist repression of Indigenous migrants both in the United States and Mexico "nurture a more collective and conscious conception of what it is to be *indígena*" (ibid.: 185) and illustrate the utility of human rights political discourse (Nagengast, Stavenhagen, and Kearney 1992; Nagengast and Kearney 1990). Furthermore, an international community of scholars, whose work is embedded in transnational networks involving NGOs, universities, and private foundations, uses their positions to examine and empower the ethnopolitics of cultural plurality in Oaxaca (e.g., Bartolomé and Barabas 1996).

Additionally, the transnational relations shaping structural adjustment programs and related institutional decentralization dramatically revamp state development programs in rural Mexico. According to Jonathon Fox (1996), since the early 1980s changes in bargaining relations between rural development agencies and Indigenous organizations have, to varying degrees, empowered local social actors and led to the thickening of civil society in Oaxaca. That is to say that increasingly (but sporadically), action orchestrated by civic groups and cultural collectives concerned with development unfolds outside the purview of the state.[5] While authoritarian clientelism ("the threat of the stick") continues to discourage translocal linkages in some places, in others it is increasingly replaced by semiclientelism ("the threat of the withdrawal of carrots") that fosters independent organization and greater local control of resource allocation. These changing state-society relations contribute to greater social capital and regional linkages that empower community development initiatives. Although diminished funding and political shifts in the last few years have reduced state support, community-based organizations utilize the skills they learned through their participation in state programs to engage with the growing numbers of development NGOs operating in Mexico.

In the early 1980s, the Mexican government established Culturas Populares, a new bureau in its public education system (Reuter 1983). Stefano
Varese, an Italian-Peruvian anthropologist, became the first director of
Culturas Populares in Oaxaca. Varese brought with him the desire to
reform state policies of cultural assimilation. Like many of his Latin
American colleagues, Varese emphasized the violent disruption of Indigenous life through the intrusion of colonialism and the continued assault
of state neocolonialism. In the name of cultural plurality, these researchers advocated the rescue and revitalization of ethnicity (e.g., Varese 1983;
Bonfil Batalla and Rojas Arevena 1982; La cuestión étnica, 1981). Varese set
out to arm Indigenous peoples with a theoretical tool they could use to
analyze their socioeconomic locations. He sought to educate a "militant
ethnic nucleus" about the historical processes of the " 'ghettoization' of
Indian culture and language . . . because this nucleus will provide the
intellectuals and leaders who will develop an active consciousness of the
different self, a militant ethnic consciousness" (Varese 1985: 204–8). While
director of Culturas Populares from 1981 to 1986, Varese supervised the
training of thirty-six bilingual individuals from Indigenous communities.
The goal was to equip these individuals with the skills "to systematize
'popular ethnic knowledge and thought' and enhance its value by critically comparing it with universal knowledge, and enriching it thereby"
(ibid.: 212). Culturas Populares then employed many of the participants as
"cultural promoters," whose job was to research and implement *etnodesarrollo* (ethnic development), or culturally appropriate development
projects in Indigenous communities.

Eucario Angeles Martínez was one of the original thirty-six participants in the Culturas Populares training program. In 1969, when he was
eleven, Angeles Martínez left Quiatoni, following his older brothers to
the capital city of Oaxaca, where they had gone to finish their education
and find employment.[6] As he grew up, Angeles Martínez was very active
in the base community centered in his urban church parish. Drawing on
the liberation theology movement in the Catholic Church, base communities sought the spiritual and material betterment of their members
(MacNabb and Rees 1993). Angeles Martínez's activities and related travels shaped his goals of organizing collective action and morally encouraging those faced with the hardships of socioeconomic marginalization. His

experience, in tandem with his settlement in the city, equipped Angeles Martínez for the training program that he entered in 1983, and then led to his position with Culturas Populares. Angeles Martínez linked the cultural revitalization aims of etnodesarrollo with his own goals and, in 1984, he helped establish the Grupo Solidario de Quiatoni. Throughout the 1980s, the group undertook agricultural projects that were supported by state development agencies and later by international aid agencies and NGOs.[7] Most of these development initiatives required initial group financing and voluntary labor. They also entailed filling out numerous forms in Spanish, traveling to far away institutional headquarters and often waiting hours to appeal for support in person. Because of his location and bilingual literacy, Angeles Martínez often represented Grupo Solidario, and he usually spearheaded their petitions for resources.

Grupo Solidario benefited from Angeles Martínez's urban bureaucratic position and connections to researchers and institutions based far from Quiatoni. For example, after making Angeles Martínez's acquaintance, the U.S. anthropologists Martha Rees and Arthur Murphy brought students to Quiatoni for a summer field course in 1989 (Murphy 1989), and in 1999 Rees brought Angeles Martínez to the United States to speak about his work with Grupo Solidario. Earlier, after learning of the group's desire for computers to further their collection of local history, legends, and myths, Rees and Murphy had arranged for the donation of second-hand computers (Rees, personal communication, January 24, 2002). Eventually the results of these long-term investigations appeared in two books published by Culturas Populares (Angeles Martínez 1997a, 1997b). Paola Sesia (1990), an Italian researcher pursuing participatory research projects in the region, also visited Quiatoni and assisted members of Grupo Solidario with their compilation of traditional healing practices. Sesia also helped edit the history of the group that Angeles Martínez wrote in order to share their experiences in self-organization and community development (Angeles Martínez 1994). With Sesia's assistance, Grupo Solidario submitted a grant proposal to the U.S.-based Kellogg Foundation that led to the group's acquisition of a video camera and the undertaking of self-evaluations in 1994 (Sesia, personal communication, February 8, 2002).

While membership numbers had always fluctuated, around this time the organization underwent a crisis of confidence that left only a core of about twenty members (from its peak of more than 100). Many disengaged themselves from the group because their development projects had repeatedly proven unprofitable. Indeed, due to the lack of promised technical assistance, unfavorable prices, and costly transportation, many were outright disasters. Debates over the misuse of organizational funds also reduced enthusiasm and the group's size. Finally, some members withdrew from the organization because they were tired of the forceful yet often absentee leadership by Angeles Martínez who, along with his extended family, lived in the city of Oaxaca. Those who remained with the Grupo Solidario decided to be far more cautious about outside funds and initiatives. Continuing to work with Angeles Martínez, they founded the Centro de Investigación, Experimentación y Desarrollo Indígena (Center for Indigenous Research, Experimentation, and Development). They focused their efforts on researching and applying local knowledge about practices such as water divination and curing.

Also in 1994, the Instituto Nacional Indigenista (INI, National Indigenous Institute) established the Centro de Video Indígena (CVI, Indigenous Video Center) in the city of Oaxaca. Guillermo Monteforte, an Italian Canadian who had been working in INI's Audiovisual Archives Department, was the founding director. Monteforte collaborated in INI's Media Transference Program, which provided thirty-seven Indigenous organizations with video production and editing equipment and training for organization members. Monteforte and others at the CVI worked to enhance Indigenous self-representation by facilitating access to video technology. While the Grupo Solidario did not participate in the initial transference program, Angeles Martínez's activism and Monteforte's advocacy brought them into contact, and eventually their work began to overlap. Angeles Martínez was eager to produce a documentary with the many hours of video footage shot in Quiatoni. Toward this end, Monteforte accessed financial resources from INI to add to the support by Culturas Populares.

In the summer of 1997, two women from Quiatoni, María Santiago Ruiz and Eugenia Martínez Reyes, became involved with the video. Both women were heavily involved in Grupo Solidario's collection of local knowledge. Partly because Santiago Ruiz and Martínez Reyes were single women and thus able to spend weeks away from home, they were willing to participate in workshops at the CVI, where they learned to shoot and edit video. Angeles Martínez, Santiago Ruiz, Martínez Reyes, and Monteforte worked together to record more material and edit it together with previously shot footage to produce the twenty-seven-minute video *Buscando bienestar* (1997). All editing, production, and postproduction took place at the CVI, since this is where the equipment and assistance were located. Monteforte and other CVI personnel provided technical support, and Angeles Martínez contributed input on content, but it was Santiago Ruiz and Martínez Reyes who spent weeks at the CVI, sequestered in the editing suite wrestling with the new technology. They found the process arduous and tedious (especially Martínez Reyes, who had her infant with her), but fruitful and ultimately satisfying.

The first shots of *Buscando bienestar* locate Quiatoni: its hillside location, the central plaza filled with people watching dancers perform, people working in their homes and the fields, and "San Pedro Quiatoni" written across the municipio's administrative headquarters. Accompanied by the camera's pan across dry terrain, a man remembers how there used to be more rain, how houses were built with materials that withstood mudslides, and there was always plenty to eat. Seated next to a dry creek bed, an old man testifies about the fish that used to swim there when he was a boy. Against the backdrop of three photographs—two of which feature Angeles Martínez addressing group members—a woman (the credits indicate it is Martínez Reyes) narrates the establishment of Grupo Solidario. They came together in 1984 "to think and talk about the problems we had" and to solicit funds from "outsiders" in order "to get ourselves out of poverty." With images and interviews, *Buscando bienestar* details the outcomes of some of these development projects. It shows insect-infested tomato plants and offers insight into a pig-raising initiative that fizzled because it overextended water supplies. Following this overview of frustrations is a head and shoulder shot of Angeles Martínez delivering a monologue about Grupo Solidario. This scene stands out from the rest of the video because of its professional lighting and because, at almost three minutes, it is much longer than any other interview. Recorded in the CVI, this is the only scene not shot in Quiatoni. Here Angeles Martínez recalls the failure of development projects and notes that, in addition to low prices and sales, "we were having problems because money is not part of our culture."

The remainder of the video examines the activities of the Center for Indigenous Research. In between montage and music, members describe the group's dynamics, review their experiments, and outline their research methods. One man reviews his experiments on rain prediction, and viewers are introduced to the Zapotec calendar that resulted from them. Other men dig a well and use the water to irrigate corn planted with organic fertilizer. Yet another man notes how the combination of low prices and the high cost of transporting the tomato harvest to the city made the venture unprofitable. We see a group of women including Santiago Ruiz and Martínez Reyes examining plant samples. As narrator, Martínez Reyes tells us they classify the plants to learn about and utilize their qualities for medical balms and soap. A man's voice says, "We all work . . . all family members have been working. Here the elderly, the children and women work, the whole family."

During scenes of people gathered for a meeting, this same man continues by pointing out that, while not everyone attends the meetings, "We all participate." He then explains their research methods. "We want the work to turn out well; this is why we take three years to do it. We repeat the experiment to see if we get the same results . . . that is why we programmed three years for the project, so we can be sure." At this point, a young woman named Carmen Martínez addresses the camera, observing that not everyone has the power to heal, but some of us do. She is followed by Santiago Ruiz, who briefly talks to viewers about the relationship between the moon's position and healing practices. Then comes footage of traditional cures such as bleeding. An elderly man reminisces that "my grandparents used to say that we should plant when the moon is full." In response to questions from Angeles Martínez, a man describes the organic fertilizers he is using to grow garlic and herbs. Accompanied by music, shots of women boiling and pounding plant leaves fade into the finished products with handwritten labels identifying them as soaps or healing ointments. Next is a still shot of local produce laid out on a small woven mat. The music stops as Carmen Martínez once again addresses the camera saying: "We have already begun, we have it all set up, though there is no money to support this project. We will continue to work as long as we can, even if it takes a long time." The music starts again as we see the final series of images—someone measuring an ear of corn with their hand span, women admiring harvested carrots, children eating at the table and then playing, and finally young boys and girls performing a dance in the central plaza where the video began.

From the start, *Buscando bienestar* points to the past as a site of guidance during uncertain times. The video revalorizes local practices and knowledge by connecting them to a time when the community did not have to cope with shortage and the need to migrate, and by comparing them to failures of imported practices and knowledge. *Buscando bienestar* defines development as a profoundly cultural project that should include wide community participation and follow local criteria for success and happiness. That is, development projects must culturally fit the place where they are undertaken. Although this video visualizes Quiatoni-based collective action, it is far from a strictly local project, largely due to Angeles Martínez's mediation. His long speech and photographic presence suggest how he functions as a cultural broker whose ideas and activities are central to the organization. In his monologue, Angeles Martínez appropriates the scholarly concept of etnodesarrollo with his calls for the investigation of traditional approaches to land management and production through research and testing. The scientific methods used to interrogate the usefulness of Indigenous knowledge and the utilization of video technology to disseminate Grupo Solidario's efforts also reflect institutional linkages and connections to networks of advocacy.

CONCLUSIONS ABOUT IMPACT

Journeying through transnational networks orchestrated and maintained by advocates and activists between 1998 and 2000, *Buscando bienestar* was screened at international Indigenous film and video festivals in Ecuador and Guatemala (where the video won awards) and then later in Madrid, New York City, and Paris. These travels and Monteforte's assistance led to funding from the MacArthur and Rockefeller Foundations for the production of two more videos by Grupo Solidario. Their subsequent video, *El árbol de jabón (The Soap Tree)*, suggests that women in Quiatoni should turn off their televisions and consider locally produced soap products. This video has in turn led to an environmental impact study and the possibility of manufacturing health and beauty commodities in Quiatoni. Both *Buscando bienestar* and *El árbol de jabón* demonstrate how comtech-mediated transnational networks of advocacy project a community's struggles with, and its proposed solutions to, globalization far beyond the local scale.

Production of the second video for which Grupo Solidario has received funding has been stalled for a year now, which draws our attention back to the local scale. Although Angeles Martínez continues to credit his Culturas Populares projects to Grupo Solidario and remains a strong presence in their favorable coverage in the local press (Esteva 2001a, 2001b), he did not travel to Quiatoni between 1999 and 2000. He says that his absence was an effort to address accusations of paternalism and a reflection of his current focus on the urban children of migrants from Quiatoni. Other people familiar with the situation suggest that Angeles

Martínez did not visit Quiatoni because he had so alienated local authorities and residents with his claims to speak for them that he was no longer warmly welcomed. The recent shift in local community leadership in Quiatoni at the start of 2002 had everyone hoping the postponed video's production will begin soon.

The ways in which entangled institutional linkages and the concept of etnodesarrollo shaped the production of *Buscando bienestar* reveal the importance of urban, bureaucratic nodes in the networks of advocacy seeking to facilitate Indigenous self-representation in Mexico. As the recent tensions in Quiatoni suggest, however, jumping scales and transnational success at making development cultural cannot alone solve problematic sociospatial relations at the local level. Indeed, due to the politics of representation, it may exacerbate them. Although *Buscando bienestar* never directly mentions Indigenous ethnicity per se, theorizations of Indigenous identity and place-based politics of representation help explain the video's look at community development. Grupo Solidario utilizes ethnopolitics to ground its representations of Quiatoni. While its representation cautiously attempts to police borders (identify what fits this place), mine has focused on the ways place and geographies of belonging are rewritten through video and the relations that made its production and mobility possible.

NOTES

This essay grew out of a project funded by a Dissertation Research Grant, no. SES-0136035, from the National Science Foundation's Science and Technology Studies Program and was previously published in slightly different form in another book (Cresswell and Verstraete 2003). I greatly appreciate the encouragement of that and this book's editors and am forever grateful for the generosity of the people whose work and experiences I explore here.

1. The video's Zapotec title is *Been rgil gialnzak*. This is also the Zapotec name of Grupo Solidario de Quiatoni (Quiatoni Solidarity Group), often translated as "People Looking for Well-Being." Although the video's dialogue is in Zapotec, and the video was originally released with Spanish subtitles, I relied on the English translations finalized by Martha Rees, an anthropologist who has long-standing relations with Grupo Solidario de Quiatoni.

2. All quotes are directly from the film's English subtitles.

3. Activists lobby for causes with which they self-identify and advocates lobby on the behalf of the identity and livelihood of others.

4. The federal government has since effectively stalled their implementation and intense debate continues to hinder legislation based on the signed accords.

5. See the discussion by Fox (1996) regarding the concept of the "thickening" of civil society.

6. Information about Angeles Martínez's life stems from interviews and conversations with him and people in Oaxaca who have worked with him.

7. Grupo Solidario worked with Mexican institutions such as the Secretaría de Agricultura, Ganadería, Desarrollo Rural, Pesca y Alimentación, and the Instituto Nacional Indigenista. The group also drew on the support of the Dutch Embassy, the Italian NGO Movimiento Laico América Latina, and Grupo de Apoyo al Desarrollo Etnico, an NGO established by Varese and other advocates in the mid-1980s in order to channel resources garnered from the U.S. Inter-American Foundation.

CHAPTER 10

"TO BREATHE TWO AIRS":

EMPOWERING INDIGENOUS SÁMI MEDIA

Sari Pietikäinen

Sámi media exist so that it would be possible for the Sámi people to live as Sámi.

—Niila, *veteran Sámi journalist, personal communication, March 2003*

To be a Sámi today is "to breathe two airs," to quote a Sámi saying.[1] Sápmi, the Sámi homeland spreading across four countries—Norway, Sweden, Finland, and Russia—is a region in which majority and Indigenous cultures, languages, and ways of living have coexisted in the same territory for centuries. Today, the Sámi community is transnational, multilingual, pluricultural, and partly diasporic, including—depending on the criteria used—approximately fifty thousand to eighty thousand people, of whom seven thousand to seventy-five hundred live within the borders of Finland and nearly half of them outside the Sámi homeland (Aikio and Aikio 2001; Aikio-Puoskari 2001).[2] According to the legal definition, which is primarily based on linguistic criteria, a Sámi is a person who identifies himself or herself as a Sámi and who has, or at least one of whose parents or grandparents has, learned Sámi as a first language. Being Sámi also means belonging to and participating in a complex network of families, shared histories and circumstances, and cultural practices. Definitions of Sámi have been contested and renegotiated from time to time, a typical consequence of both colonialization and the self-empowering goals and aspirations of the Sámi people (cf. Kulonen, Seurujäriv-Kari, and Pulkkinen 2005).

Sámi history provides a story of how Indigenous culture and language become endangered. Starting in the sixteenth century with wider political and cultural transformations—such as the migration of settlers from the south, the formation of the states of Norway, Sweden, Finland, and Russia, and the strengthening of the church—the traditional Sámi communal organization (a network of villages with exclusive right to use a specific area for hunting and reindeer herding) was gradually broken, and Sámi claims to ancestral lands were ignored by the states. By the nineteenth century, the states claimed ownership of the northern areas (Lehtola 1997: 30–34). The result has been a gradual loss of cultural, economic, and juridical autonomy among the Sámi. With this loss, and with assimilation, the Sámi have witnessed the marginalization of their languages, ways of living, and societal organization (Aikio and Aikio 2001; Scheinin 2001). Today, Sápmi is divided by four different state borders and by four different political and legal systems—a discontinuity that disrupts traditional Sámi communal life and livelihoods. Within two generations, all ten Sámi languages have become endangered or nearly extinct. Presently, nine Sámi languages are still spoken. Today, all Sámi people speak the majority language(s) of their particular nation-state, while approximately half of the Sámi people also speak one of the Sámi languages (Aikio-Puoskari 2001). Contrary to popular imagery, a minority of Sámi make a living by herding reindeer. Rather, in the north—for Sámi and non-Sámi alike—the service industry (and tourism in particular) provides the majority of the jobs. This small transnational minority community faces challenges of high unemployment, an aging population, and a lack of resources.

Despite these challenges, the Sámi experience also provides a story of the strength, endurance, and flexibility of an Indigenous community and its empowering activities to ensure survival. To counteract colonializing practices and harmful modernization processes, the Sámi have sought out ways to advance their rights socially and politically as well as novel ways to articulate the dynamic Sámi cultural experience and transmit languages to the next generation. The pan-Sámi movement, particularly strong since the 1950s, has actively promoted these objectives.

The Sámi people have been recognized as an Indigenous people with due rights according to the 1989 ILO Convention number 169 on Indigenous and Tribal people. The pan-Sámi, nongovernmental Sámi Council works to further secure and promote Sámi rights and culture.[3] The Sámi Council has also taken an active role in the United Nations, in the Council of Indigenous Peoples, and in the Arctic Council. In addition, in all three Nordic countries, the Sámi now have representative Sámi Parliaments, whose purpose is to oversee Sámi rights and to enhance the economic, social, and cultural conditions of the Sámi (Aikio-Puoskari 2001: 20–21; Lehtola 1997: 78–83). Furthermore, in 1997, a joint parliamentary council was founded, including the Sámi Parliaments of Norway, Sweden, and Finland. In these countries, Sámi organizing has resulted in legislation securing linguistic (e.g., Finland's 1991 Language Act) and cultural rights and autonomy (Finland's 1995 Act on the Sámi Parliament). Furthermore, Sámi politics have been manifested in the establishment and reinforcement of various Sámi institutions and organizations—including Sámi-language education and daycare, Sámi arts and handicrafts, and Sámi media. One empowering goal of pan-Sámi politics is to continue to contribute to a sense of a shared transnational Sámi identity and the construction of symbolic Sámi nationhood, symbolized by a flag, national day, and anthem—and, significantly, by the existence of Sámi media. To borrow Benedict Anderson's (1983) idea of imagined communities, Sámi community is "imagined" in the sense that both the Sámi nation and Sámi national identity have been socially constructed, and in this process, the media have played a central role.

These different circumstances contribute to what it means to be Sámi today. They also highlight the importance of Sámi media in providing a space for voicing the community's agenda and concerns, as well as in serving as a resource for communal and linguistic revitalization. Sámi Radio has been a lifeline for endangered Sámi languages, and new media forms—the Internet, television news broadcasts, rap music, etc.—address the Sámi community across national borders. Sámi media now offer a significant public voice for the transnational Sámi nation, reaching out to its own people and outsiders alike.

A multiplicity of practices and experiences characterize the ongoing transformations among the Sámi and in Sámi media. My ethnographic research focuses particularly on the possibilities for and constraints on Sámi-language media as they empower communal organizations and revitalize the Sámi language.[4] I hope to show the variety of forces and tendencies that work, often simultaneously, for either the survival and empowerment of the Sámi community or its further endangerment. Being a majority member myself, this research is also my small attempt to continue a dialogue between different positions of knowing, sharing, and working together.

Theoretically and methodologically, this research draws on critical discourse analysis (Fairclough 1992, 2003; Scollon 2001; Wodak and Myers 2001), dialogism (Bakhtin 1986; Dufva 2004), and participatory journalism

(Cadiz 2005). Thus, I attempt to bring together the perspectives of both individual experiences and social practices, including institutional policies, professional practices, and power relations (see Pietikäinen and Dufva 2006). In so doing, I see Sámi media as part of a larger network of culturally and politically significant forms and processes that contribute to the production and circulation of a repertoire of images and narratives paramount for the construction of identities, nations, and communities (cf. Appadurai 1986; Ginsburg, Abu-Lughod, and Larkin 2002; and Rantanen 2005). I conceptualize the Sámi media as a space of experiences, contestations, and negotiations, signifying and carrying along certain perspectives and seeking out and voicing communal, political, and individual voices in a historic, political, and cultural context. My goal is to reveal the places where empowering practices for journalists exist, emerge, or are particularly needed. These fall under the topics of visibility, Indigenous information, community building, and language revitalization.

THE SÁMI MEDIA SPACE

The Sámi media space[5] is diverse but uneven. Radio is the strongest medium, while the press languishes due to lack of resources and subscribers. Television programs in Sámi languages or produced by and for Sámi are quite rare. However, the continuously developing Internet is showing interesting potential for the Sámi.

The development of Finnish Sámi radio in the state-owned Finnish public broadcasting company Yleisradio Oy (YLE) resulted from years of persistent work by the Finnish Sámi community. Veli-Pekka Lehtola (1997) describes the various stages of Sámi radio development, from the first sporadic programs in the Sámi language in 1936, to the beginning of a regular schedule of Sámi broadcasting in 1947, to the dynamic Sámi radio of the present. Today, the radio has its own channel and broadcasts a wide range of programs, about forty-eight hours each week, in all three Sámi languages spoken in Finnish Sápmi. In Norway and Sweden, the development of Sámi radio has been roughly the same (see Greller 1996; Skogerbø 2001; and Solbakk 1997). These Sámi radio systems have, over time, established a successful policy of cooperation among themselves, and today they have an extensive program exchange (Greller 1996: 52; Solbakk 1997: 178).

Sámi television programs are still rare. Until 2001, in Finland and

Sweden, Sámi programs were broadcast sporadically and often outside of prime time. The situation in Norway was only slightly better; in 2000, there was a weekly children's program and one satirical talk-show series, both Sámi-produced in a Sámi language (Skogerbø 2001: 163). In the fall of 2001, after years of preparation, jointly produced transnational Sámi television news broadcasts were launched. A fifteen-minute television news program, *tv-Oddasat,* is broadcast nationwide on weekdays in Norway and Sweden, with subtitles in majority languages. In Finland, it is broadcast in the northern part of the country without subtitles, while a subtitled version airs later in the evening in Finnish on the YLE24 digital television channel.

A chronic lack of resources restricts the potential of newspapers published in Sámi languages. There are no daily Sámi newspapers in Finland and Sweden. The newspapers *Aššu* and *Min Ággi* come out twice a week in Norway, with more than one thousand subscribers throughout Sápmi (Solbakk 1997: 174–75). In Finland, one magazine, *Anarâš,* is published quarterly. There are also many other periodical publications and youth and children's magazines published only a few times a year (see Greller 1995: 47–48; Kauranen and Tuori 2001; Lehtola 1997; and Suihkonen 2003: 15).

The Internet offers interesting opportunities for Sámi-language media: various Sámi organizations and groups have been developing their own Web sites in recent years. Today, Sámi radio programs and TV news broadcasts can also be listened to or watched via the Internet. As Internet access is provided free at libraries, workplaces, and schools—and as an increasing number of households gain access, too—the Internet is becoming a viable media alternative for members of the Sámi community.

SÁMI ALTERNATIVES: BECOMING VISIBLE

The Sámi media function in a complex and paradoxical terrain of language endangerment and revitalization and of political struggle and negotiation of Indigenous Sámi rights. This terrain, furthermore, is affected by larger, partly global, partly national economic and transnational changes affecting all people living in this northernmost part of the European Community. The everyday experiences of the Sámi are shot through with empowerment and powerlessness, creativity and exhaustion, hope and despair.

To illustrate the territory where the Sámi media work, particularly the

Pekka's illustration of his usage of Sámi and Finnish languages. (In this black and white reproduction, gray = red and black = blue.) COURTESY OF THE AUTHOR.

multivalent relationships that inhere between Indigenous and majority languages and communities in Sápmi, let us look at a drawing (fig. 10.1) made by Pekka, a Sámi-language activist and journalist interviewed in April 2005. Pekka depicts the places and people with whom he can use a Sámi language (in red)—a right guaranteed by the Finnish Sámi Language Act in 1991—and in which situations he needs to use majority languages (in blue).

According to his personal language policy, Pekka always starts his conversation in Sámi as a way to resist language shift. He continues using Sámi when in Sámi-community domains—e.g., political organizations such as the Sámi Parliament (*Sämitigge*), Sámi-language classrooms (*škovla*), or Sámi-language media (*Anarâš*). Also, he uses Sámi in his private life: with his family, some of his friends, and with his cat. But whenever he has dealings with majority institutions or authorities—municipal authorities (*kieldâ*), police (*poolis*), church (*kirkko*), as well as with much of the mainstream media—he is forced to shift into the majority language. And if he were to choose to exercise his right to use his own language when speaking to the authorities, an interpreter would be called on—that, ironically, being Pekka.

Pekka's drawing also maps the multilayered postcolonial situation in which the hybrid experiences and conditions of the Indigenous Sámi people—and their media—are located. From the perspective of discourse analysis, Sámi media are seen as an emergent and shifting site of dominant and alternative cultural, journalistic, and linguistic practices: narrating, representing, and resisting constructions of what it means to be Sámi today. Such media activities also contribute to ongoing processes of imagining and culturally establishing a transnational Sámi nation. Against these positive tendencies, the economic conditions and imperatives severely limit the possibilities of Sámi media. Also, Sámi media are understaffed, with limited resources and a fragmented audience. Sirpa, a female TV journalist, described these contradictions:

> Sometimes I feel great pride in the fact that I work expressly in Sámi-language news. We are something great, something that functions in three countries regardless of the borders. At times, though, I'm ashamed of the quality of our broadcasts, but one cannot always do better and better. In Finland, the reason for insufficient work is, above all, lack of resources. Now the furthest parts of Sápmi are not covered, because nobody has time to go there. The production obligation—five stories and five news flashes per week—for two journalists is totally impossible to carry through. This causes unnecessary stress and dreams about giving my notice. Now we are totally exhausted, and I get nightmares. At times, I am terrified when I think that I am not even thirty yet and still, I feel killing exhaustion. (personal communication, August 2005)

Given these complications, the mere existence of Indigenous media signals the vitality and cultural legitimacy of the Sámi community. Minority media typically go hand-in-hand with political mobilization and organization, increased cooperation, and demands for recognition of Indigenous rights (see, e.g., Browne 2005; Cottle 2000). Now the struggles are to gain wider visibility for negotiations about financial resources, broadcasting times, and channels in national media space (Prins 2002a; Roth 2000).

Gaining more and wider media visibility enhances opportunities to get (better) recognized as an Indigenous community entitled to specific rights, while controlling media production provides possibilities for achieving that recognition (more) on one's own terms. The Sámi-language media locate the Indigenous community as a part of a national or transnational mediascape. This, in turn, enables both the minority and majority members to see and recognize the Indigenous community as a part of the (trans)national assemblage (cf. Ginsburg 2003: 78). From a journalistic perspective, media construct a public space that is critical for political processes and democratic activities (see Hartley and McKee 2001; Hartley 2004; and Howley 2005). For example, Mike Cormack (1998: 49) emphasizes that minority media are never merely linguistic or cultural resources but are always crucial for the political activity and participation of the community. In the case of the Sámi, their media reaffirm the existence and vitality of the Indigenous community, as these journalists attest. Heta, a female Sámi TV journalist interviewed in 2003, noted: "We are also a sign saying, 'Hi, we are here, we do exist'—a sign both to our own people as well as to the outsiders" (personal communication, March 2003). Niila, a male Sámi radio journalist, also interviewed in 2003, added, "As the radio is 'around the clock' almost, you hear it here and there, so that must be a signal that our culture is not going to be destroyed at all, but that it is something worth putting your money on" (personal communication, March 2003).

Alternative, radical, and oppositional representations of the Sámi are needed. Colonialist discourses about the Sámi, stemming from historical and anthropological studies done in the nineteenth and twentieth centuries, represent the Sámi as uncultivated, mystic, erotic, and disconnected from their own history, culture, political organization, and achievements. Although these representations are often disputed, they still circulate in dominant popular media, advertisements, tourism, and folklore in Finland, Sweden, Norway, and Russia (Lehtola 1999; Pietikäinen and Leppänen 2006). Although mainstream news journalism—framed by journalistic ideals of impartiality and neutrality—avoids blatant stereotyping, it is still rare for Sámi political movements to get mainstream coverage of internal and transnational processes and of Sámi achievements (cf. Pietikäinen 2000, 2003). Sámi journalists describe the mainstream media publicity on Sámi people and Sámi issues as superficial, one-sided, and often negative. And such publicity underscores the need for counterpublicity. The journalist Niila explained in an interview: "Well, our own media were really important for us because we do not have national or local press. Those majority media were blind, clearly taking their side with the majority society. What they told about the Sámi were, should I say, amusing things, stereotyping the Sámi people. And they did not report anything about the Sámi movement or the internal affairs here" (personal communication, March 2003).

The long-standing stereotypical representation of the Sámi people, combined with their very limited visibility in contemporary national media space, is also manifest in scant and inaccurate knowledge about them among the majority members. Given that in a relatively small Finnish society (5.2 million inhabitants), Sámi is one of the four officially recognized language minorities, awareness and knowledge about them might be expected. An extract from a focus group discussion about Finnish majority students' reception of *tv-Ođđasat* illustrates the invisibility of the Sámi community for majority students:

> [Student 1]: I wonder why it is so difficult to realize how many people are actually living up there. Somehow you just keep on thinking that maybe one or two people live somewhere in there.
>
> [Student 2]: Right. And then, you think, it is just that Lapland where nothing happens except there are those reindeers there.
>
> [Student 1]: Yeah. Right.
>
> [Student 3]: And those mountains where you can do downhill skiing.
>
> [Student 1]: Right. So you don't actually realize that, yes, they need to have all these administrative and other stuff organized in there too.
>
> [Student 3]: And from this news broadcast you get the picture that "Hi, we are organized and we can take care of these things." (Focus Group 2, personal communication, March 2005)

The students' reactions illustrate the contemporary consequence of colonialist and marginalizing representations of the Sámi. For the majority of Finns, this northern part of the country continues to be only "Lapland": a place for tourism, Santa Claus, vast sceneries, and untouched nature. Sápmi, existing simultaneously at the same geographic location, continues to be unrecognized and unfamiliar. Because the majority society, to a large extent, makes the decisions regarding laws and finance, Indigenous people must raise awareness and gain recognition among the majority. It becomes a matter of survival to establish that Indigenous people have special rights and their own culture.

The basic journalistic task—to provide accurate and relevant information—is, of course, a central task for Sámi journalists, too, but the information must also be delivered in Sámi languages and about Sámi topics. News reporting in the Sámi context includes a mixture of new happenings as well as daily life events in the Sámi community combined with a group of culture-specific Sámi news topics that are continuously followed: "language issues, language rights, hunting, reindeer, fish, reindeer husbandry and traditional livelihoods" (journalist Heta, personal communication, March 2003). This kind of an Indigenous news agenda rearticulates and recontextualizes traditional aspects of the Sámi culture in contemporary media space. This usually also means incorporating these topics into situations in which both majority and Sámi interests and cultural practices are intertwined, mixed, and embedded. Stories of language shift and crossings, popular culture and contemporary art, employment and economic interests in tourism, reindeer herding, and fishing are some examples of the meeting points of two cultures.

A pressing challenge for Sámi journalists seems to be whether to include in *TV-Oḏḏasat* major national and international news events that do not have any direct link to or impact on the Sámi community. So far, major events such as the tsunami in December 2004, or the wars in Iraq or Palestine in 2004–5 have been covered in Sámi news. Arguments for inclusion stem from the "full service principle"—echoing the national broadcasting company's ideologies. The 2001 Sámi news policy stated that *TV-Oḏḏasat* should cover all important news events so that the viewer should have no need to watch any other news. The scope has since been narrowed to focus on Sámi issues: in the latest news policy from 2005, the goal of the television news is to cover relevant events in Sápmi and report other news events only when something very exceptional happens in other parts of the world.

This development points toward the multiple preferences and loyalties of audiences and the unique role and nature of Indigenous media space. Sámi journalists considered the idea that the Sámi audience would only watch Sámi TV news unrealistic. Rather, their experience was that the "market value" of the Sámi news is that it provides distinctive Indigenous information unavailable anywhere else. Since there is no audience research available on Sámi television news in Finland, the journalists in their negotiations rely on their own experiences and feedback obtained from the audience. In daily reality, the tension between goals and resources often comes head-to-head.

These various tendencies and conditions are constantly being negotiated as the Sámi media news editors and journalists jointly create and readjust Sámi news policy and practices that will implement practical journalistic work. This means finding a place for Sámi media in local, national, and global mediascapes as well as identifying audiences and defining the mission for the Sámi news. It also means reevaluating traditional journalistic news criteria that do not seem altogether compatible when situated in transnational Sámi experiences and community.

BRIDGING TRANSNATIONAL SÁMI COMMUNITY

The need to rewrite and rethink the role and criteria of Sámi news indicates the ongoing process of searching for, and articulating, common grounds for shared Sámi identity and the symbolic Sámi nation. Among journalists, to contribute to this sense of "Sáminess" is also an important part of the mission of the Sámi media, as Sirpa, the female TV journalist, explained: "We are one same big nation, although scattered in different countries. I believe that joint TV news binds us together as a nation. The news is also a good way to learn about neighboring societies, although that is not the main goal" (personal communication, August 2005). This power of media to connect people and to reinforce a sense of belonging has made them a vital part of Indigenous community building and identity politics (see Browne 2005; Georgiou 2001; Rantanen 2005; Roth 2000; and Sreberny 2002). Also, Sámi media attempt to bridge localized experiences and dialogue across national, cultural, and language borders (Lehtonen 1997; Sara 2004). Since their foundation, the Sámi media have tried to be inclusive rather than exclusive. Their language policy, for instance, embraces and promotes all Sámi languages, regardless of the fact that some of the languages have only three hundred to four hundred speakers.

New technologies have contributed to the potential for the media to connect the Sámi community. Virtual visits to the homeland are one way to strengthen the sense of belonging and Indigenous identity, particularly in a diasporic situation (Tufte 2003). By crossing cultural and geographical borders, the Internet has become an increasingly important Sámi medium, reaching out particularly to those Sámi people (more than half the Sámi population) living outside of Sápmi.

Producing a voice audible across various national (state) borders presents a challenge to Sámi journalists. Sirpa provided an example of one possible solution: "We could improve our TV news by connecting the stories to our neighboring countries, too. In this way, we would better address the audience in Norway and Sweden. For example, in Finland, a reindeer herdsman earns this much from one reindeer, but in Sweden, the sum is this. We don't manage to do this often, but perhaps things will get better once the cooperation between countries functions better" (personal communication, August 2005).

Differences in news routines, journalistic practices, and resources between Sámi newsrooms in three countries make working together rather difficult (Rasmussen 1999; Sara 2004). The national broadcasting companies hosting the Sámi media differ in their news ideologies, and these differences filter into Sámi journalistic practices. Heta, a TV journalist, summarized the difference as follows: "YLE [the Finnish public broadcasting company]: factual, neutral. NRK [Norwegian Broadcasting Corporation]: tabloid, sensational" (personal communication, August 2005). Negotiations between localized information and journalistic practices are tense at times, and changes happen slowly. Sirpa expressed her frustration: "The different perspectives on news among the countries handicaps our job. This topic is loudly discussed in the meetings, and the fact that the 'real' news falls in the shadow of scandal news shakes the foundation of the cooperation. These issues are always talked about, but nothing ever changes" (personal communication, August 2005).

These incompatibilities mean that, at times, stories by YLE Sámi journalists are put on hold or are never broadcast by NRK-run broadcast news management. According to the feedback they have received from the news editors in Norway, who are responsible for the final cut of TV-Oddasat, this is because the editor has perceived their stories as too local, addressing too small an audience, or otherwise not newsworthy enough. To think and act across national borders, to address a Sámi audience, and to reflect one Sámi nation is also challenging, simply because this ongoing process of constructing cultural identity is necessarily happening in hectic newsrooms in the midst of many competing processes.

REVITALIZING COMMUNITY AND ENDANGERED LANGUAGES

The comment by the veteran Sámi journalist Niila, quoted at the beginning of this chapter, also captures one of the clearest distinctions between minority and mainstream media, namely, their relationship to their audience. Browne (2005: 113) argues that many ethnic minority media services, rather than *speak to* their audience, consider it essential to *work with* their audience, a community. For the Sámi media, close collaboration with their community is both a guiding principle and a practical consequence due to its small population. Close collaboration, in turn, is needed for endorsement of goals for communal and linguistic revitalization.

This idea of participatory media and empowering journalistic practices has been developed in minority media, but also in new social and civic journalism movements, which seek to make journalism more relevant and meaningful to its community (see Atton 2002; Couldry 2003; and Sirianni and Friedland 2001). Alternative practices often aim to enable community members to participate in journalism by, for example, giving more power to community members to set their own agendas. Multivocal, participatory Sámi media open up the airwaves to everyday experiences, to the smallest events and achievements of the community. A news report can be, for example, about the first person in the world passing an examination in Skolt Sámi. Participatory programs in endangered languages create a vibrant Indigenous-language domain where one's own language can be used and heard: a public proof that one's own language is good and vital enough to be used in the media context and by new generations of speakers. Due to the closeness of the community, multivocality in Sámi programs can be put into practice rather easily. In a 2003 interview, Niila estimated that "the majority of the Sámi people have participated in our programs in a one way or another" (personal communication, 2003). At the same time, however, Sámi journalists are acutely aware of the lack of young people's and children's voices in their programs. Irja, a female radio journalist, described the significance of children's voices in Sámi programs in a 2003 interview: "I have received feedback many times about interviewing the children. Their parents call back to me and say that 'our Ville indeed speaks Sámi' and 'Mikko speaks Sámi so well.' They have been surprised by how well the children speak Sámi. And this means that all of them are listening to the programs as well" (personal communication, 2003).

At the moment, only one weekly children's radio program is broadcast in Sámi in Finland. There are, however, serious plans to start joint Sámi children's broadcasts in the near future. In Inari, the Sámi journalists worry about not reaching the young audience partly because of a lack of programs, partly due to competition with national and global media and, ultimately, because of the language endangerment and shift. Given

Johanna's representation of herself as a Sámi and Finnish speaker. COURTESY OF
THE AUTHOR.

that Sámi children are the next generation of Sámi language and media
users, the worry is understandable.

An example of this may be seen in a 2005 case study examining language and media usage among multilingual Sámi school pupils. The
study was comprised of questionnaires, self-portraits, and interviews
with twenty-nine students. Twelve-year-old Johanna's self-portrait of her
language usage illustrates a central finding (fig. 10.2).

As a Sámi speaker, Johanna depicts herself facing the viewer with a
smile. In addition, she has drawn her family and a reindeer herd. When
asked about the picture, Johanna explains that she likes to speak Sámi
and that she uses it with her family and when reindeer herding. Yet
Johanna portrays herself as a Finnish speaker in the living room at her
home, watching television alone and listening to music. In the interview,
Johanna says that she watches Finnish TV channels and listens to Finnish
pop music. When asked explicitly about her usage of Sámi-language
media, Johanna mentions that she watches *TV-Oḏḏasat* at times in case
somebody she knows has gotten on a news broadcast, but otherwise she
does not care that much about Sámi media. Johanna's drawing illustrates
a visual pattern noticeable in other children's drawings as well: Sámi

language is visually connected with nature, family, and a traditional Sámi way of life, notably reindeer herding, while Finnish is associated with leisure time spent with Finnish (or English) television programs, books, popular music, and computer games. The case study fuels the worry of the journalists: Sámi media do not have a footing among young Sámi.

However, popular Sámi music provides a sign of hope. Inari Sámi rap musician Amoc is very popular among the Sámi children in the study. His music has inspired some children to create their own rap lyrics in Sámi, and one of the schoolchildren in the study has been on stage with Amoc. Journalist Pekka explained Amoc's popularity in an interview:

> Of course Amoc is quite an idol among the young people. Besides, rap is fashionable. That's why rapping in Inari Sámi is influential, because it already has a place, let's say, in kids' and in young people's lives. It's just like the missionaries who build their churches on the old sacrificial sites. People were accustomed to visit those places. And the place was the same, but suddenly the contents were changed. It's a bit like this with rapping in Inari Sámi, though of course it is not necessarily consciously planned that way. (personal communication, 2005)

For the whole Sámi community, the maintenance and revitalization of Sámi languages is one of the utmost worries. By doing programs in Sámi languages, the journalists hope to strengthen the usage of endangered languages in contemporary conditions. If we take seriously the Sapir-Whorf hypothesis—that our ways of thinking and seeing the world are shaped by the language we use—then Sámi-language media facilitate Indigenous ways of knowing, sharing, and being (Maffi 2002; Dufva 2004; see also Lee 1960).

From a language revitalization perspective, then, Sámi media can, on the one hand, be a language reservoir: a space for remembrance that enables reliving and transmitting past experiences, places, and ways of speaking and knowing. The popularity of rebroadcasts from the early days of Sámi radio speaks volumes about the importance of longing and remembering. In daily journalistic work, remembering is manifested in the importance of knowing the "elders' language"—in particular, the correct pronunciations of words used in traditional ways of hunting, fishing, and herding. At the same time, however, Sámi media are also like language workshops where ways of speaking Sámi are continuously translated and transformed / transposed into present situations. New words are invented, and Sámi languages are used in new contexts including, for example, the Internet, popular music, and tourism. New language domains are ways to revitalize endangered languages—the heritage and resources that the Sámi community cherish. Niila summarized the importance of Indigenous languages when he said, "It is the social significance of language. It is not only a tool for information, but is also a tool for thinking and important for self-esteem. It is socially significant both to the community as a whole and to each individual personally" (personal communication, 2003).

CONCLUSION

Sámi media provide one viable way for the Sámi community to represent, negotiate, and construct Sámi identity and a symbolic Sámi nation. Although the scarcity of resources limits this potential, the production and programming of media on the community's own terms has opened up new possibilities. For Sámi media in Inari, the main goals seem to be to increase visibility, to provide good quality Indigenous information, to contribute to Sámi nation-building, and to enhance language revitalization. At the same time, due to the daily practices and challenges of the journalistic profession, these goals are at times difficult to achieve. Moreover, different Sámi newsrooms have pursued these goals and navigated these challenges in distinct ways. These different approaches sometimes complicate efforts at pan-Sámi cooperation.

In terms of their audience, the Sámi media also seem to be approaching a crossroads: will the future Sámi media focus on Sámi-speaking audiences only, or will they try to address people without Sámi language skills or even people without Sámi background? These questions are located in a complex terrain of audience rating, production financing and communal and language revitalization. Perhaps a translation of the Sámi saying "to breathe two airs" into a media context would necessitate a mixture of programs addressing a variety of audiences—Sámi voices dialoguing across borders and territories.

NOTES

1. Sámi are historically better known as Lapps, a term no longer preferred due to its derogatory connotations.
2. This latter group is the focus of this study. Although the Indigenous status of

the Sámi people is recognized in all Scandinavian countries and their rights are partly secured by legislation, only Norway has signed the International Labor Organization (ILO) Convention no. 169 on Indigenous Peoples. Consequently, land rights are disputed in both Sweden and Finland, where the traditional Sámi lands are presently owned by the state (Scheinin 2001). As my data mainly derive from daily practices and experiences around Sámi media in Inari, Finland, I focus primarily on the Sámi in Finland, but when possible I discuss the situation in Sweden and Norway.

3. See their Web site at www.saamicouncil.net.

4. This article is part of a fieldwork-based research project in progress (2003–present), Empowering Potential of Ethnic Minority Media, funded by the Academy of Finland. The data so far include interviews with Sámi journalists (n = 29), focus-group discussion (n = 4) with the journalists and with the majority audience members (n = 19), and related questionnaires (n = 38), drawings by Sami children and their interviews (n = 29), and drawings and essays by the journalists (n = 7).

5. Here, I use the term *media space* to describe the specific cultural and political negotiations taking place between Sámi groups and Sámi media producers. I reserve Appadurai's (1990) concept of "mediascape" to situate Sámi media in the broader flows of national and global institutions, though the distinction is a heuristic one. As I argue here, Sámi nationhood is already dynamic and transnational.

CHAPTER 11

INDIGENOUS MEDIA AS

AN IMPORTANT RESOURCE FOR

RUSSIA'S INDIGENOUS PEOPLES

Galina Diatchkova

Across the vast northern lands of the Russian Federation, scores of Indigenous media producers dedicate their words and work to helping their peoples make positive social and political changes in their own Indigenous communities as well as in the larger Russian society. In this capacity, they serve as significant advocates and mediators with government officials and larger nongovernmental organizations. Among them, Valentina Uspenskaya was instrumental in establishing Kamchatka's Aboriginal newspaper, *Aborigen Kamchatki*, in the mid-1990s, and under her leadership, *AK* has become a significant vehicle for addressing the Indigenous issues of Kamchatka.[1] Elena Timonina, a Chukchi television journalist in Anadyr City, Chukotka, produced Chukchi-language TV programs, including news and documentaries about Chukchi issues. Audiences across Russia—non-Indigenous and Indigenous alike—were impressed by *When the Men Cry*, a film about the education of a Chukchi boy as a reindeer herder that Timonina coproduced with Alexander Rudoy, a non-Indigenous Russian. In 2005, her work as a journalist and editor was recognized by a prestigious award from the Sovet Federatsii (Federation Council of Russian Federation). Representing many local Indigenous people, the Chukchi journalist Margarita Belichenko produces radio news programs in the Chukchi language. In spite of the hard conditions and very low salary that characterize her work, Belichenko strives, like many journalists in the northern regions, to provide high quality and interesting reports in dialogue with the Indigenous peoples of Chukotka.

The 1990s witnessed the growth of the Indigenous movement in northern Russia and the increasingly vital role that media is playing in this groundswell. Because of the dedicated work of people like Uspenskaya, Timonina, and Belichenko, Indigenous media in the 1990s and early 2000s have flourished and supported Aboriginal mobilization. In this chapter, I provide background on the growth of the Indigenous movement in the past decades, partnered with the development of Indigenous broadcasting and journalism and now strongly supported in some regions by a network of computer-based information centers. While discussing the development of these media networks, I provide insight into the cultural and institutional politics of Indigenous media in post-Soviet Russia, the challenges facing Indigenous media initiatives (both political and financial), the development of professional Indigenous media networks across the Arctic and in the Russian Federation, and the development of international networks of support for the Indigenous movement and its media.

INDIGENOUS MOBILIZATION BY MEDIA

The Soviet period of perestroika ("changing the political ideas") during the second half of the 1980s led to an intensification of Indigenous identity in Russia's northern, Siberian, and far eastern regions, home to more than forty Indigenous groups representing about 250,000 people.[2] From this social and political movement emerged the nongovernmental organization (NGO) RAIPON (Russian Association of Indigenous Peoples of the North), formed by the first Congress of Indigenous Peoples of the North, Siberia, and Far East in 1990. One of RAIPON's goals was general recognition by the dominant society of Indigenous interests and rights.

By dominant society, I mean institutions and ideologies that have furthered the interests of the state and have brought the outside social environment to bear on Russia's northern Indigenous peoples. In recent centuries, the northern Indigenous peoples had been subjects of, and colonized by, the Russian Empire, whose 1822 charter outlined how the Indigenous peoples of Siberia were to be managed and linked Indigenous rights to Native territories and their resources. Throughout this imperial period, during which time Christian missionaries (both Orthodox and Protestant) also introduced their religion to the peoples of the north, the Indigenous peoples were able to preserve and maintain much of their traditional heritage and nomadic lifestyle (Diatchkova 2005: 220–22; Alekseenko 1979: 50).[3]

Following the formation of the Union of Soviet Socialist Republics in 1922, the Indigenous peoples became the subjects of a new regime. Over time, the policies of the Soviet state toward these peoples varied greatly. From 1924 to 1935, the Assistance Committee for the Numerically Small Peoples of the Northern Territories governed the Indigenous groups, with efforts to develop and promote written languages, national literatures, and national mass media (which would, in fact, serve as the basic propaganda channel for Communist ideas). During this period, Indigenous languages received enhanced recognition by the state and were used by government bodies, legal proceedings, and other cultural and educational institutions. However, beginning in the mid-1930s through the 1950s, these policies were replaced by a state policy emphasizing the integration of Indigenous peoples into larger Soviet industrial society (Pika and Prokhorov 1994: 3). State campaigns intensified against religious belief systems, traditional customs, cults, and the rites of Indigenous peoples. The state enforced property ownership and collectivization, often in violent ways. Indigenous people were in many cases forcibly resettled from their traditional territories into new, compact settlements. In many cases, these processes transformed nomadic societies into sedentary ones, as the state also intensified the industrial development of the northern region during this time (Diatchkova 2005: 223).

By the late twentieth century, the dominant Soviet society exhibited an array of industrial and postindustrial features and institutions such as urbanization, rationalization, bureaucratization, the importance of market relations, and in particular, a high level of dependence on the rapid transfer of information. Although Soviet officials initially supported the emerging Indigenous movement during the early 1990s, that support soon gave way as political opposition to regional authority and local self-government developed. A history of paternalistic control, coupled with disregard for international standards for human and Aboriginal rights, prevailed. In this transitional perestroika period, the transformation of the country's economic and political system led to a severe economic crisis.[4] During this time, the growing Indigenous movement focused on issues of sustainable development and on attaining social equality in the dominant society.

In his discussions of modernization processes and their effects on traditional societies (in this case, Indigenous ethnic groups), Samuel Huntington (1968) noted that the highest political mobilization occurs during such transitional periods, pointing out that urbanization, education, and media generate the new needs and ideas of Indigenous peoples to help these groups to achieve their rights. The Russian realities of the 1990s validated this thesis. During perestroika the associations in the villages, districts, and areas (*okrug*) were organized and the pan-Russian Congress of Indigenous Peoples was first held. During this critical period, Indigenous peoples began to use the media to express their ethnic interests.

While adapting to the industrial and postindustrial society of dominant Russian society, Indigenous activities during the 1990s were closely connected to the development of institutions representing Indigenous interests in Russia as well as internationally (e.g., RAIPON; parliament committees on the North; offices addressing the needs of Indigenous peoples in the United Nations; the Arctic Council, an intergovernmental body with eight member states; and regional governmental structures in Russia). International organizations aided in the development of an Indigenous infrastructure with modern equipment and using new communication technologies.

Among the important directions of RAIPON activities—institutional, ecological, ethnic, legislative, and informational—the latter have become most essential, as I have discussed elsewhere (Diatchkova 2005). During perestroika, the Indigenous peoples of Russia found a compelling need to generate information in the social sphere. Media became a critical means of sustainability for Indigenous peoples. The development of ethnic or Indigenous media—along with the broadening of existing creative media activities—demonstrates the rapid changes that occurred in the cultural space of Indigenous peoples in the last decade of the twentieth century with regard to the density of information available to them. Many ethnic groups began undertaking efforts to develop a broadcasting industry, using these channels for maintaining or recovering Native languages and cultures as well as for establishing a journalistic space for news on the Indigenous Peoples' Movement. In the mass media (newspapers, magazines, broadcasting, and online), the overall volume of information on and for different Indigenous groups and cultures enlarged significantly during this period. These media have primarily addressed issues of social and cultural development of ethnic groups, interethnic relations, and the relationship between center and peripheral regions (Mal'kova and Ostapenko 2000: 42).

The Growth of Indigenous Broadcasting in Russia
From the late 1960s through the 1990s, Russia established a number of different television and broadcast committees (GTRK) in Indigenous regions that were the agencies of the state and administered by local autonomous authorities. Although not under strict Indigenous control, they have been devoted to Indigenous interests due to the Aboriginal journalists who contribute to these committees. These Native-language broadcasts are very significant for Indigenous people—it is the way they express their voice. The programming consists of news (mostly local, Indigenous issues as well as comments on regional events) and documentary films.

As table 11.1 demonstrates, television broadcasting transmissions in the Chukchi language commenced in 1967.[5] By the 1990s, the GTRK of Chukotka, one of the first regions to have Indigenous broadcast programs, ran broadcasting six hours per month in the Chukchi language and over three hours per month in the Eskimo (Yupik) language. Chukotka GTRK produced weekly radio transmissions *Today in Okrug*; *In Districts, Villages, and Brigades*; *Nunavut* ("Land," in Eskimo); and *We Are Aboriginals*. By 1999, the time allotted for TV programs in the Chukchi language was expanded by four hours every month. Every week, the Chukotka station broadcast the TV news *Pynylte* ("News," in Chukchi) and *Eygyskin* ("Native Land"), as well as the TV documentary programs *Tradition* and *Rodoslovnaya* ("Lineage"). During the 1990s, the station aired the festival of throat songs and rapid speech called *Eynet* ("Songs"). The state TV and Broadcasting Foundation (Moscow), noting the professionalism of Chukotka journalists, obtained and broadcast nationwide the documentary films produced by the Chukotka GTRK on Indigenous culture and contemporary issues, including *The Feast of Language*, *When the Men Cry*, and *The Stone Sail*.

Indigenous Newspapers in the 1990s
In many northern regions, Indigenous groups partnered with local governments to establish Indigenous newspapers. For example, during the 1990s, the Koriakskiy Autonomous Oblast began to issue the newspaper *Narodovlastie (People's Power)* in four Indigenous languages (Koriak, Itelmen, Chukchi, and Even). In the Kamchtskaya Region, the Indigenous peoples of Kamchatka established the newspaper *Aborigen Kamchatki* in 1995 with the support of RAIPON. In Chukotka in the 1990s, the newspaper *Murgin Nutenut* ("Our Land," in Chukchi) was published by the local Indigenous organization, with the financial backing of the local

TABLE 11.1: Russian Federation Indigenous Television and Radio Stations
(by the end of the 1990s)

Name of TV & radio station	Location (region & city)	Broadcast language	Date of establishment
Chukotka GTRK	Chukotskiy AO, Anadyr'	Chukchi (TV, radio), Eskimo (Yupik) (radio)	1967
Koriakskiy GTRK	Koriakskiy AO, Palana	Koriak, Chukchi, Even (radio); Koriak (TV)	1990s
Ugoria GTRK	Khanty-Mansiyskiy AO, Khanty-Mansiysk	Khanty, Mansy	1990s
Dal'nevostochnaya GTRK	Primorskiy Kray (region)	Ul'chi, Negidal	1990s
Komsomol'sk GTRK	Khabarovskiy Kray, Komsomol'sk-na-Amure	Nanay	1990s
Zapoliarie GTRK	Nenetskiy AO, Narian-Mar	Nenet	1990s
Yamal GTRK	Yamalo-Nenetskiy AO, Salekhard	Nenet	1960s
Kheglen GTRK	Evenkiyskiy AO, Tura	Evenk	1990s
Gevan GTRK	Republisk Sakha (Yakutia), Yakutsk	Evenk, Even, Yukagir (radio, TV)	1990s
Taymyr GTRK	Taymyrskiy (Dolgano-Nenetskiy AO), Dudinka	Nenet, Dolgan, Enet, Nganasan	1990s

government, in the Chukchi, Eskimo, and Even languages. During 1998, across the Russian Federation, the number of periodicals in Native languages increased by 35 percent from 300 to 406 (Mal'kova and Ostapenko 2000: 42).

The need for a network to implement RAIPON's informational politics led to the establishment of the Information Center (IC) in December 1999.[6] The IC began to publish the journal *Mir Korennykh Narodov—Zhivaya Arctika* (*Indigenous World—Vivid Arctic*), with attachments on different themes. The creation of the RAIPON Web site (www.raipon.net) in 2000 allowed RAIPON to receive and disseminate information on the association's activities and Indigenous community issues to Indigenous groups across Russia.

So, the establishment and development of Indigenous media began to open up many channels for expressing ethnic identities during the transitional 1990s. This in turn created an increasingly important informational space for and about Indigenous peoples in the media, as well as a space for Indigenous media producers to produce media forms in their own languages and from their own cultural perspectives.

Indigenous Information Centers

The increasing cooperation between Indigenous organizations both domestically and internationally led to a need for improved informational and communication technologies. The financial support of international Indigenous advocacy organizations and foundations provided the Russian regional organizations with computers, Internet access, and training workshops. The years following 2000 were an intensive period of building electronic informational space to address the issues of the Russian Indigenous movement.

During this time, RAIPON's Information Center stimulated the establishment of regional Information Centers into a network united by the Agreement on Partnership and Cooperation. The members of this agreement are RAIPON Information Center (www.raipon.net); the Ethnoecological Information Center *Lach* in Kamchatka, located in Petropavlovsk-Kamchatskiy in the Kamchatskaya region; the Youth Information Center *Severnyi Ochag* in Saint Petersburg (www.raipon.net / piter); the Youth Center *Fenix Amura* and Informational and Legal Center under the Indigenous Association of Khabarovskiy Area (ulchi@mail.kht.ru); the Information Center of the Indigenous Association of Magadan Region; the Information Center *Yasavei Manzara* in Narian-Mar, Nenetskiy Autonomous Area (www.raipon.net / yasavey); the Informational and Legal Center *Sibir'-Diu* of the Indigenous Association of Krasnoyarskiy Area and Evenkia; the Informational and Legal Center *Turgar* under the auspices of the Kemerovskaia regional community organization of *Teleuts Nabat* in Kemerovo (www.turgar.ru); and the Informational and Legal Center of the Indigenous Peoples of Primorskiy Area *Suneyni* in Vladivostok (www.udege.ru). Other centers joining the Indigenous Network in 2005 included the Republic Sakha (Yakutia) Information Center and the Center for Conservation and Development of Indigenous Culture *Kykhkykh* in Nekrasovka village, Sakhalin Area.[7]

Most ICS address the legal issues and interests of the communities, providing legal and Indigenous rights information and advocacy. For example, the main goal of *Sibir'-Diu* Information Center (established in February 2003) has been to organize the territories regarding traditional land use; to help in drawing up the documents for registration of the communities; to report about the projects; and to advocate for supplemental education for Indigenous representatives. The ic in the Magadan region (established in 2003), funded by the International Work Group for International Affairs (iwgia), has focused its efforts on the economic development of communities, creating a legal database and holding workshops for Indigenous representatives.

In addition to distributing information through electronic media, information centers also issue printed materials. For example, *Lach* issues an attachment to the newspaper *Aborigen Kamchatki*, while *Yasavei Manzara* publishes a monthly bulletin, as do the information centers in Khabarovsk and in the Magadan region. Subscription circulation of bulletins runs between two hundred and six hundred copies. The citizens of rural districts, communities, and other Indigenous organizations are the main readers of these bulletins, since they often lack Internet access.

The protection of Indigenous rights has grown into one of the most important components of raipon activities during the intensive industrial development of northern territories. These kinds of activities are documented on raipon's Web site and in its journal, *Mir Korennykh Narodov—Zhivaia Arctica (Indigenous World—Vivid Arctic)*. The Web site and journal maintain current listings of legislative acts, comments regarding the federal laws, and information about special practices, such as roundtables and conferences, that are devoted to the protection of Indigenous rights.

The current legal situation in the Russian Federation is characterized by reforms of federal legislation (and Indigenous legislation particularly) for delineation between public authorities at all levels. raipon's operative measure in conjunction with the work of the Russian Federation Commission for the development of proposals on this issue in 2002–3 resulted in discussion of Indigenous rights and the issuing of proposals and amendments for changing eighteen federal laws, all of which were prepared by raipon for the Russian government (Todyshev 2004: 254).

On the whole, the main information provided by Indigenous ics, through electronic media as well as printed materials, reflects not only the establishment of a database on Indigenous legislation issues affecting the Indigenous movement but also vigorously maintains informational support for conflict situations that may arise. These include cases in which the habitat of Russia's Indigenous peoples needs to be protected legally and preserved from actions of large oil and gas companies and others. For example, a widespread information campaign through Indigenous media was mobilized at the beginning of the 2000s to support the

Primorskaia Association of Indigenous Peoples in their conflict with the transnational Hyundai corporation and the Primorsklesprom company (Aksenova 2004: 78). The association's activities were supported by legal and nature protection organizations. Such cases of maintaining information support in conflict situations also occurred in Sakhalin, Kamchatka, and other regions of the Russian Federation.

IDENTITY AND INSTITUTIONAL POLITICS
OF INDIGENOUS PEOPLES IN MEDIA

Indigenous Media in Chukotka

Provoked by the democratization of Soviet society during the late 1980s and early 1990s, the success of Chukotka's Indigenous peoples in preserving and revitalizing their ethnic identity stimulated many Indigenous communities to use media to express their Indigenous interests. Since the early 1950s, translated materials from the Russian newspaper *Soviet Chukotka* had been used to create the Chukchi-language newspaper *Sovetken Chukotka*. Then, due to perestroika, the latter began to publish original materials (contributions) prepared by Indigenous journalists, and it became an independent newspaper that, in 1990, was renamed *Murgin Nutenut* (*Our Land*), published weekly with a circulation of 690. In practically every issue during the first five years, we could read words of appreciation and joy over the existence of an original Native newspaper. For example, one reader wrote: "We have to remember that a national gift is to know our native language and traditions" (June 4, 1994). This newspaper was popular not only in Chukotka, but also in the Republic of Sakha (Yakutia). One reader from Yakutia, Khristofor Dutkin, wrote: "I think, in any case, the Indigenous newspaper has to exist. Due to it, we learn about language, culture, and life. The newspaper is our eyes, ears, and conscience" (May 23, 1992).

The first pages of the Native newspaper were published in the Chukchi language, with additions around 1990 of contributions in the Eskimo and Even languages. This up-to-date Indigenous newspaper, staffed by Aboriginal journalists, reflected social, cultural, economic, and political events among Chukotka's Indigenous peoples, and *Murgin Nutenut* became the main means for expression of the ethnic interests of Chukchi, Eskimos, Even, Yukagir, and others.

During the second half of the 1990s, however, the situation changed. Governor A. V. Nazarov of the Chukotskiy Autonomous Area closed the newspaper for "financial reasons." The journalists were sacked, and *Murgin Nutenut* was transformed into an attachment to a Russian newspaper *Krayniy Sever* and staffed by only one journalist. The contents no longer reflected Indigenous activities and politics. Nazarov scorned the appeals of Indigenous peoples about the need and desire to preserve the original status of their Native newspaper. This disruptive interference by the regional administration into the social channel connecting Chukotka's Indigenous peoples and the dismantling of the creative collective of Indigenous journalists resulted in the fall of the Indigenous movement against the background of social and economic crisis in Russia and especially in Chukotka.

In the early 2000s, I carried out a sociological survey to learn about the condition of local Indigenous organizations, about awareness of their rights and access to media (see Diatchkova 2001). Later, the survey results were introduced at the roundtable "Chukotka Indigenous Movement—Problems and Tasks" in August 2005 during World Indigenous Peoples Days in Anadyr. Representatives of Indigenous communities, the Duma (parliament), the Chukotka government, and journalists participated in the roundtable.

My report showed the involvement of local Indigenous organizations —associations, elders' councils, women's councils, the Chukotka Union of Reindeer Herders, the Chukotka association of marine hunters, societies of *Upik* ("true man" in Eskimo), and *Chichetkin Vetgav* ("Native Word" in Chukchi)—in regional cultural politics. My findings showed that (1) rural Indigenous associations had been in a formal relationship (without engaging) with different Indigenous organizations and did not vigorously present Indigenous issues to authorities; and (2) most Indigenous persons were not fully aware of their Indigenous rights and laws. The participants in the survey stressed that the next tasks of the Chukotka Indigenous association should be to (1) discuss the laws and law drafts, social programs, and information from different organizations; (2) raise issues at the community meetings; (3) maintain Indigenous representation in the district Duma and government; and (4) collaborate with administrations and other organizations.

After listening to the report, the roundtable participants noted the absence of information as a main reason for the weakness of Chukotka Indigenous organizations, and in conjunction with it the need to spread information on Indigenous rights. They told about maintaining the status of the Chukotka indigenous association as a coordination center to participate in area social politics and emphasized the need to continue to monitor the activities of Indigenous organizations. These findings underscore the significance of systematically transmitting information via special media channels, such as Indigenous ics, and also demonstrate the cumulative role of information in the development of the Indigenous movement.

The Kamchatka Indigenous Peoples Network

To illustrate, we can point to the activities of two publications, *Aborigen Kamchatki*[8] and ic *Lach*.[9] These two Kamchatka-based Indigenous media resources have created a significant informational space on Indigenous issues by maintaining collaborative media activity with international institutions. Their influence on the cultural politics of the region has put Indigenous rights issues squarely on the social agenda.

At the beginning of the 2000s, *Aborigen Kamchatki* and *Lach* had played a significant role in institutional politics, especially by disseminating information about conservation and Indigenous rights and facilitating the construction of the Kamchatka Indigenous Peoples Network (which includes Koriaks, Itelmens, Chukchi, Evens, and Kamchadals) to solve environmental problems together. In September 2002, an international conference, "Traditional Indigenous Land Use and Environment," was held in Petropavlovsk-Kamchatskiy, and the regional pact on building the network of Kamchatka Indigenous organizations was signed at this meeting.[10] Twenty-four organizations entered into this network, and they jointly adopted an appeal to Russian Federation President Vladimir Putin about the network's goals. Participants at this conference also discussed legislative issues affecting Indigenous peoples.[11]

The establishment of the Kamchatka Network as a means for joint collaboration stimulated attention to environmental and political problems, such as questions of development versus traditional land use; conservation of the Kamchatskiy Shelf of the Bering Sea (an area targeted for oil and gas drilling); and the organization of discussion and referendums on Indigenous and environmental issues at the local, regional, or federal parliament.

The network provides a number of measures most relevant to the social and ecological situation in the area in the framework of the International Decade of the World's Indigenous People (1995–2004), proclaimed by the U.N. General Assembly. With the help of a grant from the U.S. Agency for International Development (USAID), the Kamchatka

Indigenous Peoples Network used new technologies to develop a Web site (www.ttp.klie.ru) to supply information about the ways of developing the Indigenous territories according to federal laws. The site contains standardized documents, contributions about experiences, and accounts of the problems of development of the territories of traditional land use.[12]

In 2003, the network organized the meeting "The Ways of Inter-relationships between Authorities, Local Self-Government Institutions, and Social Organizations for Protection and Maintaining of Indigenous Rights in Kamchatskaya Oblast." The main topics of this meeting were the problems of forming a standardized legal base to protect Indigenous rights; legislative initiatives of Indigenous organizations; and problems of regional land use. *Aborigen Kamchatki* vigorously informed the populace about the preparation for the meeting, in addition to providing information about other events.[13]

The years 2004 and 2005 were marked by large-scale actions of the network that were highlighted in *Aborigen Kamchatki* and *Lach:* the formation of the Council of Indigenous Representatives in Kamchatskaya Oblast[14] and the appeal to the Russian Federation prosecutor general about the nonobservance of legislation in the Oblastnaya (Areas) program Ecology and Natural Resources,[15] adopted by the Council of People's Deputies in Kamchatskaya Oblast (March 2, 2005) and certified by a Kamchatskaya Oblast governor resolution (no. 436; November 11, 2004). The development of this program had disregarded Indigenous interests, and the ecological and ethnoecological examinations had not been carried out. The appeal by the Council of Indigenous Representatives requested the inclusion of an Indigenous representative on the program's expert council. As a result, the prosecutor general's judgment forbade the implementation of the resolution of the Kamchatskaya Oblast governor. Another action of the network during this time was an initiative for holding a referendum for conservation of the Kamchatskiy shelf and the inadmissibility of geological surveyance.

The process of unifying two Russian Federation territories—Kamchatskaya Oblast and Koriakskiy Autonomous Okrug—was one of the most highlighted topics in the media during this time. The network took an active role in preparing for the unity of these two territories, considering the observance of Indigenous rights as a main issue. This position was expressed in the appeal to the Russian Federation president and to the different authorities.[16]

Thus, the Kamchatka media, primarily *Aborigen Kamchatki* and *Lach,* have enabled the creation of an important informational space updating the people on Indigenous rights and other interests of Indigenous peoples of the area. These media have provided the necessary information to empower the local Indigenous peoples to actively and effectively participate in solving political, environmental, social, and economical problems. This social channel stimulated the networking of Indigenous organizations and the formation of new Indigenous institutions.

THE STRENGTHENING OF INDIGENOUS MEDIA RESOURCES

Informational resources as well as information technologies and computer skills have become essential for all of the regional Indigenous organizations in Russia; unfortunately, many of the local organizations are not yet equipped with computer technology. Financing is the greatest stumbling block to the maintenance of an Indigenous press organ. Thus, Indigenous media producers find it essential to exchange information about and creative solutions for acquiring funds if they are to reserve their positions in the informational public sphere.

The *Aborigen Kamchatki* team had to obtain funding to save the newspaper in the 1990s. Continuing this practice, in September 2004, the newspaper office acquired funding to realize the next project, For the Development of Northern Indigenous Peoples Ecological Press, supported by the Initiative for Social Action and Renewal (ISAR)–Far East within the framework of the program Support for Social Ecological Movement in Far East. The goals of the project were widening the environmental focus of the newspaper, improving design, and holding training seminars for the journalists. This project resulted in many contributions by Indigenous representatives in environmental activity, as well as in the transfer of traditional knowledge to the younger generations. Finally, in December 2004, the newspaper staff held a workshop on journalism with the participation of public correspondents, which facilitated the improvement of the local press.[17]

The past decade has witnessed an increase in international attention to, and concern about, the status of Russia's Indigenous peoples, especially due to the involvement of Russia in the International Decade of the World's Indigenous People. One of the major results of activities by state authorities was the development of Indigenous legislation and the establishment of different regional institutions representing Indigenous interests under regional governments in the Russian Federation.

Professionalization and Networking of Indigenous Journalists
Once small presses had achieved a measure of stability, they sought to develop a professional network of journalists from different territories. In April 2005, the RAIPON Information Center held a workshop to advance training of IC members, coordinate IC activities, and discuss information exchanges between ICs.[18]

A popular international network, Barents Press International, was established ten years ago when journalists in the Barents Region joined forces. This organization held the conference "The Role of Media in Light of Indigenous Peoples and Ethnic Problems" in May 2005, with participants from Norway, Finland, Sweden, and Russia.[19] Participants discussed tasks for the coming decade and the immediate future, as well as issues such as freedom of the press, distinctions between the media of different countries and Indigenous media, and the development of tolerance in society.

Such networking by journalists facilitates the increasing professionalization of Indigenous journalism and the opportunity for dialogue about how Indigenous problems might best be approached and solved. The training of Indigenous journalists has provided new levels of professionalism and knowledge of broader Indigenous issues, international and state politics regarding Indigenous peoples and media, international nongovernmental and governmental organizations and available external funds and sources of assistance, how to develop information centers, and networking for the internal development of Indigenous media.

Transnational and International Resources
International organizations (IWGIA, the World Wildlife Fund, the World Bank, ministries of Arctic countries, etc.) have helped stabilize Indigenous informational resources by funding Indigenous media and the Indigenous movement. For instance, the United Nations held an international conference "Information for Everybody" in September 2003 in Petropavlovsk-Kamchatskiy that permitted local journalists to receive training, gain valuable experience, and develop contacts with different organizations.[20]

Some sources of international attention are the Web sites set up by various research institutions in different countries with a focus on Indigenous issues. For example, the Web site siberian-studies.org, developed by the German anthropologist Erich Kasten and his compatriot the linguist Michael Dürr, presents and disseminates case studies about Siberia and the Russian north by leading social and cultural anthropologists, with a special focus on Kamchatka. This Web site publishes the proceedings of academic conferences, the programs of sustainable development of traditional land use, and information about self-government. It facilitates a productive dialogue between Indigenous representatives and academics who have done fieldwork in the Indigenous regions. The Web site receives about nine thousand to ten thousand hits per month. Its developers believe that putting the information on the Internet is more accessible, more effective, and more cost-efficient than publishing printed materials (Kasten 2004).

Another significant transnational project is the Arctic Network for the Support of the Indigenous Peoples of the Russian Arctic (ANSIPRA), originally founded by the Norwegian Polar Institute and expanded in conjunction with RAIPON but still under the auspices of the Norwegian Ministry of the Environment. ANSIPRA describes itself as "a communication network linking Russian Indigenous Peoples' Organisations (IPOs) with international institutions and organisations alarmed about the future of the Indigenous peoples of the Russian North" (www.npolar.no / ansipra). Among ANSIPRA's goals is providing information from Indigenous representatives and others on the state of Indigenous peoples, as well as providing Indigenous groups with intermediation and funding assistance. ANSIPRA issues a semiannual bulletin, in English and Russian (with downloadable copies on the Web site), which is distributed among 270 Indigenous representatives, international organizations, and administrations in Russia. Although ANSIPRA is primarily supported by the Norwegian Polar Institute, financial support was also granted by bodies such as the Barents Region, Norway's Department on Nature Management, Tromsø Museum (Norway), and the Canadian Embassy in Norway.

The Problems of State Support
The state politics of the Russian government and the relation of local authorities to the media have an effect on the development of media for and by Indigenous peoples. Officially, the government is supposed to develop media across the country. On the whole, according to the 2004 report of the Federal Agency for the Press and Mass Communications (the first systemic analysis by the state of trends and prospects for the development of a Russian periodical press market), an advantageous economic situation has emerged in Russia. Liberal legislation on the press was created during the 1990s; the demand for quality journalism con-

tinues to rise; the technologies have been improving; no restrictions have been imposed on foreign companies seeking to own Russian press and media assets; and the flow of investment has been growing. Thanks to this climate, the informational and advertising role of online media has enjoyed continuous growth (Russian media market 2005). The report indicates that the media market in the Russian Federation has developed on the whole; however, it remains below the world standard.

Among the factors that restrict the development of an Indigenous media market, the report names the lack of state support of the Aboriginal-language periodical press as well as the regional and local presses. The federal budget stopped financing regional newspapers at the beginning of 2005. The report also notes the technological constraints on the Russian printing industry and the shortage of printing press managers trained to work in the market conditions. Meanwhile, for most of Russia's population, the regional newspapers are the only accessible printed media. This has created a critical situation for newspaper publishing and has led to restrictions on freedom of the press imposed by local authorities, who are now financing the local editions.

During this same period, the regional TV and radio companies experienced some interference from GTRK, the state TV and radio company. Many regional broadcasting companies were forced to discontinue or shorten their Indigenous-language broadcasts because of job cuts and reduced broadcasting time. As a result, the Indigenous population's access to information has been diminished, especially in rural areas, where radio is generally the only source for information in Native languages.[21]

CONCLUDING WORDS

Although threatened, many Indigenous media have been able to survive thanks to fundraising projects by journalists with the special support of international advocacy organizations. Networking and training are increasingly preparing journalists for professional tasks in information exchange. The intensity of the Indigenous movement's need for informational support has become increasingly obvious. At the federal level, however, Indigenous media development in the regions, and the financial support of the state, are issues that loom large.

The media of Indigenous peoples across Russia are an indispensable resource, providing access to information on Indigenous rights. Examining the media's ability to illuminate the activities of Indigenous movements

nationally and regionally provides insights into its influence on Indigenous identity, into its ability to build up adequate treatment by state and
community agencies of Indigenous issues, and into the broader possibility
for distributing international and regional expertise to solve the problems
of Indigenous communities. The Indigenous media play an essential role
in stabilizing the social and cultural conditions of Indigenous peoples.

NOTES

I would like to thank the editors of this collection and the readers from Duke
University Press for their helpful feedback, with special thanks to Pam Wilson for
improving my English.

1. Valentina Uspenskaya was a representative of the Itelman people of Kamchatka and a powerful force for Indigenous journalism in Russia's north.
   Canadian journalist Jane George of the Nunatsiaq News profiled Uspenskaya
   in an article titled "Reporter's Notebook: Journalist Keeps Aboriginal Languages Alive in Russian Arctic" (June 8, 2001), which can be found at www
   .nunatsiaq.com / archives / nunavut010630 / nvt10608__07html. I sadly received word in late 2005 of Uspenskaya's death.

2. For a listing of these Indigenous groups, see the Web site for the Russian Association of Indigenous Peoples of the North (RAIPON) at www.raipon.net /
   english / index.html. Those officially designated by the government as "Indigenous Small-Numbered Peoples of Russia" are listed in the ЕДИНЫЙ
   ПеречеНЬ кореННЫХ МаЛОчИсЛеННЫХ НароДоВ РоссИИ (Com-
   mon List of Indigenous Small Peoples of Russia) approved by the government
   of the Russian Federation on March 24, 2000. Criteria for recognition include
   living in historically traditional territory, preserving a traditional way of life,
   self-designation as a separate ethnicity, and having a population of fewer than
   50,000 members. Indigenous groups not considered among the "numerically
   small peoples" may be considered titular nations associated with republics.

3. In 1926, according to Gurvich 1961: 45, 54.4% of the Indigenous peoples of the
   region still maintained a nomadic lifestyle. Prior to the birth of the Soviet
   Union, Russian Orthodoxy was the leader in missionary efforts. In the post-
   Soviet era, other denominations have gained ground.

4. See RAIPON Web site for history (www.raipon.net); see also Kriukov, Seliverstov, and Tokarev 2004.

5. The information in table 11.1 was kindly provided to me by the leaders of the
   Indigenous regional associations at the end of the 1990s. It appears that some
   stations have subsequently closed due to a lack of financing.

6. RAIPON project partners: UNEP / GRID-ARENDAL and Sámi Council. Sponsor: Norwegian Ministry of Foreign Affairs.

7. Information was kindly provided by the RAIPON IC staff employee I. Kurilova, personal communication.

8. *Aborigen Kamchatki* (hereafter *AK*), Press Organ of RAIPON, Kamchatka Area Association of Indigenous Organizations of the North, and Regional Institution Informational Center Aborigen of Kamchatka. Issued from June 11, 1995, circulation 1,000 copies; published in Petropavlovsk-Kamchatskiy.

9. *Lach*, besides dissemination of its information in electronic version and printed materials across Kamchatka (about 200 recipients), has the table at *AK* (one page).

10. *AK*, no. 9 (68), September 17, 2002.

11. *AK*, no. 12 (71), December 24, 2002.

12. *AK*, no. 2 (73), February 25, 2003.

13. *AK*, no. 4 (75), April 29, 2003.

14. *AK*, no. 15 (99), December 30, 2004.

15. Informational Issue *Lach*, April 26, 2005.

16. Informational Issue *Lach*, no. 10 (166), February 15, 2005.

17. *AK*, no. 1 (100), February 2, 2005.

18. *AK*, no. 4 (103), May 6, 2005.

19. See www.raipon.org / news / 13 / 05 / 2005 / .

20. *AK*, no. 9 (80), September 19, 2003.

21. *AK*, no. 1 (100), February 2, 2005.

CHAPTER 12

INDIGENOUS MINORITY-LANGUAGE MEDIA:
S4C, CULTURAL IDENTITY, AND THE WELSH-
LANGUAGE TELEVISUAL COMMUNITY

Ruth McElroy

Because the United Kingdom was, at least until the Second World War, a global center of imperial power, it may seem peculiar to locate a discussion of Indigeneity in one of its home nations, Wales, rather than in the context of its former colonies. Contemporary Wales is part of a state that retains substantial global power—its permanent seat on the U.N. Security Council, for example—and tremendous wealth. The United Kingdom's economy is one of the largest in Europe, which means that Wales, its people, and its traditional culture are hardly facing the same realities that Indigenous peoples such as the Maori or Aboriginal Australians daily encounter. Discussions of Indigeneity, media, and cultural identity are more likely to surface in those parts of the globe that have been marked by and responded to waves of imperial migration and enforced subjection to colonial rule. For some nationalists, however, this description applies to Wales, inasmuch as Wales has experienced migration from the empire since at least the nineteenth century, meaning that it has had ethnic minority communities for a considerable period. Wales itself was colonized by England (see Hechter 1975), most obviously through the 1536 Act of Union that included a clause outlawing the Indigenous Welsh language as an official language of justice and state administration. What, then, can examining the case of Welsh-language broadcasting offer practitioners, artists, and scholars of global Indigenous media?

Concentrating on the case of the Welsh-language television broadcaster, Sianel Pedwar Cymru (s4c), I address this question by exploring the dynamic relationship between Welsh cultural identity, the preservation and enhancement of the Welsh language (a Celtic language distinct from the Gaelic spoken in Scotland and Ireland), and the role of television in the construction and maintenance of a national community. "The growing power of the broadcast media in contemporary Europe," Niamh Hourigan (2001: 77) has argued, "has created a cultural environment where television and radio services have become the focus of controversy and protest. Indigenous European linguistic minorities have placed themselves at the center of a number of these controversies by asserting the need for television services for minority language communities." Following such scholars, I employ the term *Indigenous minority language* to specify the minority language(s) of Indigenous people (e.g., Welsh) as opposed to the language(s) of both Indigenous majority-language groups (e.g., English) and minority ethnic groups in the United Kingdom (e.g., Punjabi, Urdu, Somali), many of whom have arrived since the nineteenth century as part of extensive imperial and postimperial migrations. However, as this essay will demonstrate, the meanings and deployment of Indigeneity in political and cultural discourses in Wales and the United Kingdom extends beyond this scholarly definition to reveal complex imbrications of race, nationalism, and cultural belonging.

s4c, launched in 1982, is a commissioning broadcaster, broadcasting an average of thirty-two hours a week of Welsh-language programming across a full range of genres from news to soap opera to children's TV, most of which air during peak hours (6–10 p.m.).[1] In 1998, s4c Digital was added, carrying more than eighty hours of Welsh-language programming and providing the first opportunity for Welsh speakers outside of Wales to watch television, via satellite, in their native language. A second digital channel, s4c2, carries broadcasts of the proceedings of the Welsh Assembly.

In the political discourse of contemporary Wales, language, culture, and national identity have become inextricably intertwined. s4c is a channel born out of political protest, a testament to the capacity of individuals to work in cultural groups both to contest their own cultural erosion and, more positively, to develop a media institution that may speak to that community in its own tongue (see K. Williams 2003). s4c began broadcasting in 1982 following an extensive political campaign conducted by both a political party, Plaid Cymru, and a social protest group, Cymdeithas yr Iaith Gymraeg (Welsh Language Society, *Cymraeg* being the Welsh term for the Welsh language, and here mutated for reasons of grammar to "Gymraeg"), which had been established in 1962. The Welsh

Language Society is a pressure group whose members have been prepared to break the law and undertake nonviolent direct action as a means to campaign for the preservation of the language in a range of areas, from the right to have bilingual road signs to campaigning for Welsh-medium education. From a position in 1911, when the census recorded one million speakers of Welsh (representing just under half the population), by the middle of the twentieth century, the Welsh-language culture of Wales appeared to be in terminal decline, seemingly one of many victims of the complex transformations wrought by industrial capitalism on Indigenous cultures. While urbanization, migration, and education were the principal drivers of this change, social protest groups began to recognize that the mass media were further establishing the primacy of English as the dominant language of both the home and the public sphere.

The success of the first two decades of Welsh-language television programming is reflected in linguistic data: the 2001 census showed a reversal in the decline of Welsh speakers, noting a small increase in the number of Welsh speakers in Wales, at that time comprising 20.8 percent of the population. Some key points regarding the Welsh language and its speakers may be noted here. First, all Welsh speakers are bilingual. However, speakers whose mother tongue or first language is Welsh may well be more fluent in Welsh than English. Second, data gathered since the 2001 census suggests that the growth in Welsh speakers is continuing. The Welsh Language Board's 2004 *Welsh Language Use Survey* (2006) cites an increase from the 20.8 percent in 2001 to 21.7 percent in Welsh speakers. Third, the question of fluency of speakers—together with the extent of regular usage in family, work, and social life—makes for a complex and shifting picture. For example, of the 21.7 percent Welsh speakers cited by the above report, 57 percent describe themselves as fluent. While children between three and fifteen make up the highest percentage of Welsh speakers at 37 percent (of which 44% are "fluent"), fluency rates increase by age such that the highest percentage of fluent speakers are in the sixty-five or over age group, with fluency levels at 72 percent.

The growth in Welsh speakers has many causes, including increased esteem enjoyed by the language after devolution in 1997[2] and the policy since 1999 for Welsh to be a compulsory subject for all school children up to the age of sixteen. These findings accord generally with another report, *Living Lives through the Medium of Welsh Study*, commissioned by s4c, the Welsh Language Board, bbc Wales, and the Arts Council of Wales, which found that "fewer 22–45 year old Welsh speakers describe themselves as fluent . . . than people in other age groups," but that Welsh speakers in this age group believe that "the Welsh Language has a more positive image and is in a stronger position now than ever before," such that it is perceived to be "cool" and fashionable to be able to speak Welsh (Beaufort Research 2006: 2). Thus "the general view . . . was that the language has greater visibility now and broader acceptance, with much more Welsh spoken in places like Cardiff and with a steady growth in Welsh medium education" (11). Finally, the geography of the Welsh language is also shifting. While the highest density of speakers is still to be found in North and West Wales, away from the Eastern border with England, some of the highest growth rates are to be found in the Anglicized South East in which the capital, Cardiff, is located. As I explore below, these reconfigurations pose challenges for s4c.

Nonetheless, other minority- and Indigenous-language groups in Western Europe commonly cite s4c's success as an example of how the mass media can help maintain linguistic and cultural heterogeneity and foster a modern sense of community. Some argue that the success of the Welsh campaign has paved the way for other Indigenous Celtic minorities (see Hourigan 2001).[3] s4c challenges pessimistic views about the decline of minority languages and cultures and provides evidence of how Indigenous European linguistic minorities have levered support from regional, national, and international policy makers. Indigenous communities have often deftly deployed emerging discourses of cultural diversity (especially prominent in European Union policy debates) for their own ends, yet in doing so, they sometimes risk maintaining elements of cultural essentialism and national exclusivity. s4c, as a relatively mature broadcasting entity, offers evidence of the strains inherent in any media project that is so deeply imbricated in broader political projects. This is especially so when, in their impulse for cultural preservation, such political projects risk acting as the agents of cultural exclusions.

FROM CULTURAL EROSION TO CULTURAL DIVERSITY: INDIGENOUS MINORITY-LANGUAGE COMMUNITIES AND SHIFTING CRITIQUES OF THE MASS MEDIA

The mass media have long been regarded as a powerful threat to the world's linguistic and cultural minorities. Such fears have emerged along distinct lines. One trajectory of critique positions the mass media as tools of the dominant classes under capitalism, the use of which aims at the erosion of all political and cultural alternatives. The very technology of the media is thus suspect because of its role in a broader ideological formation. Saunders Lewis, a leading literary figure and one of the founding fathers of modern Welsh nationalism, wrote in 1951 of television's dangers: "Bringing the cinema into the home every day of the week is a moral danger. . . . It could totally destroy all culture" (quoted in Davies 1994: 173). In 1950, the director of programs in the BBC's Welsh region, John Tudor Jones, spoke of the small screen as a technology of oppression: "It frightens me to see the BBC's Welsh Council and others calling so irresponsibly for television stations in Wales. . . . The Welsh should oppose the development of television or work to postpone it" (quoted in Davies 1994: 173).

A second trajectory of critique shifts the focus from the technological threat of television and centers, instead, on the process of cultural domination. In the Welsh nationalism of the mid-twentieth century onward, this critique has commonly been articulated through the discourse of colonization, with England cast in the role of colonizer at roughly the same historical point at which the British Empire itself was waning. In an edited volume contesting Wales's position as both colonizer and colonized, Dylan Phillips quotes Cynog Dafis's contribution to the 1972 manifesto of the Welsh Language Society, the protest group credited with spearheading the campaign for Welsh-language television:

> Just as the Welsh language has been downgraded in its own land in order to bind the Welsh people closer to England and to lose their own identity in the new "British" identity, so also the Welsh economy has been bound to that of England. A colonial function has been forced on it. It has been a source of raw materials, coal, slate, iron, steel and water. Now it is being turned into a playground, a picturesque wilderness at the service of the sprawling conurbations along its borders. The subjection of Wales is all one and the same— its ravished culture and its exploited economy. (Dafis quoted in Phillips 2005: 102)

Indigeneity operates in Welsh nationalist discourse of the period under the specific guise of colonization. In 1975, for example, Michael Hechter notoriously—and with enduring contest—proposed the model of internal colonialism as a way of explaining the different relations of Scotland, Ireland, Wales, and England to the British state. For Hechter, the Celtic periphery was kept economically and politically dependent on the English core even as their resources—both mineral and human—were exploited. The rooted and closely bound relationship of the people to both land and language were disrupted by the colonizing force of England, a process that may be dated back to the early-sixteenth-century Acts of Union. From this perspective, Celtic nationalisms are forms of anticolonial resistance. Thus, writing in 1982, the same year that s4c first broadcast, the veteran language campaigner Angharad Tomos (1982: 40) argued that "English is the language of broadcasting in Wales and TV and radio sets are being used to Anglicize our home and kill our language. A Welshman is thus educated to look at life through English eyes."

A third critical trajectory approaches the mass media from within the frame of globalization. From this perspective, globalization and cultural imperialism become, not unproblematically, intertwined. For example, the Council of Europe's explanatory report produced to accompany the European Charter for Regional or Minority Languages (1992) notably shifted its attention from state-based policies to the homogenizing effects of the media:

> The demographic situation of such regional or minority languages varies greatly, from a few thousand speakers to several million, and so does the law and practice of the individual states with respect to them. However, what many have in common is a greater or lesser degree of precariousness. Moreover, whatever may have been the case in the past, nowadays the threats facing these regional or minority languages are often due at least as much to the inevitably standardizing influence of modern civilization and especially of the mass media as to an unfriendly environment or a government policy of assimilation. (Council of Europe n.d.)

The deft shifting of responsibility from government to a conveniently amorphous "modern civilization" in the above quotation downplays the complex interrelationship between government's trade, communications, and culture policies, on the one hand, and the international trade in media commodities, including intellectual property and actual media content, on the other.

Government ministers often praise the economic benefits of selling U.K. television abroad, while U.K. government policy on deregulation—ongoing from the Thatcher years and the overhaul of the BBC—provides the vital context for a globalized media industry. The disavowal of governmental power, especially in cross-national or regional bodies such as

the Council of Europe and the European Union, belies this reality. However, at the discursive level, deploying notions of heritage, culture, and
diversity may provide a space of cultural value that Indigenous minority-
language groups can mobilize in both academic and policy spheres. Mike
Cormack (2005), for example, argues that this is a distinctly postmodern
space and draws on Hourigan (2001) for his argument:

> Indigenous minority language communities are not victims of post-
> modernity (in the sense that many were victims of modernity),
> but—at least in some aspects—examples of it. . . . Minority lan-
> guages are not a remnant of some out-of-date world-view, frag-
> ments of now superseded linguistic, political or cultural structures.
> Rather, they fit into the current global structure very easily, with
> their emphasis on cultural choice and their focus on identity. Those
> who use, defend and adopt minority languages are better seen as the
> prototypes of the new global citizens of the twenty-first century,
> rather than as atavistic cultural dinosaurs. (Cormack 2005: 120)

While the upbeat tone here is wonderfully energizing, the rhetoric of
choice carries an uneasy echo of consumer culture's aestheticization of
cultural difference as a precursor for its use of difference as an attribute to
be traded (see Lury 1996; Skeggs 2004).

Postimperial, multicultural British identity is currently being reformu-
lated through the discourses of both diversity and cosmopolitanism (see
Gilroy 2004; for a critique of cosmopolitanism's exclusions, see Skeggs
2004). While this narrative of a diverse, cosmopolitan Britain operates at
the level of the *British* state and society, it may reconfigure the context in
which policy makers hear the claims of Indigenous media. We may see
this complex set of moves, for example, in a U.K. parliamentary debate in
2004 on Gaelic broadcasting, in which the minister for Europe, Denis
MacShane, declared:

> One of the most positive aspects of the European Union that we are
> shaping is precisely its diversity. When I attend Council of Ministers
> meetings for Foreign Ministers I hear Maltese, Slovakian and Slove-
> nian spoken. Such languages, which, like the Baltic tongues, were to
> some extent lost under the dominance of one or two giant Euro-
> pean languages, are now flourishing. Britain, which is perhaps the
> most cosmopolitan country and open to foreigners of all the Euro-
> pean nation states, is where so many foreign languages jostle for

attention. Not for one second would I say that Gaelic in Scotland or Welsh in Wales were foreign languages. They belong to our country and deserve the support and respect that their speakers give them. (United Kingdom Parliament 2004)

The blind alley into which the minister leads himself at the end of this quotation reveals how the claims of Indigenous minority-language communities may both be set in potentially inclusive narratives of cosmopolitanism and, at the same time, may rapidly be drawn into enduring notions of "our country" as opposed to the foreign and other, a context in which claims to Indigeneity sit in uneasy proximity to racialized anti-immigration politics.

In Wales today, the nationalist deployment of a rooted Indigeneity is subject to contest. Paradoxically, this is partly a result of the nationalists' own successes. In 1997, Wales and Scotland voted in favor of the devolution of specific political powers from Westminster, the seat of the U.K. central government, to Cardiff and Edinburgh (the respective seats of Wales and Scotland, which, along with Northern Ireland, constitute the three devolved governments of the United Kingdom), thereby leading to some of the most fundamental changes in the structure of the British political state. The referendum resulted in the establishment of a National Assembly for Wales in 1999. Devolution has therefore meant that nationalists (and others) have had the opportunity and responsibility to demonstrate what a more inclusive national community might look like. In terms of forging a new national political culture, Indigeneity may carry too many connotations of rooted and hierarchical authenticity to act effectively in building a civic culture of inclusion.

Furthermore, if devolution has necessitated a reevaluation of the discourse of Indigeneity, it is also the case that debates concerning Britain as a postimperial and multicultural society have necessitated critical self-examination in Wales of its own colonial past and multiracial present. In particular, the dichotomies of Indigenous Welsh culture versus colonial Anglicized culture come unstuck when non-Indigenous minorities—such as those of African, Caribbean, and Asian descent—articulate their cultural identities and demand representation in the narratives of the nation. This is especially the case for those born in Wales, for whom the notion that place of birth may not confer belonging is most obviously unreasonable and grievous. Charlotte Williams, the daughter of a Welsh mother and Guyanese father, is a good example of a writer who has publicly contested the mythology of Wales as a tolerant nation. For Williams (2005: 28), the belief that racism is an English phenomenon mitigates against an honest assessment of the politics of race and racism in Welsh society, since, as she says, "it fosters a distinctive and characteristic culture in relation to racism based on disassociation, denial, and disbelief." Welsh debates on racism thus frequently disassociate Wales from colonialism and imperialism except as its victim, deny the role played by the Welsh in building empire and its concomitant racisms, and finally deny that racism exists in Wales. The assumption that victims of colonization may not also be its perpetrators goes unchallenged; it is a story that resists neat binaries and, as a consequence, both the imperial past and racism in the present often remain unspoken.

S4C TODAY: CONTEMPORARY CHALLENGES FOR INDIGENOUS MINORITY-LANGUAGE TELEVISION

s4c has itself sought to address the dynamics of race and multiculturalism in Wales. In its Race Equality Scheme—a response to the Race Relations (Amendment) Act 2000—s4c addresses the areas of training, employment, audiences, and broadcasting as central to its delivery of meaningful race equality. Nonetheless, for s4c, as with other public employers in industries and communities where the ability to speak Welsh is deemed important, matters of race often come up against matters of language and Indigeneity. In such instances, the question of what it means to be part of both an Indigenous minority-language community and part of a postimperial state, still grappling with the changes empire has wrought on British society, becomes especially acute and complex.

These tensions are visible in s4c's Race Equality Scheme. On the one hand, for example, s4c cites the overrepresentation of ethnic minorities in the audiovisual workforce (3.5%) as compared to the ethnic minority Welsh population as a whole (2.1%) (s4c Race Equality Scheme n.d.). On the other hand, when the focus shifts from employment per se to broadcasting, greater tensions are revealed, particularly when race gets overdetermined by Indigenous language issues. In its discussion of drama programming, for example, s4c articulates a commonly heard "problem" of a lack of sufficient Welsh-speaking ethnic minority candidates: "Members of the ethnic minority communities are an integral and a growing part of the Welsh speaking community and this needs to be reflected in the fictional communities we portray on screen. Increasing the number of Welsh speaking actors from ethnic minority communities will be a crucial factor influencing our ability to succeeding [*sic*] in this area" (ibid.).

In the logic of media text as cultural reflection, this argument may just hold. However, looked at from the angle of cultural politics, such a formulation both sidesteps the question of responsibility for engendering an ethnically diverse acting community, and, perhaps even more important, sets a linguistic barrier to inclusion in the cultural representation of the Welsh national community. s4c's policy document is caught then between wishing to recognize the diversity of contemporary Welsh society and at the same time preserve its Welsh-language ethos, in which language operates as "a key marker of authentic Welsh identity" (C. Williams 2005: 30). An implicit associative chain links Indigeneity to authenticity to being a Welsh speaker and, in the process, establishes hierarchies of belonging that exclude many—including quite possibly the 1 percent of Welsh speakers from nonwhite ethnic groups (Welsh Language Board 2006).

Nonetheless, s4c, through its programming, has sought to address some of the exclusions and amnesia of Welsh cultural nationalism. In a landmark documentary series, *Cymru Ddu* (*Black Wales*) (2003), the poet Alan Llwyd fronted an extensive assessment of the silenced history of Black and Asian people in Wales from the sixteenth century onward. The documentary, broadcast in 2003, has since led to a book of the same title, both of which emerged out of a joint project between s4c, the program producers, AntenaDocs, and the Butetown History and Arts Centre (Butetown, in Cardiff, is one of the oldest black communities in Europe and the site of what are often regarded as the first "race riots" in Britain, in 1909). Single programs and books, no matter how accomplished, do not change a national mindset, let alone a set of practices habitually reproduced to preserve racial privilege. However, such a project exemplifies how a broadcaster established in one political reality may find itself needing to deliver in a new political environment, one where there is a need for new cultural representations of what it means to be a silenced minority in a place one calls home. Even if s4c were itself founded on a relatively secure understanding of what Welsh cultural identity meant in the specific context of Indigenous linguistic-minority campaigns of the 1960s to 1980s, cultural identity itself cannot be stabilized in this way; it is a dynamic process and not a fixable commodity or attribute.

The dynamism of cultural identity inflects the constitution of the media audience and a broadcaster's relationship to it. Two reports, an internal review undertaken by s4c and an independent review of s4c undertaken for the Department of Media, Culture, and Sport by Roger Laughton (both published in 2004), highlighted some of these changes and the challenges that s4c faces in maintaining its appeal and value in the Welsh mediascape. Like many broadcasters, s4c inhabits a new multi-channel environment, one in which the close affinities between audience and channel—and according to John Hartley (2004), between nation and television—are subject to disruption. On the one hand, digital technologies have led to the emergence of more channels. This has been accompanied by a fragmentation of the audience and greater competition for public service broadcasters, who may remain committed to the provision of mass audience programming. Choice may diminish audiences and may potentially diminish future diversity. The arrival of digital broadcasting is a mixed blessing for s4c, a channel launched in a more stable, modernist era. As for many public service broadcasters, digital television has led to falling audience shares for s4c, but it has also enabled s4c to reach the Welsh-speaking audience beyond Wales and to offer a broader range and more hours of Welsh-language programming.

Neither Indigenous minority-language media nor their audiences operate in a vacuum. Just as there are no longer monoglot Welsh speakers, so there are no viewers of s4c who have not seen the output of English-language channels, both terrestrial and satellite. s4c thus speaks to an audience that is not only bilingual, but also bicultural, in the sense that viewers are used to switching between the cultural codes of different national broadcasters. A particular tension for s4c is the question of its comparability with and relationship to other U.K. broadcasters, both public service and commercial. For example, in a context where advertising streams are diminishing, s4c's revenue is not keeping up with that of Channel 4, the U.K. fourth terrestrial channel set up shortly after s4c with the charge of addressing a range of minority and specialist audiences. Thus, critical viewers of s4c point to both a lack of programming innovation (in contrast with Channel 4 and its importation of high-profile U.S. shows, for example) and lower production values, which are the outcome of tighter budgets.

The question of how s4c may address these broadcasting developments is compounded by changes in the Welsh-language community itself. How one counts and constitutes a Welsh speaker, and the community of which they are a part, is no easy matter. The independent review of s4c notes, for example, that s4c's audience is comprised of speakers with widely varying levels of fluency in the language. This is partly a consequence of the growth and increased eminence of the Welsh language. Since Welsh became compulsory in schools up to the age of sixteen, many children in Wales have learned a language that one or more of their parents cannot speak, and as a result, many Welsh-speaking children live in non–Welsh-speaking homes. Thus, while according to the independent review, 57 percent of Welsh speakers live in "Wholly Welsh Speaking homes," there are significant variations in how people access and enact their membership in the Welsh-language community. The success of this community's battle for public acknowledgment is further evidenced by the Welsh Language Act (1993), which requires public bodies to treat English and Welsh on a basis of equality. Some private companies have opted to make the language visible; the mainstreet retailer Marks and Spencer and the supermarket Tesco's, for example, use Welsh in some of their signage in Wales.

Taken together with the establishment of the Assembly and the relative success of the media industries, the Welsh language has gained currency and value—cultural, political, and economic—even for those who do not speak it themselves (see Beaufort Research 2000). This is especially marked in terms of region and demography, as Phillips (2005: 106) notes: "There are positive signs of a particularly substantial rise in the number of young people between the ages of three and fifteen who can speak the language, especially in the Anglicized south-east." Some of these border areas, many of which are urban, have, according to Phillips, "seen staggering increases in excess of 300 per cent in the numbers of Welsh-speakers during the last decade" (106).

The geography of this shift is significant because it details growth in areas not normally regarded as nationalist; the language's growth pattern challenges the geography of the older Welsh nationalism out of which s4c emerged. Those who have learned the language, those who speak the language but live in households where it is not daily spoken, and those who enjoy professional working lives lived predominantly through the medium of Welsh—all pose challenges distinct from the audiences for Welsh media in the 1970s and 1980s, when the campaigns of Indigenous minority-language media were being fought and won. As s4c's internal review recognizes, "The Welsh language tends to play a different role in the lives of a new generation of Welsh speaker than it does for the traditional Welsh communities that still constitute a significant part of s4c's audience" (Stephens 2004: 5). The independent review similarly cites these new challenges when it argues, "There is a new professional class emerging who will only buy into Welsh events if they are high quality and suit their tastes" (cited in Laughton 2004: 41). In the older discourse of Welsh nationalism, such consumer choice may be read as a sign of de-politicization and disloyalty, yet it might equally be seen as a broadening out of the community, a shift that preserves but does not fossilize the language.

Class has always mattered in Welsh society. Left-wing in its political climate, Wales's class politics have for decades been entwined in its cultural politics of both language and nation. Language campaigns and nationalist groups have been disproportionately peopled by the middle classes. The discourse of the final comment cited above, however, suggests a notable shift in political discourse away from the overt political activism of the 1970s and 1980s to a more consumerist and taste-based expression of cultural identity in the present.

BROADCASTING LIFESTYLE ON THE NATIONAL SCREEN

The new professional class of Welsh speakers may have something in common with the new middle classes identified by social scientists, most especially perhaps by the French sociologist Pierre Bourdieu. For Bourdieu (1984: 326), a key element in the new middle classes involves people he describes as "cultural intermediaries": people who work in expressive communication industries and who accrue power and influence from their capacity to shape styles and tastes: "The new cultural intermediaries (the most typical of whom are the producers of cultural programs on TV and radio or the critics of 'quality' newspapers and magazines and all the writer-journalists and journalist-writers) have invented a whole series of genres halfway between legitimate culture and mass production." One of the most visible expressions of this prominence of taste is to be found in the rise of lifestyle television. Lifestyle television has been among the most striking developments in the schedules of many European and North American broadcasters since the 1990s. Its rise to prominence has been understood in terms both of cultural shifts towards a more aestheticized, aspirant mode of identity formation, and, more industrially, as a consequence of the deregulation of broadcasting in a multichannel and globalized age of television (Bell and Hollows 2005).

Lifestyle television may offer a way of suturing older forms of belonging with newer performances of cultural identity. For instance, in an episode of *Pedair Wal* (*Four Walls*, produced by Fflic Production Company for s4c, 2001), we meet a woman who has returned to Wales from London in order to teach in a local school. Her home is a converted primary school in a village in Wales' most sparsely populated county, Powys, and is one of the three homes in which the episode unfolds. In an early scene-setting sequence, *Pedair Wal* provides the following sequence of shots:

1. Long shot of silhouetted animals on a hillside
2. Shot of a blue sky with clouds
3. A mid-shot image of a window of the school / house looking through to an old church
4. Mid-shot of the roof and restored eaves of the school / house
5. Close-up of a new hook with a rope holding down what we presume is a blind
6. Mid-shot of an old Celtic cross in a graveyard

At this point, we hear the presenter, Aled Samuel, ask Anne, "Is there comfort in living next to a graveyard?"—a question quite unimaginable in English-language programs in the United Kingdom. Such moments offer the audience opportunities to cue in to a shared and specifically Welsh sense of tradition, even if this tradition is felt at times to be stifling. The image then cuts to the interior to show both persons standing on newly varnished wooden floors in a kitchen comprised of an Aga range, reclaimed sycamore wooden tops, and MDF cupboards—all of which comprise the habitual branded iconography of middle-class home improvement.

Visually and discursively, the program invites us to witness (and thereby participate in) the negotiation of the modern, signified by the familiar icons of home design, such as wooden flooring, chrome metal hooks, and the historic—signified both through a naturalized landscape and by iconic images of an old Wales in the form of the cross, the graveyard, and the church. Taste here is a matter of selecting the right objects, styles, and brands to create the right "look" (and thereby a pleasing lifestyle), but taste is also occurring in another narrative—that of the migrant returnee whose sense of place goes beyond faithfulness to architecture and extends instead to a materialized sense of belonging conveyed on screen by the graveyard. An older form of belonging, one that is both place- and linguistically based, is being played out here alongside a familiar scene of a fashionably designed lifestyle. While some of the actual objects, such as the flooring, are common to programs in the genre, the chain of signification in which *Pedair Wal* casts them tells a more complex story of how we produce our home. As Frances Bonner (2003: 20) argues, "Television programmes do not remain the same when surrounded by material originating elsewhere and watched by audiences with different cultural backgrounds." While the program's formal, respectful tone seems extraordinary when set alongside the vigor and acerbic critique of many English-language U.K. shows of this kind, *Pedair Wal* demonstrates that the ways of achieving ordinariness on television differ from one cultural context to another.

Importantly, both the producers and s4c can assume that the audience will itself have some cognizance of this diversity. The audience not only encounters, but also brings to bear, a range of televisual and identificatory repertoires to the viewing of cross-cultural formats. s4c's audiences are viewers also of other U.K. channels, and their expectations and competencies are shaped in this bicultural broadcasting reality. Changes in U.K. broadcasting impact on s4c and its audience in distinct ways. The s4c internal review, for example, notes that "Welsh language television needs to modernise so that it equates more closely to that which viewers expect from television in the digital age. Such modernisation will be essential if s4c is to continue operating successfully in what is already a far more competitive broadcasting environment" (Stephens 2004: 27).

"Ordinary" can appear extraordinary when looked at from a different cultural perspective. In a sense, the viewers are already intimate because they constitute a minority in a small nation. In this context, intimacy may only be part of the point; distance might also be required to avoid the ennui of familiarity. Voyeurism requires some sense of distance, and if the chances of knowing the participant, the place, or even the house are relatively high, then this distance may be all the more important for all concerned. The reasons why viewers opt to watch s4c and its specific programs are necessarily diverse. However, choosing to watch the only Welsh-language channel in a televisual landscape filled with English-language programming remains, at some level, an intervention in the field of cultural politics. While this means that the audience has something in common, it does not mean that the audience is homogenous.

We can explore this further by looking at the representation of place in *Pedair Wal* and the cultural work that such representations play. These representations of place are slightly different from those in the English-language programs; they differ not only in what they do or what they show but also in the opportunities and possibilities they offer their audience. Whereas U.K.-wide house shows tend to examine the specificities of places in the country often barely known by the audience, the mode of address of *Pedair Wal* is often familiar in that it anticipates the audience knowing where the chosen places are, and as such, often mentions them only once. This assumption may well be wrong and, at one level, may exclude that segment of the audience that does not possess such knowledge. Nonetheless, because in Welsh cultural life, especially in the Welsh-language community, an affiliation for local place (*bro-garwch*) is a banal form of Welsh nationalism, the gaining of this shorthand knowledge of place is itself a potential route into the Welsh community. *Pedair Wal* has been broadcast on s4c Digital and has also attracted a significant audience among non-Welsh speakers and learners who are able to follow it through subtitles. What at one level appears as staged and laborious talk may, on another, be read as educative, not simply of house design but of how to be at home in a linguistic and cultural community from which the viewer is either geographically apart or is yet to fully comprehend linguistically. At the same time, the production of Welsh-language lifestyle programming makes available to a specifically middle-class audience the experience of being contemporary through the medium of the Welsh language. It enables Welsh viewers to feel simultaneously at one with the wider U.K. TV culture and at home in the distinctiveness of being a Welsh speaker.

CONCLUSION

This chapter has explored how s4c has developed its conversation with the Welsh-speaking community of Wales, in the process sometimes closing down the routes to belonging among others in Wales. In her detective poem, *Y Llofrudd Iaith* (*The Language Murderer*), Gwyneth Lewis sets out to answer the question, "Who killed the Welsh language?" One of the most striking images from the sequence is one in which the appointed detective—a biracial Welsh/Japanese man—stands looking at a typical rural scene of Welsh life. Rather than confirming the ideals of this traditional scene, however, Lewis has the detective reflect on community, posing a powerful rhetorical question to us the readers, and perhaps, posing a question that Indigenous-media producers and scholars need to keep in mind if we are to avoid neglecting the internal differences that give communities their shape and force:

Beth yw perthyn
Ond perthi sydd yn cau
dieithriaid allan?
Dyw cymuned glos
ddim yn cynnwys pob enaid

What is belonging
but the longing to shut out
strangers?
A close community
does not include all souls.

NOTES

1. s4c does not have in-house production. Instead, it commissions programs from producers. Of the thirty-two hours a week broadcast in the Welsh language, ten are provided by the British Broadcasting Corporation (BBC), a commitment enshrined in the Broadcasting Act 1990. Remaining hours are commissioned from independent producers, including HTV, the terrestrial commercial channel in the United Kingdom. The English-language schedule is filled by programming from the U.K.-wide English-language broadcaster, Channel 4. Non–Welsh speaking communities of Wales express frustration at not being able to access the full Channel 4 output. For further discussion of the two languages in Welsh media, see Barlow, Mitchell, and O'Malley 2005.

2. The United Kingdom is a multinational state comprising four nations: England, Northern Ireland, Scotland, and Wales. Devolution occurred in 1997–98, following majority referenda in Scotland and Wales, under the newly elected Labour government of Tony Blair. Devolution entailed the statutory granting of powers from the U.K. central government based in Westminster to national bodies in Northern Ireland, Scotland, and Wales. The powers granted vary considerably and remain a source of debate. Devolution in Scotland, for example, entailed the establishment of both a Scottish Parliament, which may pass acts and vary levels of income tax by up to 3%, and an executive that can make secondary legislation in a limited number of areas. In Wales, devolution entailed the establishment of a National Assembly which does not have power to make primary legislation (this remains with Westminster) although it can make secondary legislation. In Northern Ireland, devolution is inextricably bound with the peace process and here, devolution has been repeatedly suspended. Unlike federalism, devolution means that central government retains the power to reverse the devolving of powers. The U.K. Parliament at Westminster is thus deemed sovereign and retains

responsibility for matters such as foreign policy, macroeconomic policy, constitutional matters, and, especially significant in this context, broadcasting.

3. A comparative Celtic framework remains in play in U.K. policy debates. For instance, in a 2004 parliamentary debate on a report regarding the implementation of the European Charter for Regional or Minority Languages (to which the U.K. government became a signatory in 2000), Member of Parliament Brian Wilson argued that, "on the issue of public usage of the language, in Scotland we are light years behind Wales and Ireland." Wilson went on to cite the difference in treatment of Scots Gaelic and Welsh-language communities: "We have no ambitions to match the £92 million currently paid by the Department for Culture, Media and Sport to s4c to provide a terrestrial Welsh language service" (United Kingdom Parliament 2004).

PART IV

NEW TECHNOLOGIES, TIMELESS KNOWLEDGES:

DIGITAL AND INTERACTIVE MEDIA

RECOLLECTING INDIGENOUS THINKING

IN A CD-ROM

Priscila Faulhaber and Louis Forline

How might Indigenous knowledge, artifacts, and rituals be encoded, encapsulated, or archived in an electronic medium? What issues and considerations might the process of digitally "inscribing" an Indigenous cosmology onto a new medium raise, both for the Indigenous peoples themselves and for anthropologists and museum staff collaborating with them? How might the very concept of digitizing Indigenous knowledge be perceived and conceptualized in the belief system of an Indigenous culture as a form of ritual and magical communication that transports participants to other worlds via a shamanic voyage? How might such digitized forms be utilized by members of the Indigenous cultural group, and for what purposes? The case study of the development of the CD-ROM *Magüta Arü Inü: Recollecting Magüta Thinking*, a collaborative project between representatives of the Indigenous Ticuna communities of Brazil and the Museu Paraense Emílio Goeldi (MPEG, Emílio Goeldi Museum of Pará), provides valuable insights into these questions.[1]

The CD-ROM *Magüta Arü Inü: Recollecting Magüta Thinking* has brought the Indigenous Ticuna culture of Brazil into a virtual communication network. The Goeldi Museum produced the CD-ROM in 2002 in collaboration with Ticuna representatives wishing to "put a new face" on the ethnographic artifacts stored in the museum's technical reserve. For Ticuna representatives, collaboration in the project meant reflecting on how to transpose significant elements of their culture into a multimedia format as well as reflecting on the very nature of cultural and intercultural communication in general. Within the purview of Ticuna belief, the electronic medium presents itself as a magical resource for disseminating cultural information on a wider scale. Thus, Ticuna representatives consider the CD-ROM initiative as a means to circulate new ethnographic contents to new audiences, including other Ticuna artisans. The Ticuna value the opportunity for the kind of interactive feedback offered by the new medium. It is in this light that the Ticuna contemplate the significance of introducing their culture and identity to the global community.

ON THE MULTIMEDIA PROJECT

The *Magüta Arü Inü* project emerged in response to a Ticuna demand to evaluate existing anthropological research on their own culture. In 1997, Priscila Faulhaber had conducted the first part of her fieldwork among the Ticuna, observing a female puberty rite in the community of Barro Vermelho, located on the indigenous land Evare. Yaunapetüna, a Ticuna bilingual teacher, and Ngopacü, the community leader—a "captain" (*capitão*) at Brazil's Fundação Nacional do Indio (National Indian Foundation)—introduced Faulhaber to the puberty ritual, explaining each element of the ritual and contextualizing the puberty rite in the logic of "Magüta Thinking," or the "thinking of the people who were fished out of the Eware." The latter refers to the Ticuna foundation myth, in which Yoi'i, one of a pair of mythical twin brothers, caught some fish in the primordial Eware stream. When brought on land, these fish transformed into the first Ticuna. It is for this reason, along with the preservation of the language, that the puberty ritual constitutes a major source of Ticuna cultural belonging and that many Ticuna communities still perform it.[2]

At the climax of the ritual, community members wearing masks enter the house reserved for this initiation ceremony and dance with the young woman who is the focal point of the ritual. When Faulhaber asked about the meaning of the ceremonial masks, the school teacher and the captain explained that many ceremonial masks, such as the ones being used at that moment, as well as many other cultural artifacts of the Ticuna, had been taken from the villages and had been placed in museums by anthropologists and other outsiders. These community leaders expressed interest in visiting those museums to become reconnected to the removed cultural artifacts of their deceased relatives, since many among the Ticuna were beginning to forget the history told by their elders.[3] Yaunapetüna and the captain believed that the sight of those items on display would remind the Ticuna of the teachings of their cultural heroes.

The word *tchiga* in Ticuna means both "story" and "history" and encompasses tales of adventure, of love, and of intrigue, as well as elders' narratives about the genesis of the Ticuna people. Thus, the tales of Yoi'i, Too'ena, and Tchowico, which we will discuss later, are examples of *tchiga*. For the Ticuna, looking at the photographs and ritual artifacts in the museum was akin to consulting their elders and invoking their parted relatives. In short, the museum's collection offered a chance to have the wisdom of previous generations translated into the world of the living. Nevertheless, among the Ticuna there is no continuity between the living and their dead relatives, nor is there any possibility for the living to access by normal terrestrial pathways the mythical territory of Eware, since deceased relatives live in their own realm, a domain off limits to the living. The iconography recalled a long history of war and territorial struggle between the Ticuna and their enemies. Ceremonial instruments were associated with ancient weapons, and the masks with invisible beings that mediate relationships among people and between people and the environment. The Ticuna vision of the cosmos focuses on the movements of celestial bodies; this vision appears on all icons in order to orient the Ticuna in this world and in the world of the dead inhabited by the Magüta, the immortalized dead relatives of the Ticuna.

The richness of Ticuna cosmology and the needs of the community drew a number of interested parties to the CD-ROM project. Faulhaber, the primary author of this article and an anthropologist with the Museu Paraense Emílio Goeldi, conceived the project, conducted most of the fieldwork, and coordinated the making of the CD-ROM. The project received funding from Brazil's National Council for Scientific and Technological Development. The videographer Ilma Bittencourt, of the Centro de Pesquisa e Documentação Popular, shot and edited the video footage. The anthropologist Hugo Camacho, of the Instituto Colombiano del Bienestar Familiar, accompanied Faulhaber on field trips into Colombia. The linguist Marília Facó Soares, a Ticuna-language expert with the Museu Nacional do Rio de Janeiro, and the Web designer Carlota Brito (of the Goeldi Museum) also joined the project. Louis Forline, the coauthor of this article and then a researcher at the Goeldi Museum, followed the project activities and took part in many theoretical and practical discussions, sharing his Indigenist and anthropological views with the team.

The team of scholars proceeded to compile an inventory of the Ticuna ritual artifacts housed at the Goeldi Museum, mostly masks and musical instruments collected in the early 1940s by the German ethnologist Curt

Unkel (1883–1945), better known by his adopted Indigenous name, Curt Nimuendaju.[4] Ticuna elders acquainted with Nimuendaju still remember episodes related to his death in 1945 during fieldwork among the Ticuna. They value Nimuendaju's ethnographic work to preserve the rituals as part of their struggle for cultural survival. The Ticuna memory of Nimuendaju also sheds a light on the still fragmentary history of his work in Brazil as an ethnologist, archeologist (Nimuendaju 2004), linguist, and indigenist. An ethnography of Ticuna mythology by Nimuendaju was published after his death, in the early 1950s (Nimuendaju 1952), and it closely follows both the iconography of Ticuna ritual artifacts (collected by Nimuendaju himself for the Goeldi Museum), as well as the symbolism of the puberty rituals of today. He studied more than fifty Indigenous peoples in Brazil and corresponded with renowned scholars such as Erland Nordenskiöld and Robert Lowie (Nunes Pereira 1946; Grupioni 1998; Welper 2002; Hemming 2003).

Six Ticuna representatives undertook the final identification of the Nimuendaju material at a workshop held at the Goeldi Museum in Belém in late 2002 and made significant contributions to the project (see fig. 13.1). Ngematucü Pedro Inácio Pinheiro (age 60), an important leader and activist in the struggle for land demarcation since the 1970s and a former president of honor of the General Council of the Ticuna Tribe, acted as the main interpreter and translator of the significant contents of the Ticuna culture (see fig. 13.2). Daütchina (age 61), Ngematucü's wife, who knows shamanism and is closely bound to the values of the Magüta people, was very much involved. Paütchina (age 80), Daütchina's mother, who is very knowledgeable about Ticuna cosmology, has lived since 1997 in the Enepü Ticuna community in the indigenous land Evare 2, as do her daughter and her son-in-law. Dawegukü (age 48), from Resguardo Arara, Colombia, is a bilingual Ticuna-Spanish teacher and a compiler of Ticuna myths. Dui (age 46), from Resguardo Progreso, Colombia, is a skilled artist and artisan and the brother of Dawegukü. Rounding off the Ticuna group was Wochankü (age 30), from Resguardo Nazaré, Colombia, a student of linguistics at the Instituto de Investigaciones Amazónicas who worked on the lexical inventory.

The 2002 workshop in Belém resulted in the collectively authored script for the CD-ROM. Also, at this time, we participants began to understand that the myths conveyed by Ticuna ceremonies and reported by Nimuendaju made sense in the logic of Magüta magical thinking. Ticuna representatives assisted in selecting the images and in determining the

(*above*) Ticuna participants at work planning the CD-ROM *Magüta Arü Inü*.

(*left*) Ngematucü at work designing the CD-ROM *Magüta Arü Inü*.

PHOTOS BY MIGUEL CHIKAOKA.

sequence in which they would be displayed. They also explicated Ticuna iconography and made the final decisions in editing the video and selecting the voice-over commentary. In addition to revitalizing the Nimuendaju archives, the multimedia presentation covered the following items: (1) an essay on land and Ticuna territoriality in the face of interethnic contact; (2) images of artifacts from the Nimuendaju collection and ethnographic items collected in the current project; (3) the Ticuna interpretation—beyond the linguistic dimension—of the artifacts collected by Nimuendaju in 1941–42; (4) the "turning of the sky," the Ticuna view of the cosmos and mythical references to their perception of the movement of constellations, the changing of the seasons, and associated strategies for subsistence; (5) the video recording of a puberty ritual performed in July 2002 in the Enepü community; (6) a gallery of songs and images from the puberty ritual; and (7) a lexicon of pronounced and written words related to the images shown.

In what follows, we focus on the task of cultural translation,[5] which entailed transforming Magüta thought into a digitized databank—in other words, systematizing the meaning of Ticuna rituals, iconography, and artifacts.

Maiden Initiation and Shamanic Initiation

Maiden initiation among the Ticuna is similar to shamanic initiation in that the novice takes a sort of "mind trip" across successive worlds that make up Indigenous cosmogony. Ritual initiation in both cases is a pathway for understanding cosmogony and constitutes the foundational roots of social organization in each Indigenous community. Communicative games allow the novice access to supernatural beings. The novice represents her people in this ritual collaboration between humans and nonhumans, thus guaranteeing an alliance between the human and supernatural worlds. Both shamanism and the puberty festival are rituals that constitute dynamic social, cultural, and ethnic identities. The voyage of initiation traverses the upper aerial and atmospheric worlds, the in-between terrestrial level, and the underground and underwater realms. The initiate's voyage becomes a kind of mental cartography, linking individual and cultural memories in a manner analogous to an electronic network (Chaumeil 2000).

Ritual entails a prescribed formal performance, constructed as a system of symbolic communication both in the pragmatic sense (associating word and deed) as well as in the actors' experience of ritual statements

(Tambiah 1985). It is a generalized medium of social intervention in which the vehicles for constructing messages convert socially shared experiences into a chain of communication. The iconic symbols of ritual action—the patterns, meaning, and continuity they create—establish a cultural code.

The puberty festival for a Ticuna girl begins soon after her first menstruation. Her small seclusion room, made of straw, is attached to her father's house, and she remains inside it for up to six months. During this time, she is visited only by the older women, who teach her the new responsibilities of womanhood. The older women counsel the young woman through stories and songs about the adventures of cultural heroes; these help to describe her new social obligations as an adult woman. Throughout the ritual, the girl must not ingest certain foods considered impure, as she is considered to be in a state of extreme fragility.

At a certain point, the older women transfer the maiden to another reserved enclosure in the "house of the festival." There she waits until she is painted and introduced to the group. The ritual marks the transition between childhood and puberty and serves as an initiation into Ticuna social life. The ceremony spans the moment of passage from one state into another, symbolically playing out significant life experience.

Among the mythical events expressing the Ticuna imaginary, it is important to mention the primordial puberty ritual of To'oena, daughter of the cultural hero Yoi'i. Curiosity impelled her to leave her seclusion and wander to the place where ritual instruments forbidden to women were displayed. Enraged by this sacrilege, the spirits who played those instruments (the female and male *uaricana*, respectively a trumpet and a wooden loudspeaker) employed invisible forces that quartered her body. On that day, the mythical Eware stream turned blood red; all of the people, including To'oena's mother and sister, were forced to eat the meat of the transgressor; and Yoi'i himself forbade them to mourn her passing by threatening them with death.

The Making of the Video

With this mythic story in mind, our CD-ROM team decided to record the puberty festival for a girl named Tueguna, which took place at the Enepü Ticuna Village in the indigenous land Evare 2 in Brazil on July 30 and 31, 2002. The script for the video was intended to illuminate ritual artifacts by including, in voice-over, an ensemble of Ticuna translations of selected stories, sung in unison by hosts and ritual specialists.

Though the ritual is mostly banned for the uninitiated, the Ticuna specialists invited our videographer, Ilma Bittencourt, to film the event because they were interested in having a thorough record of the festival. Nevertheless, they advised her of the danger involved in being excessively curious, reminding her of To'oena's punishment. Later, Bittencourt confided that seeing and handling the tools—as well as the weight of the possible misappropriation of Indian images without just compensation for property rights—frightened her.[6]

In the field, we recorded a song about To'oena's punishment in the Eware stream, which became the musical leitmotiv for the project. Tuegucü, a Ticuna referred to by Brazilian nationals as Ildo, had an electric keyboard at home, and we asked him to play the Eware song on it. He invested long hours in this task, as he was determined to find the right chords for this mythical melody. His performance serves as an overture on the CD-ROM, as this song appropriately symbolizes this joint project. The soundtrack also includes songs performed by youth and adult choirs that we recorded in Enepü.

A draft version of the video was later shown to the Ticuna representatives who attended the 2002 workshop. They gave suggestions on narrative construction and chose Ngematucü as the narrator for his translating skills.

The Translation of Magüta Thinking into Electronic Text

While running a multimedia program on a computer monitor, a black screen usually indicates a pause in the showing of contents. One of our Ticuna hosts, Daütchina, told us about the *genipa*, a vegetable pigment used in Ticuna facial and body painting to protect the body, mind, and person against evil influences. Since the Ticuna specialists used the iconography of ritual artifacts as a key for cultural translation, we all decided that the background screen of the CD-ROM should also have the color of genipa so as to protect those who participated in its production.

Computational aesthetics affect digital editing, which in turn imposes a new form of interaction with written text that differs markedly from printed material. Comparing printed and electronic texts, Antonio Rodríguez de Las Eras (cited in Chartier 2002) points out that, in the latter case, the texts successively emerge from the depths of the three-dimensional screen to reach the luminous surface. In digital space, the text browser is a roll similar to a scroll, and the navigator can choose the path of his / her reading in the same way as one would with a codex with numbered pages, where the reader follows the already ordered sequence of thinking (Chartier 2002; Eckert and Rocha 2005). The transposition of human thinking into electronic devices implies a pulverization of the "author function" (Foucault 2004) in a twofold way: (1) the transposition into digital codes renders property rights looser and more accessible, better allowing for their public consumption, and (2) in media language, precise quotes are not necessarily prescribed if the former idea is transformed. Electronic texts, located in a domain of knowledge built differently from printed matter, do not flow in accordance with linear, deductive logic (Chartier 2002). As such, the texts are analogous to the mythical thinking characteristic of people without an alphabet, as is the case of many Amazonian Indians.

According to Michael Fischer (1999), narratives and institutionalized discourses act as switches and circuits of thought, behavior, action, organization, and cultural forms. The Ticuna specialists elaborated a "native theory" to show how electronic devices could serve as tools for a communicative ritual that would enable its participants to travel to other worlds. Thus, through ritual action, the Ticuna view access to an "electronic society" as a kind of shamanic voyage.

THE DATABANK, THE ETHNOGRAPHIC COLLECTION, AND RITUAL ARTIFACTS

The databank developed for the *Magüta Arü Inü* project systematizes iconographic interconnections by using classificatory criteria consistent with the logic of Magüta thinking. In so doing, we attempted to harmonize these classificatory criteria with the vision of the Ticuna as they scrutinized and described the ritual artifacts used in the female puberty ritual.

The Goeldi Museum holds 444 Ticuna objects collected by Curt Nimuendaju between 1941 and 1942. This is one of the most significant Brazilian collections of the material culture of the Ticuna people. Included in this current databank are also 11 objects that Faulhaber collected between 2000 and 2002: masks and clothes, as well as a wheel and a cloth used in the puberty ritual. These artifacts demonstrate a continuity through time of the meanings contained in Ticuna culture.

In one sense, the ordering of Ticuna artifacts in this databank primarily follows the guidelines of ethnographic criteria in attempting to record how Magüta thinking establishes the iconography of a given sociocultural organization. The description of each artifact, provided in both Portuguese and Ticuna, identifies its constituent materials, use, manufacturing process, dimensions, collection data, and decorative motifs, and also includes a Ticuna account of its most salient features with regards to iconography and symbolism. The images of humans, animals, plants, and mythological motifs refer to zoological, botanical, and astronomical criteria of classification. Though interpretations produced by different disciplines and using different parameters often conflict, our interdisciplinary focus entailed the analytical organization of the collected materials as "boundary objects" containing elements that are understood to have different meanings in different worlds (Star and Griesemer 1989).

Thus, we attempted to understand Ticuna artifacts in terms of their ritual use, which includes two categories: (1) dancing implements, such as masks and mask dressings, barkcloths and wheels, and (2) symbolic/ signaling instruments, such as ceremonial batons, drums, flutes, and wooden staves.

Ticuna Ritual Artifacts and Travel to Other Worlds
The Ticuna produce artifacts that serve as ritual instruments representing weapons, musical instruments, or mythical entities. The Ticuna word that corresponds to "ritual artifact" is translated as "an instrument or something that is useful for war training, for knowledge, for lore, for science"—a definition that reflects the conflict in Ticuna interpretations of their own material culture. Ticuna elders assigned this meaning to the photograph of an artifact, a piece of barkcloth used in the ritual as a cosmogonic wheel that shields the girl and her reference group against threats (see figs. 13.3 and 13.4). This artifact—registered among the Goeldi Museum's holdings—iconographically expresses the symbol that corresponds, in our society, to the opposition between "fortune" and "misfortune." Associated with the learning of warfare, this artifact guards memories of fights against enemies both mythical and real, and can thus be interpreted as a talisman for vanquishing the opposition, both symbolic and potential.

The icon of converging and diverging arrows controls navigation on the CD-ROM, allowing for advances and retreats much like in a video war game. This icon joins images and meanings, helping the navigator to become familiar with Ticuna culture. Such knowledge, an index of good fortune, is an affirming factor of identity. Conversely, the Ticuna believe

(*top*) Barkcloth used on a cosmogonic wheel in Ticuna puberty ritual. Design by Dui. (*bottom*) Color rendering of the pictorial narrative on the barkcloth above. Design by Dui.

PHOTOS BY MIGUEL CHIKAOKA.

that ignorance of this culture will bring misfortune and tragedy to those who forget their purpose and lose their frame of reference.

In puberty rituals, artifacts become a means of communication. This communication embraces the ritual life of those who celebrate their family members and neighbors, the dead, and those living in the world beyond. Ritual often addresses enemies as well, since enemies also populate the world of the dead and, in certain situations, are transformed into allies. Barriers between the worlds of the living and the dead are crossed by the initiates—pubescent girls, potential candidates—through magical acts made possible by those artifacts. Thus, Magüta thinking itself also appears as an artifact: as a logical construction, a puzzle through which the Ticuna can interpret the relationship between worlds. According to the Ticuna representatives, ritual artifacts taken from them during conflicts were later used in battle episodes between enemies, prior to the colonial conquest, and in interethnic contact. Today, such conflicts are alive in the memories of family, clan, moiety, and community. To explain the meaning of their iconography, Ticuna often evoke a scenario of warfare. In their accounts of border conflicts, they update the war scenario, visualizing it as a framework for understanding the tensions between representatives of the dominant national society and of Indigenous peoples. These confrontations are also internalized in intraethnic rivalry between clans, communities, and Indian organizations.

For Tueguna's ceremony, we acquired a single ceremonial costume, or mask, called Tchowico and fabricated by Ngematucü (see fig. 13.5). The Ticuna consider the mask to consist of two parts—the mask's head / face and the mask's body covering (see figs. 13.6a, 13.6b). After the ceremony, this mask was presented to the Ethnographic Collection of the Goeldi Museum. According to Ngematucü, the Tchowico's body covering design evokes the story of the two brothers who decide to avenge the death of their sister. Some versions of this narrative return to the cosmogonic myth, according to which the three siblings are children of the incestuous union between the Moon (male) and the Sun (female). Other versions of the myth address the moment of contact. In this sense, revenge against the killer affirms the Ticuna identity of the Moon's children despite the presence of the colonizer. The mask gives the wearer the magic power to penetrate the depths of the earth and to escape from the minions of his sister's murderer. The fact that a single mask in Tueguna's ceremony represents the two brothers in the ritual can be explained by a logic of multiplication: one mask symbolizes all the masks appearing in Ticuna

(*above*) A Ticuna girl looking at Tchowico, alongside a couple of elders entering the festival house. PHOTO BY MIGUEL CHIKAOKA.

Tchowico body sheath, front view (*below left*) and back view (*below right*). PHOTOS BY MIGUEL CHIKAOKA.

ceremonies. In this ceremony, the song of Tawemacü, the Moon, joins the narrative leitmotif as a complement to Yoi'i's song about the punishment of To'oena.

Social Organization and Journeys into Identity

We must reemphasize that the Ticuna are revitalizing their forms of ethnic and cultural representation. They regard the inscription of digital codes in a multimedia system and the Internet connection as analogous to a phone call. Thus, they understand electronic communication as a form of ritual communication, one that creates conditions for journeys into the cosmos and for interactions between humans and other beings residing in other worlds.

The Ticuna have two exogamic moieties. The first half includes those clans anthropologically classified as being "birds," "feathers," "feathered," or "of the air." The other half contains clans identified as being "not feathered," "without feathers," i.e. "with skin," "shell," "fur," or "of the earth." Nimuendaju pointed out that these moieties correspond to the Ticuna division of the universe, so there is a "western moiety" and an "eastern moiety." The complementary relation between the moieties expresses a mechanism for the consolidation of group identity. Even non-Indian representatives of the national Brazilian society are incorporated into this social organization: the children of non-Indian men with Ticuna women are said to belong to the nation of the bull (*woca* in Ticuna). This division signals a logic of opposition between moieties. For this reason, the incorporation of the opposite side was vital in the construction of our multimedia product as a dynamic, image-based reenactment of the disputes and alliances between moieties, factions, and different organizations.

In intercultural dynamics, one should not speak in terms of a "loss" of Ticuna culture as a whole or of a loss of the artifacts collected for museum holdings. In Ticuna culture, a father only keeps the masks and related instruments until the puberty festival of his youngest daughter: after that, he destroys the implements. Thus, when artifacts are sent to a museum, they cannot be used in the ritual context for which they were designed. By offering artifacts to the museum, the Ticuna express a desire to enter and engage the field of their "other": the "cultivated" men and women who manage communicative tools in the dominant culture's society of knowledge.

The Ticuna represent those artifacts as tools that transport them across space and time, travels perceived as similar to shamanistic voyages, traversing the borders separating them from other worlds. These tools are living objects, devices of intervention that mediate between humans and nonhumans. So our multimedia product took the shape of a device for communication between the social world of the Ticuna and the other worlds, including that of European thinking. By extension, this representation of ritual includes the world of museums to which the artifacts are destined.

Those artifacts relay the expressive and communicative experiences that construct the Ticuna self-image through daily practices relating territory to culture. As such, they enact a process that affirms identity *and* that manages the influence of the "white" world on Ticuna terms by means of ritual instruments and magical operations that transpose the mythical thinking into digital media. The logic of vengeance (of the murdered sister) and punishment (of the careless sister), proper to the Ticuna myth and conceived in the field of relations of intimacy between relatives and guests at the celebration, begins to take on ethical connotations related to the protection of the culture and of the moral integrity of Ticuna girls. Thus, even before Ticuna mythical thinking enters the political arena of the public sphere that characterizes the society of knowledge in the twenty-first century, Ticuna mythology and ritual have marked out a space for interaction between the Ticuna and others that still affords a sense of the integrity of Ticuna culture.

DISTRIBUTION OF INDIGENOUS MEDIA AND EXPECTATIONS
OF AUDIENCE RESPONSE

On completion of the CD-ROM *Magüta Arü Inü: Recollecting Magüta Thinking*, the Goeldi Museum sent twelve hundred copies to the Ticuna, including three hundred each for the following entities: the General Council of the Ticuna Tribe in Brazil, the General Organization of Ticuna Teachers in Brazil, the Ticuna communities in Colombia, and the Ticuna community in Enepü, Brazil, located in a remote area near the Brazil-Colombia border, where the filming took place. Those copies are being utilized in instruction courses for Ticuna teachers and artisans. With resources obtained by Brazil's Instituto do Patrimônio Histórico e Artístico Nacional (Institute for National Historic and Artistic Patrimony) through the 2003 Rodrigo de Melo Franco de Andrade Award, the Museum purchased computer equipment that was donated directly to the

Ticuna community in Enepü, where some bilingual teachers already have learned to access the Internet.

Electronic media allow one to delve into a virtual framework of planetary communication. Reading texts and perceiving sounds and images on a screen in a nonlinear sequence creates a new relationship with the audience. The possibility of transposing Indigenous thinking into digital media allows for the propagation of ritual meanings to new audiences, audiences different from those for whom the rituals were originally intended. This dissemination, then, fosters the possibility of feedback from Ticuna artisans and bilingual teachers. Thus, the Ticuna anticipate a new way of sharing knowledge, as their own culture could be inserted into a planetary chain that includes programs of scientific dissemination or public exhibition of expressive forms germane to specific Indigenous peoples.

Some Indigenous communities in various parts of the world have become wary of being the objects of visual media and the implications these images convey in the ideology of "vanishing natives" (cf. Prins 2004). Although some Indigenous communities still refrain from such a perceived objectification, others, such as the Ticuna, have embraced this as a form of self-expression and seen it as a method to reproduce the cultural knowledge that is meaningful to them and others. It is in this sense that the Ticuna regard the CD-ROM *Magüta Arü Inü* as an instrument for virtual communication and a way to overcome barriers they perceive between themselves and the dominant cultures that sponsor the museums to which their artifacts have for many years been shipped. As Ngematücü expressed on the release of the CD-ROM in Belém in 2003, it is impossible to return to a prior situation when the Magüta people lived at the headwaters of the Eware stream. "The damage has already been done," he proclaimed. In turn, he had traveled a long way to take part in the CD-ROM launching event, hoping to make new allies for his people, as this product now serves as an instrument that bridges different worlds. Transferring Magüta thinking into an electronic medium implies translating and updating meaningful cultural contents in consonance with the Ticuna, the main readers of this "text."

NOTES

We express much gratitude to Eliseo Altunaga for his theoretical suggestions about the imagery connections between script and fictional narrative construction. We are grateful to Horácio Higuchi for his hand in editing the article. We also appreciate the assistance of Michelle Stewart and Pamela Wilson, who helped improve the manuscript in no small measure.

1. The Ticuna territory is about 600 kilometers long, and runs west to east from the Chimbote region in Peru, along the Amazonas-Solimães Valley (Oliveira 1988; Goulard 1998, 2002), in the so-called Colombian-Amazonian Trapezoid, to the Barreira da Missão region in the municipality (county) of Tefé, in the Brazilian state of Amazonas (Faulhaber 2001). The Ticuna population resides in three countries: some 26,000 in Brazil, 10,000 in Colombia, and up to 6,000 in Peru (Oliveira 1988; Goulard 1998, 2002). Together, they constitute the most populous Indigenous group in Amazonia. Aside from their own Ticuna language, they also speak the official language of the country in which they reside—either Portuguese or Spanish (López 2000).

2. Although the Ticuna have never ceased to practice the ritual, they were forced to practice it secretly for many years in remote communities, fearing the missionaries and rubber tappers, who stigmatized it. Anthropologists, however, have been considered allies by the Ticuna, as they helped affirm the Ticuna's Indigenous identity and their distinctive cultural traits. Anthropologists galvanized a movement for the positive valuation of Ticuna ethnicity in 1992, when a large portion of their territory was officially demarcated by the Brazilian government.

3. Among the Ticuna, dead relatives cease to be consanguines and are classified alongside their enemies in the symbolic territory of Otherness. According to Manuela Carneiro da Cunha (1978), among lowland Indian groups of South America, such as the Kraho and Canela, there is an opposition between the dead and living and not a continuum, properly speaking.

4. This surname is not accented in Portuguese. In the Guarani language, it means "he who built his own home among us." Unkel adopted this name when he naturalized himself as a Brazilian.

5. Here we consider the definition of cultural translation to be an unceasing quest for harmony between different points of view, which implies a constant recreation of significant contents, in the perspective proposed by Talal Asad (1984) from a reading of Benjamin 1992.

6. An alternative to resolving issues of copyrighting would have been to hold a video workshop for the Ticuna to engage in their own filmmaking, as is done by a project underway in Brazil known as Vídeo nas Aldeias (VNA, Video in the Villages). We encouraged some of the Ticuna to film their activities but they indicated that they did not feel adequately prepared to do so. Thus, to document their rituals they requested that our video staff film these events. Additionally, because of budget constraints, we were not able to embark on such a project. As a result, our solution was to document events in a participatory manner, accompanying the Ticuna's ritual performance.

CHAPTER 14

DIGITAL TOOLS AND THE MANAGEMENT OF
AUSTRALIAN ABORIGINAL DESERT KNOWLEDGE

Michael Christie

What is the contemporary status of Australian Aboriginal knowledge traditions? Some claim that they are alive and well in communities throughout Australia, where Aboriginal people continue to celebrate their identities through persistence and resistance. Others claim that they are threatened with extinction. Some Aboriginal people insist on keeping their knowledge exclusively for themselves and their kin, while others are keen to share and commercialize. This chapter examines Aboriginal knowledge in the context of a large Australian research institution, with particular reference to the role of databases and digitizing technologies in the ongoing life of ancestral knowledge traditions.

AUSTRALIAN ABORIGINAL DESERT KNOWLEDGE
IN A COOPERATIVE RESEARCH CENTER

Alice Springs, in the desert heart of Australia, is the home of a cooperative research center (CRC) working on desert knowledge.[1] According to the Desert Knowledge CRC Web site, desert knowledge is "the unique knowledge Australians have about prospering in the hot, dry and isolated inland that makes up two thirds of their continent" (www.desertknowl edge.com.au /). The research center's mission is clear, according to its Web site:

> A virtual network of researchers from 28 partner organisations nationwide links traditional knowledge and local desert skills with cutting edge Western science. . . . Marketing the products of our unique research brand to some 1.5 billion people around the globe

who also live in hot, dry and isolated places, our innovative research partnership will pave the way for Australia's next major export sector. [The Desert Knowledge CRC] is supported by over $20 million of Australian Federal funding as well as cash and in-kind commitments from its 28 partner organizations to create a research effort worth a total of $90 million over the next seven years.[2]

Interestingly, while over half of the total desert population is Aboriginal (and Aborigines account for 80 percent of the population outside of urban centers), the Web site's "About Us" section makes no mention of Aborigines, and there is little representation of Aboriginal people on the research or administrative staff of the CRC.

This is a story of my work as a member of a small group set up in the CRC to develop a "scoping"[3] study of Indigenous knowledge, its role in research, and its protection under law. My involvement as a non-Indigenous member of the group was through the Charles Darwin University, a partner in the CRC. My previous experience in other parts of Australia had concerned Aboriginal knowledge and education particularly in Arnhem Land with "saltwater people" (Christie 1994, 2000; Christie and Perrett 1996). The most recent was a "collective memory" project in which I looked at digital technologies and the intergenerational transmission of Aboriginal knowledge traditions (see www.cdu.edu.au / ik).

The scoping group included Aboriginal and non-Aboriginal members and continues its work, now trying to make sure that the findings and recommendations that we develop become ratified by the CRC governing board. The leader of the group was my former boss, an Aboriginal woman who was concerned by the misappropriation of Aboriginal knowledge. My own concern centered on how information technologies were (re)configuring and commodifying (and thus generally misrepresenting) Aboriginal knowledge throughout the vast desert area, where outbreaks of "archive fever" (Derrida 1995) are increasingly common. Other members of the group, including one traditional owner of desert knowledge, were researching traditional plant use in the desert and preparing a database of plant names and uses for potential commercialization. Another was working to help articulate the traditional cultural values of water in a particular desert region and to find pathways by which Aboriginal owners might begin negotiating with government and industry over their traditional water resources, utilizing their own cultural ways of representing their perspectives and values. Other group members were Aboriginal lawyers and academics from more southern parts of Australia whose communities have their own knowledge traditions and their own struggle to "grow up" young people inside those traditions.

We all worked hard to agree on and make clear the politics of representation at work in our negotiations and writing. Australian Aboriginal knowledge is governed by strict rules concerning the right to make representations, so we wrote our papers in "an objective, distanced style" and with the recognition that they did not represent an Indigenous voice or claim an Indigenous authority—nor could they, being official documents for the CRC. The position paper made a point of acknowledging "the institutionalised silencing, and marginalizing of Aboriginal people's voices, that is a consequence of the textual representation of Indigenous people's cultures, societies and ways of knowing." In recognizing the tendency for research and academic discourse to "speak for" Indigenous people— often without those peoples' consent or involvement—the position paper sought to "advocate on behalf of Indigenous peoples, in the knowledge that it cannot, by its nature, adequately represent their voices."[4]

CHARACTERIZING DESERT ABORIGINAL KNOWLEDGE

We had trouble from the beginning developing a unified position paper on the many discrete knowledge traditions of various peoples for whom we had already admitted we had no legal right to speak (legal, that is, under traditional Aboriginal law). In responding to the institutional mandates of the CRC, we acknowledged that from an Aboriginal perspective, we were applying an alien and totalizing epistemological framework.

The natural inclination of the group was to identify Aboriginal knowledge as a special case for the CRC, by defining it. I began to resist this process, because it seemed inevitably to produce a reading of Indigenous knowledge as something that could be contained in, or recognized by, a Western research agenda, without a fundamental commitment to ongoing negotiated translation work between the two working traditions.[5] A definition would further enable Western researchers to reduce ancestral knowledge traditions to *content*. We could not define Aboriginal knowledge without emphasizing its commodifiability, becoming complicit in the marginalization that we had already decided would be a consequence of textual representation. Perhaps we should abandon the goal of defining Aboriginal knowledge and try instead to characterize it. I suggested some characterizations that might be accepted as representative of the Australian case (and hopefully the desert case) along the following lines:

1. Aboriginal knowledge, like all other knowledge, comes out of the routine practices of everyday life and makes those practices possible. Sometimes particular representations of knowledge become codified in particular ways, as in art and painting—and in databases, university textbooks, and research papers—but normally, knowledge is embedded in the ways people live out their daily lives. It is performative. It should be understood more as something that you *do* than as something that you *have*. Therefore, ensuring the successful transmission of knowledge traditions into the future generations has more to do with young people learning how to construct, rehearse, perform, and celebrate knowledge collectively than it has to do with specific content, such as place names and species names and facts about their usefulness.

2. Aboriginal knowledge traditions differ from place to place. They derive from and enable culturally specific and context-specific practices. Australian Aboriginal knowledge is possibly different from many other Indigenous knowledge systems around the world, because language, land, and identity are interdependent in a unique way in the Australian Aboriginal world and in a distinctive way in each context. We should not assume that there is something universal about Aboriginal knowledge, even though there is important work being done protecting Indigenous knowledge globally. Like all knowledge, desert knowledge is fundamentally local. It comes from place and relates people to place in their everyday lives. When it is abstracted and generalized, it loses some of its richness, quality, and usefulness. It is at work in urban as well as remote settings, embedded in place and practice. The natural environment is an embodiment of both ancestral and recent histories. The species it holds participate in making the world both intelligible and meaningful. People are only part of the knowledge system at work in the world.

3. Aboriginal knowledge is owned. Laws concerning who can say what, and who can profit from particular performances, existed throughout Australia for millennia before colonization. Western laws cannot define Aboriginal knowledge adequately or accommo-

date its requirements. They may go some way toward linking tradi-tional knowledge systems with Australian law, but they will never replace or take precedence over the need for local respectful agree-ments over place and history, and agreements over what knowledge is, who it belongs to, and what can be done with it.

4. Aboriginal knowledge is collective. It is owned and performed by groups of people, and its representation depends on the collective memory at work in Aboriginal languages and attendant social prac-tices, structures, and performance traditions, as well as in the phys-ical features of their land, its species, and other "natural" phe-nomena. It is also often (but not always) protected by a system of "managers" or "caretakers" who have rights through kinship to supervise and control the performance of particular knowledge tra-ditions. People who share it must account for their right to represent it. People who receive it must account for the use to which it is put. Laws and acceptable practices that govern knowledge use are local and need to be understood and negotiated at the local level. None of this changes when digitizing technologies (and all the problems they create and solve) arrive in an Aboriginal community. Social groupings are constituted through shared knowledge, and Aborigi-nal identity depends as much on practices of exclusion—making only some knowledge available freely, and controlling the avail-ability of other knowledge—as it does on sharing and inclusion.

5. Aboriginal knowledge is responsive, active, and constantly re-newed and reconfigured. It continues to embrace and make use of new technology. It is eco-logical. What becomes sequestered on a database or a DVD or a book is only ever already a trace of some encounter, waiting to be called on as a resource in a new knowledge production episode.

The working group accepted my efforts to have us characterize this complexity with mixed enthusiasm. It was clear to everyone that I had a problem with the uncritical use of databases in Aboriginal knowledge work, and I had made clear what I was hoping would be better alterna-tives (Christie 2005). People in the working group who were already involved in database projects quite naturally felt under attack and felt that I was ignoring the fact that traditional knowledge in the desert was threatened and in danger of extinction.

As we pored over the documents we were working on together, the people involved in databasing projects pointed out several times that we had been talking on some pages about desert knowledge as being threatened, and on other pages we had been declaring it alive and well.[6] We were able to agree that the processes whereby knowledge traditions are renewed in each generation are still at work, even if some of the specific knowledge of the medical and nutritional uses of plants, for example, may be dying out. While many people are still living in the desert, the more settled and externally supported life they lead today is much less dependent on bush tucker (wild foods) and bush medicine, and thus less dependent on specific botanical and pharmacological knowledge. Clearly something is threatened with extinction even if some of the traditional knowledge practices are being renewed in these radically changed circumstances.[7]

The focus on the vibrancy of contemporary Aboriginal knowledge was particularly enthusiastically embraced by the Aboriginal team members from southern states whose traditional languages had been lost and whose environmental and religious knowledge practices had been decimated a hundred or more years ago. They were clear that their knowledge practices were distinctively Aboriginal and were properly considered traditional, even if their "content" (i.e., their words, artifacts, technologies) was not. Our work characterizing (rather than defining) Aboriginal knowledge brought the discussions around to empirical questions—"Which knowledge practices?" "Where are they at work?" "Who does them?"

The ethnobotanical work is clearly motivating for the participants and brings Aboriginal people together in discussion about knowledge, history, the environment, and sustainable livelihoods. In terms of the ethnobotanical documentation (some call it "knowledge harvesting"), it is really no different than what was being done in Australia even before it was Australia. Robert Brown did similar collecting in Arnhem Land in 1803, and his data and samples went into the imperial archive and just sat there.[8] The actual content of the databases, and its usefulness, remains largely unexamined. At another Desert Knowledge CRC research meeting, it became clear that there was nothing in any of the Aboriginal-owned databases that was not already in the public domain (in books on Aboriginal pharmacology or bush tucker, for example), but this does not deter the researchers. Twenty years ago, pharmaceutical companies were interested in working with Aboriginal knowledge, but these days they prefer to set up laboratories that process and interrogate every bit of every species in a search for profitability, without any need to negotiate over intellectual property.

RESEARCH AGENDAS AND THE POLITICS
OF SCALE AND REPRESENTATION

We took a trip to a desert community to meet the Aboriginal elders working on a plant project. Everyone had a great time meeting the land-owners and seeing their country, and quite different knowledge production agendas crystallized. The two Toyotas carried a very diverse group of interested people, including Aboriginal people from other desert areas, who ended up deciding among themselves to make arrangements for further collaboration over knowledge, skills, research agendas, and commercialization. We did not get to see the database, but Aboriginal people from all over were exchanging stories, reflections, and agendas.

Back in Alice Springs, it became clear that our task was to find ways of activating concepts of desert Aboriginal knowledge that accommodated both the commodifiable hard facts of the nutritional and medical potentials of desert plant species (where required) and the soft, intangible, embodied knowledge practices embedded in the places and routine practices of everyday life. A focus on one perspective seemed inevitably to compromise the viability of the other.

In this undecideable context, the important thing for our group was to agree on (and convince the Board about) ways in which the Aboriginal knowledge owners themselves could make informed decisions about how their knowledge could be shared, strengthened, and utilized in the context of the CRC research agenda. But since knowledge is to some extent collectively held, who is to make these decisions on behalf of whom? And how can the CRC make sure that the negotiations are done properly according to both Australian and Aboriginal law?

My intuition is that the presence of digitizing technologies in the research context could greatly enhance both the positive and the negative practices aimed at access to Aboriginal knowledge and benefit sharing. The acceptance of digitizing technologies as either a "good thing" or at least as politically neutral made their uncritical use even more worrying, especially seeing that the Aboriginal knowledge owners themselves were rarely finding opportunities to explore and configure the cameras, computers, softwares, and so on themselves, for their own cultural purposes.

There is often a power struggle at work in making agreements and enforcing accountability over Indigenous intellectual property, a struggle hidden by a politics of scale. Powerful parties assume (and less powerful parties accept) the scale at which they are working to be the best or only or most natural scale, without proper negotiation. Scales (e.g., local, regional, national, global, or individual, family, clan, phratry, tribe, community) are not given. They are socially and politically constructed, and thus they can hide unequal power relations and allow people to avoid their responsibilities. For example, it may be convenient for some to assume that intellectual property is held by a whole community rather than by an individual. Or conversely, it may be convenient to assume that an individual can give permission or receive payment for something that belongs to a group. Or it may be convenient for some to assume that international protocols should have a more primary focus in making arrangements than the traditional rules that are already at work governing intellectual property in a particular local context. Different scales imply different systems and relationships of accountability, and these need to be identified and negotiated rather than assumed.

I made a list from my experience of examples of scales in use by academic researchers working with Australian Aboriginal Knowledge. These include, first, a group of people who tell a particular story or share a particular named landscape with all its histories, and second, an individual who has knowledge of a particular place or plant, for example. Both of those examples have been governed by Aboriginal intellectual property law for countless generations before the establishment of Australian law.

But if we look at a slightly larger scale, we find that projects may also be at work in a particular Aboriginal community, made up of a number of different language and cultural groups and the knowledge that is collectively at work in that community. This is not a "traditional" Aboriginal scale, because contemporary governance of Aboriginal communities is a product of a Western colonial and bureaucratic system.

We ourselves were working on the scale designed to represent desert Aboriginal people in general, the way in which their knowledge traditions work, and the practices that embody and regulate them. We were advising at the scale of the overall aegis of the Desert Knowledge CRC and the way in which Aboriginal knowledge is collected and operationalized there. The CRC itself had a particular ecologically determinist line, avowing that the unique ecological characteristics of the desert environment implied something homogeneous about the knowledge systems that it had produced.

Others in our group were mostly experienced at working with the knowledge systems and intellectual property rights of Aboriginal people at the Australian national level. There is again some argument for the viability of an Australian scale, which may include all Australian Aborigines but may not account, for example, for New Zealand Maori, because Australian accounts of Aboriginal knowledge derive from their autochthonous origins, whereas Maori origin stories are of migration and settlement, traceable through genealogy to a point in historic time.

But Australian Indigenous people include both Torres Strait Islanders and Aboriginal people, and together their experiences and needs may comprise a scale without much ontological coherence; in fact, this scale really reflects the conceptualization of intellectual property as constituted, recognized, and governed by Australian law. Others in the group helped the CRC understand the protective measures that derive from significant conventions concerning the rights of Indigenous people at the global level, to which national governments around the world may or may not subscribe.

I was keen to draw the CRC's attention to the tendency of researchers to operationalize their research at the particular scales that suit their own interests and render them immune to some of the complexities of accountability that would emerge if the research were differently negotiated from the outset under the aegis of properly constituted traditional Aboriginal governance.

The problem here, the team agreed, is that non-Aboriginal researchers draw up the research agenda, then solicit Aboriginal research partners at a location and scale that is convenient to them as researchers (in terms of funding, accountability, accessibility, the presence or absence of "gatekeepers," etc.).

The urban center tends to constitute the locus of research agenda negotiation and supervision, where there is no sense of inequity in the disjunction between the unified, centralized, mostly non-Aboriginal research machine, on the one hand, and the diverse, scattered, and very grounded population of desert knowledge owners, on the other. This inequity is exacerbated by the fact that the Desert Knowledge CRC creates its unity partially through the use of digital technology in the form of its Web site, electronic discussion groups, e-mails, and so on, despite the fact that almost none of the Aboriginal constituents have private access to the Internet, much less ownership of personal computers.

The group came to argue that resolving the hidden disadvantage to Aboriginal knowledge holders requires considerable support for the development of an Indigenous research agenda. This requires, first of all, rethinking the role of Aboriginal people in the Desert Knowledge CRC as mere "stakeholders" (along with pastoralists, mining companies, and government departments) and repositioning them as key owners of the research programs.

The first steps toward a healthy Indigenous research agenda, we decided, would be for groups of Aboriginal people in the desert to come together to discuss the research program—to share their experiences of research (and being researched) and to articulate their own vision for possible useful research in the future. The Desert Knowledge CRC needs to fund and facilitate many such meetings that will allow traditional scales and practices of knowledge production and negotiation to balance and inform its work. The Desert Knowledge CRC had, in our brief trip to a desert community, accidentally facilitated a small example of this networking that allowed scale to be determined through an Aboriginal polity.

POSITIONING ABORIGINAL KNOWLEDGE

The international and national legal protective measures with which we were dealing seemed to have the unintended effect of configuring only certain parts of Aboriginal desert knowledge as legible. My concern with the politics of scale and its relation to local Aboriginal knowledge practices led me to James Scott's book *Seeing Like a State* (1999), which describes the particular sort of vision that is implied by the modern phenomenon of the nation-state—and particular blindnesses that this vision produces. Scott uses the ancient Greek notion of *mètis* as a means of "comparing the forms of knowledge embedded in local experience with the more general, abstract knowledge deployed by the state and its technical agencies" (311).

As an example, Scott offers the contrast between the general knowledge of *navigation* with the particular knowledge of *piloting*, which replaces navigation each time a large ship approaches a port and the controls are handed over to a local knowledge holder. What the pilot knows are the local cycles of winds and tides, the local traffic conditions, hidden rocks and currents—not to mention the local politics and economies of the port. Some of the pilot's knowledge could be abstracted and made useful elsewhere, but some of it is utterly specific. Some of it could be verbalized, while some of it is incommunicable. It can only be inferred after its performance. I had focused on such tacit aspects of Aboriginal knowledge that were alive and well in Arnhem Land and supported the socialization of young people in the old traditions. But my experience in the desert made me more conscious of how I had ignored the more objective and transferable manifestations of Aboriginal knowledge.

In an essay on the role of "oblique knowledge" in the identification and solution of problems in organizations, Philippe Baumard (1994: 2) describes mètis as

> a persistent model of knowing and perceiving . . . at all levels of society, from the fisherman and the hunter to the sophist and the politician. The *mètis* is that form of practical intelligence, using conjectural and oblique knowledge, which anticipates, modifies and influences the fate of events in adversity and ambiguity. When abstract generalizations (*episteme*) are unable to handle a changeable and unpredictable situation; when know-how (*techne*) does not have any grip on a chancy and fluid reality; when practical wisdom, drawn from social practice (*phronesis*) does not come with any solution to a mutable and unsure event, here comes the fourth dimension of knowledge, . . . that no words can fully contain, a knowledge of short-cuts, of sagacious envisioning, of perspicuous intervention, even more mutable than the situation it has to cope with, discreet, operative, conjectural: the *Mètis*. . . . [It is] a form of knowledge at the opposite end of metaphysics, with no quest of ideal, but a search for a practical end; an embodied, incarnate, substantial form of knowledge.

Baumard's diagram, which represented the four Greek forms of knowledge along two continua (fig. 14.1), immediately reminded me of my much earlier attempts to characterize the ways information technologies (in this case softwares) bias users toward particular ways of perceiving, configuring, and engaging Aboriginal knowledge. Previous work in the Collective Memory project (see www.cdu.edu.au / ik) had convinced me that digital technologies could be used to support Aboriginal ways of making collective memory and of teaching new generations to use it

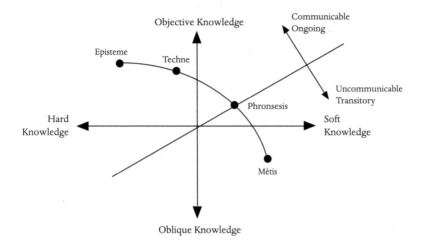

"Attempts to position *mètis*, phronesis, techne and episteme." From Baumard (1994, 3).

respectfully and effectively and to renew it carefully. But these solutions in the first instance would have to be negotiated locally according to local agendas and protocols, and the required technical systems (hardware, software) would need to be appropriated and "reinvented" in culturally consistent ways.

At a collective memory seminar a couple of years before, I had addressed the question that now arose again in the context of desert knowledge: If Aboriginal knowledge is embedded in the land, language, and people's relation to history, the environment, and everyday being-in-the-world, how can a computer help keep alive these connections in each new generation? Could it be that the computer might actually erode and subvert the viability of knowledge traditions?

At the seminar, I had presented a critique of the digital archive and advocated the development of locally grown and controlled appropriations of digitizing technology to support traditional knowledge practices. I had used two continua to represent the tensions between local versus general software configurations, on the one hand, and the complex versus more simple or "flat" metadata structures, on the other. I placed the general tendency toward complex one-size-fits-all solutions in one sector and the more specifically localized and ad hoc solutions we were proposing in another (fig. 14.2). My resistance to the commodification of Aboriginal knowledge (a commodification that information technologies imply and enable, and which may give rise to the possibility of exploitation

General applicability

MOST
PROPRIETARY
SOFTWARE

Complex
data and
metadata
structures

Simple
data and
metadata
structures

INDIGENOUS
USER FRIENDLY
DATA MANAGEMENT
SYSTEM

Specific applicability

Software options for Indigenous digital resource management.

without properly negotiated accountability, access, and benefits agreements) had biased me toward representing Aboriginal knowledge as mètis: always local, tacit, nontransferable, and performative.

For me, considering Aboriginal knowledge to be mètis means recognizing it as alive, well, and under the control of Aboriginal people. In the context of the Desert Knowledge project, my colleagues pointed out to me on a number of occasions that the idea of "indigenous user-friendly data management systems" reflected my experience on the north coast. There, Aboriginal groups had more government resources, many Aboriginal people had more experience and were thus more confident in their interactions with outsiders, and the coastal mode of traditional economic adaptation, with its rich marine resources, was still relatively easy to engage and reproduce (as compared with a hunting and gathering lifestyle in the much harsher desert areas). My analysis and my agenda did not account for the many cases in other areas like the desert, in which older Aboriginal people were passing away without having been able to renew in the younger generation their rich knowledge of the environment and all the healing and nourishing it provided (Christie 2004).

The resonance between the two diagrams allowed me, somewhat reluctantly, to accept that databases may well have a useful purpose for Aboriginal knowledge makers and owners. They do not distort or deny Aboriginal knowledge traditions; they merely represent small, commodifiable, transferable parts of it: the *episteme*, and to some extent the *techne* (although the techne would be more difficult to render as information).

They can be understood as collections of resources, much like a dilly bag or a billabong[9] (both of which have been used in Aboriginal Australia as metaphors for digital data management systems). But databases are not innocent objects. They shape the ways we see the world (Bowker 2000), and they bias us toward understanding knowledge as a commodity (van der Velden 2005).[10]

CONCLUSION: DIGITIZING TECHNOLOGIES, DESERT ABORIGINAL KNOWLEDGE, AND THE CRC

As a mixed group of Aboriginal and non-Aboriginal academics and lawyers, scoping Desert Aboriginal Knowledge for a cooperative research center, we experienced collaborative research as a complex and controversial phenomenon. The group leader pointed out after some months that she was surprised that a fight had not yet broken out between those members of the group who were "sharers" (i.e., those who were keen for desert knowledge to be shared as equitably and efficiently as possible in the interests of all) and those who were "protectors" (who were keen for knowledge owners to keep their knowledge to themselves until they were completely convinced of the justice and profitability of the access and benefit sharing arrangements they were being offered).[11] There is little wonder that our work is resisted by some who see it as a regrettable outbreak of political correctness.

The knowledge practices at work in the desert and the CRC are so complex that we could not agree on a definition. They are so subjugated (Foucault 1980), existing outside of books, and eluding the forces of inscription that would legitimate them, that we could hardly agree on a characterization. Concentrating on uncommunicable embodied aspects of an Aboriginal knowledge tradition drew attention away from the commercial potential of ethnopharmaceutical and ecological knowledge. Concentrating on the potential of ethnopharmaceutical knowledge to produce sustainable livelihoods for desert Aboriginal people drew attention away from the everyday knowledge practices that keep knowledge traditions alive from one generation to the next. Every part of the knowledge tradition needs to be acknowledged as a matter of "cognitive justice."

As Maja van der Velden (2005) makes clear, "cognitive injustice" is exacerbated by the uncritical embrace of digitizing technologies. Knowledge is conceptualized in a system's design, and the bias thus affects issues of legibility (Scott 1999), control, access, trust, and accountability.

The information found on a database—"knowledge that can be expressed in words and numbers"—is "only the tip of the iceberg of the entire body" of Aboriginal knowledge (Nonaka as cited in Baumard 1994: 2).

Information technology is everywhere invested in producing and reproducing particular social, cultural, and political interests. Aboriginal people in the desert need access to a range of targeted technologies, integrated into and adapted to a context of local supervision and access. The control of information and communication technology (for representing owners' views of the cultural values of water, for example) needs to be central to the research agenda of the CRC. The desert Aboriginal people are not stakeholders. They are the owners of the desert and their knowledge. Currently, the CRC sets the research agenda without a significant Aboriginal authority. Research collaborations at the CRC engage with Indigenous "stakeholders" on the margins rather than the other way around. The agenda-setting process whereby non-Aboriginal researchers are (with few exceptions) the initiators of the research agendas automatically positions the Indigenous knowledge holders at the margin.

The wider the purview of a databasing system, the greater the hegemony.[12] There is a tension between the always-grounded always-partial nature of (Aboriginal) knowledge (adapting Donna Haraway's 1995 concept) and the need for the mobilization of a wider desert Aboriginal research agenda. This could be partially addressed if the CRC were to finance and facilitate network meetings of Aboriginal people from desert communities to talk together about the research in which they are involved (or not) and their ideas for useful research. Juggling between emerging local solutions (see, e.g., *www.cdu.edu.au / centres / ik / databases .html*) and wider Aboriginal engagement and supervision of research is a scale of politics yet to be taken seriously by the CRC. My colleagues pointed out that my insistence on the always-local, always-grounded, always-performative nature of Aboriginal knowledge did not help to generate a unified Aboriginal research agenda. We need to consider this problem particularly in the context of the burgeoning use of digitizing technologies, especially databases.

There are lots of different sorts of databases, and the development of savvy systems needs to be researched. Even where an Indigenous research agenda is at work, we still need to identify ways to engage the uncommunicable and transitory dimensions of knowledge (see fig. 14.1), the ability of individuals in networks to "double-cross" the structural arrangements in place to solve problems by illuminating shortcuts and furtive, sagacious, deviant, and oblique knowledge in the practices or routine negotiations with outsiders.

Preserving the episteme on a database (for example, the abstracted generalizations about the medicinal uses of a plant species) is not a difficult thing to achieve, but making that information work to keep traditional knowledge practices alive is much harder. Difficult also is keeping both alive and equitable the networks of rights and responsibilities that customary law attaches to the electronic artifacts and traces of knowledge practices. Rights management systems that work through computer passwords have been attempted, but no Aboriginal knowledge owner in my experience is confident that passwords can keep private knowledge private. Information on a computer is never completely safe if the computer is shared in a public space, much less if its contents are backed up on the Internet.

Increasingly, Aboriginal knowledge owners are using their own computers to assemble their own collections of digital resources. These collectors have the advantage of being small enough not to require more than the most basic metadata protocols to locate them. Their owners know what they contain and exercise the same stewardship as they do over their "natural" resources. File management softwares allow the owners to assemble and display configurations of digital resources on the fly. People are at work negotiating user-friendly systems for facilitating these engagements (including fuzzy searches for languages that are not often written or read; see, e.g., Tami at www.cdu.edu.au / centres / ik / db _TAMI.html; see also Christie 2005). With increasing control of the digital technologies now normally in the hands of non-Aboriginal researchers, Aboriginal people can continue to renew their traditional knowledge practices, keeping digital resources to themselves for their own purposes, and making pathways for engagement with outsiders—using resources in particular, lively contexts, tailored for particular audiences and particular agendas. Many different sorts of knowledge practices need to be strengthened and supported in a cooperative research center. Digital resources need to be put into many different sorts of hands.

NOTES

I wish to acknowledge the valuable assistance of Helen Verran and the good will of the other members of our Desert Knowledge working party: Sonia Smallacombe, Michael Davis, Robynne Quiggin, Donna Craig, Darryl Cronin, Jocelyn

Davies, Megan Davis, Josephine Douglas, Michael Duffy, Tahnia Edwards, Louis Evans, Josie Guy, Lucas Jordan, Kado Muir, Margaret Raven, Kathy Rea, and Juanita Sherwood. My views may not necessarily reflect theirs.

1. The CRC Programme was established in 1990 to improve the effectiveness of Australia's research and development effort in six sectors: environment, agriculture, information and communications technology, mining, medical science, and technology and manufacturing. It links researchers, the users of research, and industry to focus research and development efforts on progress toward utilization and commercialization. See www.crc.gov.au /.

2. Quotes taken from the CRC Web site: www.desertknowledge.com.au.

3. A scoping process is a study that presents a position paper to authorities.

4. All quotes are from our scoping documents which will appear on the Desert Knowledge CRC Web site at www.desertknowledgecrc.com.au / publications / downloads / DKCRC-Report-22-Traditional-Knowledge.pdf.

5. I acknowledge Helen Verran's help working through these ideas.

6. This sort of disagreement, of course, is a typical and healthy problem to be solved when any position paper is put together by a committee of busy people from all around the continent.

7. The vision of loss increased the sense of urgency for the databasers and their project to record specific facts about specific plants and put these facts onto a database with the view of a potential commercial use of the plants. Theirs were Aboriginal-initiated, Aboriginal-controlled projects in three different contexts (two of them remote desert contexts) where old people, mostly grandparents, were sharing their knowledge of plants and allowing representations of that knowledge to be databased. Their children and grandchildren were, by and large, just not interested in the ongoing engagement with and dependence on the environment that a deep localized traditional knowledge requires. These researchers were most concerned about knowledge loss, and they were also interested in the commercialization potential of Aboriginal plant knowledge for sustainable livelihoods for desert Aborigines.

8. I am grateful to Helen Verran for pointing this out to me.

9. Dilly bag is a traditional bag or basket for carrying food; a billabong is a lake or pool of water.

10. Ironically, as we pointed out in our paper on legal intellectual property protection measures, it is this rendering of knowledge into information that is seen to protect it as "prior art" against being patented as "invention" by others.

11. There were Aboriginal and non-Aboriginal people in both "factions," and the discussions were always cordial and lively.

12. See van der Velden 2005 for a description of the problem and possible solutions at the global level.

CHAPTER 15

RETHINKING THE DIGITAL AGE

Faye Ginsburg

In March 2005, the United Nations inaugurated a long-awaited program, a "Digital Solidarity Fund," to underwrite initiatives that address "the uneven distribution and use of new information and communication technologies" and "enable excluded people and countries to enter the new era of the information society" (Digital Solidarity Fund Foundation 2005). What this might mean in practice—which digital technologies might make a significant difference and for whom and with what resources—is still an open and contentious question. Debates about plans for the fund at the first meeting of the World Summit on the Information Society (WSIS) in December 2003 are symptomatic of the complexity of "digital divide" issues that have also been central to the second phase of the information summit held in November 2005 in Tunisia.[1]

In this chapter, I consider the relationship of Indigenous people to new media technologies that people in these communities have started to take up—with both ambivalence and enthusiasm—over the last decade. To give a sense of that oscillation, let me start with three quotes that articulate the range of stakes. The first—a statement leaning toward the technophilic—is from Jolene Rickard (1999), a Tuscarora artist, scholar, and community leader, introducing an online project, called CyberPow-Wow,[2] that began in 1996 in order to get more Native American art on the Web:

> Wasn't it the Hopi that warned of a time when the world would be circled by a spiders' web of power lines? That time has come. . . . There is no doubt that First Nations Peoples are wired and ready to surf and chat. It seems like a distant memory when the tone of discussion about computers, interactivity, and aboriginal people was filled with prophetic caution. Ironically, the image of Natives is still

firmly planted in the past. The idea that Indians would be on the frontier of a technology is inconsistent with the dominant image of "traditional" Indians.

The second, more skeptical, quote is from Alopi Latukefu (2006: 4), regional manager of the Outback Digital Network (www.odn.net.au /), a digitally based broadband network that began in 1996, linking six Aboriginal communities in Australia:

> So seductive is the power of the ICT medium that it might only appear to remove centralized control out of the hands of government and into the hands of the people, giving them the notion of . . . empowerment. While ongoing struggles for self-determination play a complex role in the drive to bring the information age to indigenous communities in Australia and around the world, it can be argued that self-determination within one system may well be a further buy in to another. . . . The issue that needs to be raised before any question of indigenous usage of the Internet is addressed is: whose information infrastructure or "info-structure" determines what is valued in an economy—whether in the local community or the greater global economy which they are linked to? . . . Associated with this is the overarching issue of who determines knowledge within these remote communities and for the wider indigenous populations throughout Australia and beyond?

The third quote is from the Indigenous Position Paper for the 2003 WSIS and the discussion of its implications in the cultural commons debates by Kimberly Christen in her essay "Gone Digital" (2005). She first quotes the position paper: "Our collective knowledge is not merely a commodity to be traded like any other in the market place. We strongly object to the notion that it constitutes a raw material or commercial resource for the knowledge-based economy of the Information Society." Commenting on that quote, Christen points out that,

> like some of their corporate counterparts, international indigenous representatives want to limit the circulation of particular ideas, knowledge and cultural materials. In fact, they "strongly reject the application of the public domain concept to any aspect related to our cultures and identities" and further "reject the application of IPR [intellectual property rights] regimes to assert patents, copyrights, or trademark monopolies for products, data or processes

derived or originating from our traditional knowledge or our cultural expressions." (328)

The issues raised in these quotations echo those I have heard in my own research with Indigenous media makers, positions that are not necessarily in contradiction. Fundamentally, they ask who has the right to control knowledge and what are the consequences of the new circulatory regimes introduced by digital technologies. Rickard articulates a desire, as an Indigenous artist, to work with digital technologies in order to link Indigenous communities to each other on their own terms, objecting to stereotypes that suggest traditional communities should not have access to forms associated with modernity. Latukefu cautions that one must take into account the power relations that decide whose knowledge is valued, while the statement of the Indigenous People's Working Group offers a strong warning against the commodification of their knowledge under Western systems of intellectual property.

Why are their concerns barely audible in discussions of new media? I would like to suggest that part of the problem has to do with the rise of the term *the digital age* over the last decade and the assumptions that support it. While it initially had the shock of the new, it now has become as naturalized for many of us—Western cultural workers and intellectuals— as a temporal marking of the dominance of a certain kind of technological regime ("the digital") as is "the Paleolithic's" association with certain kinds of stone tools for paleontologists. This seems even more remarkable given certain realities: only 12 percent of the world was wired as of January 2005 (according to statistics from the 2005 World Economic Forum in Davos, Switzerland), and only sixteen of every one hundred people on the planet were serviced with telephone land lines.[3] Digerati may see those numbers and salivate at the possibilities for entrepreneurship. But for an anthropologist who has spent a good portion of her career looking at the uptake of media in remote Indigenous communities, the unexamined ethnocentrism that undergirds assumptions about the digital age is discouraging; indeed, the seeming ubiquity of the Internet appears a facade of First World illusions. I am not suggesting that the massive shifts in communication, sociality, knowledge production, and politics that the Internet enables are simply irrelevant to remote communities; my concern is with how the language smuggles in a set of assumptions that paper over cultural differences in the way things digital may be taken up—if at all—in radically different contexts and thus serve to further insulate thinking against recognition of alterity that different kinds of media worlds present, particularly in key areas such as intellectual property.

In this chapter, I examine how concepts such as the digital age have taken on a sense of evolutionary inevitability, thus creating an increasing stratification and ethnocentrism in the distribution of certain kinds of media practices, despite prior and recent trends to de-Westernize media studies (see Curran and Park 2000). Work in new (and old) media that is being produced in Indigenous communities might expand and compli- cate our ideas about "the digital age" in ways that take into account other points of view in the so-called global village.

A HISTORY OF DIGITAL DEBATES

Let me first briefly review some of the recent debates around the rhetoric of the digital age—for certainly I am not alone in my concern, though mine may be shaped in a particular way. Within the ranks of those who have been writing and worrying about "cultural production in a digi- tal age" and its global implications, there is some contestation as to "whether it is appropriate, given unequal access to advanced technolo- gies (let alone more basic goods)" in different parts of the world, that the term *the digital age* be used to define the current period (Klineneberg and Benzecry 2005; 10). This debate occurs in tandem with that attached to the digital divide, the phrase invented to describe the circumstances of inequality that characterize access (or lack of access) to resources, tech- nological and otherwise, across much of the globe. Although its users want to express well-intentioned concern about such inequities, the term invokes neodevelopmentalist language that assumes that less privileged cultural enclaves with little or no access to digital resources—from the South Bronx to the global South—are simply waiting, endlessly, to catch up to the privileged West. Inevitably, the language suggests, they are simply falling farther behind the current epicenter—whether that be Silicon Valley or the MIT Media Lab.

Some exemplary cases that have made it to the *New York Times* and the *Wall Street Journal* provide charming counterpoints of hopeful possibility, stories of far-flung villages "catching up" to the West. For example, in a *New York Times* article, James Brooks (2004) describes the work of Ber- nard Krisher, representing both MIT's Media Lab and the American Assis- tance for Cambodia group in O Siengle, Cambodia, a village of fewer than eight hundred people on the edge of the forest that is emblematic of life for the millions of Asians who live on the unwired side of the digital divide. Through the Motoman project, the village connects its new elementary school to the Internet. Since they have no electricity or phones, the system is powered by solar panels, and, as Brooks describes it:

> An Internet "Motoman" rides a red motorcycle slowly past the school [once a day]. On the passenger seat is a gray metal box with a short fat antenna. The box holds a wireless Wi-Fi chip set that allows the exchange of e-mail between the box and computers. Briefly, this schoolyard of tree stumps and a hand-cranked water well becomes an Internet hot spot [a process duplicated in five other villages]. At dusk, the motorcycles [from five villages] converge on the provincial capital, Ban Lung, where an advanced school is equipped with a satellite dish, allowing a bulk e-mail exchange with the outside world. (n.p.)[4]

Tellingly, this story was in the business section of the *Times*, suggesting that part of its charm is the possibility of new markets, the engine that drives even such idealistic innovation in consumer technologies; computers and the Internet are hardly exceptional.

This techno-imaginary universe—of digital eras and divides—has the effect, I argue, of reinscribing onto the world a kind of "allochronic chronopolitics" (to borrow a term from Johannes Fabian's *Time and the Other* [1983]), in which "the other" exists in a time not contemporary with our own. This has the effect of restratifying the world along lines of a late modernity, despite the utopian promises by the digerati of the possibilities of a twenty-first-century, McLuhanesque global village. For the last two decades, scholars have argued about (and mostly for) the transformative power of digital systems and their capacity to alter daily life, democratic politics, and personhood. That sense of a paradigm shift is perhaps most evident in Manuel Castells's *The Rise of the Network Society* (1996). The premise of his work, of course, is that the Internet has more or less created a new era by providing the technological basis for the organizational form of the information age: *the network*. In *The Internet Galaxy* (2003), Castells's scale seems to have expanded from society to the cosmos. While he celebrates the Internet's capacity to liberate, he also cautions us about its ability to marginalize and exclude those who do not have access to it and suggests that we need to take responsibility for the future of this new information age.

Taking that critique a bit farther, no less a luminary than Bill Gates, founder of Microsoft and once the personification of new media evangelism, has become an outspoken critic of that attitude. Initially, he was part of the group of U.S. executives who, at the 1998 World Economic Forum in Davos, dedicated themselves to closing the digital divide. By 2000, however, in a speech at a conference titled "Creating Digital Dividends," Gates demonstrated a remarkable change of heart, offering blistering criticism of the idea of the digital divide and its capacity to blind people to the reality of the conditions of the globe's poorest people. As he put it at the time,

> O.K., you want to send computers to Africa, what about food and electricity—those computers aren't going to be that valuable. The mothers are going to walk right up to that computer and say, "My children are dying, what can you do?" They're not going to sit there and like, browse eBay or something. What they want is for their children to live. They don't want their children's growth to be stunted. Do you really have to put in computers to figure that out? (quoted in Verhovic 2000)[5]

His clear disdain for the notion that the world's poorest people constitute a significant market for high-tech products has had an impact. The priorities of the $21-billion Bill and Melinda Gates Foundation are with health care, in particular the development and distribution of vaccines. At the January 2005 World Economic Forum, while technology guru Nicholas Negroponte was marketing a mock-up of a one-hundred-dollar laptop computer, hoping to capture China's 220 million students as possible consumers of digital technology, Gates was reported to be "in the thick of plenary discussions . . . considering ways of eliminating poverty and disease that do not encompass information technology. . . . 'I think it's fascinating,'" Gates commented, "'that there was no plenary session at Davos this year on how information technology is changing the world'" (quoted in Markoff 2005).[6]

The Internet, of course, has been met with some optimism by those sharing concerns of broader access for freedom of expression and social movements. Manuel Castells in *The Power of Identity* (1997) noted the range of dissident social actors, such as the Zapatistas in Mexico. Today, we would add to that list an array of groups from the grassroots leftist political sentiments organized by moveon.org to right-wing Christians and militant Islamists to the Falun Gong in China. These and scores of other groups have used the Internet to shape what some call "the network logic" of anti-[corporate]-globalization movements and smart mobs, as well as its uptake by loosely linked Islamic terrorists. Additionally, a number of researchers have noted how the Internet has in many cases reduced the "price of entry" into a cultural field, creating openings for actors and organizations who were previously unable to get their work into the public, as the inclusion and insidious impact of bloggers during the 2004 U.S. presidential campaigns makes clear (Massing 2005). Clearly then, digital networks can enable the global dispersion of creative and political activity.

In the cover story for its March 12–18, 2005, issue, no less an advocate of free enterprise than the *Economist* features a rethinking of the term (and terms of) "the real digital divide," along with a compelling photo of a young African boy holding an ersatz cell phone made of mud to his ear. Its lead opinion piece states that "the debate over the digital divide is founded on a myth—that plugging poor countries into the Internet will help them to become rich rapidly. . . . So even if it were possible to wave a magic wand and cause a computer to appear in every household on earth, it would not achieve very much: a computer is not useful if you have no food or electricity and cannot read" (*Economist* 2005).

Ideas about what "the digital age" might offer look different from the perspective of people struggling to manage to make ends meet on a daily basis. As the *Economist* notes, research suggests that radio and cell phones may be the forms of digital technology that make the difference, once basic needs are addressed (Norris, Bennett, and Entman 2001). My concern here, however, is to ask whether terms like *the digital divide* too easily foreclose discussion about what the stakes are for those who are out of power. Rather than imagining that we know the answers, clearly, we need to keep listening to the large percentage of the earth's population that is on the unwired side of the so-called digital divide.

GOING DIGITAL: INDIGENOUS INTERNET "ON THE GROUND"

So what does "the digital age" feel and look like in Indigenous communities in remote regions of the world where access to telephone land lines can still be difficult? As Kyra Landzelius asks in her collection, *Native on the Net* (2006: 1): "Can the info-superhighway be a fast track to greater empowerment for the historically disenfranchised? Or do they risk becoming 'roadkill': casualties of hyper-media and the drive to electronically map everything?" Recent developments give some insight into what it might actually mean for Indigenous subjects. As Harald Prins (2001: 306) has argued regarding the place of Indigenous people in "Cyberia,"

> although indigenous peoples are proportionally underrepresented in cyberspace—for obvious reasons such as economic poverty, technological inexperience, linguistic isolation, political repression, and / or cultural resistance—the Internet has vastly extended traditional networks of information and communication. Greatly enhancing the visibility of otherwise marginal communities and individuals, the information superhighway enables even very small and isolated communities to expand their sphere of influence and mobilize political support in their struggles for cultural survival. In addition to maintaining contact with their own communities, indigenous peoples also use the Internet to connect with other such widely dispersed groups in the world. Today, it is not unusual for a Mi'kmaq in Newfoundland to go on the Internet and communicate with individuals belonging to other remote groups such as the Maori in New Zealand, Saami in Norway, Kuna in Panama, or Navajo in Arizona. Together with the rest of us, they have pioneered across the new cultural frontier and are now surfing daily through Cyberia.

Clearly, Prins points to the circumstances in which use of the Internet —and more broadly the cross-platformed use of digital technologies—is being taken up in Indigenous communities on their own terms, furthering the development of political networks and the capacity to extend their traditional cultural worlds into new domains. It is that latter enterprise that I address in the following examples.

Recent initiatives demonstrate what some of these possibilities look like in three very different parts of the world: Inuit regions of Nunavut through the work of Igloolik Isuma; the work of Arrernte living in town camps in Alice Springs, Australia, creating an innovative interactive project called "UsMob"; and a digital animation project by Canadian-based Northwest Coast Aboriginal artists and storytellers who have created an animated version of the Raven tales. All are exemplary of community-based groups collaborating with a number of agencies to indigenize the use of digital technologies in the interests of storytelling as a way to generate broader understandings of their histories and cultures, for wider audiences but, most important, for their own cultural futures.[7]

Igloolik Isuma and Sila.nu

During the 1970s, as satellite-based television made its way into the Canadian Arctic, Inuit people began exploring the possibilities that these combinations of media forms offered for local productions that could be distributed over the vast expanses of Canada's north. Zacharias Kunuk, a young Inuit man, had the vision to turn these technologies into vehicles for cultural expression of Inuit lives and histories, forming a media production group called *Igloolik Isuma* (see www.isuma.ca). Kunuk worked with friends and family members, creating a remarkable team of non-professional actors who recreated the stories of the transformation of their lives over the last century, starting with works such as *Qaggig* in 1988 and quickly moving on to create the remarkable television series *Nunavut*, which is also the name of the recently formed Inuit-controlled territory where Kunuk's home settlement is located. The series *Nunavut* was not only a staple of TV Northern Canada (the pan-Arctic satellite station that preceded the first national Indigenous cable television station, Aboriginal Peoples Television Network [APTN]), but it also screened at the Museum of Modern Art in New York and the Pompidou Center in Paris.

Fast forward to 2001 and the premiere at the Cannes Film Festival of Kunuk's first feature, the epic recreation of a well-known Inuit legend, *Atanarjuat: The Fast Runner* (see www.atanarjuat.com); there, this first film ever made by an Inuit director in the Inuktitut language received the coveted Caméra d'Or for best first feature and went on to stunning critical and theatrical success, picking up many more awards along the way. In 2005, Kunuk and his crew shot their second feature, a Danish coproduction titled *The Journals of Knud Rasmussen*, based on the writings of the famous Inuit-Danish explorer who traveled throughout the Arctic in the 1920s exploring the transformations of Inuit life that were occurring in the early twentieth century, when Inuit shamans first encountered Christian missionaries. The journals provide the storyline for a film that provides an Inuit perspective on that fateful historical encounter.

Never content to think conventionally, Kunuk and company established an incredible Web site from the film's production location (www .sila.nu / live) that allowed us to follow what was happening on the set on a daily basis while also sending us back to Rasmussen's journals and the key characters he met in his journeys through the Arctic.[8] Daily blogs by an "embedded" journalist and (of course) their own anthropologist provided different perspectives, while QuickTime movies showed us how multiple languages (English, French, Inuktitut, Danish) were negotiated, as well as how props and food were managed in this remote Arctic locale. Pop-ups offered a linked glossary for foreign or more arcane words. Background bios on key personnel—on and off screen—illuminated the community-based approach to filmmaking that Kunuk and his partner Norman Cohn have perfected. (My personal favorite was the interview with the lead sled dog, Tooguyuk, who "described" the trials of learning commands in both "Greenlandic" and "Igloolik" and talked about looking forward to his "girlfriend having puppies so I'm excited to be a daddy.") Inuit Web site producer Katarina Soukup explained the project and its origins:

> Isuma has wanted for a long, long time to use the Internet to connect the remote Arctic with people around the world, a way to bring people to Igloolik without the extreme expense and inconvenience of traveling here, as well as to allow Inuit to remain in their communities and out on the land without losing touch with the 21st century. One dream is a nomadic media lab / TV station out on the land connected to the Internet. It just has not been technically possible until now, thanks to a high-speed data satellite phone and wireless broadband in Nunavut, making remote, nomadic computing much less expensive. The goals with the educational website are to connect people to Inuit culture through the Internet and our films. We have been creating materials for the educational market for about 2 or 3 years (e.g., the Isuma Inuit Culture Kit), and the site is another step in this direction. The project employs an innovative technical infrastructure to deliver to the world priceless Inuit cultural content, such as interactive e-learning activities, video-on-demand, customizable teacher resources, and Inuktitut language lessons. It is a platform for North-South communication and collaboration. In addition to educating the public about Inuit culture, another goal of the site is to develop a youth and educational market for our films. (quoted in Ginsburg 2005b)

The site was beautifully designed in every sense. The project had two teams, one in the Arctic at Igloolik and another in Montreal. In Igloolik, the team was made up of about nine members: three videographers, one audio reporter, one photographer, and three writers who did the daily blogs, as well as eight youth trainees from the community who were learning about media production. The Sila Web site presented a remarkable demonstration of how this technology might be successfully "indigenized" to help Inuit school kids, college students in New York, Maori colleagues in New Zealand, and many others, learn about their filmmaking, the Arctic, Indigenous lives, missionization, and new ways of "understanding media" (McLuhan 1994 [1964]) and its possibilities in the twenty-first century.

Us Mob: Central Australia

A recent digitally based project has been developed by activist lawyer and documentary maker David Vadiveloo in collaboration with Arrernte Aboriginal youth living in Hidden Valley, a town camp outside of Alice Springs in central Australia. Us Mob is Australia's first Aboriginal children's television series and interactive Web site. On the site, users interact with the challenges and daily lives of kids from the camp—Harry, Della, Charlie, and Jacquita—following multipath storylines, activating video and text diaries, forums, movies, and games that offer a virtual experience of the camp and surrounding deserts, and uploading their own video stories. The site, in English and Arrernte with English subtitles, was launched at the Adelaide Film Festival on February 25, 2005, and simultaneously on Australian Broadcasting Corporation (ABC) TV and ABC online (see figs. 15.1–15.3; for Web site see www.usmob.com.au).

The project had its origins in requests from traditional elders in the Arrernte community in central Australia to David Vadiveloo, who first worked with that community as their lawyer in their 1996 historic Native Title claim victory. Switching gears since then to media activism, Vadiveloo has made six documentaries with people in the area, including the award-winning *Trespass* (2002), *Beyond Sorry* (2003), and *Bush Bikes* (2001). Us Mob is the first Indigenous project to receive production funding under a new initiative from the Australian Film Commission and ABC New Media and Digital Services Broadband Production Initiative (BPI); it received additional support from the Adelaide Film Festival, Telstra, and the South Australian Film Corporation.

The Us Mob project was motivated by Vadiveloo's concern to use media to develop cross-cultural lines of communication for kids in the camps. As he put it: "After ten years of listening to many Arrernte families in Town Camps and remote areas, I am trying to create a dynamic communication bridge that has been opened by the Arrernte kids of Alice Springs with an invitation extended to kids worldwide to play, to share, and to engage with story themes that are common to all young people but are delivered through Us Mob in a truly unique cultural and physical landscape" (quoted in Ginsburg 2005a). In keeping with community wishes, Vadiveloo needed to create a project that was not fictional. Elders were clear: they did not want community members referred to as "actors"—they were community participants in stories that reflected real life and real voices that they wanted heard. To accomplish that, Vadiveloo held workshops to develop scripts with more than seventy nonactor Town Camp residents, who were paid for their participation. The topics they raised range from Aboriginal traditional law, ceremony, and hunting to youth substance abuse and other Aboriginal health issues. Building bush bikes is the focus of one of the two Us Mob games, while the second one requires learning bush skills as players figure out how to survive in the outback.

Establishing a sense of partnership has been essential to the project. According to Vadiveloo, "The creative, executive and editorial role taken by the community at every stage was paramount to the production process. Respecting protocols and ensuring community ownership and profit-share meant the relationship between community and screen producers was always a partnership" (personal communication, February 11, 2007). The producer, Heather Croall, and the interactive producer, Chris Joyner, were integral partners for Vadiveloo. Apart from raising finance, they wrote the project together with Vadiveloo; then final scripts were written by the Indigenous screenwriter Danielle McLean. Camera work was by Allan Collins, the Indigenous, award-winning cinematographer and Alice Springs resident. Every stage of the project was supervised and approved by traditional owners and the peak Indigenous organization, Tangentyere Council, which has a profit-share agreement with the producers, on behalf of the community.

With this project Vadiveloo hoped to create a television series about and by Aboriginal youth, raising issues relevant to them, as well as an online program that could engage these young people to spend time online acquiring some of the skills necessary to be computer literate. He was particularly concerned to develop an alternative to the glut of single-shooter games online and the constant diet of violence, competition, and destruction that characterize the games they were exposed to in town. "When kids play and build together," Vadiveloo explains, "they are learning about community and consequence and that is what I wanted to see in the project" (quoted in Ginsburg 2005a). And rather than assuming that the goal is for Aboriginal children in central Australia to catch up

The cast of Us Mob (http://usmob.com.au). PHOTOS COURTESY OF DAVID VADIVELOO.

(*above left*) Clockwise from left: Jacquita (Letitia Bartlett), Della (Cassandra Willams), Charlie (Selwyn Anderson), and Harry (Ishmael Palmer) in Hidden Valley Town Camp, Alice Springs.

(*top right*) Clockwise from front left: Harry (Ishmael Palmer), Della (Cassandra Willams), Jacquita (Letitia Bartlett), and Charlie (Selwyn Anderson) in Alice Springs.

(*bottom right*) Left to right: Harry (Ishmael Palmer), Grandpa Jack (Max Stuart), Charlie (Selwyn Anderson), and Mervin (Gibson Turner) on location—Titjikala Road, Alice Springs.

with the other side of the digital divide, based on someone else's terms, he wanted to help build a project that dignified their cultural concerns. This is charmingly but emphatically clear in the first encounter with the Us Mob home page (see www.usmob.com.au), which invites you in but notifies you that you need a permit to visit:

> Everyone who wants to play with us on the full Us Mob website will need a permit. It's the same as if you came to Alice Springs and wanted to visit me and my family, you'd have a get a permit to come onto the Town Camp. Once you have a permit you will be able to visit us at any time to chat, play games, learn about Aboriginal life and share stories. We love going out bush and we're really looking forward to showing you what it's like in Central Australia. We'll email you whenever we add a new story to the website. We really hope you can add your stories to the website cos we'd love to learn about your life too.

Us Mob and Hidden Valley suggest another perspective on the digital age, one that invites kids from "elsewhere" to come over and play on their side.

Raven Tales: Northwest Coast
Raven Tales: How Raven Stole the Sun (2004) is the first of a series of experiments in digital animation by Simon James (Kwakwaka'wakw) and Chris Kientz (Cherokee) that create new versions of centuries-old stories to be shown across Canada on APTN. This work reworks famous Northwest Coast myths from the Kwakwaka'wakw, Squamish, and Haida peoples—in particular Raven, a trickster figure, along with Eagle, Frog, and the first humans. It includes voices ranging from those of well-known Native actors such as Evan Adams of *Smoke Signals* (Chris Eyre, 1998) fame to that of Hereditary Chief Robert Joseph. Cutting across centuries and generations, it uses the playful spirit of animation to visualize and extend the lives of these myths. These stories and the distinctive look of Northwest Coast design have been proven, as James, the series producer, joked during the question and answer session at the New York premiere of this work in the fall of 2004, by "10,000 years of local market research" (quoted in Ginsburg 2005c; see also Joanna Hearne's essay in this collection).

Spicing up these stark and complex traditional stories with some contemporary humor and the wonders of digital animation is always a risk.

But clearly it was a risk worth taking, when the murky darkness of the Myth Time is suddenly (and digitally) transformed from barren smoky grays to brilliant greens, the result of Raven's theft of the gift of light and its release into the world.[9]

At the New York premiere, James's father, a Kwakwaka'wakw artist and elder, came on stage with his drum, embellished with the distinctive raven design. Inviting other Native media makers who were present to join him on stage, he sang "Wiping the Tears" to remember those who have come before and are gone and to praise the work of this new generation. When Pam Belgarde, a Chippewa woman who had produced another work shown in the session, came up, he dressed her in the traditional black and red regalia, a stunning full-length button cape with appliqués of wild roses, and a regal fur hat. As he draped the cape across her shoulders, he explained: "When we meet someone we are honored to meet, we dress them to show that we are willing to go cold in order to keep our guests warm." Simon began to beat the drum and asked us to look at the empty seats in the theater and think of those who came before; the media producers on stage lowered their eyes. At the conclusion of his song, he addressed the audience and said, "All our ceremonies need witnesses. And as witnesses, we ask you to be part of that tradition, and go and share with others what you have seen today."

In each of these cases, digital technologies have been taken up because of the possibilities they offer to bring younger generations into new forms of Indigenous cultural production and to extend Indigenous cultural worlds—on their own terms—into the lives of others in the broader national communities and beyond who can serve, in the way that Simon James expressed, as virtual witnesses to their traditions, histories, and daily dilemmas.

CONCLUSION

To return to the concern that motivated this chapter, I want to underscore the way that the term *the digital age* stratifies media hierarchies for those who are out of power and are struggling to become producers of media representations of their lives. It is an issue that is particularly salient for Indigenous people who, until recently, have been the object of other peoples' image-making practices in ways damaging to their lives. They do not experience these practices in the same way as other minorities: questions of the digital age look different to people struggling to control land and traditions appropriated by now dominant settler societies for as long as five hundred years.

To underscore what their work is about, I use the term *cultural activist* to describe the self-conscious way in which they—like many other people—use the production of media and other expressive forms not only to sustain and build their communities but also to transform them through what one might call a "strategic traditionalism" (to borrow from Bennett and Blundell 1995). This position is crucial to their work but is effaced from much contemporary cultural theory addressing new media that emphasizes dislocation and globalization. The cultural activists creating these new kinds of cultural forms have turned to them as a means of revivifying relationships to their lands, local languages, traditions, and histories, and of articulating community concerns. They also see media as a means of furthering social and political transformation by inserting their own stories into national narratives as part of ongoing struggles for Aboriginal recognition and self-determination.

Increasingly the circulation of these media globally—through conferences, festivals, coproductions, and the use of the Internet—has become an important basis for a nascent but growing transnational network of Indigenous media makers and activists. These activists are attempting to reverse processes through which aspects of their societies have been objectified, commodified, and appropriated; their media productions and writings are efforts to recover their histories, land rights, and knowledge bases as their own cultural property. These kinds of cultural productions are consistent with how the meaning and praxis of culture in late modernity has become increasingly self-conscious of its own project, an effort to use imagery of Indigenous lives to create an activist imaginary. One might think of media practices as a kind of shield against the often unethical use or absolute erasure of their presence in the ever increasing circulation of images of other cultures in general, and of Indigenous lives in particular, as the Indigenous position paper for the wsis makes clear. At every level, Indigenous media practices have helped to create and contest social, visual, narrative, and political spaces for local communities and in the creation of national and other kinds of dominant cultural imaginaries that, until recently, have excluded vital representations by First Nations peoples within their borders. The capacity of such representations to circulate to other communities—from Indigenous neighbors to NGOs—is an extension of this process, across a number of forms of mediation, from video and film to cyberspace (Danaja and Garde 1997).

Indigenous digital media have raised important questions about the politics and circulation of knowledge at a number of levels; within communities this may be about who has had access to and understanding of media technologies, and who has the rights to know, tell, and circulate certain stories and images. Within nation-states, media are linked to larger battles over cultural citizenship, racism, sovereignty, and land rights, as well as struggles over funding, airspace and satellites, networks of broadcasting and distribution, and digital broadband that may or may not be available to Indigenous work. The impact of these fluctuations can be tracked in a variety of places—in fieldwork, in policy documents, and in the dramas of everyday life in cultural institutions.

I explore the term *the digital age* because it so powerfully shapes frameworks for understanding globalization, media, and culture, creating the "common sense" discourse for institutions in ways that disregard the cultural significance of the production of knowledge in minoritized communities, increasing an already existing sense of marginalization. Rather than mirroring the widespread concern over increasing corporate control over media production and distribution, and the often parallel panic over multiculturalism (Appiah 1997), can we illuminate and support other possibilities emerging out of locally based concerns and speak for their significance in contemporary cultural and policy arenas? Institutional structures are built on discursive frameworks that shape the way phenomena are understood, naturalizing shifts in support for a range of cultural activities. In government, foundations, and academic institutions, these frameworks have an enormous impact on policy and funding decisions that, for better or worse, can have a decisive effect on practice.

Other scholars who recognize, more generally, the significance of locally situated cultural practices in relation to dominant models point instead to the importance of the productions / producers who are helping (among other things) to generate their own links to other Indigenous communities through which local practices are strengthened and linked. For example, Rob Wilson and Wimal Dissanayake (1996: 14) point to such processes as part of "an aesthetic of rearguard resistance, rearticulated borders as sources, genres, and enclaves of cultural preservation and community identity to be set against global technologies of modernization or image-cultures of the postmodern." Indeed, simultaneous to the growing corporate control of media, Indigenous producers and cultural activists are creating innovative work, not only in the substance and form of their productions, but also in the social relations they are creating through this practice, that can change the ways we understand media and its relationship to the circulation of culture more generally in the twenty-first century.

Such efforts are evidence of how Indigenous media formed over the last decades now find themselves at the conjuncture of a number of historical developments: these include the circuits opened by new media technologies, ranging from satellites to compressed video and cyber-space, as well as the ongoing legacies of Indigenous activism worldwide, most recently by a generation comfortable with media and concerned with making their own representations as a mode of cultural creativity and social action. They also represent the complex and differing ways that states have responded to these developments—the opportunities of media and the pressures of activism—and entered into new relationships with the Indigenous nations that they encompass.

I conclude on a note of cautious optimism. The evidence of the growth and creativity of Indigenous digital media over the past two decades, whatever problems may have accompanied it, is nothing short of remarkable. Formations such as these, working out of grounded communities or broader regional or national bases, offer an important elaboration of what the digital age might look like, intervening in the "left behind" narrative that predominates.

Indigenous media offer an alternative model of grounded and increasingly global interconnectedness created by Indigenous people about their own lives and cultures. As we all struggle to comprehend the remapping of social space that is occurring, Indigenous media offer some other coordinates for understanding what such an interconnected world might be like outside a hegemonic order. Terms such as *the digital age* gloss over such phenomena in their own right or as examples of alternative modernities, resources of hope, new dynamics in social movements, or as part of the trajectory of Indigenous life in the twenty-first century. Perhaps it is time to invent new language.

NOTES

I would like to thank the following people for the ongoing conversations that helped me to write this article, in particular Leo Hsu, David Vadiveloo, Katrina Soukoup, and Barbi Zelizer. This piece grew out of a column first written for the online journal *Flow* in January 2005, and a lecture of the same title delivered February 22, 2005, at the Annenberg School for Communication at the

University of Pennsylvania in its Scholars Program series. Thanks to Pam Wilson and Michelle Stewart for encouraging me to write this piece, and to Pam in particular for her skilled editing and patience.

1. For information on the 2005 WSIS, see www.itu.int / wsis / index-p1.html.
2. As the site's founders explain at www.cyberpowwow.net / about.html, "The CyberPowWow project, conceived in 1996, is part Web site and part palace—a series of interconnected, graphical chat rooms which allow visitors to interact with one another in real time. Together, the Web site and palace form a virtual gallery with digital (and digitized) artworks and a library of texts."
3. For discussion of these statistics at the 2005 World Economic Forum, see www.weforum.org / site / knowledgenavigator.nsf / Content / New + Technologies. For an excellent discussion of the complexity of accounting for telephone statistics, see Shirky 2002.
4. The system, developed by First Mile Solutions, based in Boston, uses a receiver box powered by the motorcycle's battery. The driver need only roll slowly past the school to download all the village's outgoing e-mail and deliver incoming e-mail. Newly collected information is stored for the day in a computer strapped to the back of the motorcycle.
5. Thanks to Leo Hsu for passing this reference on to me.
6. Thanks to B. Ruby Rich for this reference.
7. For other examples, see Landzelius 2006; Prins 2002a; and Christen 2005.
8. See sila.nu / swf / journal and www.sila.nu / live. The Web site is financially supported by Telefilm Canada's New Media Fund, Government of Nunavut (Department of Sustainable Development), Nunavut Community Economic Development, Heritage Canada (Canadian Studies Program), National Research Council (Industrial Research Assistance Program). The Nunavut Independent Television Network (NITV) is a collaborating partner, along with sponsorships from Ardicom Digital Communications, SSI Micro, and Stratos Global Corporation.
9. *Raven Tales* premiered in Los Angeles in 2005 at the National Geographic's All Roads Film Festival (www.nationalgeographic.com / allroads), which gave the project completion funds, the only digital animation in that project. The first six episodes aired on Canada's Aboriginal People's Television Network in 2006; the next seven starting in November of 2007. The final thirteen episodes will broadcast in November of 2008; overall, the twenty-six episodes include stories from tribal communities from across North America (Chris Kientz, personal communication, October 2007).

REFERENCES

Aikio, P., and A. Aikio. 2001. Saavatko saamelaiset elää rauhassa [Are the Sámi allowed to live in peace?]. In M. Scheinin and T. Dahlgren, eds., *Toteutuvatko saamelaisten ihmisoikeudet? [Are the human rights of the Sámi carried out?]*. Pp. 92–119. Helsinki: Helsinki University Press.

Aikio-Puoskari, U. 2001. About the Saami and the domestic legislation on their language rights. In U. Aikio-Puoskari and M. Pentikäinen, eds., *The language rights of the Indigenous Saami in Finland: Under domestic and international law*. Pp. 3–70. *Juridica Lapponica 26*. Rovaniemi: University of Lapland.

Aksenova, O. V. 2004. Korennye malochislennye narody Severa: Uroki samoorganizatsii I social'nogo partnerstva [Indigenous small-numbered peoples of the North: The lessons of self-organization and social partnership]. *Seria: Biblioteka korennykh narodov Severa [Seria: Library of Indigenous Peoples of the North]* (Moscow), no. 2.

Albers, P., and B. Medicine, eds. 1983. *The hidden half: Studies of Plains Indian women*. Washington, DC: University Press of America.

Alekseenko, Y. A. 1979. Khristianizatsia na Turukhanskom Severe i eye vlianie na mirivizrenie i religioznye kul'ty ketov [Christianization in the Turukhansk North and its influence on the worldview and religious cults of the Kets]. In I. S. Vdovin, ed., *Khrisctianstvo i lamaizm u korennogo naselenia Sibiri, vtoraya polovina XIX—nachalo XX v. [Christianization and Lamaism of Siberia's Indigenous population, second half of the nineteenth and beginning of the twentieth century]*. Pp. 50–85. Leningrad: Nauka.

Alfredsson, G., and M. Stavropoulou, eds. 2002. *Justice pending: Indigenous peoples and other good causes (Essays in honour of Erica-Irene A. Daes)*. Leiden, the Netherlands: Martinus Nijhoff.

Alia, V. 1999. *Un/covering the North: News, media and Aboriginal people*. Vancouver: University of British Columbia Press.

Allen, C. 2002. *Blood narrative: Indigenous identity in American Indian and Maori literary and activist texts*. Durham, NC: Duke University Press.

Alvarado, M., P. Mege, and C. Baez. 2001. *Fotografías mapuche siglos XIX y XX: Contrucción y montaje de un imaginario [Mapuche photographs of the nineteenth and twentieth centuries: Construction and montage of an imaginary]*. Santiago:

Pehuén. Retrieved January 6, 2006, from www.puc.cl / proyectos / mapuches / html / frameportada.html.

Anaya, S. J. 2004. *Indigenous peoples and international law.* 2nd ed. Oxford: Oxford University Press.

Anderson, B. 1983. *Imagined communities: Reflections on the origin and spread of nationalism.* New York: Verso.

Anderson, K. 2001. *A recognition of being: Reconstructing Native womanhood.* Toronto: Sumach.

Ang, I. 1991. *Living room wars: Rethinking media audiences for a postmodern world.* London: Routledge.

Angeles Martínez, E. 1994. *"Been rgil guialnzak" (Gente que busca el bienestar): La historia del grupo solidario de San Pedro Quiatoni, Oaxaca* [*"Been rgil guialnzak" (People who search for well-being): The history of the solidarity group of San Pedro Quiatoni, Oaxaca*]. Oaxaca: Unidad Regional Oaxaca de Culturas Populares and Consejo Nacional para la Cultura y las Artes.

———, ed. 1997a. *Cuentos, leyendas y sucesos históricos de Quiatoni* [*Stories, legends, and historical events of Quiatoni*]. Municipio de San Pedro Quiatoni, Tlacolula, Oaxaca: Culturas Populares.

———, ed. 1997b. *Historia, cuentos y leyendas* [*History, stories, and legends*]. Soledad Salinas, Agencia Municipal de San Pedro Quiatoni, Oaxaca: Culturas Populares.

Animated News. 2004a. *Raven Tales:* The first all Native American computer animated short film. May 22. Retrieved October 15, 2005, from www.animated-news.com / archives / 00001550.html.

———. 2004b. *Raven Tales* wins book contract to document production. 2004. June 17. Retrieved October 15, 2005, from www.animated-news.com / archives / 0000 1743.html.

Appadurai, A. 1996. *Modernity at large: Cultural dimensions of modernity.* Minneapolis: University of Minnesota Press.

Appiah, K. A. 1997. The multiculturalist misunderstanding. *New York Review of Books,* October [electronic version]. Retrieved October 15, 2005, from www.ny books.com / articles / article-preview?article _id=1057.

Arnait Video Productions. N.d. *Arnait Video Productions: Voicing a unique Canadian view.* Retrieved November 28, 2005, from www.isuma.ca / about_us / arnait / index.html.

Asad, T. 1984. The concept of cultural translation in British social anthropology. In J. Clifford and G. E. Marcus, eds., *Writing culture: The poetics and politics of ethnography.* Pp. 141–64. Berkeley: University of California Press.

Asch, M., ed. 1997. *Aboriginal and treaty rights in Canada: Essays on law, equity, and respect for difference.* Vancouver: University of British Columbia Press.

Asian Indigenous Peoples Pact. 1989. *Indigenous peoples in Asia: Towards self-determination.* Bombay: Asian Indigenous Peoples Pact.

Askew, K., and R. R. Wilk, eds. 2002. *The anthropology of the media: A reader.* Malden, MA: Blackwell.

Atton, C. 2002. *Alternative Media.* London: Sage.

Aufderheide, P. 1995. The Video in the Villages Project: Videomaking with and by Brazilian Indians. *Visual Anthropology Review* 11(2): 83–93.

Ausubel, D. 1960. *The fern and the tiki—An American view of New Zealand national character, social attitudes, and race relations.* London: Angus and Robertson.

Avelar, I. N.d. *Toward a genealogy of Latin Americanism.* Retrieved January 6, 2006, from www.tulane.edu / avelar / genealogy.html.

Babcock, B. 1977. The story in the story: Metanarration in folk narrative. In R. Bauman, ed., *Verbal art as performance.* Pp. 61–79. Prospect Heights, IL: Waveland.

Bakhtin, M. 1986. *Speech genres and other late essays.* Austin, TX: University of Texas Press.

Balikci, A. 1970. *The Netsilik Eskimo.* Garden City, NY: American Museum of Natural History, Natural History Press.

Bannerji, H. 1999. A question of silence: Reflections on violence against women in communities of colour. In E. Dhua and A. Robertson, eds., *Scratching the surface: Canadian anti-racist feminism.* Pp. 261–77. Toronto: Women's Press.

Banning, K. 1991. Local channels: Zach Kunuk remodels T.V. *Parallelogramme* 17: 24–30.

Barclay, B. 1988. The control of one's own image. *Illusions* 8: 8–14.

——. 1992. Amongst landscapes. In J. Dennis and J. Bieringa, eds., *Film in Aotearoa New Zealand.* Pp. 116–29. Wellington, N.Z.: Victoria University Press.

——. 2002. Fourth Cinema. Paper presented at the Auckland University Film and Media Studies Department, September.

——. 2003. Exploring Fourth Cinema. Paper presented at the NEH Summer Institute in Hawaii, July.

——, M. Mita, and T. Stephens. 2003. Mana Maori Paepae / Maori cinema: A plan for growth. Unpublished brief.

Barlow, D. M., P. Mitchell, and T. O'Malley. 2005. *The media in Wales: Voices of a small nation.* Cardiff: University of Wales Press.

Bartolomé, M. A., and A. M. Barabas. 1996. *La pluralidad en peligro: Procesos de transfiguración y extinción cultural en Oaxaca* [*Plurality in danger: Processes of cultural transfiguration and extinction in Oaxaca*]. Mexico City: INAH.

Bataille, G. M., and C. L. P. Silet, eds. 1980. *The pretend Indians: Images of Native Americans in the movies.* Ames: Iowa State University Press.

Baumard, P. 1994. Oblique knowledge: The clandestine work of organizations. Retrieved September 1, 2005, from www.iae-aix.com / cv / enseignants / baumard / pages / oblique_knowledge.htm.

Beaufort Research. 2000. *State of the Welsh language research report.* Cardiff.

——. 2006. *Living lives through the medium of Welsh study summary report.* Cardiff.

Becker, M., C. Vivier, and P. d'Errico. 2002. *The history of NativeWeb*. Retrieved January 15, 2007, from www.nativeweb.com / info / history.php.

Bell, D., and J. Hollows, eds. 2005. *Ordinary lifestyles: Popular media, consumption and taste*. Maidenhead, U.K.: Open University Press.

Bellinghausen, H. 2007. Thousands rebel against neoliberalism in Chiapas. *La jornada*, January 5. Trans. from the Spanish and reposted by *Narco News Bulletin*, January 12, 2007. Retrieved January 13, 2007, from www.narconews .com / Issue44 / article2480.html.

Benjamin, W. 1968. *Illuminations*. Trans. H. Zohn. New York: Harcourt, Brace and World.

———. 1992. The task of the translator. In R. Schulte and J. Biguenet, eds., *Theories of translation: An anthology of essays from Dryden to Derrida*. Pp. 71–82. Chicago: University of Chicago Press.

———. 1999 [1934]. The author as producer. In M. W. Jennings, H. Eiland, and G. Smith, eds., *Walter Benjamin: Selected writings*. Vol. 2, *1927–1934*. R. Livingstone et al., trans. Pp. 768–82. Cambridge: Harvard University Press.

Bennett, J., and S. Rowley, eds. 2004. *Uqalurait: An oral history of Nunavut*. Montreal: McGill-Queen's University Press.

Bennett, T., and V. Blundell. 1995. First Peoples. *Cultural Studies* 9: 1–24.

Bergquist, C., R. Peñaranda, and G. Sánchez, eds. 1992. *Violence in Colombia: The contemporary crisis in historical perspective*. Wilmington, DE: SR.

Bonfil Batalla, G., and F. Rojas Arevena, eds. 1982. *América Latina: Etnodesarrollo y etnocidio* [*Latin America: Ethnodevelopment and ethnocide*]. San José, Costa Rica: FLACSO.

Bonner, F. 2003. *Ordinary television: Analyzing popular TV*. London: Sage.

Bordwell, D. 1989. Historical poetics of cinema. In R. B. Palmer, ed., *The cinematic text: Methods and approaches*. Pp. 369–98. New York: AMS.

Bourdieu, P. 1977. *Outline of a theory of practice*. Cambridge: Cambridge University Press.

———. 1984. *Distinction: A social critique of the judgement of taste*. Cambridge: Harvard University Press.

———. 1993. *The field of cultural production*. New York: Columbia University Press.

Bowker, G. C. 2000. Biodiversity, datadiversity. *Social Studies of Science* 30(5): 643–83.

Brooks, J. 2004. Digital Pony Express links up Cambodia. *New York Times*, January 27.

Brooten, L. 2004. Human rights discourse and the development of democracy in a multi-ethnic state. *Asian Journal of Communication* 14(2): 174–91.

Browne, D. R. 1996. *Electronic media and indigenous peoples: A voice of our own?* Ames: Iowa State University Press.

———. 2005. *Ethnic minorities, electronic media, and the public sphere: A comparative study*. Cresskill, NJ: Hampton.

Brysk, A. 2000. *From tribal village to global village: Indian rights and international relations in Latin America.* Stanford, CA: Stanford University Press.

Buddle, K. 2004. Media, markets and powwows: Matrices of Aboriginal cultural mediation in Canada. *Cultural Dynamics* 16(1): 29–69.

———. 2005. Aboriginal cultural capital production and radio production in urban Ontario. *Canadian Journal of Communications* 30(1): 7–40.

Burma Issues. 1994a. *BI organisation.* Retrieved October 1, 2005, from burmaissues .org/ En / BI%20Organisation.html.

———. 1994b. *Video project.* Retrieved October 1, 2005, from burmaissues.org / En / video1.html.

Butler, J. 1999. Performativity's social magic. In R. Shusterman, ed., *Bourdieu: A critical reader.* Pp. 113–28. Malden, MA: Blackwell.

Cache Collective. 2005. Persevering realpolitik: A conversation with Marie-Hélène Cousineau of Arnait Video Productions. *Fuse* 28(3): 15–19.

Cadiz, M. C. 2005. Communication for empowerment: The practice of participatory communication for development. In O. Hemer and T. Tufte, eds., *Media and glocal change: Rethinking communication for development.* Pp. 145–59. Nordicom: Clacso.

Cairns, B., and Martin, H. 1994. *Shadows on the wall: A study of seven New Zealand feature films.* Auckland: Longman Paul.

Calderón, F., A. Piscitelli, and J. L. Reyna. 1992. Social movements: Actors, theories, expectations. In A. Escobar and S. E. Alvarez, eds., *The making of social movements in Latin America: Identity, strategy, and democracy.* Pp. 19–36. Boulder, CO: Westview.

Caldón, J. D. 2005. Los indígenas y el conflicto armado en Colombia: A propósito de las acciones bélicas de las FARC en Toribío, Caldono y Jambaló [Indigenous people and the Colombian armed conflict: Regarding the bellicose actions by the FARC in Toribio, Caldoso, and Jambalo]. *Etnias y política* 1: 26–34.

Campbell, H., ed. 1996. *The politics of ethnicity in Southern Mexico.* Nashville: Vanderbilt University.

Capdevila, G. 2005. No declaration for indigenous peoples this year—maybe next. Inter Press Service News Agency, December 22. Retrieved December 31, 2005, from www.ipsnews.net / news.asp?idnews=31549.

Carelli, V. 2004. *Moi, un Indien [I, an Indian]—Mostra Vídeo nas Aldeias: Um olhar indígena [Video in the Villages: Through Indian eyes.* Retrieved January 6, 2006, from www.videonasaldeias.org.br / textos_ok / moi_un_indien_ok.htm.

Carneiro da Cunha, M. 1978. *Os mortos e os outros [The dead and the others].* São Paulo: Hucitec.

Carpenter, E. S. 1955. Space concepts of the Aivilik Eskimos. *Explorations* 5: 131–45.

———. 1956. The timeless present in the mythology of the Aivilik Eskimos. *Anthropologica* 3: 1–4.

———. 1973. *Eskimo realities.* New York: Holt, Rinehart and Winston.

——. 2004. Eskimo. In G. Robinson, ed., *Isuma Inuit studies reader: An Inuit anthology*. Pp. 149–63. Montreal: Isuma.

——, and McLuhan, M., eds. 1960. *Explorations in communication*. Boston: Beacon.

Castells, M. 1996. *The rise of the network society*. London: Blackwell.

——. 1997. *The power of identity: The information age*. London: Blackwell.

——. 2003. *The Internet galaxy: Reflections on the Internet, business and society*. London: Oxford University Press.

Castells i Talens, A. 2003. Cine indígena y resistencia cultural [Indigenous cinema and cultural resistance]. *Chasqui: Revista latinoamericana de comunicación* [*Chasqui: Latin American Review of Communication*] 84. Retrieved January 6, 2006, from chasqui.comunica.org / content / view / 124 / 61 / .

Chaliand, G. 1989. Minority peoples in the age of nation-states. In G. Chaliand, ed., *Minority peoples in the age of nation-states*. Pp. 1–11. Trans. T. Berrett. London: Pluto.

Champagne, D. 2005. Rethinking native relations with contemporary nation-states. In D. Champagne, K. Torjesen, and S. Steiner, eds., *Indigenous peoples and the modern state*. Pp. 3–23. Walnut Creek, CA: Altamira.

Chartier, R. 2002. *Os desafios da escrita* [*The challenges of writing*]. São Paulo: UNESP.

Chassen-López, F. R. 2001. *The view from the South: An insurgent reading of Mexican history*. Lexington: University of Kentucky Committee on Social Theory Working Papers Series.

Chaumeil, J.-P. 2000. *Voir, savoir, pouvoir: Le chamanisme chez les Yagua de l'Amazone péruvienne* [*To see, to know, to have power: Shamanism among the Yaguoa of the Peruvian Amazon*]. Geneva: Georg.

Christen, Kim. 2005. Gone digital: Aboriginal remix in the cultural commons. *International Journal of Cultural Property* 12: 315–44.

Christie, M. 1994. Grounded and ex-centric knowledges: Exploring Aboriginal alternatives to Western thinking. In J. Edwards, ed., *Thinking: International interdisciplinary perspectives*. Pp. 24–34. Heatherton, Australia: Hawker Brownlow Education.

——. 2000. Galtha: The application of Aboriginal philosophy to school learning. *New Horizons in Education* 103: 3–19.

——. 2004. Computer databases and Aboriginal knowledge. *Learning Communities: International Journal of Learning in Social Contexts* 1: 4–12.

——. 2005. Words, ontologies and Aboriginal databases. *Multimedia International Australia* 116: 52–63.

Christie, M., and W. Perrett. 1996. Negotiating resources: Language, knowledge and the search for "Secret English" in northeast Arnhem Land. In R. Howitt, J. Connell, and P. Hirsch, eds., *Resources, nations and Indigenous peoples*. Pp. 57–65. Melbourne: Oxford University Press.

Churchill, W. 1996. *From a Native son: Selected essays on indigenism, 1985–1995*. Boulder, CO: South End.

——. 1998. *Fantasies of the master race: Literature, cinema, and the colonization of American Indians*. San Francisco: City Lights.

Cobo, José Martínez. 1986. *Study of the problem of discrimination against Indigenous populations*. United Nations Economic and Social Council, Commission on Human Rights. U.N. Document E / CN.4 / Sub.2 / 1986 / 7 / Add.4. New York.

Communication Initiative. 2002. Making waves: Stories of participatory communication for social change—Kayapó Video. August 21. Retrieved October 25, 2005, from www.comminit.com / strategicthinking / pdsmakingwaves / sld -1865.html.

Confederación de Nacionalidades Indígenas del Ecuador (CONAIE). N.d. El Festival de Cine y Video: Nuestro punto de encuentro. Retrieved from conaie.native web.org / cine.html.

Consejo Nacional de Cultura (Ecuador) (CNC). N.d. II Festival de Cine y Video de las Naciones AbyaYala: Premiación de videos ganadores del II festival—Obras premiadas. Retrieved from www.cncultura.gov.ec / cultura / HTML / FESTIVALA LABY.HTM#arriba.

Controversia. 1978. *Consejo Regional Indígena del Cauca: Diéz años de lucha, historia y documentos* [*Indigenous Regional Council of Cauca: Ten years of struggle, history and documents*]. Bogotá: CINEP.

Convenio Unión Europea / Universidad del Valle. 2004. *En minga con los pueblos indígenas y por el derecho a su palabra: Monitoreo de medios de comunicación masiva* [*In struggle with the Indigenous communities and their right to self-expression: Monitoring the mass communication media*]. Cali, Colombia.

Córdova, A., and G. Zamorano. 2003. Mapping Mexican media: Indigenous and community video and radio. *Native Networks* (Smithsonian National Museum of the American Indian). Retrieved January 6, 2006, from www.nativenet works.si.edu / eng / rose / mexico.htm.

Cormack, M. 1998. Minority language media in Western Europe: Preliminary considerations. *European Journal of Communication* 13(1): 33–52.

——. 2005. The cultural politics of minority language media. *International Journal of Media and Cultural Politics* 1(1): 107–22.

Cottle, S. 2000. *Ethnic minorities and the media: Changing cultural boundaries*. Buckingham, U.K.: Open University Press.

Couldry, N. 2003. Beyond the hall of mirrors? Some theoretical reflections on the global contestation of media power. In N. Couldry and J. Curran, eds., *Contesting media power: Alternative media in a networked world*. Pp. 39–56. London: Rowman and Littlefield.

Council of Europe. N.d. *European charter for regional or minority languages*. ETS no. 148. Retrieved November 7, 2005, from conventions.coe.int / TREATY / EN / Reports / Html / 148.htm.

Coyes, G. 2003. *Shared visions: The art of storytelling*. Storytellers Productions.

Cresswell, T., and G. Verstraete, eds. 2003. *Mobilizing place, placing mobility: On the politics of representation in a globalized world.* Amsterdam: Rodopi.

Crofts, S. 1993. Reconceptualizing national cinema / s. *Quarterly Review of Film and Video* 14(3): 49–67.

Cultural Survival Quarterly. 1983. The electronic era. Special issue, 7(2).

——. 1994. Native American journalism. Special issue, 17(4).

——. 1998a. The Internet and Indigenous groups. Special issue, 21(4).

——. 1998b. Aboriginal media, Aboriginal control. Special issue, 22(2).

——. 2006. Indigenous peoples bridging the digital divide. Special issue, 29(2).

Curran, J., and Park M.-J., eds. 2000. *De-Westernizing media studies.* New York: Routledge.

Daes, E.-I. A. 1993. *Discrimination against indigenous peoples: Explanatory note concerning the draft declaration on the rights of indigenous peoples.* United Nations Economic and Social Council, Commission on Human Rights, July 19. U.N. Document E / CN.4 / Sub.2 / 1993 / 26 / Add.1. New York.

——. 1996. *Working paper by the chairperson-rapporteur, Mrs. Erica-Irene A. Daes, on the concept of "indigenous people."* United Nations Economic and Social Council, Commission on Human Rights, June 10. U.N. Document E / CN.4 / Sub.2 / AC.4 / 1996 / 2. New York.

Danaja, P., and M. Garde. 1997. From a distance. In C.E. Smith and H. Burke, eds., *1997 Fulbright Symposium: Indigenous cultures in an interconnected world.* Pp. 179–88. Precirculated papers.

Davies, J. 1994. *Broadcasting and the BBC in Wales.* Cardiff: University of Wales Press.

Dawson, A. S. 1998. From models for the nation to model citizens: *Indigenismo* and the "revindication" of the Mexican Indian, 1920–1940. *Journal of Latin American Studies* 30: 279–308.

de Certeau, M. 1984. *The practice of everyday life.* Berkeley: University of California Press.

Decker, S. 1999. Imagination on fire: First Nations tales of trickster, teacher and nature told on Christmas Day. *Jam! Showbiz,* December 24. Retrieved October 29, 2005, from jam.canoe.ca / Television / TV _Shows / S / Stories_ From _the _Seventh_ Fire / 1999 / 12 / 24 / 733359.html.

Declaración de Iquique de los Pueblos Originarios. 2002. *Red Regional de Comunicación Indígena Kujkuj Zugun,* February 28. Retrieved September 28, 2007, from http://www.cuestiones.ws / revista / n8 / abro2-indigenas-serpal.htm.

de Costa, R. N.d. Indigenism. *Globalization and autonomy online compendium.* Social Sciences and Humanities Research Council (Canada). Retrieved March 7, 2006, from anscombe.mcmaster.ca / globalı / glossary _print.jsp?id=CO.0027.

Deleuze, G. 1989. *Cinema 2: The time-image.* Trans. H. Tomlinson and R. Galeta. London: Athlone.

Deloria, P. 1998. *Playing Indian*. New Haven, CT: Yale University Press.

Department of Communications, Information Technology and the Arts (DCITA), Commonwealth of Australia. 2005. *Indigenous television review report: Report of the review into the viability of establishing an indigenous television service.* Retrieved January 15, 2007, from www.dcita.gov.au / indigenous_programs / publications_and_reports / recent / previous_publications_and_ reports / indigenous_television_review_report.

d'Errico, P. 2000. Native Web: Internet as political technology. January. Retrieved January 15, 2007, from jurist.law.pitt.edu / lessons / lesjanoo.htm.

Derrida, J. 1995. *Mal d'archive: Une impression freudienne [Archive fever: A Freudian impression]*. Paris: Galilée.

Diatchkova, G. S. 2001. Dvizhenie korennykh narodov Chukotki i etnicheskoe samosoznanie [Chukotka Indigenous movement and ethnic identity]. *Zhurnal prikladnoy psikhologii [Journal of Applied Psychology]* 4–5: 80–100.

———. 2005. *Models of ethnic adaptation to the natural and social environment.* Retrieved August 15, 2005, from www.siberian-studies.org / Themes / Identities.

Digital Solidarity Fund Foundation. 2005. From the digital divide to the need for a worldwide solidarity movement. Retrieved January 1, 2006, from www.dsf-fsn .org / en / 02-en.htm.

Dinoff, D. 2000. Stories from the seventh fire. *Playback*, June 12. Retrieved October 29, 2005, from www.playbackmag.com / articles / magazine / 20000612 / 29424.html.

Dirlik, A. 2000. *Postmodernity's histories: The past as legacy and project.* Lanham, MD: Rowman and Littlefield.

Dobrow, J. R., and C. L. Gidney. 1998. The good, the bad, and the foreign: The use of dialect in children's animated television. In A. B. Jordan and K. H. Jamieson, eds., *Children and television.* Pp. 105–19. *Annals of the American Academy of Political and Social Science.* Thousand Oaks, CA: Sage Periodicals Press.

Dorado, M., and Radio Payu'mat Staff. 2004. Radio Payu'mat: Una experiencia de comunicación en la zona norte del Cauca [Radio Payu'mat: An experience of communication in the northern zone of Cauca]. M.A. thesis, Universidad Pontificia Bolivariana.

Downing, J. D. H. 2001. *Radical media: Rebellious communication and social movements.* Thousand Oaks, CA: Sage.

Dufva, H. 2004. Culture, language and thinking: Whorf, Bakhtin, Merleau-Ponty and situated embodiment. In F. Bostad, C. Brandist, L. S. Evensen, and H. C. Faber, eds., *Bakhtinian perspectives on language and culture: Meaning in language, art and new media.* Pp. 133–46. Houndsmills, U.K.: Palgrave Macmillan.

Dyck, N., ed. 1985. *Indigenous peoples and the nation-state: "Fourth World" politics in Canada, Australia and Norway.* St. Johns, NF: Institute of Social and Economic Research.

Earthwatch Institute. 2001. Diversity in the age of globalization: Roundtable—Indigenous Internet, April. Retrieved January 15, 2007, from www.wadsworth .com / anthropology_d / special_features / ext / earthwatch / rt.html.

Eckert, C., and A. L. C. Rocha. 2005. Escrituras hipermidiáticas e as metamorfoses da escrita etnográfica na era das "textualidades" eletrônicas [Hypermedia scriptures and the metamorphoses of ethnographic writing in the age of electronic "textualities"]. Paper presented at the Nineteenth Annual Meeting of ANPOCS: Associação Nacional de Pós-Graduação e Pesquisa em Ciências Sociais, October. Caxambu, Brazil.

Economist. 2005. Technology and development: Editorial. March 10 [electronic version]. Retrieved December 12, 2005, from www.economist.com.

Embassy of the Peoples Republic of China in Switzerland. 1997. China concerned with protection of indigenous peoples' rights, April 1. Retrieved December 15, 2005, from www.china-embassy.ch / eng / ztnr / rqwt / t138829.htm.

Encounter between the Zapatista Peoples and the Peoples of the World—3. 2007. *IndyMedia.uk*, January 2. Retrieved January 14, 2007, from www.indymedia .org.uk / en / 2007 / 01 / 359192.html.

Esteva, D. 2001a. Cosecha escarlata [Scarlet harvest]. *Noticias de Oaxaca*, March 23.

———. 2001b. Sabia convivencia [Wise coexistence]. *Noticias de Oaxaca*, March 25.

European Commission. 1996. Sixth European Union–Rio Group Ministerial Conference: Cochabamba Declaration. Bulletin EU 4–1996. July 19. Retrieved from europa.eu / bulletin / en / 9604 / p000347.htm.

Fabian, J. 1983. *Time and the other.* New York: Columbia University Press.

Fairclough, N. 1992. *Discourse and social change.* Cambridge, U.K.: Polity.

———. 2003. *Analysing discourse: Textual analysis for social research.* London: Routledge.

Faulhaber, P. 2001. Réfractions de mémoire dans un processus d'identification ticuna [Refractions of memory in a process of Ticuna identification], Terre Indigène Tupã-Supé, Cours Moyen du Fleuve Solimões, December. In P. de Robert and L. Forline, eds., Dialogues amazoniens: Etudes indigénistes du Museu Paraense Emilio Goeldi. Special issue, *Ateliers de Caravelle* 18: 63–74.

Favre, H. 1999. *El indigenismo.* Mexico City: Fondo de Cultura Económica.

Festa, R., and L. F. Santoro. 1991. New trends in Latin America: From video to television. In N. Thede and A. Ambrosi, eds., *Video the changing world.* Pp. 84–93. Montreal: Black Rose.

Fickling, D. 2003. The return of the native. *Guardian unlimited*, July 10 [electronic version]. Retrieved January 10, 2004, from film.guardian.co.uk / features / fea turepages / 0,4120,995725,00.html.

Fischer, M. M. 1999. Worlding cyberspace: Toward a critical ethnography in time, space and theory. In G. Marcus, ed., *Critical anthropology now: Unexpected contexts, shifting constituencies, changing agendas.* Pp. 245–304. Santa Fe, NM: School of American Research Press.

Fleming, K. 1996. Marie-Hélène Cousineau: Videomaker. *Inuit Art Quarterly*. Retrieved December 20, 2005, from www.isuma.ca / news / press_clipping / .

Fleras, A., and J. L. Elliot, eds. 1992. *The "nations within": Aboriginal-state relations in Canada, the United States, and New Zealand*. New York: Oxford University Press.

Foucault, M. 2004. *Philosophie: Anthologie*. Paris: Gallimard.

Fox, J. 1996. How does civil society thicken? The political construction of social capital in rural Mexico. *World Development* 24(6): 1089–14.

Froehling, O. 1997. The cyberspace "War of ink and Internet" in Chiapas, Mexico. *Geographical Review* 87(2): 291–307.

Frota, M. N.d. Taking Aim e a Aldeia Global: A apropriação cultural e política da tecnologia de vídeo pelos índios kayapós [Taking Aim and the global village: The cultural appropriation and politics of video technology for the Kayapó Indians]. Retrieved from www.mnemocine.com.br / osbrasisindigenas / frota .htm.

García Canclini, N. 1995. The future of the past. In N. García Canclini, ed., *Hybrid cultures: Strategies for entering and leaving modernity*. Pp. 107–44. Minneapolis: University of Minnesota Press.

García Espinosa, J. 1983 [1970]. For an imperfect cinema. In M. Chanan, ed., *Twenty-five years of Latin American cinema*. Pp. 28–33. London: British Film Institute.

Gardiner-Garden, J. 2000. *The definition of aboriginality*, December 5. Research Note 18 2000–01. Parliament of Australia, Parliamentary Library. Retrieved February 7, 2007, from www.aph.gov.au / library / pubs / rn / 2000–01 / 01RN18 .htm.

Garduño Cervantes, J., ed. 1985. *El final del silencio: Documentos indígenas de México* [*The end of silence: Indigenous documents of Mexico*]. Mexico City: Ediciones del Centro Cultural Mazahua.

Garnham, N. 1992. The media and the public sphere. In C. Calhoun, ed., *Habermas and the public sphere*. Pp. 359–76. Cambridge: MIT Press.

Geiogamah, H., and D. M. Pavel. 1993. Developing television for American Indian and Alaska Native children in the late twentieth century. In G. L. Berry and J. K. Asamen, eds., *Children and television: Images in a changing sociocultural world*. Pp. 191–204. Newbury Park, CA: Sage.

Georgiou, M. 2001. Crossing the boundaries of the ethnic home: Media consumption and ethnic identity construction in the public space—The case of the Cypriot Community Centre in North London. *Gazette* 63(4): 311–29.

Gilroy, P. 2004. *After empire: Multiculture or postcolonial melancholia*. London: Routledge.

Ginsburg, F. D. 1991. Indigenous media: Faustian contract or global village? *Cultural Anthropology* 6(1): 92–112.

———. 1993. Aboriginal media and the Australian imaginary. *Public culture: Bulletin of the Project for Transnational Cultural Studies* 5: 557–78.

———. 1994. Embedded aesthetics: Creating a space for indigenous media. *Cultural Anthropology* 9(3): 365–83.

———. 1995. Production values: Indigenous media and the rhetoric of self-determination. In D. Battaglia, ed., *The rhetoric of self making.* Pp. 121–38. Berkeley: University of California Press.

———. 1997. "From little things, big things grow": Indigenous media and cultural activism. In R. G. Fox and O. Starn, eds., *Between resistance and revolution: Cultural politics and social protest.* Pp. 118–44. New Brunswick, NJ: Rutgers University Press.

———. 1998. Institutionalizing the unruly: Charting a future for visual anthropology. *Ethnos* 63(2): 173–201.

———. 1999. Shooting back: From ethnographic film to indigenous production / ethnography of media. In T. Miller and R. Stam, eds., *A companion to film theory.* Pp. 295–322. London: Blackwell.

———. 2000 [1997]. Resources of hope: Learning from the local in the age of globalization. In C. Smith and G. Ward, eds., *Indigenous cultures in an interconnected world.* Sydney: Allen and Unwin.

———. 2002. Screen memories: Resignifying the traditional in Indigenous media. In F. Ginsburg, L. Abu-Lughod, and B. Larkin, eds., *Media worlds: Anthropology on new terrain.* Pp. 40–56. Berkeley: University of California Press.

———. 2003. Screen memories and entangled technologies: Resignifying Indigenous lives. In E. Shohat and R. Stam, eds. *Multiculturalism, postcoloniality and transnational media.* Pp. 77–98. New Brunswick, NJ: Rutgers University Press.

———. 2005a. Rethinking the digital age. *Flow: A critical forum on television and film* 1(8). Retrieved January 23, 2006, from jot.communication.utexas.edu / flow / ?jot=viewandid=528.

———. 2005b. Move over Marshall McLuhan! Live from the Arctic! *Flow: A critical forum on television and film* 2(4). Retrieved January 23, 2006, from jot.communication.utexas.edu / flow / ?jot=viewandid=779.

———. 2005c. Ten thousand years of media flow. In *Flow: A critical forum on television and film* 1(4). Retrieved January 23, 2006, from jot.communication.utexas.edu / flow / ?jot=viewandid=491.

———, L. Abu-Lughod, and B. Larkin. 2002. Introduction to F. D. Ginsburg, L. Abu-Lughod, and B. Larkin, eds., *Media worlds: Anthropology on new terrain.* Pp. 1–36. Berkeley: University of California Press.

Giroux, H. 1998. Are Disney movies good for your kids? In S. R. Steinberg and J. L. Kincheloe, eds., *Kinder-culture: The corporate construction of childhood.* Pp. 53–67. Boulder, CO: Westview.

Gladney, D. 2003. *China's minorities: The case of Xinjiang and the Uyghur people.* Geneva: United Nations High Commission on Human Rights.

——. 2004. *Dislocating China: Muslims, minorities, and other subaltern subjects*. Chicago: University of Chicago Press.

Gluck, C. 2005. Taiwan Aborigines get TV channel. *BBC News Online*, July 1. Retrieved January 15, 2007, from news.bbc.co.uk / 2 / hi / asia-pacific / 4640567.stm.

González, G. 2005. Latin America: Advances on paper no guarantee of real progress, June 13. *Inter Press Service News Agency*, retrieved February 3, 2007, from ipsnews.net / news.asp?idnews=29059.

Goodman, D. S. G. 2004. The campaign to "open up the West": National, provincial-level and local perspectives. *China Quarterly* 178: 317–34.

Goulard, J. P. 1998. *Les genres du corps: Conceptions de la personne chez les Ticuna de la Haute Amazonie* [*Genres of the body: Conceptions of the person among the Ticuna of the Upper Amazon*]. Paris: Ecole des Hautes Etudes en Sciences Sociales.

——. 2002. Un objeto ritual: El chine o escudo de baile de los Ticuna [A ritual object: The *chine* or dance shield of the Ticuna]. In T. Myers and M. S. Cipoletti, eds., *Artifacts and society in Amazonia*. Pp. 47–62. Bonner Americanistische Studien 36. Bonn: Bonner Universtität Verlag.

Government of New Zealand. 1995. *New Zealand Film Commission Act*. Wellington: New Zealand Government.

——. 2000. *The Film Fund*. Retrieved January 12, 2006, from www.filmfund.co.nz / about / .

Grande, S. 2004. *Red pedagogy: Native American social and political thought*. Lanham, MD: Rowman and Littlefield.

Greller, W. 1996. *Provision and regulation of the Sámi languages*. Aberystwyth, Wales: Centre for Educational Studies.

Grupioni, L. D. B. 1998. *Coleçães e expediçães vigiadas: Os etnólogos no Conselho de Fiscalização das expediçães artísticas e científicas no Brasil* [*Collections and expeditions under surveillance: The ethnologists of the Council for the Inspection of the Artistic and Scientific Expeditions in Brazil*]. São Paulo: ANPOCS.

Guissé, El H. 2004. *Globalization and indigenous peoples*. United Nations Economic and Social Council, Commission on Human Rights, Working Group on Indigenous Populations. U.N. Document E / CN.4 / Sub.2 / AC.4 / 2004 / 3, June 10. New York.

Gurvich, I. S. 1961. O putiakh dalneyshego pereustroystva ekonomiki i kultury narodov Severa [On the ways of further reconstructing northern peoples' economics and culture]. *Sovetskaya Etnografia* [*Soviet Ethnography*] 4: 45–57.

Hale, C. 1994. Between Che Guevara and the Pachamama: Mestizos, Indians and identity politics in the anti-quincentenary campaign. *Critique of Anthropology* 14(1): 9–39.

Hall, S. 2000. Cultural identity and cinematic representation. In R. Stam and T. Miller, eds., *Film and theory: An anthology*. Pp. 704–14. Oxford, U.K.: Blackwell.

——. 2001. Constituting an archive. *Third Text* 54: 87–110.

Hanson, R. D. 2004. Contemporary globalization and tribal sovereignty. In

T. Biolsi, ed., *A companion to the anthropology of American Indians*. Pp. 284–303. Malden, MA: Blackwell.

Haraway, D. 1995. The science question in feminism and the privilege of partial perspective. In A. Feenberg and A. Hannay, eds., *Technology and the politics of knowledge*. Pp. 175–94. Bloomington: Indiana University Press.

Harrell, S. 2001. *Ways of being ethnic in Southwest China*. Seattle: University of Washington Press.

Hartley, J. 2004. Television, nation and Indigenous media. *Television and new media* 5(1): 7–25.

——, and A. McKee. 2000. *The Indigenous public sphere: The reporting and reception of Indigenous issues in the Australian media, 1994–1997*. Oxford: Oxford University Press.

Hearne, B. 1993. Cite the source: Reducing cultural chaos in picture books. Part 1. *School Library Journal*, July, 22–27.

Hearne, J. 2005. "John Wayne's teeth": Speech, sound and representation in *Smoke signals* and *Imagining Indians*. *Western Folklore* 64(3–4): 189–208.

——. 2006. Telling and retelling in the "ink of light": Documentary cinema, oral narratives, and indigenous identities. *Screen* 47(3): 1–20.

Hechter, M. 1975. *Internal colonialism: The Celtic fringe in British national development, 1536–1966*. London: Routledge and Kegan Paul.

Heider, K. 1976. *Ethnographic film*. Austin: University of Texas Press.

Hemming, J. 2003. A fresh look at Amazon Indians: Karl von den Steinen and Curt Nimuendaju, giants of Brazilian anthropology. *Tipiti: Journal of the Society for the Anthropology of Lowland South America* 1(1): 163–78.

Hendrick, S., and K. Fleming. 1991. Zacharias Kunuk: Video maker and Inuit historian. *Inuit Art Quarterly* 6: 24–28.

Hernández Díaz, J. 1992. El movimento indígena y la construcción de la etnicidad en Oaxaca [The Indigenous movement and the construction of ethnicity in Oaxaca]. *Cuadernos del Sur* 1(2): 47–66.

——. 1993. Etnicidad y nacionalismo en Mexico: Una interpretación [Ethnicity and nationalism in Mexico: An interpretation]. In *Etnicidad, nacionalismo, y poder: Tres ensayos* [*Ethnicity, nationalism and power: Three essays*]. Pp. 9–64. Oaxaca: Universidad Autónoma Benito Juárez.

Hocking, P., ed. 1975. *Principles of visual anthropology*. The Hague: Mouton.

Hourigan, N. 2001. New social movement theory and minority language television campaigns. *European Journal of Communication* 16(1): 77–100.

Howell, P. 2002. Northern exposure. *Toronto Star*, April 12.

Howley, K. 2005. *Community media: People, places and communication technologies*. Cambridge: Cambridge University Press.

Human Rights Watch. 2005. UN Security Council should take up Burma's human rights crisis, October 15. Retrieved October 15, 2005, from hrw.org / english / docs / 2005 / 10 / 14 / burma11873.htm.

Huntington, S. P. 1968. *Political order in changing societies*. New Haven, CT: Yale University Press.

Hylton, J., ed. 1994. *Aboriginal self-government in Canada: Current trends and issues*. Saskatoon: Purich.

Igloolik Isuma International. 1996. Nunavut (Our Land): (Unpublished) proposal to telefilm, MTL. 1993. In P. Gale and L. Steele, eds., *Video re/view: The (best) source for critical writings on Canadian artists' video*. Pp. 69–71. Toronto: Art Metropole and Vtape.

Igloolik Isuma Productions. N.d. *Igloolik video on-line catalogue: Igloolik video by artists*. Retrieved December 11, 2004, from www.isuma.ca / catalogue / isuma _view.php?what=28.

Ihimaera, W. 1987. *The Whale Rider*. Auckland: Heinemann.

Imam, A. M. 1991. Ideology, the mass media, and women: A study from Radio Kaduna, Nigeria. In C. Coles and B. Mack, eds., *Hausa women in the twentieth century*. Pp. 244–52. Madison: University of Wisconsin Press.

Indian Country Today. 2005. Support the Draft Declaration on the Rights of Indigenous Peoples. December 15 [electronic version]. Retrieved December 31, 2005, from www.indiancountry.com / content.cfm?id=1096412114.

Indigenous position paper for the World Summit on the Information Society (WSIS). 2003. *Indigenous peoples and the information society* [Draft version], December. Geneva. Retrieved from www.un-ngls.org / WSIS%20-%20Indigenous-PositionPaper-EN.rtf.

Instituto Nacional Indigenista (INI). 1990. *Hacia un video índio [Toward Indian video]*. Mexico City: Cuadernos del INI.

International Labour Organisation (ILO). 1989. *C169 Indigenous and Tribal Peoples Convention*. Retrieved January 15, 2007, from www.ilo.org / ilolex / cgi-lex / convde.pl?C169.

Jaimes, M. A., ed. 1992. *The state of Native America: Genocide, colonization, and resistance*. Boston: South End.

Jakubowicz, A. 2006. Indigenous media and global futures. Unpublished ms.

James, S. D. N.d. Simon Daniel James, CBC Aboriginal: Personalities. Retrieved October 5, 2007, from www.cbc.ca / aboriginal / personalities_sub_7.htm.

Jhala, J. 1998. The shaping of Gujarati cinema: Recognizing the new in traditional cultures. *Visual Anthropology* 11: 373–85.

Kampe, K. 1997. Introduction: Indigenous peoples of Southeast Asia. In D. Mc-Caskill and K. Kampe, eds., *Development or domestication? Indigenous peoples of Southeast Asia*. Pp. 1–25. Chiang Mai, Thailand: Silkworm.

Kapur, Jyotsna. 2005. *Coining for capital: Movies, marketing, and the transformation of childhood*. Brunswick, NJ: Rutgers University Press.

Kasten, E. 2004. *The cultural heritage of the peoples of Kamchatka and Internet: Returning knowledge to Indigenous communities*. Retrieved September 7, 2005, from www.siberian-studies.org / publications / PDF,kasten2004f.pdf.

Kauranen, R., and S. Tuori. 2001. Mapping minorities and their media: The national context—Finland. Retrieved June 28, 2005, from www.lse.ac.uk / collections / EMTEL / minorities / reports.html.

Kearney, M. 1996. *Reconceptualizing the peasantry: Anthropology in global perspective.* Boulder, CO: Westview.

———. 2000. Transnational Oaxacan Indigenous identity: The case of Mixtecs and Zapotecs. *Identities: Global Studies in Culture and Power* 7(2): 173–95.

———, and S. Varese. 1995. Latin America's Indigenous peoples: Changing identities and forms of resistance. In S. Halebsky and R. L. Harris, eds., *Capital, power, and inequality in Latin America.* Pp. 207–31. Boulder, CO: Westview.

Kearns, Rick. 2006. Indigenous Latin America: Progress in '06. *Indian Country Today,* December 29. Retrieved February 3, 2007, from www.indiancountry .com / content.cfm?id=1096414275.

Keck, M. E., and K. Sikkink. 1999. Transnational advocacy networks in international and regional politics. *International Social Science Journal* 51(1): 89–101.

Keeshig-Tobias, L. 1997. Stop stealing native stories. In B. Ziff and P. V. Rao, eds., *Borrowed power: Essays on cultural appropriation.* Pp. 71–73. New Brunswick, NJ: Rutgers University Press.

Kilpatrick, J. 1999. *Celluloid Indians: Native Americans and film.* Lincoln: University of Nebraska Press.

King, M. 1985. *Being Pakeha.* Auckland: Hodder and Stoughton.

Klineneberg, E., and C. Benzecry. 2005. Introduction: Cultural production in a digital age. *Annals of the American Academy of Political and Social Science* 597(1): 6–18.

Kraeger, P. 1991. Aung San Suu Kyi and the peaceful struggle for human rights in Burma. In M. Aris, ed., *Freedom from fear and other writings.* Pp. 318–59. London: Penguin.

Kriukov, V., V. Seliverstov, and A. Tokarev. 2004. Problemy socialno-ekonomicheskogo razvitiya syrievykh territoriy i nedropolzovania v federativnoy sisteme i regionalnoy politike Rossii [The problems of social and economical development of primary producing territories and subsurface use in federal system and Russian regional politics]. In V. E. Seliverstov and A. V. Novikov, eds., *Federalizm v Rossii i Kanade: Pravovye i economicheskiy aspekty* [*Federalism in Russia and in Canada: Legal and economical aspects*]. Pp. 77–99. Moscow: International Center for the Projects and Programs on Development of Federal Relationship and Regional Politics.

Kulonen, U.-M., I. Seurujärvi-Kari, and R. Pulkkinen. 2005. *The Saami: A cultural encyclopaedia.* Helsinki: sks.

Kunuk, Z. 1992. Zacharias Kunuk. In *Revisions.* Pp. 14–15. Banff, AB: Walter Phillips Gallery.

———. N.d. *The art of Inuit storytelling.* Retrieved November 28, 2005, from www.isuma.ca / about_us / isuma / our_style / kunuk.html.

La cuestión étnica en América Latina [The ethnic question in Latin America]. 1981. Special issue, *Revista mexicana de ciencias políticas y sociales* [*Mexican Review of Political and Social Sciences*] 27(103).

Landzelius, K. M., ed. 2006. *Native on the Net: Virtual diaspora in the digital age.* London: Routledge.

Langton, M. 1993. *"Well, I heard it on the radio and I saw it on the television. . . ." An essay for the Australian Film Commission on the politics and aesthetics of filmmaking by and about Aboriginal people and things.* Sydney: Australian Film Commission.

Lansing, J. S. 1989. The decolonization of ethnographic film. In R. M. Boonzajer Flaes, ed., *Eyes across the water.* Pp. 10–17. Amsterdam: Het Sinhuis.

Latukefu, A. 2006. Remote Indigenous communities in Australia: Questions of access, information, and self-determination. In K. Landzelius, ed., *Going native on the Net: Indigenous cyber-activism and virtual diasporas over the World Wide Web.* Pp. 1–42. London: Routledge.

Laughton, R. 2004, July. *s4c: An independent review.* Department of Culture, Media and Sport. Retrieved 7 November 2005, from www.s4c.co.uk / abouts4c / authority / pdf / e_adolygiad_laughton.pdf.

Lee, D. 1960. Lineal and nonlineal codifications of reality. In E. Carpenter and M. McLuhan, eds., *Explorations in communication: An anthology.* Pp. 136–54. Boston: Beacon.

Lehtola, V.-P. 1997. *Saamelaiset: Historia, yhteiskunta, taide* [*The Sámi: History, society, art*]. Jyväskylä, Finland: Gummerus.

———. 1999. Aito Lappalainen ei syö haarukalla ja veitsellä. Stereotypiat ja saamelainen kulttuurintutkimus [Stereotypes and Sámi cultural studies]. In M. Tuominen, S. Tuulentie, V.-P. Lehtola, and M. Autti, eds., *Pohjoiset identiteetit ja mentaliteetit. Outamaalta tunturiin* [*Northern identities and mentalities*]. Pp. 15–22. Osa 1. Lapin yliopiston taiteiden tiedekunnan julkaisuja C. Katsauksia ja puheenvuoroja.

Lewis, G. 1999. *Y Llofrudd Iaith.* Llandybie: Barddas.

Lindvall, T. R., and J. M. Melton. 1997. Towards a post-modern animated discourse: Bakhtin, intertextuality and the cartoon carnival. In J. Pilling, ed., *A reader in animation studies.* Pp. 203–20. Sydney: John Libbey.

Llacta. N.d. IV Festival Continental de Cine y Video de las Primeras Naciones de Abya Yala. Retrieved from www.llacta.org / notic / 010507a.htm.

Llwyd, A. 2005. *Cymru ddu / Black Wales.* Cardiff: s4c and Butetown Arts Centre.

Loizos, P. 1993. *Innovation in ethnographic film: From innocence to self-consciousness, 1955–1985.* Chicago: University of Chicago Press.

Lomas, R. 1987. A first for the Maori: *Ngati. Illusions* 5: 2–5.

López de La Roche, F. 2001. Medios de comunicación y movimientos sociales: Incomprensiones y desencuentros [Communications media and social movements: Misunderstandings and disconnects]. In M. Archila and M. Pardo, eds., *Movimientos sociales, Estado y democracia en Colombia* [*Social movements, the state, and democracy in Colombia*]. Pp. 475–94. Bogotá: Centro de Estudios Sociales, Universidad Nacional de Colombia.

López, C. L. 2000. Etnicidade e nacionalidade nas fronteiras: Ticunas brasileiros, colombianos e peruanos [Ethnicity and nationality on the borders: Brazilian, Colombian, and Peruvian Ticunas]. PhD diss., Universidade de Brasília.

Lury, C. 1996. *Consumer culture.* Cambridge, U.K.: Polity.

Macdonald, T. 2006. New U.N. Human Rights Council approves Declaration of the Rights of Indigenous Peoples, September 13. *Cultural Survival Quarterly* 30(3). Retrieved January 15, 2007, from www.culturalsurvival.org / publica tions / csq / csq-article.cfm?id=1916.

MacDougall, D. 1992–93. When less is less: The long take in documentary film. *Film Quarterly* 46(2): 36–46.

——. 1998. *Transcultural cinema.* Princeton, NJ: Princeton University Press.

MacNabb, V. A., and M. W. Rees. 1993. Liberation or theology? Ecclesial base communities in Oaxaca, Mexico. *Journal of Church and State* 35: 723–50.

Maffi, L. 2002. Endangered languages, endangered knowledge. *International Social Science Journal* 54(173): 385–93.

Maldonado, B. 2000. El indio y lo indio en el anarquismo magonista [The Indian and indigenousness in Magonista anarchism]. *Cuadernos del Sur* 6(15): 115–37.

Mal'kova, V. K., and L. V. Ostapenko. 2000. Etnicheskaya journalistika i problemy tolerantnosti [Ethnic journalism and tolerence problems]. In *Pressa i etnicheskaya tolerantnost'—posobie dlia zhurnalistov [Press and ethnic tolerance–a grant for journalists].* Pp. 41–56. Moscow: Akademia.

Malpas, J. 1999. *Place and experience: A philosophical topography.* Cambridge: Cambridge University Press.

Mamber, S. 1976. *Cinéma vérité in America: Studies in uncontrolled documentary.* Boston: MIT Press.

Mankekar, P. 1999. *Screening culture, viewing politics: An ethnography of television, womanhood, and nation in postcolonial India.* Durham, NC: Duke University Press.

Manuel, G., and M. Posluns. 1974. *The Fourth World: An Indian Reality.* New York: Free Press.

Maracle, S. 2003. The eagle has landed: Native women, leadership and community development. In K. Anderson and B. Lawrence, eds., *Strong women stories: Native vision and community survival.* Pp. 70–80. Toronto: Sumach.

Markoff, J. 2005. Taking the pulse of technology at Davos. *New York Times,* January 31. Retrieved December 25, 2005, from cel.media.mit.edu / press / mirrors / NYT100DollarPC.html.

Marks, L. 2000. *The skin of the film: Intercultural cinema, embodiment, and the sense.* Durham, NC: Duke University Press.

Martin, H., and S. Edwards. 1997. *New Zealand film, 1912–1996.* Auckland: Oxford University Press.

Masayesva, V. 2000. Indigenous experimentalism. In J. Lion, ed., *Magnetic north: Canadian experimental video*. Pp. 226–39. Minneapolis: University of Minnesota Press.

Massing, M. 2005. The end of news? *New York Review of Books*, December 1. [electronic version]. Retrieved December 25, 2005, from www.nybooks.com / articles / 18516.

Mato, D. 1997. On global and local agents and the social making of transnational identities and related agendas in "Latin" America. *Identities: Global studies in culture and power* 4(2): 167–212.

———. 2000a. Not "studying the subaltern," but studying *with* subaltern social groups, or, at least, studying the hegemonic articulations of power. *Nepantla: Views from South* 1(3): 479–502.

———. 2000b. Transnational networking and the social production of representations of identities by Indigenous peoples' organizations of Latin America. *International Sociology* 15(2): 343–60.

McLuhan, M. 1994 [1964]. *Understanding media: The extensions of man*. Boston: MIT Press.

Michaels, E. 1986. *The Aboriginal invention of television in central Australia, 1982–1986*. Canberra: Australian Institute of Aboriginal Studies.

———. 1994. *Bad Aboriginal art: Tradition, media, and technological horizons*. Minneapolis: University of Minnesota Press.

———, and F. J. Kelly. 1984. The social organization of an Aboriginal video workplace. *Australian Aboriginal Studies* 1: 26–84.

Miller, J. 2005. Native voices, Native visions: Native cinema showcase brings Indigenous films to Santa Fe Indian market. *Crosswinds Weekly*, August 17. Retrieved October 15, 2005, from www.crosswindsweekly.com / archives / cover / 75.htm.

Mita, M. 1992. The soul and the image. In J. Dennis and J. Bieringa, eds., *Film in Aotearoa New Zealand*. Pp. 36–54. Wellington, N.Z.: Victoria University Press.

Molnar, H., and M. Meadows. 2001. *Songlines to satellites: Indigenous communications in Australia, the South Pacific and Canada*. Annandale, NSW: Pluto.

Mon Forum. 2000. SPDC's MI no. 5 attempted to close Mon national schools. October 30. Retrieved December 6, 2001, from www24.brinkster.com / themonforum / MONFORUM / 2000 / 10 _ 00.pdf.

Mondragón, H. 2005. Disuasión y corrosión: La política del gobierno de Alvaro Uribe Vélez para los pueblos indígenas [Prevention and corrosion: Indigenous policy of President Alvaro Uribe Vélez]. *Etnias y política* (Bogotá), July: 15–26.

Murg, W. 2004. May I suggest . . ."The beginning they told" by Joseph Erb. *Indian Country Today* [electronic version], March 18. Retrieved December 26, 2005, from www.indiancountrytoday.com / content.cfm?id=1079625931.

Murillo, M. A. 2003. Community radio in Colombia: Civil conflict, popular media and the construction of a public sphere. *Journal of Radio Studies* 10(1): 120–40.

——. 2004. *Colombia and the United States: War, unrest, and destabilization*. New York: Seven Stories.

Murphy, A. D. 1989. Field notes from San Pedro Quiatoni. *Baylor Line*, September. Waco, TX: Baylor University.

Nagengast, C., and M. Kearney. 1990. Mixtec ethnicity: Social identity, political consciousness, and political activism. *Latin American Research Review* 25(2): 61–91.

Nagengast, C., R. Stavenhagen, and M. Kearney. 1992. *Human rights and Indigenous workers: The Mixtecs in Mexico and the United States*. La Jolla: Center for U.S.-Mexican Studies, University of California, San Diego.

Narayan, K. 1993. How native is a "native" anthropologist? *American Anthropologist* 95: 671–86.

Nichols, B. 1994. *Blurred boundaries: Questions of meaning in contemporary culture*. Bloomington: Indiana University Press.

Niezen, R. 2003. *The origins of indigenism: Human rights and the politics of identity*. Berkeley: University of California Press.

Nimuendaju, C. 1952. *The Tukuna*. Berkeley: University of California Press.

——. 2004. *In pursuit of a past Amazon: Archaeological researches in the Brazilian Guyana and in the Amazon region*. Trans. S. Rydén and P. Stenborg. Ed. P. Stenborg. Etnologiska Studier 45. Gothenburg, Sweden: Världskulturmuseet.

Nora, P. 1989. Between memory and history: *Les lieux de mémoire*. *Representations* 26: 7–24.

Norris, P., W. L. Bennett, and R. Entman. 2001. *Digital divide: Civic engagement, information poverty, and the Internet Worldwide*. Cambridge: Cambridge University Press.

Nunes Pereira, M. 1946. *Curt Nimuendaju: Aspectos de uma vida e uma obra* [*Curt Nimuendaju: Aspects of a life and work*]. Belém, Brazil: Oficinas Gráficas.

O'Connell, P. J. 1992. *Robert Drew and the development of cinéma vérité in America*. Carbondale: Southern Illinois University Press.

Oliveira, J.P. 1988. *'O Nosso Governo': Os Ticuna e o regime tutelar* [*Our government: The Ticuna and the tutelage system*]. Rio de Janeiro: Marco Zero / MCT / CNPq.

Ong, A. 1999. *Flexible citizenship: The cultural logics of transnationality*. Durham, NC: Duke University Press.

Onsman, A. 2004. *Defining Indigeneity in the twenty-first century: A case study of the free Frisians*. Lewiston, NY: Edwin Mellen.

Pack, S. 2000. Indigenous media then and now: Situating the Navajo Film Project. *Quarterly Review of Film and Video* 17(3): 273–86.

Parekowhai, C. 1987–88. Te Poho o Paikea: Barry Barclay and *Ngati*. *Art New Zealand* 45: 75–77.

Parra Mora, L. J. 1993. Indios y mestizos: Un esquema explicativo [Indians and mestizos: An explanatory scheme]. In *Etnicidad, nacionalismo y poder: Tres ensayos* [*Ethnicity, nationalism, and power: Three essays*]. Pp. 67–109. Oaxaca: Universidad Autónoma Benito Juárez.

Paulson, S., and P. Calla. 2000. Gender and ethnicity in Bolivian politics: Transformation or paternalism? *Journal of Latin American Anthropology* 5(2): 112–49.

People's Daily. 1999. Editorial: Centennial prelude to opening up the western region of China. December 8 [electronic version]. Retrieved December 25, 2005, from http://english.peopledaily.com.cn/english/199912/07/eng199912 07B101.html.

Pérez Montfort, R. 1994. El estereotipo del indio en la expresión popular urbana (1920–1940) [The stereotype of the Indian in urban popular expression (1920–1940)]. In R. Pérez Montfort, ed., *Estampas de nacionalismo popular mexicano: Ensayos sobre cultura popular y nacionalismo* [*Stamps of Mexican popular nationalism: Essays on popular culture and nationalism*]. Pp. 161–76. Mexico City: Centro de Investigaciones y Estudios Superiores en Antropología Social.

Phillips, D. 2005. A new beginning or the beginning of the end? The Welsh language in postcolonial Wales. In J. Aaron and C. Williams, eds., *Postcolonial Wales*. Pp. 100–113. Cardiff: University of Wales Press.

Pietikäinen, S. 2000. *Discourses of differentiation: Ethnic representations in newspaper texts*. Studies in Communication 12, Jyväskylä University. Jyväskylä, Finland: Jyväskylän Yliopisto.

———. 2003. Indigenous identity in print: Representations of the Sámi in news discourse. *Discourse and Society* 14(5): 581–638.

———, and H. Dufva. 2006. Voices in discourses: Dialogism, critical discourse analysis, and ethnic identity. *Journal of Sociolinguistics* 10(2): 205–24.

———, and S. Leppänen. 2006. Saamelaiset toisin sanoin [The Sámi in other words]. In M. Lehtonen, O. Löytty, and J. Kuortti, eds., *Suomi ja jälkikolonialismi* [*Finland and postcolonialism*]. Unpublished ms.

Pika, A. I., and B. B. Prokhorov, eds. 1994. *Neotraditsionalism na Rossiyskom Severe (Etnicheskoye vozrozdenie malochislennyh narodov severa i gosudarstvennaya regionalnaya politika)* [*Neotraditionalism in the Russian north (Ethnic revival of small-numbered northern peoples and state regional politics)*]. Moscow.

Polan, D. 1985. A Brechtian cinema? Towards a politics of self-reflexive film. In B. Nichols, ed., *Movies and methods*. Vol. 2. Pp. 661–71. Los Angeles: University of California Press.

Povinelli, E. A. 2002. *The cunning of recognition: Indigenous alterities and the making of Australian multiculturalism*. Durham, NC: Duke University Press.

Prins, H. E. L. 1977. The paradox of primitivism: Native rights and the problem of imagery in cultural survival films. *Visual Anthropology* 9: 243–66.

———. (1989). American Indians and the ethnocinematic complex: From native participation to production control. In R. M. Boonjazer Flaes, ed., *Eyes across the water*. Pp. 80–89. Amsterdam: Het Sinhuis.

———. 2001. Digital revolution: Indigenous peoples in Cyberia. In W. Haviland, ed., *Cultural anthropology*, 10th ed. Pp. 306–8. Fort Worth, TX: Harcourt College.

———. 2002a. Visual media and the primitivist perplex: Colonial fantasies, indigenous imagination and advocacy in North America. In F. D. Ginsburg, L. Abu-Lughod, and B. Larkin, eds., *Media worlds: Anthropology on new terrain*. Pp. 58–74. Berkeley: University of California Press.

——. 2002b. Guidelines for the evaluation of ethnographic media: Historical background. *American Anthropologist* 104(1): 303–14.

——. 2004. Visual anthropology. In T. Biolsi, ed., *A companion to the anthropology of American Indians*. Pp. 506–25. Malden, MA: Blackwell.

Radcliffe, S. A. 1999. Reimagining the nation: Community, difference, and national identities among Indigenous and mestizo provincials in Ecuador. *Environment and Planning A* 31(1): 37–52.

Rantanen, T. 2005. *The media and globalization*. London: Sage.

Rappaport, J. 2005. *Intercultural utopias: Public intellectuals, cultural experimentation, and ethnic pluralism in Colombia*. Durham, NC: Duke University Press.

Rasmussen, T. 1999. Tied hands write lies. In F. Horn, ed., *Sami and Greenlandic media*. Northern Institute for Environmental and Minority Law. *Juridica Lapponica* 22: 39–46.

Reid, B., and R. Bringhurst. 1984. *The raven steals the light*. Vancouver: Douglas and McIntyre.

Reese, D. 1998. Mom, look! It's George, and he's a TV Indian! *Horn Book Magazine* 74(5): 636–43.

Renov, M. 1993. The poetics of documentary. In M. Renov, ed., *Theorizing Documentary*. Pp. 12–36. New York: Routledge.

Reuter, J., ed. 1983. *Indigenismo, pueblo y cultura [Indigenism, community and culture]*. Mexico City: Consejo Nacional Técnico de la Educación, SEP.

Rickard, J. 1999. First Nation territory in cyber space declared: No treaties needed. *CyberPowWow: An Aboriginally determined territory in cyberspace*. Retrieved February 7, 2007, from www.cyberpowwow.net / nation2nation / jolenework .html.

Rizvi, H. 2006. U.N. delays vote on native self-determination. Inter Press Service News Agency, November 28. Retrieved January 15, 2007, from www.ipsnews .net / news.asp?idnews=35638.

Robinson, G., ed. 2004. *Isuma: Inuit studies reader*. Montreal: Isuma.

Rodríguez, C. 2001. *Fissures in the mediascape*. Cresskill, NJ: Hampton.

Rofel, L. 1994. Yearnings: Televisual love and melodramatic politics in contemporary China. *American Ethnologist* 21(4): 700–722.

Rollins, P. C., ed. 2003. *Hollywood's Indian: The portrayal of the Native American in film*. 2nd ed. Lexington: University Press of Kentucky.

Roncagliolo, R. 1991. The growth of the audio-visual imagescape in Latin America. In N. Thede and A. Ambrosi, eds., *Video the changing world*. Pp. 22–30. Montreal: Black Rose.

Roth, L. 2000. Bypassing of borders and building of bridges: Steps in the construction of the Aboriginal Peoples Television Network in Canada. *Gazette* 62(3–4): 251–69.

———. 2005. *Something new in the air: The story of First Peoples television broadcasting in Canada*. Montreal: McGill-Queen's University Press.

———, and F. Ginsburg. 2003. Thinking outside the box: Indigenous television in Australia and Canada. In T. Miller, ed., *The television book*. London: British Film Institute.

Rouch, J., and S. Feld. 2003. *Cine-ethnography*. Minneapolis: University of Minnesota Press.

Roy, D. 2005. Statement on behalf of the Indigenous Peoples Caucus on provisional adoption of articles. Eleventh session of UN Working Group on a Draft Declaration on the Rights of Indigenous Peoples, Geneva, December 5–16. Retrieved December 31, 2005, from www.unpo.org/news_detail.php?arg=02 andpar=3306.

Ruby, J. 1992. Speaking for, speaking about, speaking with, or speaking alongside: An anthropological and documentary dilemma. *Journal of Film and Video* 44(1–2): 42–66.

Ruiz, R. 1995. *The poetics of cinema*. Paris: Dis Voir.

Russian media market (Rossiyskiy rynok periodicheskoy pechati). 2005. *Sostoyanie, tendentsii i perspectivy razvitiia—Doklad Federalnogo agenstva po pechati i massovym kommunikatsiam [The state, trends, and prospects of development—Report of the Federal Agency for the Press and Mass Communications]*, May. Moscow. Retrieved September 12, 2005, from www.fapmc.ru/docs/Report_12.05.doc.

s4c Race Equality Scheme. N.d. Retrieved November 7, 2005, from www.s4c .co.uk/abouts4c/authority/pdf/e_cyd_hiliol.pdf.

Sara, I.-A. 2004. *Saamelaisuutta vahvistamassa: Sámi Radion toimittajien käsitykset saamelaismedian tehtävistä [The Sámi Radio journalists' views on the role of the Sámi media]*. MA thesis, University of Jyväskylä.

Sarmiento Silva, S. 2001. El movimiento indio mexicano y la reforma del Estado [The Mexican Indian movement and the reform of the state]. *Cuadernos del Sur* 7(16): 65–96.

Sassen, S. 1998. *Globalization and its discontents*. New York: New Press.

Schein, L. 2000. *Minority rules: The Miao and the feminine in China's cultural politics*. Durham, NC: Duke University Press.

Scheinin, M. 2001. Saamelaisten ihmisoikeudet, kulttuuri ja maankäyttö [Sámi human rights, culture, and land usage]. In M. Scheinin and T. Dahlgren, eds., *Toteutuvatko saamelaisten ihmisoikeudet [Are the Sámi human rights carried out?]*. Pp. 92–119. Helsinki: Helsinki University Press.

Scollon, R. 2001. *Mediated discourse: The nexus of practice*. London: Routledge.

Scott, J. C. 1999. *Seeing like a state: How certain schemes to improve the human condition have failed*. New Haven, CT: Yale University Press.

Sesia, P. 1990. Salud y enfermedad en Oaxaca [Health and disease in Oaxaca]. *América indígena* 50(2–3): 291–308.

Shirky, C. 2002. Sorry, wrong number. *WIRED*, October 10 [electronic version]. Retrieved from www.wired.com / wired / archive / 10.10 / view.html?pg=2.

Shohat, E. 1991. Notes on the "post-colonial." *Social Text* 31–32: 99–113.

———, and R. Stam. 1994. *Unthinking Eurocentrism: Multiculturalism and the media*. New York: Routledge.

Silva, R. 2000. Ondas nacionales: La política cultural de la república liberal y la Radiodifusora Nacional de Colombia [National waves: The cultural politics of the liberal republic and the Radiodifusora Nacional of Colombia]. *Análisis político*, December, 3–22.

Simpson, J. A., and E. S. C. Weiner, eds. 1989. *The Oxford English Dictionary*, 2nd ed. London: Oxford University Press.

Sirianni, C., and L. Friedland. 2001. *Civic innovation in America: Community empowerment, public policy and the movement for civic renewal*. Berkeley: University of California Press.

Skeggs, B. 2004. *Class, self, culture*. London: Routledge.

Skogerbø, E. 2001. Sami media—Identity projects in a changing society. In K. Ross and P. Playdon, eds., *Black marks: Minority ethnic audiences and media*. Pp. 157–75. Aldershot, U.K.: Ashgate.

Smith, L. T. 1999. *Decolonizing methodologies: Research and indigenous peoples*. London: Zed.

Smith, M. 1991. *State of fear: Censorship in Burma (Myanmar)*. London: Article 19.

———. 1999. *Burma: Insurgency and the politics of ethnicity*. 2nd ed. London: Zed.

Solbakk, J. T. 1997. Sami mass media: Their role in a minority society. In H. Gaski, ed., *Sami culture in a new era: The Norwegian Sami experience*. Pp. 172–98. Karasjok, Norway: Davvi Girji os.

Spickard, P., ed. 2005. *Race and nation: Ethnic systems in the modern world*. New York: Routledge.

Sreberny, A. 2001. Gender, globalization and communications: Women and the transnational. *Feminist Media Studies* 1(1): 61–65.

———. 2002. Collectivity and connectivity: Diaspora and mediated identities. In G. Stald and T. Tufte, eds., *Global encounters: Media and cultural transformation*. Pp. 217–234. Luton, U.K.: University of Luton Press.

Sreberny-Mohammadi, A., and Mohammadi, A. 1994. *Small media, big revolution: Communication, culture, and the Iranian Revolution*. Minneapolis: University of Minnesota Press.

Star, S. L., and J. R. Griesemer. 1989. Institutional ecology, "translations" and boundary objects: Amateurs and professionals in Berkeley's Museum of Vertebrate Zoology, 1907–1939. *Social Studies of Science* 19: 387–420.

Statistics New Zealand: Tatauranga Aotearoa (Government of New Zealand). 2002. Census Snapshot: Maori, April. Retrieved November 18, 2005, from www.stats.govt.nz / products-and-services / Articles / census-snpsht-maori-Apro2.htm.

——. 2005. Maori. June 8. Retrieved October 27, 2006, from www.stats.govt.nz/ people / communities / maori.htm.

Steinberg, D. I. 2001. *Burma: The state of Myanmar*. Washington, DC: Georgetown University Press.

Stephen, L. 1996. The creation and re-creation of ethnicity: Lessons from the Zapotec and Mixtec of Oaxaca. *Latin American Perspectives* 23(2): 17–37.

Stephens, E. C. 2004. *s4c internal review: A Welsh language service fit for the twenty-first century?* Retrieved November 7, 2005, from www.s4c.co.uk / e_index .html.

Stewart, M. 2001. Sovereign visions: Native North American documentary. PhD diss., University of Minnesota.

——.2007. The Indian film crews of Challenge for Change: Representation and the state. *Canadian Journal of Film Studies* 16(2): 49–81.

Stockes, B. 2000. Federal recognition an unresolved issue. *Indian Country Today*, December 13. Retrieved January 23, 2006, from www.indiancountry.com / content.cfm?id=504.

Strong, P. T. 1998. Playing Indian in the nineties: *Pocahontas* and *The Indian in the Cupboard*. In P. C. Rollins and J. E. O'Connor, eds., *Hollywood's Indian: The portrayal of the Native American in film*. Pp. 187–205. Lexington: University Press of Kentucky.

Suihkonen, M. 2003. *"Kukaan ei halua elää semmoista elämää, jossa omaa ääntä ei kuulu": Haastattelututkimus etnisten vähemmistöjen omasta mediasta ja vähem-mistötaustaisten toimittajien pääsystä valtamediaan ["Nobody wants a life with-out a voice of their own": A study of ethnic minority media and employment of ethnic minority journalists]*. Tampere: Tampereen yliopisto, Journalismin tutki-musyksikkö [University of Tampere, Research Centre for Journalism].

Tambiah, S. J. 1990. *Magic, science and the scope of rationality*. Cambridge: Cam-bridge University Press.

Thede, N., and A. Ambrosi. 1991. Introduction to N. Thede and A. Ambrosi, eds., *Video the changing world*. Pp. 1–20. Montreal: Black Rose.

Thomas, N. 1994. *Colonialism's culture: Anthropology, travel and government*. Prince-ton, NJ: Princeton University Press.

Ticona, A., and I. Sanjinés. 2004. *Las cámaras de la diversidad [Cameras of diversity]*. Report from UNESCO intercultural dialogue project ICT4ID: The training of indigenous people in audiovisual and community television production. La Paz: CEFREC Bolivia.

Todyshev, M. A. 2004. Sovershenstvovanie federal'nogo zakonodatel'stva o pra-vakh korennykh malochislennykh narodov Severa Rossii [Improving the fed-eral legislation on Indigenous rights of small-numbered peoples of the Rus-sian north]. In V. E. Seliverstov and A. V. Novikov, eds., *Federalizm v Rossii i Kanade: Pravovye i economicheskie aspekty [Federalism in Russia and Canada: Legal and economical aspects]*. Pp. 238–60. Moscow: International Center for the

Projects and Programs on Development of Federal Relationship and Regional Politics.

Tomos, A. 1982. Realising a dream. In S. Blanchard and D. Morley, eds., *What's this Channel Fo(u)r? An alternative report.* Pp. 37–53. London: Comedia.

Tsai, J. 2007. TBS merges with three TV stations, seeks to "create synergy." *Taiwan Journal,* January 12. Retrieved January 15, 2007, from taiwanjournal.nat.gov .tw / ct.asp?CtNode=122andxItem=23691.

Tufte, T. 2003. Minority youth, media uses and identity struggle: The role of the media in the production of locality. In T. Tufte, ed., *Medierne, minoriterne og det multikulturelle samfund: Skandinaviske perspektiver* [*Media, minorities and multicultural society: Scandinavian perspectives*]. Pp. 181–98. Nordicom, Sweden: Göteborgs Universitet.

Turner, T. 1990. Visual media, cultural politics, and anthropological practice: Some implications of recent uses of film and video among the Kayapó of Brazil. *Commission on Visual Anthropology Review* 1: 9–13.

——. 2002. Representation, politics, and cultural imagination in indigenous video: General points and Kayapó examples. In F. Ginsburg, L. Abu-Lughod, and B. Larkin, eds., *Media worlds: Anthropology on new terrain.* Pp. 75–89. Berkeley: University of California Press.

UN adopts declaration on rights for Indigenous peoples worldwide. 2007. *International Herald Tribune,* September 13 [electronic version]. Retrieved September 13, 2007, from http://www.iht.com / articles / ap / 2007 / 09 / 13 / news / UN-GEN-UN-Indigenous-Peoples.php.

Unidad de Radio del Ministerio de Cultura. 2000. *Memorias: Radios y pueblos indígenas—Encuentro Internacional de Radios Indígenas de América* [*Report: Radio and indigenous peoples—International Meeting of Indigenous Radio Stations in the Americas*]. Bogotá: Ministro de Cultura.

United Kingdom Parliament, House of Commons, Hansard Debates. 2004. Column 65WH, June 8. Retrieved January 23, 2006, from www.parliament.the-stationery-office.co.uk / pa / cm200304 / cmhansrd / vo040608 / halltext / 40608h05.htm#40608h05_spmino.

United Nations Economic and Social Council, Commission on Human Rights. 1994. *Draft UN Declaration on the Rights of Indigenous Peoples,* October 28. U.N. Document E / CN.4 / 1995 / 2, E / CN.4 / Sub.2 / 1994 / 56, pp. 105–15. New York.

——. 2001. *Promoting the rights and cultures of Indigenous peoples through the media,* June 6. U.N. Document 2001E / CN.4 / Sub.2 / AC.4 / 2001 / 3. New York.

——. 2002. *The role of the media in combatting discrimination against Indigenous peoples,* May 16. U.N. Document E / CN.4 / Sub.2 / AC.4 / 2001 / 3. New York.

van der Velden, M. 2005. Programming for cognitive justice: Towards an ethical framework for democratic code. *Interacting with Computers* 17: 105–20.

Varese, S. 1983. *Proyectos étnicos y proyectos nacionales* [*Ethnic projects and national projects*]. Mexico City: Fondo de Cultura Económica.

———. 1985. Cultural development in ethnic groups: Anthropological explorations in education. *International Social Science Journal* 37(104): 201–16.

———. 1996. The ethnopolitics of Indian resistance in Latin America. *Latin American Perspectives* 89(2): 58–71.

Verhovic, S. 2000. Bill Gates turns skeptical on digital solution's scope. *New York Times*, November 3.

Villa, W., and J. Houghton. 2005. *Violencia política contra los pueblos indígenas en Colombia, 1974–2004 [Political violence against the Indigenous peoples of Colombia, 1974–2004]*. Bogotá: CECOIN.

Viswanath, K., and P. Arora. 2000. Ethnic media in the United States: An essay on their role in integration, assimilation and social control. *Mass Communication and Society* 3(1): 39–56.

Wachowich, N. 2004. An overview of Iglullingmiut and Mittimatalingmiut culture and history. In G. Robinson, ed., *Isuma: Inuit studies reader*. Pp. 131–36. Montreal: Isuma.

Waisbord, S. 2001. *Watchdog journalism in South America: News accountability and democracy*. New York: Columbia University Press.

Waller, G. 1996. The New Zealand Film Commission: Promoting an industry, forging a national identity. *Historical Journal of Film, Radio and Television* 16(2): 243–62. Retrieved January 1, 2006, from findarticles.com/p/articles/mi_m2584/is_n2_v16/ai_18897250.

Weaver, S. 1993. First Nations women. In S. Burt, L. Cody, and L. Dorney, eds., *Changing patterns: Women in Canada*. Pp. 92–150. Toronto: McClelland and Stewart.

Weinberger, E. 1994. The camera people. In L. Taylor, ed., *Visualizing Theory: Selected essays from* Visual Anthropology Review, *1990–1994*. Pp. 3–26. New York: Routledge.

Wells, P. 2002. *Animation: Genre and authorship*. London: Wallflower.

Welper, E. M. 2002. Curt Unkel Nimuendaju. MA thesis, Museu Nacional and Universidade Federal do Rio de Janeiro.

Welsh Language Board. 2006. *2004 Welsh language use survey*. Retrieved October 16, 2006, from www.bwrdd-yr-iaith.org.uk/cynnwys.php?pID=109andnID=2122andlangID=2.

Willemen, P. 1994. *Looks and frictions: Essays in cultural studies and film theory*. Bloomington: Indiana University Press.

Williams, C. 2005. Emergent multiculturalism? Challenging the national story of Wales. *Journal for the Study of British Cultures* 12(1): 25–37.

Williams, K. 2003. Constructing the national: Television and Welsh identity. In M. Scriven and E. Roberts, eds., *Group identities on French and British television*. Pp. 34–40. Oxford, U.K.: Berghahn.

Wilson, P. 1996. Disputable truths: "The American stranger," television documentary, and Native American cultural politics in the 1950s. PhD diss., University of Wisconsin, Madison.

——. 1998. Confronting "The Indian Problem": Media discourses of race, ethnicity, nation and empire in 1950s America. In S. Torres, ed., *Living color: Race and television in the United States.* Pp. 35–61. Durham, NC: Duke University Press.

——. 1999. All eyes on Montana: Television audiences, social activism, and Native American cultural politics in the 1950s. *Quarterly Review of Film and Video* 16 (3–4): 325–56.

Wilson, R., and W. Dissanayake. 1996. Introduction to R. Wilson and W. Dissanayake, eds., *Global / local: Cultural production and the transnational imaginary.* Pp. 1–20. Durham, NC: Duke University Press.

Wodak, R., and Myers, M. 2001. *Methods of critical discourse analysis.* London: Sage.

Woods, C. 1996. Native Netizens: A special report. December 2. Retrieved on January 15, 2007, from www.netizen.com / netizen / 96 / 48 / index3a.html.

Wortham, E. 2000. Building Indigenous video in Guatemala. *Jump Cut* 43: 116–19.

——. 2004. Between the state and Indigenous autonomy: Unpacking *video indígena* in Mexico. *American Anthropologist* 106(2): 363–68.

Yang, M. M. 1999. *Spaces of their own: Women's public sphere in transnational China.* Minneapolis: University of Minnesota Press.

Yashar, D. J. 1999. Democracy, indigenous movements, and the postliberal challenge in Latin America. *World Politics* 52(1): 76–104.

Zimmerman, L. J., K. P. Zimmerman, and L. R. Bruguier. Cyberspace smoke signals: New technologies and Native American ethnicities. In C. Smith and G. K. Ward, eds., *Indigenous cultures in an interconnected world.* Pp. 69–88. Vancouver: University of British Columbia Press.

ABOUT THE CONTRIBUTORS

Lisa Brooten is an assistant professor at Southern Illinois University Carbondale, College of Mass Communication and Media Arts. Her regional area of expertise is Southeast Asia, and in particular Burma / Myanmar. In her research she investigates the ways gender, ethnicity, global discourses (such as the discourse of human rights), and rhetorical strategies are used to perpetuate divisive media practices, and how people resist such practices.

Kathleen Buddle is an assistant professor of anthropology at the University of Manitoba in Winnipeg. Her community-based research places gender, agency, and social change at the center of an analysis of Aboriginal social movements. Buddle has published scholarly journal articles on Aboriginal cultural capital creation; radio production; the first Aboriginally authored newspaper in Canada; the link between the emergence of Aboriginal agricultural fairs, powwows, and media and the construction of an Aboriginal public sphere in Eastern Canada; and a host of related issues.

Michael Christie, a linguist specializing in the Yolngu languages of northeast Arnhemland, Australia, is currently associate professor in the School of Education at Charles Darwin University in Darwin, Northern Territory, Australia. His research interests include Yolngu languages, culture, and epistemology; cross-cultural communication; Indigenous epistemologies and pedagogies; and the use of digital technology with Indigenous knowledge systems.

Amalia Córdova, a Chilean artist and video producer, is the Latin American program coordinator at the Film and Video Center of the Smithsonian Institution's National Museum of the American Indian in New York City. She has produced two videos on Indigenous art in Chile, has been involved in several international Indigenous film festivals, and is an international correspondent for the Latin American Council for Indigenous Film and Communication. Córdova is currently an MA candidate in performance studies at New York University.

Galina Diatchkova, head of the history department at the Regional Museum, Anadyr, Chukotka, Russia, represents the Chukchi Indigenous people of Chukotka. Now a PhD candidate, she is a council member of the International Arctic

Social Sciences Association. Her publications concern the ethnic adaptation to the natural and social environment, the Chukchi family, and the Indigenous use of media in Russia.

Priscila Faulhaber, an anthropologist at the Museu Paraense Emilio Goeldi in Pará, Brazil, since 1984, edited the CD-ROM *Magüta Arü Inü: Recollecting Magüta Thinking* and is currently working as a researcher in the History of Science Department of the Mast / MCT / Brazil. She has written two books and has published several scientific articles in Portuguese, English, French, and Spanish. Her primary field of research is the historical and interpretive anthropology of interethnic relations between Indigenous people and Amazonian national societies.

Louis Forline is an assistant professor of anthropology at the University of Nevada, Reno. His research interests include Indigenous peoples of the Amazon, hunter-gatherer studies, sustainable development and the anthropology of health and foodways. He has conducted research in the Brazilian Amazon among the Guajá and the Indigenous peoples of Altamira, in addition to work among peasant communities.

Jennifer Gauthier is an assistant professor of communication studies at Randolph College (founded as Randolph-Macon Woman's College) in Lynchburg, Virginia, where she teaches a variety of film and cultural studies courses. Her continuing research is on film and cultural policy in Canada, Australia, and New Zealand, specifically issues of race, gender, and national identity.

Faye Ginsburg is director of the Center for Media, Culture, and History at New York University, where she is also David B. Kriser Professor of Anthropology. Her work addresses issues of cultural activism and social change in various locales, from her early work on the abortion debate to her long-standing research on the development of Indigenous media in Australia and beyond. She is the author or editor of four books and was a cocurator of the international showcase First Nations / First Features, held at the Museum of Modern Art in New York City and the National Museum of the American Indian in Washington, DC, in May 2005.

Alexandra Halkin is a documentary video producer and founding director of the Chiapas Media Project / Promedios de Comunicación Comunitaria, a binational partnership that provides video and computer equipment and training for Indigenous and campesino communities in Chiapas and Guerrero, Mexico. Halkin has consulted with various organizations such as Witness, the United Nations High Commission for Human Rights Workshop on Indigenous Media, and the Latin American Council for Indigenous Film and Communication. In 2004, Halkin was awarded a Guggenheim Fellowship for her work with the CMP / Promedios and to develop a new project, the Latin American Indigenous Video Initiative.

Joanna Hearne is an assistant professor in the Department of English at the University of Missouri-Columbia, where she teaches and writes on topics in film studies, Native American studies, and folklore. Her essays have appeared in *Screen,* the *Journal of Popular Film and Television,* and *Western Folklore,* and her current research addresses representations of Native American families on screen.

Lindsay Leitch (a member of the Cache Collective) received her MA in art history from Queen's University in Kingston, Ontario. Her research areas include the social historical analysis of tourism, contemporary craft making, and political activism.

Ruth McElroy is a senior lecturer in communication, cultural, and media studies at the University of Glamorgan, Wales. She hails from North Wales, where she benefited from a Welsh-medium education and from being among the first generation of viewers of the Welsh fourth channel, Sianel Pedwar Cymru (s4c). Her research interests lie in questions of culture, gender, and national identity. Her recent publications include a special issue of the *European Journal of Cultural Studies,* an essay on Welsh bilingual literary culture for a special issue of the *Journal for the Study of British Cultures,* and a chapter on lifestyle television in a collection of essays on representations of domestic space in modern culture.

Erin Morton (a member of the Cache Collective) is a PhD candidate and teaching fellow in the Department of Art at Queen's University in Kingston, Ontario. She specializes in Canadian visual culture and museum representation and is currently completing research on the installment and expansion of liberalism in Canada, those who reshaped and resisted this project, and the intersections of these political developments with visual culture in Atlantic Canada.

Mario A. Murillo is an associate professor in audio / video / film in the School of Communication at Hofstra University in Hempstead, New York, where he coordinates the audio production / radio studies academic program. A veteran radio journalist and feature documentarian, he has worked as a correspondent and producer in commercial, public, and community radio for the past twenty years, with a primary focus on Latin America and the Caribbean. He currently hosts and produces *Wake Up Call* on Pacifica Radio station wbai. The author of two books, Murillo has also published numerous journal and newspaper articles about Colombia's indigenous movement.

Sari Pietikäinen is a professor of discourse studies in the department of languages, University of Jyväskylä, Finland, having received her PhD in applied linguistics. Her research interests are in minority media, multilingualism, empowering discursive practices, and critical discourse analysis. She has published several articles on Sámi identity, has contributed to several Finnish books on ethnic minority and media, and has co-edited a book on multiculturalism in Finland.

Emily Rothwell (a member of the Cache Collective) is currently completing an MA in art history at Queen's University in Kingston, Ontario. She is writing her thesis about the artistic practice of Canadian contemporary artist Janet Morton in relation to social histories of urban and architectural spaces. Her research interests include Canadian contemporary art, feminist theory, histories of women artists, the social history of architecture, and art as activism in public, urban spaces.

Juan Francisco Salazar is a Chilean anthropologist and videomaker who teaches film studies at the University of Western Sydney, from which he holds a PhD in communication and media, and is a researcher at the Centre for Cultural Research. He has written several journal articles and book chapters on media anthropology, Chilean cinema in exile, and more recently Indigenous media and communication rights in Latin America. He is currently involved with several transnational advocacy groups such as OUR Media Network and the Latin American Council for Indigenous Film and Communication.

Taryn Sirove (a member of the Cache Collective) received her undergraduate training at the Nova Scotia College of Art and Design and is a PhD candidate in art history at Queen's University in Kingston, Ontario, where she also completed her MA. Her areas of interest include film and video regulation and alternative video art practices in Canada as part of her broader interest in electronic and new media art.

Laurel Smith is an assistant professor of geography and honors at the University of Oklahoma. Her research focuses on how Indigenous actors' use of visual technologies reconfigures the cultural geographies of technoscience. Her dissertation, "Mediating Indigenous Identity: Video, Advocacy and Knowledge in Oaxaca, Mexico," explored the hybrid geographies that comprise Indigenous movements, especially the contributions of Latin American traditions of academic advocacy.

Michelle Stewart is coordinator and assistant professor of cinema studies and literature at Purchase College in New York. Her dissertation from the University of Minnesota, "Sovereign Visions: Native North American Documentary," investigates the development of Native North American filmmaking as a creative form of cultural activism that is tied to a political program of cultural revival, self-determination, and national sovereignty. In general, her scholarship centers on interdisciplinary questions of cinema's relation to changing forms of sociality and political life under globalization. Her current research concerns film policy, the European state, and minor cinema, with an emphasis on the cinematic production of North and West Africans in France.

Andrea Terry (a member of the Cache Collective) is a PhD candidate at Queen's University in Kingston, Ontario, where she also completed her MA. Her research interests, which include living history museums, museum representation, and

Canadian history, stem from a childhood tradition of visiting heritage sites with her father.

Michelle Veitch (a member of the Cache Collective) is a PhD candidate in art history at Queen's University in Kingston, Ontario, and completed her MA at Concordia University in Montreal. Her research interests include site-specific practices and urban regeneration in Canada with particular focus on artistic interventions in city spaces.

Pamela Wilson is an associate professor of communication at Reinhardt College in Waleska, Georgia. She combines her dual backgrounds in anthropology and media studies in her teaching and research on various aspects of media and cultural representation, often from a historical perspective and with a special interest in the cultural politics of regional, minority, and Indigenous media representations and practices. Her work on various topics, including several articles on Native American activism and mainstream media in the mid-twentieth century based on her dissertation research at the University of Wisconsin, as well as her work on television and popular culture, has been published in numerous anthologies and journals, including *Television and New Media*; *Quarterly Review of Film and Video*; *Historical Journal of Film, Radio and Television*; *Camera Obscura*; and *South Atlantic Quarterly*.

INDEX

AAIA (Association on American Indian Affairs), 35

ABC (Australian Broadcasting Corporation), 297

Aborigen Kamchatki (newspaper), 214, 218, 224–26, 230, 231

Aboriginal peoples, 29, 40, 41; of Australia, 20, 30, 33, 35, 232, 270–86, 288, 294, 297–300. *See also* Indigenous peoples

Aboriginal Peoples Television Network (APTN), 20, 90, 101, 107, 108, 295, 300, 305

Abya Yala Network, 47, 48, 57

Access TV (Canada), 102

Acculturation, 184, 188. *See also* Assimilation

ACIN (Asociación de Cabildos Indígenas del Norte del Cauca), 145–59

Acteal Massacre, 163–64, 167–68

Activism, 7, 8, 9, 22, 23, 25–27, 28, 31, 32, 45, 54, 55, 71, 111–27, 128–44, 145–59, 160–80, 185–86, 189, 191, 194, 195, 202, 220, 297, 302, 304

Adams, Evan, 103, 300

Adelaide Film Festival, 297

Aesthetics, 20, 23–25, 29, 42, 77–78, 260–61; embedded, 40, 55, 90, 96, 97

Africa, 13, 23, 239, 241, 292, 293

African Americans, 99

Afro-Colombians, 145, 147

AICO (Autoridades Indígenas de Colombia), 149

AIM (American Indian Movement), 7

Aivilikmiut, 82, 85, 88

Alaska Natives, 17

Albin, Patricia, 94

Alice Springs, 30, 270, 276, 294, 297

Allen, Chadwick, 95

All Roads Film Project, 102

Alternative media, 42, 43, 90, 94, 106, 115, 148, 152, 156–59, 186, 201–5, 304

American Anthropological Association, 32, 175

American Assistance for Cambodia, 290–91

American Indian Movement (AIM), 7

American Indian Resource Center, 90

Amitturmiut, 74, 88

Amnesty International, 127, 134

Amoc (musician), 211

Anaana (2001), 84–87

Anarâš (magazine), 201

Anaya, S. James, 6, 9

Anderson, Benedict, 199

Angeles Martínez, Eucario, 183, 189–95

Angilirq, Paul Apak, 74,

Animation, 23, 25, 56, 89–108, 300

Animation from Cape Dorset (film series), 94,

Anishinaabeg (Anishinabe), 91, 104–5, 128, 129

ANSIPRA (Arctic Network for the Support of the Indigenous Peoples of the Russian Arctic), 228

Anthropology, 3, 4, 17, 32, 44, 91, 189, 190, 195, 204, 228, 253–69, 289, 295

Anthropology Film Center, 32

Appadurai, Arjun, 213

Appropriation, 24, 39, 45, 95, 260, 271, 302

APTN (Aboriginal Peoples Television Network), 20, 90, 101, 107, 108, 295, 300, 305

Arakan Ethnic State (Rakhine), 112

Árbol de jabón, El (The Soap Tree), 194

Archives, media, 25, 30, 48, 53–54, 76–87, 91, 253–69

Arctic, 74–88, 214–31, 295–97

Arctic Council, 198, 217

Arctic Network for the Support of the Indigenous Peoples of the Russian Arctic (ANSIPRA), 228

Argentina, 54, 56

Arnait Video Collective, 25, 75, 77–81

Arnhem Land, 271, 275, 280

Arora, Pamela, 119

Arrernte, 294, 297–300

Artists, 23–25, 29, 31, 41, 76–77, 287

Asia, 13, 16, 239, 241, 291

Así Pensamos (1983), 56

Asociación de Cabildos Indígenas del Norte del Cauca (ACIN), 145–59

Assimilation, 5, 11, 14, 16, 22, 30, 35, 41, 89, 95, 106, 111, 116, 186, 189, 198

Assistance Committee for the Numerically Small Peoples of the Northern Territories, 216

Association on American Indian Affairs (AAIA), 35

Aššu (newspaper), 201

Atanarjuat (The Fast Runner), 21, 74, 99, 295

Attagutaaluk (1992), 88

Audiences for Indigenous media, 29, 42, 91, 203, 206–8, 212, 240, 242–47; children and youth, 89–108, 297–300; global, 59, 94, 111, 114, 116, 121, 124–25, 133, 162, 165, 177–78, 214, 253–54, 268, 294, 297–300, 302; Indigenous, 25, 50, 53, 68, 74, 77, 93, 94, 111, 114, 116, 117, 119, 124, 151, 156, 162, 177, 178, 214, 268; mainstream, 20, 25, 53–54, 78, 93, 94, 125, 151, 162, 178, 204, 268, 294

Audiovisual indígena, 41

Australia, 4, 10, 16, 18, 20, 30, 33, 35, 43, 118, 232, 270–86, 294, 297–300

Australian Broadcasting Corporation (ABC), 297

Australian Film Commission, 297

Authenticity, 87, 97, 115, 199, 241

Authorship and ownership, 96–97, 102, 115, 279, 284, 298. See also Intellectual property rights

Autonomy and media production, 51–56, 75

Autoridades Indígenas de Colombia (AICO), 149

Avingaq, Susan, 75, 77, 79–81

Aymara, 16

Babcock, Barbara, 96

Balda-Lupaxi, 56

Balikci, Asen, 87–88

Banning, Kass, 78

Barclay, Barry, 24, 58–73

Barents Press International, 227

Basques, 12

Baumard, Philippe, 280–81

BBC (British Broadcasting Corporation), 234, 248

Beginning They Told, The (2000), 98

Belgarde, Pam, 301

Belgian thesis, 34

Belichenko, Margarita, 214

Bengalis, 112
Benjamin, Walter, 92
Beyond Sorry (2003), 297
Bittencourt, Ilma, 255, 260
Blackfeet Nation, 92
Blackgum Mountain Productions, 90, 107
Blogs, 293, 295–96
Blue water thesis, 13, 34
Boarding schools, 25, 74, 82, 89–95, 106
Boas, Franz, 103
Bolivia, 16, 47, 50–53, 57
Bourdieu, Pierre, 143, 244
Brazil, 16, 30, 45, 46, 51, 53, 253–69
Bringhurst, Robert, 102
Britain, 112, 232–49
British Broadcasting Corporation (BBC), 234, 248
Brito, Carlota, 255
Broadcasting, 28, 29, 90, 116, 128–44, 200, 203, 208, 214–31; community, 4, 5, 26, 33, 54, 75, 84, 133, 145–59, 232–49
Brooks, James, 290–91
Brooten, Lisa, 26, 111–27
Brown, Robert, 275
Browne, Donald, 13, 209
Buddle, Kathleen, 26, 128–44
Burdeau, George, 92
Burma (Myanmar), 26, 111–27
Buscando Bienestar (1997), 183, 191–95
Bush Bikes (2001), 297
Butler, Judith, 133

Cache Collective, 25, 74–88
CAIB (Coordinadora Audiovisual Indígena-Originaria de Bolivia), 48, 50, 53, 177
Camacho, Hugo, 255
Cambodia, 290–91
Campesino, 15, 186, 187
Canada, 3, 4, 10, 16, 18, 20, 21, 25, 26, 35, 74–88, 89–108, 123, 128–44, 165, 228, 295–97
Canadian Broadcasting Corporation (CBC), 84, 90
Canadian Indian Movement, 128
Cannes Film Festival, 62, 74, 295
Cárdenas, Marcelina, 50
Cardinal, Tantoo, 105
Carelli, Vincent, 45, 46, 53
Caribbean, 239
Caro, Niki, 58
Carpenter, Edmund, 76, 82, 85, 88
Castells, Manuel, 291
Castells i Talens, Antoni, 42
Castle-Hughes, Keisha, 58
Cauca department (Colombia), 145–59
CBC (Canadian Broadcasting Corporation), 84, 90
CDI (Comisión Nacional para el Desarollo de los Pueblos Indígenas), 51, 179
CD-ROMS, 30, 155, 253–69
Ceasefire (2005), 123
Celtic cultures, 232–49
Centro de Formación y Realización Cinematográfica (CEFREC), 48, 50, 53
Centro de Investigación, Experimentación y Desarrollo Indígena, 191, 192
Centro de Trabalho Indigenista (CTI), 45, 46, 57
Centros de Video Indígena (CVI), 46, 51, 52, 165, 191–92
Cerano, Dante, 39, 50, 57
CGI (computer-generated imagery), 91, 102, 104
Chaliand, Gérard, 35
Champagne, Duane, 14
Charles Darwin University, 271
Charles River Media Group, 102
Charley Squash Goes to Town (1969), 94
Cherokee, 90, 91, 95, 98–101, 300
Chiapas, 50, 160–80, 188

Chiapas Media Project (Promedios de Comunicación Comunitaria), 27, 51–53, 160–80
Chicanos, 167
Chikaoka, Miguel, 257, 263, 265
Children, 121, 136, 177; media for, 89–108, 201, 209–10, 233, 297–300
Chile, 39, 48, 50–51, 53–54, 57
China, 12, 23, 34, 35, 112, 292
Chin Ethnic State (Burma), 112
Chippewa, 301
Christen, Kimberly, 288
Christianity, 118, 149, 189, 198, 292, 295, 297
Christian missionaries, 118, 215, 295, 297
Christie, Michael, 30, 270–86
Christmas at Moose Factory (1971), 94
Christmas at Wapos Bay (2002), 108
Chrystos (poet), 137
Chukchi, 28, 214, 218, 219, 222, 224
Chukotka, 214, 218, 219, 222–24
Churchill, Ward, 8
Cine indígena, 41
Cinematography, 45, 64–66, 69–70, 77, 104, 298
Cinéma vérité, 3–4
Circulation, of Indigenous culture and media, 20, 23, 24, 42, 48, 51–56, 77, 84, 90, 169, 175, 177–78, 267, 302–4
Citizenship, 42, 127, 150, 184, 186
Civil rights, 24, 68, 122, 146
Civil society, 46, 139, 161, 188, 195
CLACPI (Consejo Latinoamericano de Cine y Comunicación de los Pueblos Indígenas), 43–54, 56
Cochabamba Declaration (1996), 50
Cohn, Norman, 74, 296
Collaborative media projects, 39, 52–53, 55, 106, 115, 160–80
Collective rights, 8–10, 19, 122, 150, 153, 160, 178, 184, 198, 200, 201, 203, 205, 215–17, 220–21, 223–25, 229

Collins, Allan, 298
Colombia, 16, 27, 44, 50, 54, 145–59, 256, 267, 269
Colonialism, 4, 5, 6, 8, 12, 39, 62, 70–71, 112, 130, 162, 189, 197, 198, 203–5, 232, 239–40, 277; internal, 7, 13, 14, 15, 17, 28, 34, 35, 236–37
Colonization, internal, 15, 137–38, 148–49, 215–16, 232, 236, 273
Comisión Nacional para el Desarollo de los Pueblos Indígenas (CDI), 51, 179
Commercial interests, 24, 29, 30, 156–59
Common List of Indigenous Small Peoples of Russia, 230
Communications technology, 28, 75, 139, 185, 194, 220, 284, 287. *See also* Technology: digital
Community broadcasting, 4, 5, 26, 33, 54, 75, 84, 133, 145–59, 232–49
Community Broadcasting Association of Australia, 33
Community media, 41, 43, 44, 45, 51–53, 74
Computer gaming, 91, 102, 105, 211, 297–300
Computer-generated imagery (CGI), 91, 102, 104
CONACIN (Coordinadora Nacional Indianista de Chile), 39
Concha, J. Leonard, 94
Confederación de Nacionalidades Indígenas del Ecuador (CONAIE), 47, 54, 177
Conference on Indigenous Peoples (1995), 115
Congress of Indigenous Peoples of the North, Siberia, and Far East, 215
Consejo Latinoamericano de Cine y Comunicación de los Pueblos Indígenas (CLACPI), 43–54, 56

Consejo Regional Indígena del Cauca
(CRIC), 149, 155
Constituent Assembly (Colombia,
1991), 149–50, 157
Constitutions, 42, 44, 112, 150, 160–61,
164, 187, 188
Cook, Gerri, 104
Cooperation, 39, 52–53, 55, 106, 115,
160–80
Coordinadora Audiovisual Indígena-Ori-
ginaria de Bolivia (CAIB), 48, 50, 53, 177
Coordinadora Nacional Indianista de
Chile (CONACIN), 39
Córdova, Amalia, 24, 27, 39–57, 177
Cormack, Mike, 204, 238
Cosmology, 253–69. *See also*
Knowledges
Costa Rica, 56
Council of Europe, 237–38
Council of Indigenous Representa-
tives, 198, 225
Cousineau, Marie-Hélène, 75
Coyes, Gregory, 104–6, 108
Coyote Goes Underground (1989), 94
Cree, 90–91, 104–6, 137
Creek (Muscogee), 91, 98–101
CRIC (Consejo Regional Indígena del
Cauca), 149, 155
Croall, Heather, 298
Crofts, Stephen, 67
CTI (Centro de Trabalho Indigenista),
45, 46, 57
Cuba, 24
Cufe Totkv Svtetv (The Rabbit Gets Fire),
100
Cultural autonomy, 40, 70, 185, 186,
188, 198, 299
Cultural continuity, 25, 89, 98
Cultural diversity, 19, 22, 60, 114, 147,
187–88, 235, 238, 241, 246, 258
Cultural geography, 183–96, 246–47,
270–86

Cultural identity, 25, 76, 77, 81–87, 97,
258, 271, 280–81. *See also* Memory
environment
Cultural politics, 23, 25–27, 215, 241
Cultural property, 6, 19, 96
Cultural Survival (NGO), 32, 199
Cultural Survival Quarterly, 22, 33
Culturas Populares (training pro-
gram), 189–90, 194
Culture: preservation of, 19, 25–30, 55,
114, 116, 148, 178, 215, 235, 267, 303;
revitalization of, 28, 188–90, 199,
200, 209; survival of, 22, 23, 44, 91,
97, 111, 114–18, 162, 198, 205, 256,
294
Curtis, Edward S., 137
CVI (Centros de Video Indígena), 46,
51, 52, 165, 191–92
CyberPowWow, 287, 305
Cyberspace, 21, 294, 302–4
Cymdeithas yr Iaith Gymraeg (Welsh
Language Society), 233–34, 236
Cymraeg (Welsh language), 232–49
Cymru Ddu (documentary series), 241

Daes, Erica-Irene A., 12, 33
Dafis, Cynog, 236
Dal'nevostochnaya GTRK (Russia), 219
Databases, 30, 221, 258, 261, 270–86
Daütchina, 256, 260
Davos, 292
Dawegukü, 256
Day and Night (2005), 99
De Certeau, Michel, 135
Decolonization, 13, 34, 41, 43
De Costa, Ravi, 8, 9
Deleuze, Gilles, 88
Denmark, 296
Department of Media, Culture, and
Sport (Wales), 242
Desert Knowledge Cooperative
Research Centre, 30, 270–86

Development, 14, 18, 28, 35, 41, 42, 45, 145–49, 183–96, 216, 221, 224–25, 290

Devolution, 239, 248–49

Diaspora, 5, 7, 22, 28, 76, 78, 112, 207, 242

Diatchkova, Galina, 28, 214–31

Digital age, 31, 287–305

Digital divide 22, 33, 287, 290–305

Digital media, 29–31, 50, 123, 136, 177, 233, 242, 253–69, 271, 267, 270–86, 287–305

Discrimination, 13, 14, 25

Disney Company, 1, 32, 90, 93, 103

Dissanayake, Wimal, 303

Documentary film and television, 23, 27, 39, 42, 45, 48, 50, 52, 53, 61, 77, 89, 93, 97, 122–26, 162, 164, 170, 191, 214, 241, 297; style and aesthetics of, 62–65

Dolgan, 219

Dorado, Mauricio, 159

Drumming, 133–34, 138

Duff, Alan, 59

Dui, 256, 263

Dürr, Michael, 227

DVDS, 105, 107, 274

Earthwatch Institute, 21

Echo-Hawk, Bunky, 3, 32

Economic conditions, 11, 16, 24, 29, 35, 44, 54, 75, 184, 186, 198, 216, 226, 228–29, 292, 294

Economist, 293

Ecuador, 16, 45, 47, 54, 56, 57, 139, 144, 194

Education, 25, 83, 89–108, 116, 118–19, 121, 148–49, 170, 185, 189, 199, 217, 221, 234, 243, 267, 296

Egyskin (television news program), 218

Elliot, Jean Leonard, 16, 35

El Mito de Peribo (1988), 57

Embedded aesthetics, 40, 55, 90, 96, 97

Emergence (1981), 94

Empire, 5, 7, 8, 12, 29, 35, 232–33, 237, 240

Empowerment, 25, 56, 68, 134, 188, 197–99, 201, 209, 226, 288

Environment, 8, 11, 25, 51, 119, 150, 180, 185, 194, 217, 221, 222, 224–26, 270–86; traditional knowledge of, 78, 82–87, 192–93

Erb, Joseph, 90, 98–101, 107

Eskimos (Yupik), 218, 219, 222

Espinosa, Julio García, 24, 42

Estrada, Mariano, 50

Ethics, 19, 20, 90, 302

Ethnic groups, 15, 17, 22, 34, 35, 44, 112, 114, 117, 121, 150, 217, 232, 239, 240, 241

Ethnicity, 15, 73, 185, 188, 190, 195, 269

Ethnobotany, 270–86

Ethnocentrism, 31, 115, 289–90

Ethnography, 22, 115, 199, 253–69; ethnographic film, 4, 40, 44, 45, 52, 65, 77, 87–88

Ethnopolitics, 28, 184–85, 187, 195

Etnodesarrollo (ethnic development), 189–95. *See also* Development

Eurocentrism, 41, 67

European Charter for Regional or Minority Languages (1992), 237

European Union, 235, 238

Evare (Brazil), 253–69

Even (Lamut), 218, 219, 222, 224

Evenk (Evenki; Tungus), 219

Evolution, 31, 186, 187

Exile, 5, 7, 22, 28, 76, 78, 112, 207, 242

Experimental video, 77, 85

Eynet (festival), 218

Fabian, Johannes, 291

Facó Soares, Marília, 255

Familia Indígena, La (1998), 175

Familial and kinship relations, 90, 93,

106, 132, 134, 136, 197, 254–56, 264–67, 269

FARC (Fuerzas Armadas Revolucionarias de Colombia), 155

Fast Runner, The (Atanarjuat), 21, 74, 99, 295

Faulhaber, Priscila, 30, 253–69

Feast of Language, The (television program), 218

Federal Agency for the Press and Mass Communications (Russia), 228

Festivals, 1, 4, 22, 41, 45–54, 162, 194, 302

Fiction, 50, 52, 53. See also Narrative

Film, documentary, 23, 27, 122–26, 162, 164, 170, 191, 214, 241, 297; ethnographic, 4, 40, 44, 45, 52, 65, 77, 87–88; feature, 21, 61–68, 77, 89, 93; Hollywood, 1, 2, 42, 67, 89, 95; Indigenous makers of, 19, 20, 24, 28, 42, 43, 52–54, 58–73, 89–108, 113, 177; Indigenous peoples and, 21, 41; Latin American, 39–57, 68; Maori, 58–73; New Zealand, 58–73

Finland, 28, 197–213, 227

Finnish Public Broadcasting Company (Yleisradio Oy; YLE), 200, 207, 208

Finnish Sámi Language Act (1991), 202

First Cinema, 68–69

First Nations, 68, 89–108, 287, 302. See also Indigenous peoples

First Nations / First Features (exhibition), 59

Fischer, Michael, 261

Flaherty, Robert, 65, 87, 107

Fleras, Augie, 16, 35

Ford Foundation, 1

Forline, Louis, 30, 253–69

Fourth Cinema, 7, 24, 68–71

Fourth World, 7, 8, 24, 34

Fox, Jonathan, 188

France, 194, 296

Francisco Urrusti, Juan, 45

Free Burma Coalition, 126

Free trade agreements, 150, 155, 161, 179

Frisians, 13

Frota, Mônica, 45, 57

Fuerzas Armadas Revolucionarias de Colombia (FARC), 155

Fundação Nacional do Indio (FUNAI), 46

Funding, 1, 14, 18, 19, 20, 22, 24, 25, 27, 28, 41, 43, 51–56, 59–61, 71–72, 75, 90, 102, 108, 116, 137, 165, 168–69, 171, 177, 188, 190, 194, 203, 215, 223, 226, 229, 242, 254, 267, 271, 282, 284, 298, 303, 305; international cooperation funding, 53, 154, 175–76, 227–28

García, Juan José, 50, 52

García Canclini, Néstor, 187

García Espinosa, Julio, 24, 42

Garnham, Nicholas, 156–59

Gates, Bill, 292

Gauthier, Jennifer, 24, 58–73

Geddes, Carol, 97

Gender politics, 26, 60, 124, 128–44, 176, 185

Genocide, 5, 121, 184

Geography, cultural, 183–96, 246–47, 270–86

Gerónima (1986), 56

Getino, Octavio, 42, 68

Gevan GTRK (Russia), 219

Ginsburg, Faye, 3, 4, 22, 29, 30–31, 70, 103, 115, 116, 287–306

Global cultural politics, 6, 28, 185, 186, 238

Global economy, 2, 11, 288

Global Forum of Indigenous Peoples and the Information Society, 20

Globalization, 2, 8, 11, 12, 18, 19, 162, 184–85, 194, 237–38, 293, 303

Global networks, 23, 30–31, 115, 139–40, 156, 162, 207, 209, 302, 304. *See also* International networks; Transnational networks

"Global village," 30–31, 290, 291

González, Gustavo, 16

Good Government Assemblies (Junta de Buen Gobierno), 163, 179

Goodman, David, 34

Great Western Development Program (*Xibu da kaifa*), 35

Greece, 123

Grierson, John, 65

Grupo Solidario de Quiatoni, 183–84, 190–96

GTRK (television and broadcast committees), 218, 219, 228, 229

Guambiano, 148

Guardia Indigena (Colombia), 145

Guatemala, 50, 54, 194

Guayasamin, Gustavo, 45, 56

Guerrero (Mexican state), 161, 175, 180

Guiding Star, The, 118

Guissé, El Hadji, 11

Habermas, Jürgen, 156–59

Haida, 90, 95, 102, 300

Halkin, Alexandra, 27, 52, 160–82

Hall, Stuart, 76, 81

Haniliaq, Matilda, 75

Hansen, Tom, 166

Hanson, Randel, 18

Hartley, John, 242

Haudenosaunee (Iroquois Confederacy), 129

Hawaii International Film Festival, 67

Hayward, Ramai, 61

Hayward, Rudall, 60–61

Hearne, Joanna, 25, 89–110, 300

Hechter, Michael, 236

Hegemonic media, 18, 19, 20, 23, 26, 27, 32, 39–45, 55–56, 67, 70, 89, 95, 146, 151–52, 157, 160, 161, 204, 216–17

Heritage, 41, 238

Hieleros del Chimborazo, Los (1980), 45

Hill peoples (Burma), 113

Hip Hop culture, 91

Historical continuity, 11, 12, 14, 34

Historical reenactments, 77–79, 93

Histories, 23, 41, 59, 66, 76–87, 89–92, 96, 130, 132, 149, 178, 183, 184, 187, 190, 193, 197, 241, 253–69, 274, 294, 295, 302

Hocking, Paul, 4

Hollywood, 1, 2, 42, 67, 89, 95

Hopi, 287

Hubley, Faith, 94

Human rights, 3, 7, 9, 10, 11, 19, 26, 27, 48, 54, 55, 113–16, 121–22, 164, 178, 188, 216

Human Rights Foundation of Monland (HURFOM), 118, 120–21

Human Rights Watch, 127

Huntington, Samuel, 216–17

Hybridity, 25, 64–65, 78, 90, 100, 115–16, 187, 203

Hyundai Corporation, 222

IBC (Inuit Broadcasting Corporation), 77, 84

Identity, 5, 11, 17, 19, 24, 25, 27–29, 34, 41, 48, 61, 70–71, 89, 92, 96, 106, 115, 117, 128–35, 140, 147, 184, 186, 187, 195, 199–200, 203, 207, 212, 219, 222, 229–30, 232–33, 241–42, 244, 258, 267, 269, 288

IDPS (Internally Displaced Peoples), 124

Igloolik Isuma Video Collective, 25, 74–88, 294–97

Iglulingmiut, 88

Ihimaera, Witi, 58

Ildo (Tuegucü), 260

ILO (International Labour Organization), 9, 122; Convention no. 169, 16, 33, 198, 213

Imagined community, 21, 186, 199, 203, 207, 235, 302

Imparja, 20

Imperfect cinema, 24, 42; video or media, 41, 48, 50, 55

Imperialism, 5, 7, 8, 12, 29, 35, 232–33, 237, 240

Independent production companies, 54

India, 23, 112, 123

Indígena, 184, 188

Indigeneity, 6, 12, 14, 15, 16, 23, 33, 34, 35, 40; discourses of 29, 232–49

Indigenism, 8, 9, 18, 21, 31

Indigenismo, 40–41, 45, 56, 186

Indigenist, 7, 42, 256

Indigenous Journal in Russia (Mir korennykh Narodov–Zhivaya Arctika), 219, 221

Indigenous media, 2, 6, 18, 19, 209, 269; awards for, 21, 48–50, 56, 58, 62, 72, 108, 154, 214; distribution of, 20, 23, 24, 42, 48, 51–56, 77, 84, 90, 169, 175, 177–78, 267, 302–3; nation-states and, 52, 54–55, 59–60, 71, 207–8, 226–29; political nature of, 7, 8, 9, 22, 23, 25–27, 28, 31, 32, 45, 54, 55, 69–71, 111–27, 128–44, 145–59, 160–80, 184–87, 189, 191, 194, 195, 202, 220, 294, 302; sales of, 175–76. *See also* Audiences for Indigenous media

Indigenous peoples: activism of, 7, 8, 9, 22, 23, 25–27, 28, 31, 32, 45, 54, 55, 71, 111–27, 128–44, 145–59, 160–80, 185–86, 189, 191, 194, 195, 202, 220, 297, 302, 304; aesthetics of, 20, 23–25, 29, 40, 42, 77–78, 90, 260–61; ancestral territories of, 13, 34, 198, 215, 258; artistic practices of, 23–25, 29, 31, 41, 76–77, 287; collective

memory of, 25, 76, 77, 81–87, 97, 258, 271, 280–81; collective rights of, 8–10, 19, 122, 150, 153, 160, 178, 184, 198, 200, 201, 203, 205, 215–17, 220–21, 223–25, 229; concept of, 12, 34; conferences of, 39, 52, 145, 175, 223, 227, 302; cultural autonomy of, 40, 70, 185, 186, 188, 198, 299; cultural continuity of, 25, 89, 98; cultural preservation and, 19, 25–30, 55, 114, 116, 148, 178, 215, 235, 267, 303; cultural property of, 6, 19, 96; cultural revitalization and, 28, 188–90, 199, 200, 209; cultural survival of, 22, 23, 44, 91, 97, 111, 114–18, 162, 198, 205, 256, 294; definitions of, 12, 14, 17, 33–34, 114–15, 197; familial and kinship relations among, 90, 93, 106, 132, 134, 136, 197, 254–56, 264–67, 269; globalization and, 2, 8, 11, 12, 18, 19, 162, 184–85, 194, 237–38, 293, 303; histories of, 23, 41, 59, 66, 76–87, 89–92, 96, 130, 132, 149, 178, 183, 184, 187, 190, 193, 197, 241, 253–69, 274, 294, 295, 302; intellectual property rights and, 11, 19, 96, 101, 237, 260, 269, 272–78, 285, 288–90, 302; land rights and, 3, 5, 6, 11, 14, 18, 19, 23, 24, 26, 39, 68, 106, 146, 149, 150, 194, 213, 220, 224, 225, 270–86, 302; languages of, *see* Languages; legal systems of, 34, 149–50, 276, 298; magical thinking and, 253–69; nation-states' recognition of, 14, 15, 16–17, 26, 40, 44, 148, 160, 197, 198, 203, 215, 230, 302; oral traditions of, 76, 77, 83–86, 90, 92; ownership and authorship and, 96–97, 102, 115, 279, 284, 298; policies of nation-states and, 6, 7, 8, 13, 14, 15, 16, 21, 26, 28–30, 34, 35, 42, 54, 75, 89, 119, 125, 136, 145–59, 165, 184, 186, 187, 189, 215–16, 228–29, 237, 249,

Indigenous peoples (*continued*)
303–4; political issues affecting, 20,
21, 24, 28, 41, 44, 45, 46, 50, 54, 75,
111–27, 214–31; political representation and, 149–50, 198, 199, 223; on
reservations and reserves, 15, 135–37,
139, 149; resettlement of, 7, 82, 93,
114, 149, 216; self-determination and,
3, 7, 8, 11, 17, 18, 23, 24, 25–27, 34, 40,
41, 62, 70, 114–17, 121, 188, 288, 302;
self-governance and, 16, 75, 147–50,
163, 216; self-representation and, 3, 4,
5, 19, 24, 26, 28, 40, 45, 48, 62, 90, 96,
122, 162, 185, 191, 195, 268, 302, 304;
sovereignty of, 5, 7, 8, 9, 16, 17, 18,
19, 21, 34, 97, 303; territorial autonomy of, 12, 75, 150, 185, 186, 197, 198;
territorial occupation and, 14, 34, 98,
197–98, 230; traditional culture of,
66, 79–87, 132–33, 139–40, 187, 198,
206, 211, 215–16, 230, 245, 272–75,
277, 280, 302; traditional knowledge
of, 5, 11, 19, 23, 25–27, 29, 30, 76, 78,
82–87, 89, 95, 119, 126, 133, 226, 270–
86, 288–89, 302; urban, 26, 51, 128–
44; violence against, 114–15, 121–24,
127, 128, 146–49, 162, 187; ways of
knowing among, 30, 39, 82, 85, 98,
140, 183–85, 189, 191–94, 208, 253–69,
270–86
Indigenous Peoples Forum, 114, 124
Indigenous Small-Numbered Peoples
of Russia, 230
Indigenous Television Network (Taiwan), 20
In Districts, Villages, and Brigades (radio
program), 218
Information, 19, 22, 206, 212, 217, 280,
287, 288
Information Center (IC) of RAIPON,
219
Information Center of the Indigenous

Association of Magadan Region,
220–21
Institute for American Indian Arts, 1,
32
Instituto Columbiano del Bienestar
Familiar, 255
Instituto do Patrimônio Histórico e
Artístico Nacional (Brazil), 267
Instituto Nacional Indigenista (INI), 44,
46, 165, 191
Insurgents, 113–14
Intellectual property rights, 11, 19, 96,
101, 237, 260, 269, 272–78, 285, 288–
90, 302
Interactive media, 29, 254, 297–300
Internal colonialism, 7, 13, 14, 15, 17, 28,
34, 35, 236–37
Internally Displaced Peoples (IDPS), 124
International Decade of the World's
Indigenous Peoples, 224, 226
International Film Festival of Morelia,
Mexico, 39
International Indian Treaty Council, 7
International Labour Organization
(ILO) 9, 122; Convention no. 169, 16,
33, 198, 213
International law, 6, 8, 9, 19, 34, 121,
279
International Monetary Fund, 9, 11
International networks, 18, 27, 28, 48,
52, 122, 125, 136, 161, 177, 190, 215, 217,
224, 227, 229
International Telecommunication
Union, 20
International Work Group for Interna-
tional Affairs (IWGIA), 221
Internet, 19, 20, 199, 212; access of
Indigenous groups to, 22, 29, 30, 177,
179, 200, 201, 207, 220–22, 268, 279,
287–305; blogs and, 293, 295–96;
cyberactivism and, 22, 23, 28, 160–
61, 302; web sites of Indigenous

groups and, 21, 33, 127, 146, 219, 225, 226–28, 270–71, 278, 287–305

Internet Native Peoples Conference, 21

Inuit, 25, 74–88, 143, 295–97

Inuit Broadcasting Corporation (IBC), 77, 84

Inuktitut language, 78

Ireland, 236, 248, 249

Iroquois Confederacy (Haudenosaunee), 129

Irrawady (magazine), 116, 119

Islam, 292–93

Italy, 165, 189, 190, 191

Itelmen (Kamchadal), 218, 224

Ivalu, Julie, 75

Ivalu, Madeline, 75, 79–81

IWGIA (International Work Group for International Affairs), 221

Jackson, Dennis, 108

Jaimes, Annette, 34

James, Simon, 90, 95, 102–4, 108, 300–301

Japan, 113, 247

Jones, John Tudor, 236

Jones, Pei te Hurinui, 67

Joseph, Robert, 300

Journalism, 116, 122, 151, 160–61, 163–64; Indigenous, 19, 20, 23, 28, 33, 48, 134, 200–209, 211, 214–31, 295

Journals of Knud Rasmussen, The (2005), 295

Joyner, Chris, 298

Junta de Buen Gobierno (Good Government Assemblies), 163, 179

Justice, 24, 68, 129, 142

Kaa, Wi Kuka, 63

Kachin Ethnic State (Burma), 112

Kamchadal (Itelmen), 218, 224

Kamchatka, 28, 214, 218, 220, 222, 224–25, 228, 230

Kamchatka Area Association of Indigenous Peoples of the North, 231

Kamchatka Indigenous Peoples Network, 224–25

Kamchatskaya Oblast, 218–20, 225

Karen, 111–27

Karen Education Surviving (2003), 123

Karen Environmental and Social Action Network (KESAN), 119

Karen Ethnic State (Burma), 112

Karen National Union (KNU), 122–24

Karenni (Kayah) Ethnic State, 113, 122, 125

Karen Women's Organization (KWO), 124

Karvonen, Albert, 104

Karvonen, Ava, 104

Kasauh Mon, Nai, 117, 121–22

Kasten, Erich, 227

Kawlah Films, 111, 122–24

Kayah (Karenni) Ethnic State, 112

Kayapó, 45

Kellogg Foundation, 190

Keresan, 92

Khanty, 219

Kheglen GTRK (Russia), 219

Kientz, Chris, 102–4, 300

King, Dell, 67

King, Michael, 62

Knowledges: commodification of, 30, 282–83, 288; Indigenous and Aboriginal, 5, 11, 19, 23, 25–27, 29, 30, 39, 76, 78, 82–87, 89, 95, 98, 119, 126, 133, 140, 183–85, 189, 191–94, 208, 226, 253–69, 270–86, 288–89, 302;

Kokonuco, 148

Komsomol'sk GTRK (Russia), 219

Koriak, 218, 224

Koriakskiy Autonomous Okrug, 218–20, 225

Krisher, Bernard, 290

Kuna, 294

Kunuk, Enuki, 85–86
Kunuk, Mary, 75, 86
Kunuk, Vivi, 84–86
Kunuk, Zacharias, 74, 295–97
Kwakiutl Reserve, 102
Kwakwaka'wakw, 90–91, 95, 102–3, 108, 300–301
Kway K'Lu, 117, 119–20
Kweh Say, Saw, 125

Lach Ethnoecological Information Center (Kamchatka), 220, 224, 225, 230, 231
La Duke, Winona, 8
Laguna Pueblo, 91
Lahu, 112
Lamut (Even), 218, 219, 222, 224
Land, 3, 5, 6, 11, 14, 18, 19, 23, 24, 26, 39, 68, 106, 146, 149, 150, 194, 213, 220, 224, 225, 270–86, 302
Landzelius, Kyra, 22, 293
Language Murderer, The (Y Llofrudd Iaith), 247–48
Languages, 4, 12, 14, 15, 19, 25, 28, 29, 40, 61, 62, 71, 75, 84, 90–94, 97, 100, 112, 118, 137, 148–50, 162, 175, 177, 179, 185, 187, 190, 197–213, 214, 216, 219–20, 222, 229, 232–49, 275, 293–94, 302; preservation and revitalization of, 91, 98, 201, 209–12, 217–18, 233–34
Lapps, 205, 212
Latin America, 16, 24, 27, 145–80, 183–96; film in, 39–57, 68
Latin American Studies Association (LASA), 176
Latinos, 52
Latukefu, Alopi, 288, 289
Laughton, Roger, 242
Law, 42, 220–21, 223, 228, 279; Indigenous, 34, 149–50, 276, 298
Learning Path, The (1991), 93
Lee, Dorothy, 64

Legal recognition, 14, 15, 16–17, 26, 40, 44, 148, 160, 197, 198, 203, 215, 230, 302
Lehtola, Veli-Pekka, 200
Letter from an Apache (1982), 94
Lewis, Gwyneth, 247
Lewis, Saunders, 236
Liberation Theology, 189
Literature, 41, 59, 95, 96, 118, 216
Littlebird, Larry, 91–92
Llwyd, Alan, 241
Local cultures, 2, 8, 9, 18, 21–28, 30, 41, 42, 50, 51, 55, 74, 77, 90, 130, 132, 136, 145–59, 162–63, 179–80, 183–96, 193, 198, 200, 204, 207, 229, 247, 273, 281, 303
Lowie, Robert, 256
Luzuriaga, Camilo, 56

MacArthur Foundation, 194
MacDougall, David, 65
Magazines and journals, 116–21, 201, 228
Magical thinking, 253–69
Magüta Arü Inü: Recollecting Magüta Thinking, 30, 256–58, 261, 267–68
Maktar, Martha, 75
Mana Maori Paepae (MMP), 71
Manitoba, 26
Mansi, 219
Manuel, George, 7
Maori, 16, 232, 278, 294, 297; film of, 19, 20, 24, 28, 42, 43, 52–54, 58–73, 89–108, 113, 177; television of, 20, 71, 101
Maori in Film and TV, Inc. (Nga Aho Whakaari), 71–73
Maori Merchant of Venice, The (2002), 66–67
Maori TV Fund, 67
Map of the Human Heart (1996), 93
Mapuche, 39, 50

MAQL (Movimiento Armado Quintín
  Lame), 149
Mara'acame, cantador y curandero
  (1982), 45
Marcos, Subcommander, 161
Market forces, 157–59
Marketing the Indigenous, 1, 5, 185
Marks, Laura, 78, 87
Martínez Reyes, Eugenia, 191–93
Masayesva, Victor, 77, 94
Mato, Daniel, 185
Matthews, Pamela, 93
Mauri (1988), 66
Mayans, 160, 162, 179
Maybury-Lewis, David, 33
McElroy, Ruth, 29, 232–52
McLean, Danielle, 298
McLuhan, Marshall, 291
Mead, Margaret, 88
Meadows, Michael, 43
Media: alternative, 94, 148, 156–59, 186,
  205; broadcasting, 23, 25, 56, 89–108,
  300; defined, 2, 6, 18, 19, 115, 209,
  269; digital, 29–31, 50, 123, 136, 177,
  233, 242, 253–69, 270–86, 287–305;
  Indigenous access to, 19, 208, 151–
  52; mainstream, 18, 19, 20, 23, 26, 27,
  32, 39–45, 55–56, 67, 70, 89, 95, 146,
  151–52, 157, 160, 161, 204, 216–17;
  minority, 203, 204, 209, 232–49;
  newspapers, 29, 118–21, 201, 218–
  20, 222–23, 226, 229; participatory,
  44, 120–21, 139, 199, 209, 298; political activism and, 24, 54–56, 203, 215,
  217, 220, 223–24; production centers
  for, 45–48, 51, 54, 84, 90, 170–71, 176–
  77, 179; state-owned, 19, 22; video,
  24, 26, 27, 28, 39–57, 75, 122–25, 146,
  160–80, 183–96, 255, 258–60, 297–
  300, 303. *See also* Animation; Film;
  Internet; Journalism; Radio;
  Television

Media collectives, 23, 25, 43, 44, 74–88,
  169
Media Rights Foundation, 108
Mediascape, 207, 209, 213, 242
Mekaron Opoi D'joi, 45
Meltis, Fabio, 166
Memory environment, 79–88
Messenger (2004), 95, 98, 100–101
Mestizo, 40, 56, 148, 161, 186
Métis, 143
Mètis, 279–81
Mexico, 15, 27, 28, 39, 40, 44–46, 51, 52,
  55, 160–80, 183–96
Mexico Solidarity Network, 166
Michaels, Eric, 89
Migration, 52, 135–37, 188, 194, 232, 234,
  278
Mi'kmaq, 294
Militarism, 111–27, 145–59, 163–64, 167
Military organizations, 149, 160–61, 163
Min Ággi (newspaper), 201
Mir korennykh Narodov–Zhivaya Arctika
  (*Indigenous Journal in Russia*), 219,
  221
Mita, Merata, 59, 66, 73
MIT Media Lab, 290
MMP (Mana Maori Paepae), 71
MNDF (Mon National Democratic
  Front), 117
Moana (1926), 65
Mobilization, 18, 26, 28–29, 43, 51, 52,
  92, 119, 145–59, 185, 203, 215, 217
Modernity, 30, 52, 100, 132, 139, 159, 187,
  245, 289, 291, 302
Modernization, 42, 198, 216–17, 246,
  303
Mohawk Nation, 133
Molnar, Helen, 43
Mon, 111–27
Mon Forum, The, 118, 121
Mon National Democratic Front
  (MNDF), 117

Monteforte, Guillermo, 165–66, 168, 191, 192, 194

Moore, Carmen, 103

Morales, Evo, 16

Morrisseau, Norval, 89, 91, 104

Moseley-Braun, Carol, 166

Motoman Project, 291

Movimiento Armado Quintín Lame (MAQL), 149

MPEG (Museu Paraense Emílio Goeldi), 253, 255, 256, 261, 262, 267

Muenala, Alberto, 50, 57

Multiculturalism, 59, 150, 187, 197, 238–40, 303

Multilingualism, 28, 29, 197

Multimedia, 23, 253–69

Multiracialism, 29, 239

Mune, Ian, 60

Murgin Nutenut (newspaper), 218, 222, 223

Murillo, Mario, 27, 145–59

Murphy, Arthur, 190

Murphy, Geoff, 58

Muscogee (Creek), 91, 98–101

Museums, 187, 253–69

Museu Paraense Emílio Goeldi (MPEG), 253, 255, 256, 261, 262, 267

Music, 159, 199, 210–12; rap, 199, 211; soundtrack, 79; traditional, 51, 85, 134, 159, 218, 260; videos, 48

Mutiny on the Bounty (1962), 69

Myanmar (Burma), 26, 111–27

NABC (Native American Broadcasting Corporation), 90

NAFTA (North American Free Trade Agreement), 161

Naga, 112

Nakamura, Félix, 57

Nanay, 219

Nanook of the North (1922), 87, 107

Nariño department (Colombia), 147

Narodovlastie (newspaper), 218

Narrative, 23, 25, 27, 45, 48, 50, 63, 77, 90, 96, 128, 200, 203, 261, 297, 302; style and structure in, 64, 78, 84, 260

Nasa (Páez), 145–59

Nation, The (Thailand), 118

National cinemas, 42, 43, 58–59, 67, 70

National Congress of American Indians (NCAI), 35

National Film Board of Canada (NFB), 90, 94, 108

National Film Unit, New Zealand Tourist and Publicity Bureau, 60

National League for Democracy (NLD), 113

National Museum of Anthropology (Mexico City), 187

National networks, 18, 23, 27, 46, 48, 53, 74, 111–27, 140, 145–59, 185–86, 203, 207, 304

National Womens Association of Canada, 128

Nations, Indigenous, 18, 34, 35, 45, 203, 208, 209, 213; national identity and, 184, 199, 207, 212, 232–33; nationalism and, 3, 7, 17, 26, 27, 29, 44, 116, 132, 147, 186, 187, 199–200, 232–49

Nation-states: citizenship in, 42, 127, 150, 184, 186; constitutions of, 42, 44, 112, 150, 160–61, 164, 187, 188; Indigenous media and, 52, 54–55, 59–60, 71, 207–8, 226–29; Indigenous peoples and, 6, 7, 8, 13, 14, 15, 16, 21, 26, 28–30, 34, 35, 42, 54, 75, 89, 119, 125, 136, 145–59, 165, 184, 186, 187, 189, 215–16, 228–29, 237, 249, 303–4; paternalism and, 29, 44, 132, 186, 194, 216. *See also* Law

Native American Broadcasting Corporation (NABC), 90

Native Americans, 1, 3, 32, 35, 89–108; Anishinaabeg (Anishinabe), 91, 104–

5, 128, 129; Blackfeet, 92; Cherokee, 90, 91, 95, 98–101, 300; Chippewa, 301; Haudenosaunee (Iroquois Confederacy), 129; Hopi, 287; Keresan, 92; Laguna Pueblo, 91; Mohawk, 133; Muscogee (Creek), 91, 98–101; Navajo, 294; Ojibwe, 129; Oneida, 21; Seneca, 129; Squamish, 300; Taos Pueblo, 94; Tlingit, 97; Tuscarora, 287; Tutchone, 97

Native Communications, Inc. (NCI), 137, 144

NATIVE-L, 21

Native Media Network (NMN), 137

NativeNet, 21

NativeWeb, 21

Native Women's Association of Canada, 134

Navajo, 294

NCAI (National Congress of American Indians), 35

NCI (Native Communications, Inc.), 137, 144

Negidal, 219

Negroponte, Nicholas, 292

Nenet, 219

Netsilik Eskimo (film series), 87–88

New Mexico Film Production Grant, 108

Newspapers, 29, 118–21, 201, 218–20, 222–23, 226, 229

New Zealand, 10, 16, 20, 24, 43, 58–73, 101

New Zealand Film Commission (NZFC), 59, 60, 66, 67, 71–72

New Zealand Ministry of Culture and Heritage, 71

NFB (National Film Board of Canada), 90, 94, 108

Nga Aho Whakaari (Maori in Film and TV, Inc.), 71–73

Nganasan, 219

Ngati (1987), 58, 62–67, 69–71

Ngematucü, 256, 257, 264

NGOS (nongovernmental organizations), 6, 8, 26, 27, 41, 46, 51, 53, 114, 119, 121–24, 161, 164–66, 185, 188, 190, 196, 215, 302

Nicaragua, 54

Nichols, Bill, 64

Niezen, Ronald, 9

Nimuendaju, Curt, 255–56, 258, 261, 266

Nisga'a Treaty, 16

NLD (National League for Democracy), 113

Nomadic media lab, 296

Nongovernmental organizations (NGOS), 6, 8, 26, 27, 41, 46, 51, 53, 114, 119, 121–24, 161, 164–66, 185, 188, 190, 196, 215, 302

Non-Self-Governing Territories, 34

Nora, Pierre, 88

Nordenskiöld, Norden, 256

Norsk Rikskringkasting AS (NRK; Norwegian Broadcasting Corporation), 208

North American Free Trade Agreement (NAFTA), 161

Northern Ireland, 239, 248, 249

Northwest Coast cultural groups, 294, 300–301

Norway, 197–213, 227, 228, 230

Norwegian Broadcasting Corporation (Norsk Rikskringkasting AS; NRK), 208

Norwegian Polar Institute, 228

Not Vanishing (radio program), 137–41

Noyce, Phillip, 93

Nuestra voz de tierra, memoria y futuro (1973), 45

Nunavut, 16, 25, 74–88, 294–97

Nunavut (radio program), 218

Nunavut (television series), 78, 82, 295

NZFC (New Zealand Film Commission), 59, 60, 66, 67, 71–72

Oaxaca, 28, 46, 165, 168, 171, 183–96
Obomsawin, Alanis, 93, 94
Observational cinema, 3–4
Oceania, 13
Ojibwe, 129
Ojo de Agua Comunicación, Mexico, 46, 52
Oka Crisis, 133
OMVIAC (Organización Mexicana de Videastas Indígenas), 46
Once Were Warriors (1994), 59, 66, 73
Oneida Nation, 21
ONIC (Organización Nacional Indígena de Colombia), 54
Online Burma Library, 127
Only the Devil Speaks Cree (2004), 93
Onsman, Andrys, 13
Ontario, 26, 128–29, 133–35, 138
Organización Mexicana de Videastas Indígenas (OMVIAC), 46
Organización Nacional Indígena de Colombia (ONIC), 54
Original Women's Network (OWN), 137, 144
O'Shea, John, 60–62
Outback Digital Network, 288
OWN (Original Women's Network), 137, 144
Ownership and authorship, 96–97, 102, 115, 279, 284, 298. See also Intellectual property rights

Pacific Films, 61
Pack, Sam, 115
Páez (Nasa), 145–59
Paillán, Jeannette, 50
Pakeha (non-Indigenous New Zealanders), 58–73
PAN (Partido de Acción Nacional), 163

Panama, 54
Pan-Indigenous coalitions and movements, 7, 8, 18, 22, 26, 28, 35, 132, 198–99, 217, 223–24, 225
Pa-O (Black Karen), 112
Paraguay, 54
Parbury, Nigel, 5
Participatory media, 44, 120–21, 139, 199, 209, 298
Partido de Acción Nacional (PAN), 163
Partido de la Revolución Democrática (PRD), 163
Partido Revolucionario Institucional (PRI), 163
Pastors for Peace, 166
Pastrana, Andrés, 154
Paternalism, 29, 44, 132, 186, 194, 216
Paütchina, 256
PBS (Public Broadcasting System), 90
Peaceway Foundation, 124
Peasants, 145, 147, 148, 185–87
Pedagogy, 25, 89–108. See also Education
Pedair Wal (2001), 245–47
Peoples Republic of China, 13, 15, 17, 34, 35
Perestroika, 215–17, 222
Perú, 40, 44, 45, 48, 54, 56, 189, 269
Phillips, Dylan, 236
Pietikäinen, Sari, 28, 197–213
Pinheiro, Ngematucü Pedro Inácio, 256
Pintado, Jose Manuel, 166
Plaid Cymru, 233
Plan de Vida (community development programs in Colombia), 146, 153–54
Plan Nacional Indígena de Comunicación Audiovisual (PNICA), 48, 51–53
Poata, Tama, 62, 65
Poetics of media, 24, 29, 40, 42, 48, 55
Politics, 20, 21, 24, 28, 41, 44, 45, 46, 50, 54, 75, 111–27, 214–31

Popol Vuh (1989), 94
Posluns, Michael, 7
Postcolonialism, 4, 34, 70–71, 92, 203, 239
Powwows, 128–34
PRD (Partido de la Revolución Democrática), 163
PRI (Partido Revolucionario Institucional), 163
Primorskaia Association of Indigenous Peoples, 222
Primorsklesprom Company, 222
Prins, Harald, 3, 4, 21, 294
Print media, 29, 116–21, 146, 201, 218–23, 226, 228, 229
Professional media networks, 28, 71–72, 116, 215, 227, 229
Programa Comunidad, 152–54
Project Inukshuk, 84
Promedios de Comunicación Comunitaria (Chiapas Media Project), 27, 51–53, 160–80
Protests, 113, 117, 145–46, 155, 233–34
Public Broadcasting System (PBS), 90
Public interest, 153, 157–59
Public sphere, 26, 27, 40, 148, 152, 156–59, 207, 234
Publishing, 146
Purehepecha, 39, 50
Putin, Vladimir, 224
Putumayo department (Colombian province), 147
Pynylte (television news program), 218

Qaggig (1989), 88, 295
Qarmaq (1995), 82–84
Quechua, 50
Quichua, 50
Quito Declaration (1994), 47
Qulitalik, Pauloosie, 74
Qulliq (1993), 79–82

Rabbit Gets Fire, The (Cufe Totkv Svtetv), 100
Rabbit-Proof Fence (2002), 21, 93
Racism, 15, 185, 188, 240, 241, 303
Radio, 19, 23, 26, 29, 44, 54, 115, 128–44, 145–59, 199, 200, 204, 209, 211, 218, 229; on Internet, 133, 146, 201
Radio Kawthoolei 116
Radio Nasa 147, 152, 156
Radio Payu'mat 27, 145–59
RAIPON (Russian Association of Indigenous Peoples of the North), 215, 217–19, 221, 227
Rakhine (Arakan) Ethnic State, 112
Raven Steals the Light, The (1984), 102
Raven Tales (television series), 90, 95, 101–4, 107, 108, 294, 300–301, 305
Raven Tales Productions, 90, 101–4
Real People, The (television series), 92
Reception, 26, 27
Recognition, by nation-states, 14, 15, 16–17, 26, 40, 44, 148, 160, 197, 198, 203, 215, 230, 302
Redbird, Duke, 94
Red Regional de Comunicación Indígena Kujkuj Zugun, 57
Rees, Martha, 190, 195
Refugees, 114, 119
Regional cultures, 15, 19, 23, 48, 51–53, 74, 131–36, 141, 145–59, 163, 171, 180, 186, 187, 188, 197–213, 214–31, 304
Regional Information Centers, 220, 224
Reid, Bill, 102
Religion, 14, 15, 148, 150, 162, 185, 216
Representation, political, 149–50, 198, 199, 223; by alternative media, 42, 43, 90, 94, 106, 115, 148, 152, 156–59, 186, 201–5, 304; through media, 3, 24, 25, 28, 29, 32, 40, 43, 50, 52, 68, 70, 90, 93–94, 111, 115, 151, 162, 184, 185, 187, 191, 195, 203–5, 212, 239, 240, 241, 266, 272, 302

Reservations, 15, 135–37, 139, 149

Resettlement, 7, 82, 93, 114, 124, 149, 216

Resistance, 27, 40, 111, 116, 126, 145–59, 162, 203, 303

Richard Cardinal: Cry from a Diary of a Métis Child (1986), 93

Rickard, Jolene, 287, 289

Rights, collective, 8–10, 19, 122, 150, 153, 160, 178, 184, 198, 200, 201, 203, 205, 215–17, 220–21, 223–25, 229

Ritual, 253–69, 298

Ritual Clowns (1988), 94

Rocha, Glauber, 42, 68

Rockefeller Foundation, 194

Rodoslovnaya (television documentary), 218

Rodríguez, Merta, 45

Rodríguez de Las Eras, Antonio, 260

Rudoy, Alexander, 214

Russian Association of Indigenous Peoples of the North (RAIPON), 215, 217–19, 221, 227

Russian Empire, 215

Russian Federation, 28, 197, 204, 214–31

Russian TV and Broadcasting Foundation, 218

Sahuari (1989), 56

Sakha (Yakutia) Republic, 222

Sakhalin Oblast (Russia), 222

Salazar, Juan, 24, 27, 39–57, 177

Salish, 102

Salt water thesis, 13, 34

Sámi, 28, 197–213, 231, 294

Sámi Council, 198

Sámi Radio, 199, 200, 204, 209, 211

San Andrés Accords (1996), 164, 179, 188

Sanjinés, Ivan, 53

Santa Fe Film Festival, 108

Santiago, Pedro, 183

Santiago Ruiz, Maria, 191–93

Sápmi region, 197–213

Sassen, Saskia, 136

Satellites, 4, 176–77, 179, 291, 295–96, 303–4

SAVICOM (Society for the Anthropology of Visual Communication), 32

Scandinavia, 28, 197–213

Scotland, 12, 123, 236, 239, 248, 249

Scott, James, 279

Second Cinema, 68

Sein Twa, Paul, 119

Self-determination, 3, 7, 8, 11, 17, 18, 23, 24, 25–27, 34, 40, 41, 62, 70, 114–17, 121, 188, 288, 302

Self-governance, 16, 75, 147–50, 163, 216

Self-identification, 12, 13, 14, 34, 114, 230

Self-representation, 3, 4, 5, 19, 24, 26, 28, 40, 45, 48, 62, 90, 96, 122, 162, 185, 191, 195, 268, 302, 304

Selwyn, Don, 66

Seneca, 129

Sesia, Paolo, 189

Settler states, 18, 27, 89

Shan Ethnic State (Burma), 112, 122, 125

Shohat, Ella, 92

Sianel Pedwar Cymru (S4C), 29, 232–49

Siberia, 215, 227

Siberian-studies.org, 227

Sikusilarmiut studio workshops, 94

Sila.nu, 295–97, 305

Silva, Jorge, 45

Singer, Beverly, 2

Six Nations Reserve, 128

Smith, Laurel, 28, 183–96

Smoke, Dan, 128, 133–34

Smoke, Mary Lou, 128, 133–35

Smoke Signals (radio program), 21, 129, 133–35, 300

Soap Tree, The (El Árbol de jabón), 194

Social change, 48, 75, 124–26, 162, 166, 187, 214, 302

Society for the Anthropology of Visual Communication (SAVICOM), 32
Society for Visual Anthropology, 32
Solanas, Fernando, 42, 68
Soukup, Katarina, 296
South Africa, 20
South Australian Film Corporation, 297
Sovereignty, 5, 7, 8, 9, 16, 17, 18, 19, 21, 34, 97, 303
Sovetken Chukotka (newspaper), 222
Soviet Chukotka (newspaper), 222
Soviet Federatsii, 214
Spain, 19, 147, 194
SPDC (State Peace and Development Council), 114, 121, 123–24
Spickard, Paul, 15
Squamish, 300
Starlore (1983), 94
Statelessness, 127
State Peace and Development Council (SPDC), 114, 121, 123–24
Stephens, Tainui, 71
Stereotypes, 3, 89–90, 93–94, 112–13, 162, 198, 204–5, 268, 288; master narratives and, 14, 122, 126, 186, 187, 289, 304
Stewart, Michelle, 1–38
Stolen Sisters campaign, 128, 134, 143
Stone Sail, The (television documentary), 218
Stories from the Seventh Fire, 90, 102, 104–6, 107
Storytellers Productions, 104
Storytelling, 25, 42, 48, 62, 71, 74, 76, 78–79, 85–87, 89–98, 103, 178, 183, 254–55, 259, 277, 294, 295, 297, 302
Street Level Youth Media, 167–68
Summer Television and Film Workshop, 1
Sundance Film Festival, 1, 32, 72
Sustainability, 5, 11, 27, 51, 150, 162, 166, 175, 177, 216, 217, 228, 275, 283, 286, 305
Sweden, 197–213, 227
Swiss Aid, 56

Taiwan, 20
Talens, Antoni Castells i, 42
Tamahori, Lee, 59, 66, 73
Tamil, 112
Tângata whenua, 60
Tangata Whenua (television series), 61
Tangentyere Council, 298
Taormina Festival, 62
Taos Pueblo, 94
Tariagsuk Video Centre, 75
Tauli-Corpuz, Victoria, 10
Taymyr GTRK (Russia), 219
Te Awa Marama, 62
Technology, 20, 23, 25, 46, 51, 55, 75, 81, 91, 146, 164–65, 169, 184–85, 190–94, 207, 225, 229, 236; digital, 29–31, 50, 123, 136, 177, 233, 242, 253–69, 271, 267, 270–86, 287–305; satellite, 4, 176–77, 179, 291, 295–96, 303–4
Tejido de comunicación, 145–59
Telefilm Canada, 78
Television, 19, 23, 29, 77, 81, 200, 201, 204, 205, 206, 214, 229, 232–49, 297–300; lifestyle, 244–47; news programs on, 48, 53, 199
Telstra, 297
Te Mangai Paho, 71
Te Manu Aute, 71
Temporality, 78–87, 98, 266–67
Territorial autonomy, 12, 14, 34, 75, 98, 150, 185, 186, 197, 198, 230
Territories, ancestral, 13, 34, 198, 215, 258
Te Rua (1991), 58, 66
Thailand, 112, 115, 116, 122–25
Thaw Thi, Saw, 117–18, 120–21
Third Cinema, 24, 41, 42, 43, 68, 76

Thulei Kawwei (magazine), 119, 121

Ticuna, 30, 253–69

Timonina, Elena, 214

Tiwa, 94

Tlingit, 97

Today in Okrug (radio program), 218

Todd, Loretta, 93

Tojolabal language, 162

Tolima department (Colombia), 147

To Love a Maori (1972), 61

Tomos, Angharad, 237

Tootoosis, Gordon, 105

Tosso, Raul, 56

Tourism, 5, 198, 204–6, 212

Tradition, 66, 79–87, 132–33, 139–40, 187, 198, 206, 211, 215–16, 230, 245, 272–75, 277, 280, 302

Tradition (television documentary), 218

Traditionalism, 31, 302

Training in media production, 1, 20, 27, 43, 45, 46, 48, 51–54, 62, 72, 77, 84, 90, 123, 137, 152–53, 157, 161, 165–71, 177, 189–90, 190, 191, 194, 220, 227, 229, 240, 298

Transferencia de Medios Audio-visuales a Organizaciones y Com-unidades Indígenas, 46

Transnational corporations, 8, 11; net-works and, 18, 22, 24, 27, 28, 31, 40, 42, 50, 55, 140, 160–80, 185–86, 188, 194, 195, 197–213, 215, 227–28, 302

Treaties, 7, 16, 18, 42, 106, 107

Treaty of Waitangi, 16

Trespass (2002), 297

Trickster, The (2003), 98

Trickster figure, 89, 91, 98, 104–6

Trujillo, Gary, 21

Tuegucü (Ildo), 260

Tungus (Evenk; Evenki), 219

Tunisia, 287

Turner, Terence, 45, 143

Tuscarora, 287

Tutchone, 97

TV Northern Canada, 295

TV-Oddasat, 201, 205, 206, 208, 210

Two Winters: Tales above the Earth (2004), 97, 107

Tzeltzal (Tzeltal), 50, 162

Tzotzil language, 162

Ugoria GTRK (Russia), 219

Ul'chi, 219

UNESCO (United Nations Educational, Social and Cultural Organization), 53, 154

UNHCR (United Nations High Com-mission for Refugees), 124

Unión de Organizaciones Campesinos del Azuay (UNASAY), 56

Union of Soviet Socialist Republics (USSR), 216, 222

United Kingdom, 112, 232–49

United Nations, 6, 35, 121, 198, 217; Commission on Human Rights, 9, 19, 33, 34; Declaration on the Rights of Indigenous Peoples, 10, 19; Digital Solidarity Fund, 287; Economic and Social Council, 10; Educational, Social and Cultural Organization (UNESCO), 53, 154; General Assembly, 224; High Commission for Refugees (UNHCR), 124; Human Rights Coun-cil, 10; Information for Everybody conference, 227; Least Developed Country (LDC) status and, 113; Per-manent Forum on Indigenous Issues, 10; Security Council, 232; Working Group on Indigenous Pop-ulations, 10, 11, 12, 13, 14, 88, 289, 302; Workshops on Indigenous Media, 19

United States, 3, 10, 15, 16, 18, 25, 35, 52, 77, 89–108, 114, 127, 161, 166–67, 194, 293

United States Agency for International Development (USAID), 224, 226

United States-Mexico Fund for Culture, 168, 171

Unkel, Curt, 255–56, 258, 261, 266

Urban Aboriginals, 26, 51, 128–44

Urbanization, 7, 61, 216–17, 234, 243, 273, 278

Uribe, Alvaro, 150, 155

Urrusti, Juan Francisco, 45

Uruguay, 56

USAID (United States Agency for International Development), 224, 226

Us Mob (television series), 294, 297–300

Uspenskaya, Valentina, 214, 230

USSR (Union of Soviet Socialist Republics), 216, 222

Uttuigak, Celina, 75

Utu (1983), 58

Va (Wa), 112

Vadiveloo, David, 297–300

Valle del Cauca department, 147

Vancouver Film School, 102

Van der Velden, Maja, 283

Vanishing Indian trope, 89, 106, 268, 304

Varese, Stefano, 189

Vázquez, Francisco (Paco), 166–67

Venezuela, 16, 45, 54, 56

Video, 24, 26, 27, 28, 39–57, 75, 122–25, 146, 160–80, 183–96, 255, 258–60, 297–300, 303

Video indígena, 41, 52

Video nas Aldeias (VNA; Video in the Villages), 45, 46, 51, 53, 57, 177, 269

Video popular, 44

Violence, against Indigenous peoples, 114–15, 121–24, 127, 128, 146–49, 162, 187

Visual anthropology, 4, 24

Viswanath, K. Vish, 119

Voces de Nuestra Tierra, 147, 152, 156, 158

Wa (Va), 112

WACC (World Association for Christian Communication), 53

Wales, 12, 29, 232–49

Walt Disney Company, 1, 32, 90, 93, 103

Waniandy, Johnny, 105

Ward, Vincent, 60, 73, 93

We Are Aboriginals (radio program), 218

Wells, Paul, 96

Welsh Language Act (1993), 243

Welsh Language Board, 234

Welsh Language Society (Cymdeithas yr Iaith Gymraeg), 233–34, 236

Wesakechak (trickster character), 104–6

Whale Rider (2003), 58, 73

What Becomes of the Broken-Hearted (1999), 60

When the Men Cry (television documentary), 214, 218

Wild Spaces Forum, 124

Wilk, Barbara, 94

Willeman, Paul, 68

Williams, Charlotte, 239–40

Wilson, Pamela, 1–38

Wilson, Rob, 303

Winnipeg, 137–41

Wireless technology, 116, 296

Wochankü, 256

Wolf Mother, 104–6

Women, 26, 51, 75, 79–87, 121, 124, 176, 259–60; in political process, 130–32, 223; ways of affiliating among, 128–44

World Association for Christian Communication (WACC), 53

World Bank, 9, 11, 227

World Conference against Racism, Discrimination, Xenophobia and Related Intolerance, 20
World Council of Indigenous Peoples, 7
World Economic Forum, 292, 305
World Indigenous Peoples Day, 223
World Social Forum, 123
World Summit on the Information Society (WSIS), 20, 287
World Wildlife Fund, 227
Wortham, Erica, 41, 46, 52
WSIS (World Summit on the Information Society), 20, 287

Xibu da kaifa (Great Western Development Program), 35

Yamal GTRK (Russia), 219
Yanomami (Yanomamö), 57
Yasavei Manzara Information Center, 220–21
Yleisradio Oy (YLE; Finnish Public Broadcasting Company), 200, 207, 208
Y Llofrudd Iaith (*The Language Murderer*), 247–48
Yukagir, 219, 222
Yupik (Eskimos), 218, 219, 222

Zapatistas, 7, 27, 50, 52, 160–80, 185, 187–88, 292
Zapoloarie GTRK (Russia), 219
Zapotec, 50, 52, 184, 192, 195

PAMELA WILSON is an associate professor of communication at Reinhardt College.

MICHELLE STEWART is an assistant professor of
cinema studies and literature at the State University of
New York, Purchase College.

Library of Congress Cataloging-in-Publication Data
Global indigenous media : cultures, poetics, and politics / edited by Pamela Wilson and Michelle Stewart.
p. cm.
Includes bibliographical references and index.
ISBN 978-0-8223-4291-5 (cloth : alk. paper)
ISBN 978-0-8223-4308-0 (pbk. : alk. paper)
1. Intercultural communication—Case studies.
2. Indigenous peoples and mass media—Case studies.
3. Ethnic mass media—Case studies.
4. Minorities in mass media—Case studies.
5. Communication and culture—Case studies.
I. Wilson, Pamela, 1957–
II. Stewart, Michelle, 1968–
GN345.6.G56 2008
302.23—dc22   2008007704